ALSO BY FERGUS M. BORDEWICH

America's Great Debate: Henry Clay, Stephen A. Douglas,
and the Compromise That Preserved the Union

Washington: The Making of the Nation's Capital

Bound for Canaan: The Underground Railroad
and the War for the Soul of America

My Mother's Ghost: A Memoir

Killing the White Man's Indian: Reinventing Native Americans
at the End of the Twentieth Century

Cathay: A Journey in Search of Old China

The
FIRST
CONGRESS

HOW JAMES MADISON, GEORGE WASHINGTON, AND A GROUP OF EXTRAORDINARY MEN INVENTED THE GOVERNMENT

FERGUS M. BORDEWICH

SIMON & SCHUSTER

New York London Toronto Sydney New Delhi

Simon & Schuster
1230 Avenue of the Americas
New York, NY 10020

First Simon & Schuster hardcover edition February 2016

SIMON & SCHUSTER and colophon are registered
trademarks of Simon & Schuster, Inc.

For information about special discounts for bulk purchases,
please contact Simon & Schuster Special Sales at
1-866-506-1949 or business@simonandschuster.com.

The Simon & Schuster Speakers Bureau can bring authors to
your live event. For more information or to book an event contact
the Simon & Schuster Speakers Bureau at 1-866-248-3049 or visit
our website at www.simonspeakers.com.

Interior design by Joy O'Meara

Manufactured in the United States of America

10 9 8 7 6 5 4 3 2 1

Library of Congress Control Number: 2015017286

ISBN 978-1-4516-9193-1
ISBN 978-1-4516-9213-6 (ebook)

All images are courtesy of the Library of Congress.

For Chloe
who is drawn to what was and is committed to what will be

We are in a wilderness without a single footstep to guide us.

—James Madison, June 1789

The intrigues, the cabals, the underhanded and insidious dealings of a factious and turbulent spirit are even much more frequent in this republic than in the most absolute monarchy.

—Louis-Guillaume Otto, July 1790

We are beginning to forget that the patriots of former days were men like ourselves, acting and acted upon like the present race, and we are almost irresistibly led to ascribe to them in our imaginations certain gigantic proportions and superhuman qualities, without reflecting that this at once robs their character of consistency and their virtues of all merit.

—Charles Francis Adams, 1871

Contents

———•◆•———

MEMBERS OF THE FIRST FEDERAL CONGRESS   xiii

INTRODUCTION: Nebuchadnezzar's Monster   1

CHAPTER 1:   An Ocean Always Turbulent   15

CHAPTER 2:   The Fostering Hand of Government   27

CHAPTER 3:   A New Era   43

CHAPTER 4:   Pomp and Quiddling   56

CHAPTER 5:   A Very Perplexing Business   72

CHAPTER 6:   A Great and Delicate Subject   84

CHAPTER 7:   Vile Politicks   99

CHAPTER 8:   Propositions of a Doubtful Nature   115

CHAPTER 9:   Paper Guarantees   129

CHAPTER 10:   A Centre Without Parallel   144

CHAPTER 11:   Interlude I   163

CHAPTER 12:   The Labyrinth of Finance   182

CHAPTER 13: A Gross National Iniquity   194

CHAPTER 14: The Trumpet of Sedition   213

CHAPTER 15: Cabals, Meetings, Plots, and Counterplots 227

CHAPTER 16: A Southern Position   238

CHAPTER 17: Indians   256

CHAPTER 18: Interlude II   266

CHAPTER 19: Freedom's Fav'rite Seat   274

CHAPTER 20: A Most Mischievous Engine   284

EPILOGUE: American Dawn   301

AFTERWORD   309
ACKNOWLEDGMENTS   315
NOTES   317
SELECTED BIBLIOGRAPHY   369
INDEX   379

Members of the First Federal Congress

THE SENATE

Connecticut
Oliver Ellsworth
William Samuel Johnson

Delaware
Richard Bassett
George Read

Georgia
William Few
James Gunn

Maryland
Charles Carroll
John Henry

Massachusetts
Tristram Dalton
Caleb Strong

New Hampshire
John Langdon
Paine Wingate

New Jersey
Philemon Dickinson (seated on
        December 6, 1790, after election to
        the seat of William Paterson)
Jonathan Elmer
William Paterson (resigned on
        November 13, 1790, after being
        elected governor of New Jersey)

New York
Rufus King
Philip John Schuyler

North Carolina
Benjamin Hawkins
Samuel Johnston

Pennsylvania
William Maclay
Robert Morris

Rhode Island
Theodore Foster
Joseph Stanton Jr.

South Carolina
Pierce Butler
Ralph Izard

Virginia
William Grayson (died March 12, 1790)
Richard Henry Lee
James Monroe (seated on December 6,
    1790, after election to the seat
    originally held by William Grayson)
John Walker (appointed to fill the
    vacancy left by William Grayson;
    served from March 31 to November 9,
    1790)

THE HOUSE OF REPRESENTATIVES

Connecticut
Benjamin Huntington
Roger Sherman
Jonathan Sturges
Jonathan Trumbull Jr.
Jeremiah Wadsworth

Delaware
John Vining

Georgia
Abraham Baldwin
James Jackson
George Mathews

Maryland
Daniel Carroll
Benjamin Contee
George Gale

Joshua Seney
William Smith
Michael Jenifer Stone

Massachusetts
Fisher Ames
Elbridge Gerry
Benjamin Goodhue
Jonathan Grout
George Leonard
George Partridge
Theodore Sedgwick
George Thatcher

New Hampshire
Abiel Foster
Nicholas Gilman
Samuel Livermore

New Jersey

Elias Boudinot

Lambert Cadwalader

James Schureman

Thomas Sinnickson

New York

Egbert Benson

William Floyd

John Hathorn

John Laurance

Peter Silvester

Jeremiah Van Rensselaer

North Carolina

John Baptista Ashe

Timothy Bloodworth

John Sevier

John Steele

Hugh Williamson

Pennsylvania

George Clymer

Thomas Fitzsimons

Thomas Hartley

Daniel Hiester

Frederick Augustus Muhlenberg

John Peter Muhlenberg

Thomas Scott

Henry Wynkoop

Rhode Island

Benjamin Bourn

South Carolina

Aedanus Burke

Daniel Huger

William Loughton Smith

Thomas Sumter

Thomas Tudor Tucker

Virginia

Theodorick Bland (died June 1, 1790)

John Brown

Isaac Coles

William Branch Giles (seated on
    December 7, 1790, after election to
    replace Theodorick Bland)

Samuel Griffin

Richard Bland Lee

James Madison Jr.

Andrew Moore

John Page

Josiah Parker

Alexander White

The

FIRST
CONGRESS

———◆———

Nebuchadnezzar's Monster

———•———

The vast Continent of America cannot be long subject to a Democracy, if consolidated into one Government—you might as well attempt to rule Hell by Prayer.

—Thomas Wait, November 1787

The First Federal Congress was the most momentous in American history. Had it failed in its work, the United States as we know it today would not exist. Beginning less than two years after the conclusion of the Constitutional Convention and before all thirteen states had ratified that document, the First Congress was charged with creating a new government almost from scratch. No one, neither in Congress nor outside it, knew if it would or could succeed. How it did so is an epic story of political combat, vivid personalities, clashing idealisms, and extraordinary determination. It breathed life into the Constitution, established precedents that still guide the nation's government, and set the stage for political battles that continue to be fought out across the political landscape of the twenty-first century: sectional rivalry, literal versus flexible interpretations of the Constitution, conflict between federal power and states' rights, tensions among the three branches of government, the protection of individual rights, the challenge of achieving compromise across wide ideological chasms, suspicion of "big money" and financial manipulators, hostility to taxation, the nature of a military establishment, and widespread suspicion of strong government.

Confidence in government was abysmally low. Since the end of the Revolutionary War in 1783, Congress had struggled to govern, with little actual power and even less respect. Along with many disgruntled Americans, newly elected South Carolina senator Ralph Izard complained to Thomas Jefferson of "the humiliating state into which we are plunged. The evil has arisen principally from the want of an efficient & energetic government, pervading every part of the United States." Contempt for politicians was rife: a New Englander transplanted to Georgia groaned, "The people here are as depraved as they are in Rhode Island, for Most of the Offices in the State are filled by the worst characters in it." Many political men held an equally low opinion of the voting public. "The people," condescendingly asserted Roger Sherman of Connecticut, one of the preeminent members of the House of Representatives, "should have as little to do as may be about the government. They lack information and are constantly liable to be misled."

In the late winter of 1789, the United States had only a ghost of government. The rump end of the Confederation Congress still wobbled along in New York City, where it had met since 1785, but it hadn't achieved a quorum since October. Its secretary, Charles Thomson, buttonholed members on the street, when he could find them, and dragged them into his office so that he could claim in his records that they had, technically, "assembled." The old Congress, though not formally dissolved, was literally homeless, having been ejected from its meeting rooms in what was now being called Federal Hall on Wall Street, which was being remodeled for the new Federal Congress under the direction of the French-born engineer Peter L'Enfant. (Proudly American, he no longer called himself Pierre.) Workmen were putting on a new roof, tearing out the dilapidated interior, erecting a grand, pillared balcony, and crafting a new facade in the fashionable Tuscan style. L'Enfant, remarked the French minister to the United States, Élénor-François-Élie, the Comte de Moustier, was building "a monument that can serve as an allegory for the new Constitution. Both have been entirely changed by their framers, who brought their interested clients a great deal further than they had thought to go." So impressive was the building that some suspicious members considered it to be a deliberate "trap to catch the Southern men," by inducing them to keep the seat of government in New York.

Enormous challenges confronted the men who were expected to assemble at Federal Hall in March 1789. Strident opponents of the Constitution were demanding scores of amendments, or a new constitutional convention to revise the founding document. The government lacked sources of revenue, European lenders shunned American loans, and several states teetered on the brink of fiscal collapse. Settlers were pouring by the thousands into the vast territory across the Appalachians, provoking the powerful native tribes that dwelled there, and inspiring fear among the nation's leaders that "the great Increase of New States will make so many Republics too Unwieldy to manage." From New Hampshire to North Carolina, aroused farmers had defied government attempts to tax them. Southerners were suspicious of northerners, westerners of easterners. Advocates of emancipation were organizing to press Congress to regulate the slave trade or even legislate an end to slavery, while the defenders of the "peculiar institution" contemplated secession if Congress dared to tamper with it. Where would the nation's permanent seat of government be established? The roiling debates that took place over these and other critical issues were not legalistic exercises. Every member of Congress knew that the nation's survival hung in the balance.

The United States, a shaky assemblage of eleven sovereign states—North Carolina and Rhode Island were still, in effect, foreign countries when Congress convened and would remain so for months to come—was less a reality than it was an *idea*, an argument even. "Our present Confederacy is not very unlike the Monster of Nebuchadnezzar, which was composed of Brass, Clay & Iron—It is neither completely national, federal nor sovereign," sighed William Tudor, a friend of John Adams's, in a letter to the vice president. "A Country extensive as the present united States, so differently settled, & so widely dissimilar in Manners & Ideas cannot easily be reduced to a homogeneous Body." As late as December 1790, North Carolina's legislature would vote by a large margin to reject a bill that would require it to take an oath to support the Constitution. Given the primitive and unreliable communications and transportation of the day, the prospect of governing such a diverse and far-flung country was daunting. The nation extended about twelve hundred miles from south to north, from Georgia to Maine—then still a part of Massachusetts—and about five hundred miles from the Atlantic coast to the Mississippi River. Americans mentally divided the country into four regions: the northern or, sometimes, eastern states—east of the Hudson River, that is—of Connecticut, Massachusetts, Rhode Island, and New Hampshire (and after 1791, Vermont); the middle states of New York, New Jersey, Pennsylvania (and sometimes Maryland, Delaware, and even Virginia); the South, including Georgia, the Carolinas, Virginia (and sometimes Maryland and Delaware); and the West, which roughly followed the course of the Appalachians from the middle of New York State south into Georgia, and also comprised portions of the future states of Ohio and parts of today's Upper Midwest, Virginia's western district of Kentucky, North Carolina's Tennessee district, and Alabama and Mississippi, both of which were claimed by Georgia.

Most Americans lived in what were essentially little more than hamlets that had been cut from the wilderness only a generation or two earlier, many of them far from any significant town. About half the country's population of just under 3 million was of English stock. Of the remainder, slaves made up about 18 percent, roughly equal to the number of recent immigrants, or children of immigrants, who were mainly from Ireland, Scotland, Wales, and Germany. To these may be added an unknown number of Indians, perhaps as many as several hundred thousand, who were ignored by census takers and belonged to a congeries of fractured and scattered tribes including, among others, New York's Iroquois, and the Creeks and Cherokees of western Georgia, who remained a formidable barrier to westbound settlers. Only Philadelphia, with forty-three thousand people, New York with thirty-three thousand, Boston with eighteen thousand, Charleston with sixteen thousand, and Baltimore with thirteen thousand could be considered cities in 1790, and all were dwarfed many times over by London, which had a population of almost 1 million, and by Paris, with half a million.

Americans only notionally regarded themselves as a single people. Many New Englanders thought of Pennsylvanians and their state "as opposite [to themselves] in manners and customs as light and darkness." Representative George Clymer of Pennsylvania remarked that he had less feeling for anything going on in New York than "for the transactions in Grand Cairo. The New Yorkers and I are on an equal footing— mutual civility without a grain of good liking between us." Southerners were suspicious of everyone to their north: "I fear much that whoever plays the Music—the Southern States will pay the Piper," Representative Theodorick Bland warned a fellow Virginian. Faced with such ingrained antagonisms, Fisher Ames of Massachusetts, a passionate proponent of national unity, wished every American to "think the union so indissoluble and integral that the corn would not grow, nor the pot boil, if it should be broken." Meanwhile, enemies of the untried Constitution, which was meant to bind Americans more closely together, contemptuously dismissed it as "no more than general principles thrown into form," warning that it heralded a tyranny that would soon squelch free speech and silence the press.

Could the new government be made to work? As James Madison, who would do more than anyone else to guide the First Congress along its path, put it, "We are in a wilderness without a single footstep to guide us." The powerful presidency that is today taken for granted still lay far in the future. There was an elected president, George Washington, but little agreement on what his job entailed. There were no executive departments, and no federal employees except the clerks of the Senate and the House of Representatives, and Washington's personal secretaries. Nor was there a Supreme Court, or any lower federal courts. The nature of the relation-

ship between the federal government and the states was pretty much anyone's guess. Congress had no majority or minority leaders, no organized
parties, no established rules of procedure, and no clear definition of the
relationship between the executive and the legislative branches of government. Congressional districts varied dizzyingly in size: Representative
James Jackson of Georgia represented just sixteen thousand people, while
George Thatcher of the Maine district of Massachusetts represented more
than ninety-six thousand. Slavery further skewed congressional representation. To secure ratification of the Constitution in the South, Yankee
delegates agreed that each slave would count as three-fifths of a person for
the purpose of apportioning the size of a state's delegation in the House
of Representatives. Slave states thus received bonus seats for 60 percent
of their enslaved population, giving them clout in Congress far beyond
what they would have enjoyed if bound by the same rules as the free
states, along with the presumption that they would enjoy their advantage
in perpetuity.

Though rarely addressed directly, the specter of slavery would threaten
to intrude upon some of the most crucial debates of the First Congress,
like an asteroid hurtling toward Earth whose impact could be foreseen
and was feared, but which few dared acknowledge. Under the Articles of
Confederation, which the Constitution had replaced, each state had only
one vote in the Confederation Congress, an arrangement that made slavery politically irrelevant, since it gave Virginia, with its 100,783 slaves, no
more weight than Massachusetts, which had none. At the Constitutional
Convention, the larger states had demanded that representation reflect the
size of a state's population, raising a new dilemma: Were slaves people who
should be counted, or property that should not? If only free whites were
counted, the more populous North would obviously dominate the government and would eventually have the power to bring an end to slavery, if it
wished. However, it was widely believed that the North would eventually
lose its demographic advantage as new slave states were carved from the
West. If the South could achieve sufficient leverage over the government
in the short run, periodic reapportionment would eventually cement its

hegemony. Counting slaves toward each state's representation in Congress was an exquisite solution, since no one was suggesting that slaves be actually permitted to vote for the men who would "represent" them.

If slavery was the largely unmentioned monster in the basement of the new nation, other threats could hardly be suppressed. Congress would meet in the shadow of an event that had rocked many Americans' confidence in republican government itself. Shays's Rebellion is almost forgotten today except as a footnote in American history. But it loomed large in the anxieties of many members of the First Congress. In the fall and winter of 1786–87, overtaxed farmers led by a war veteran named Daniel Shays shut down courts, ambushed judges, roughed up tax collectors, and invaded the homes of wealthy officials in western Massachusetts. Militiamen sent to suppress the rebels joined them by the scores. Conservatives feared that the rebels—"desperate and unprincipled men"—were bent on fomenting class war and on seeking an alliance with the British. The rebellion was finally put down by an armed force raised by wealthy Bostonians. But it revealed the hopeless weakness of the country's military power. It also seemed to dramatically demonstrate the dangers of unmediated democracy, free assembly, and unbridled speech. In the debates to come, members of Congress would often express a dread that America was already beginning the downward trajectory of historical republics that had collapsed into civil strife. As Virginia senator Richard Henry Lee would later opine to George Washington, Shays's uprising seemed to prove "that mankind left to themselves are unfit for their own government."

Reports of foreign subversion, cabals, and Indian attacks swirled everywhere around the country's borders. Among members of the new government anxiety was widespread that the West, in particular, bound as it was to the rest of the nation only by "lax and feeble cords," would break away and form either a separate country or ally itself with Spain or Britain. (Some Americans opposed the settlement of the west, for fear that it would depopulate the old states: "Can we retain the Western Country within the Government of the United States, and if we can, of what use will it be?" wondered the retired Revolutionary War general Rufus Putnam.) Beyond the mountains, boundaries between whites and natives were largely undefined, animosities deep, and border warfare chronic. Settlers were begging for laws and protection, which the feeble Confederation government had failed to give. Unless they were satisfied, warned Representative Thomas Scott of Pennsylvania, "They will either throw themselves on the Spanish government, and become their subjects—or they will combine, and give themselves possession of that territory and defend themselves in it against the power of the Union." To the south, hundreds of Creek warriors were said to be mobilizing to attack Georgia's frontier. General Anthony Wayne reported that the security situation there was dire, not just from Indian depredations, but also from "the insidious protection afforded by the Spaniards to our runaway Negroes . . . threaten[ing] this lately flourishing State with ruin & depopulation" unless Congress acted quickly. In the Northwest Territory, encompassing most of today's Upper Midwest, the British not only refused to relinquish their border posts, as required by the peace treaty of 1783, but had reinforced them with eight thousand troops and were reportedly fomenting discontent among the local Indians.

Even more threatening to stability was the nation's precarious financial condition. During the Revolutionary War, the Continental Congress had borrowed massively from European banks and governments, as well as Americans. The government was deeply, cataclysmically, in debt, owing almost $2 million in overdue interest, with $500,000 in new payments to overseas creditors alone falling due annually. "We are in the dark," confessed a Pennsylvania congressman. "I do believe we are now walking on the brink of a precipice that will be dangerous for us to step too fast upon." State debts, too, were a rat's nest of unsupported currency and promissory notes, some of which were unredeemable even at a discount of forty to one. The face value of all outstanding national and state government debt would eventually prove to be $74 million. In 1789, no one in Congress knew what to do about this debt. "In America we had hitherto but little experience in this science [of finance]," Massachusetts representative Elbridge Gerry gloomily observed. "We are going onward blindfolded, and have seriously to apprehend evils from every step."

The days of the United States as a world-striding titan of trade and a manufacturing powerhouse were barely a gleam in the eye of a few far-sighted financiers. Only three banks then existed in the United States, in Philadelphia, New York, and Boston, and few corporations, and those mostly to build turnpikes. Meanwhile, at least fifty bewilderingly disparate kinds of money were in use, many of them counterfeit: Spanish doubloons and pistoles, Dutch guilders, British pounds, French guineas, and a multitude of state-issued currencies. In 1787, the New York legislature declared all the copper currency in circulation to be officially fake. So many coins had already been clipped or trimmed for fractions of their value that even the simplest transactions often required a pair of scales. All this monetary bedlam tortured travelers and businessmen alike. In parts of the South, receipts for tobacco often substituted for money. In some states, such as New Jersey, travelers were obliged to accept local currency that was worse than worthless everywhere else: someone who bought Jersey money in New York at a 25 percent discount, expecting to profit by it, might well suffer a *further* discount of *50 percent* when he tried to spend it in New Jersey. This "abominable traffic," raged a French traveler, "makes a science of deceit and teaches a man to live not by honest and useful work but by dishonest and pernicious dealings."

Public confidence that the new government would be able to cope with all the "confusions, animosity and discord that now seems to dominate in the several States" was shaky at best. "Is there not danger from the imbecility of the national Govt.?" worried Vice President John Adams, who expected fully half the members of Congress to give up and resign within two years. "What has it to attract the hopes or excite the fears of the People? Has it power? Has it Force to protect itself or its Offices? Has it Rewards or Punishments in its power enough to allure or Alarm?"

The First Congress, particularly its first session, was dominated by the diminutive figure of James Madison, who often led the debates and over-awed the House of Representatives with his unrivaled command of legislative machinery and by his powers of persuasive argument. Although he held no formal position beyond that of representative from Virginia, his intimacy with Washington and his commanding grasp of the Constitution bestowed on him a tacit authority in shaping the House's agenda. The office of the House Speaker commanded little authority, and the positions of majority and minority leader would not come into being for generations, no one was surprised that Madison presumed to take the leading role in the House's deliberations. But Madison was only the first among equals in a diverse and individualistic body. The ninety-five senators and representatives who served in the First Congress were a comparatively youthful lot, mostly in their forties and thirties. A few would prove themselves far from suited to patient deliberation. The workaholic Madison tartly commented, soon after Congress opened, that he saw only "a very scanty proportion who will share in the drudgery of business," while the impatient, young Fisher Ames of Massachusetts derided "the yawning listlessness" of his colleagues and "their overrefining spirit in relation to trifles"—in other words, their pettifogging small-mindedness. But most were professional political men of talent, experience, and resourcefulness. Most had also served the patriot cause during the Revolutionary War, although a handful were tainted by allegations of wartime Loyalist sympathies.

Roger Sherman had brokered the Constitutional Convention's Great Compromise, which produced a Senate with equal representation for all states and a House of Representatives where representation was based on the population of the individual states. His Connecticut colleague, Senator Oliver Ellsworth, born poor but later Yale-educated, had served for years in the Continental Congress and would shape the creation of the judicial branch. Senator Richard Henry Lee had occupied public office for forty years, beginning with Virginia's colonial House of Burgesses, and was regarded as one of the finest orators of the age. Elbridge Gerry of Massachusetts, spartan by temperament, radical and republican by conviction, had served in public offices since 1762, signed the Declaration of Independence, and would become one of the most aggressive critics of centralized power. The philanthropic Representative Elias Boudinot of New Jersey, an evangelical Presbyterian, had spent much of his own fortune supplying the patriot army, as well as charitably providing for British prisoners of war, and later served as president of the Confederation Congress. There were plutocrats, such as Senator Robert Morris of Pennsylvania, one of the wealthiest men in America, and agriculturalists such as Senator Ralph Izard of South Carolina, who owned five hundred slaves and forty-three hundred acres of plantation land; there were soldiers such as Representative James Jackson of Georgia, who had fought Indians on the frontier, and men of faith such as Representative Frederick Augustus Muhlenberg of Pennsylvania, who had left the Lutheran ministry to join the Continental Congress and become Speaker of Pennsylvania's Assembly. Despite their competing interests and personalities, they would perform a feat of collaborative political creativity that has rarely been rivaled.

Political parties in the modern sense didn't exist. But sharp differences between supporters and opponents of the Constitution had already emerged. Self-described "Federalists," who held twenty of the twenty-two seats in the Senate, and forty-six of the fifty-nine seats in the House, were committed in differing degrees to entrenching a stronger central government. A significant minority of "Antifederalists"—enough, one Federalist wrote, to "keep [the Constitution's] friends active and vigilant"—had opposed the Constitution and now sought to curtail the federal government and to preserve as much power as they could for the states. Generally, Antifederalists believed that the national government should be allowed to operate only through the states as distinct independent republics, not directly on individual citizens, and that federal authority should be restricted to a few limited spheres of activity, such as interstate commerce, foreign affairs, high-seas navigation, coinage, and national defense. In agreeing to ratify the Constitution, one Antifederalist essayist, writing as "Federal Farmer" in a series of widely reprinted letters, charged that Americans had been hoodwinked by a cabal of "aristocratical men" who had long schemed to create a "consolidated government" upon the ruins of the states. The new system, Federal Farmer added, "was a dangerous experiment, a disaster waiting to happen," unless states retained the power to nullify laws they deemed "injurious to the people." One anonymous

New Yorker, remarkable only in his snarling ferocity, denounced the Constitution in the *New-York Daily Advertiser* as nothing less than a "monarchical, aristocratical, oligarchical, tyrannical, diabolical system of slavery." Others feared that the consolidation of powers in the presidency would make its occupant *"a King as the King of Great Britain*, and a King too of the worst kind—an elective King." The only remedy, most Antifederalists held, was a massive overhaul of the Constitution.

Federalists worried that if opponents of the Constitution succeeded in making the new government subservient to the will of the states, they would destroy the government itself. "We cannot yet consider ourselves in the Harbour of safety," the former Revolutionary War general Benjamin Lincoln of Massachusetts warned John Adams. Most Federalists considered amendments of any kind a frivolous waste of Congress's time, and liable, as the grammarian Noah Webster protested, to "sow the seeds of discord from New-Hampshire to Georgia." Others were scathing, such as an anonymous editorialist in the *Freeman's Journal*, a Philadelphia newspaper, who scoffed, "The worship of the ox, the crocodile, and the cat, in ancient time, and the belief in astrology and witchcraft by more modern nations, did not prostrate the human understanding more than the numerous absurdities" proposed as amendments. An equally sarcastic writer to the *New-York Daily Gazette* declared, "If we must have amendments, I pray for merely amusing ones, a little frothy garnish."

Despite all the complaints and anxieties, hopes for the new government were high, and popular interest was intense. "All eyes are looking up to Congress for the restoration of the golden age," a constituent wrote to Elbridge Gerry. In the months that followed, lofty ambitions for sweeping legislation would collide, sometimes violently, with sectional jealousies and commercial self-interest. Personal rivalries would at times trump the public interest. Political fissures within delegations, among states, and between regions would burst their sutures. Among some, doubts about the nation's survival would grow. Yet the output of the First Congress was prodigious, as it transmuted the Constitution from a paper charter and a set of hopeful aspirations into the machinery of a functioning government.

In its three sessions, the first two in New York and the third in Philadelphia, it would create the Departments of State, War, and Treasury, the Supreme Court, the federal court system, and the first federal criminal code. Congress would debate and pass the first amendments to the Constitution, today known as the Bill of Rights. It would enact a bold agenda of duties and tariffs to create a revenue stream for the federal government and adopt a far-reaching financial plan that rooted the nation's economic system in capitalist principles. The first national bank of the United States would be launched, the first census begun, and the patent and copyright systems established. Treaty making would be initiated through negotiations with the Indian tribes of the trans-Appalachian west, the site of the nation's permanent capital would be decided, and the last holdouts among the thirteen original states—North Carolina and Rhode Island—would be brought into the Union, along with Vermont, setting a precedent that new states would be admitted on an equal basis with the old. "In no nation, by no Legislature, was ever so much done in so short a period for the establishment of Government, Order, public Credit and general tranquillity," John Trumbull, a Hartford lawyer not to be confused with the painter of the same name, would exuberantly write to John Adams after the third session's close.

It would take months for the other parts of the government to take shape and bring their own political coloration to the dawn of the new system. During the First Congress, however, George Washington, so nervous that his hands shook at his inauguration, would gradually invent the presidency, stretch its powers, pry it away from the domination of Congress, and begin to define the parameters of the office for generations to come. John Adams would woefully fail to shape the vice presidency into an assertive force in the deliberations of the Senate, condemning that office to the diminished status that it retains today. Alexander Hamilton, the first secretary of the treasury, would devise an economic system for the US government and see it enacted by a Congress almost totally unlettered in the principles of economics. Secretary of State Thomas Jefferson, a latecomer to New York, would be instrumental in bringing into being the nation's permanent capital, and—against his own visceral instincts—Hamilton's financial plan. Henry Knox, the secretary of war, would advocate for peace with the Indians, then call for the nation's first standing army to wage war against them. Chief Justice John Jay would set the new Supreme Court on its path.

Where would it all lead? "Here are these Americans, launched onto this great sea," one of the Americans' most acute and sympathetic foreign observers, the Comte de Moustier, reflected with the almost audible sigh of a world-weary Old World cynic. "These pilots, accustomed to steering small boats with some success on water seldom and little disturbed, will have another notion of the art of governing when they will have weathered the same storms and encountered the same perils that prove formidable even for men more able and experienced than the great politicians of America. They will recognize through experience what distance and what difference lies between theory and practice and that it is just as difficult to know how to exploit a victory as it is to know how to be victorious." But now, at the birth of a government that was to defy expectations and endure beyond the hopes of even many of its creators, all was thrill and excitement. As Congress assembled that dank and chilly spring of 1789, the world seemed new, and Americans felt in their hearts that they stood at the dawn of a new epoch. "All ranks & degrees of men seemed to be actuated by one common impulse, to fill the galleries as soon as the doors of the House of Representatives were opened for the first time," recalled an elderly James Kent, who as an enthralled child had watched the Congress's first stirrings. "I considered it to be a proud & glorious day, the consummation of our wishes; & that I was looking upon an organ of popular will, just beginning to breathe the Breath of Life, & which might in some future age, much more truly than the Roman Senate, be regarded as 'the refuge of nations.'"

CHAPTER I

An Ocean Always Turbulent

——— • ———

Our Constitution is like a vessel just launched, and lying at the wharf; it is not known how she will answer her helm, or lay her course; whether she will bear in safety the precious freight to be deposited in her hold.

—Representative James Jackson of Georgia

Winter in the Potomac River Valley was unpredictable. Sheets of icy rain, sleet, and sometimes snow waterlogged much of the farmland around Alexandria and turned the roads into glutinous muck that played havoc with travelers' schedules. One of those travelers, in late February of 1789, a diminutive figure bundled against the cold, had crossed Virginia from his home near the Blue Ridge Mountains to see a friend who was also the most famous man in America. As he approached George Washington's Mount Vernon, James Madison would first have noticed the long avenue of broad-boughed, winter-bare oaks, and eventually the stately house itself, porticoed and colonnaded on its bluff overlooking the river. Madison was en route to New York City, to take up his duties in the new Congress that was about to come into being. Mount Vernon was out of his way. A more direct route would have taken him across the Potomac at

Georgetown, Maryland, and from there directly to Baltimore. But Washington had summoned him, a trusted protégé who they both knew was likely to play a central role in the great debates that were to come. Denied one of Virginia's Senate seats by his political opponents, Madison had just won a hard-fought contest against his friend James Monroe for a seat in the House of Representatives. Enemies of the Constitution, who were both passionate and powerful in Virginia, had warned that the election of Madison would produce "rivulets of blood throughout the land." Fortunately such dire predictions did not come to pass.

Washington wanted help with his inaugural address, which the president-to-be would deliver in April. He had first entrusted the job to his aide David Humphreys, who had delivered a seventy-three-page behemoth of an oration full of policy proposals that expressed Washington's support for a powerful federal government and an assertive executive. Madison told Washington, in essence, to toss Humphreys's handiwork: it was too long and tried to say too much. Instead, he urged Washington to speak more simply to a fragile nation that was about to embark on a political experiment whose outcome few could see, and many feared. They dismembered and finally discarded Humphreys's prolix draft and boiled down what Washington would say to the nation to essential ideas that every American could support. Drafting any address might have seemed like presumption on Washington's part: he was not yet president. Voting for presidential electors was still taking place in several states—no citizen could cast a vote directly for president—and the results could not be officially declared until Congress met. But since he had no opposition, the outcome was a foregone conclusion.

The two men could hardly have been more dissimilar. At fifty-seven the aging war hero, a giant by the standards of his time, with his great beak of a nose, broad shoulders, and massive thighs that seemed to have been crafted by the Almighty to fit the back of a horse, was a living demigod. During the war, he had exhibited superhuman stoicism through the years of brutal winters, hunger, battlefield defeat, and civilian disaffection. He was also brave to the point of foolhardiness, repeatedly exposing himself to enemy fire; allegedly, at one point during the rout of American troops on Long Island, with a large rock in both hands, he was said to have stormed up to a boat filled with fleeing soldiers and threatened to "sink it to hell" unless the men went back to the fight. Popular writers commonly called him the nation's "deliverer" and "savior" and occasionally even likened him to Jesus Christ. "O WASHINGTON! How do I love thy name!" declared Ezra Stiles, the president of Yale University, in a widely reprinted sermon. "How have I often adored and blessed thy God, for creating and forming thee the great ornament of human kind! Not all the gold of ophir, nor a world filled with rubies and diamonds, could effect or purchase the sublime and noble feelings of thine heart. Thy fame is of sweeter perfume than arabian spices in the gardens of *persia*." His face, which appeared everywhere—on engravings, mezzotints, dinner plates, wall plaques, jugs, and mugs—was probably the only one that was known to virtually every American. Although he had publicly professed "the most unfeigned reluctance" to take on the presidency, Washington was, as one New Englander put it, "the only man which Man, Woman & Child, Whig & Tory, Fed's and Antifed's appear to agree in."

Madison, twenty years Washington's junior, was respected in political circles for his scholarship and persuasive powers, but not much loved. Sickly and slight—he stood five feet four and weighed only a hundred pounds—and deemed "unmanly" by many of his contemporaries, it seemed as if all his vigor had been sucked into his copious and muscular mind. The wife of one prominent Virginia politician dismissed him as "a gloomy, stiff creature . . . the most unsociable creature in Existence." The two men had first met in 1781, when Madison was serving in the Continental Congress. Washington immediately recognized the Princeton-educated Madison as a young man of unusual talent. Although his wartime soldiering consisted only of a brief turn in the Virginia militia, his background in government was impressive. He had already served as a member of Virginia's revolutionary convention, and then—still only in his midtwenties—as a political adviser to Governor Patrick Henry, and to Henry's successor, Thomas Jefferson. After the war, as a member of the Virginia Assembly, Madison advocated for Washington's commercial interests in the Potomac Valley and became one of the former general's closest advisers.

Although Madison spoke in a whispery, often-difficult-to-hear voice, and without oratorical flourish, he consistently impressed those who worked with him with his "most ingenious mind," and his mastery of parliamentary strategy. He understood, as many of his more emotional colleagues did not, his biographer Richard Brookhiser acutely observed, that "losing a vote was not the same as losing the argument, because if you could then write the guidelines for implementing the decision, you could nudge it in a better direction." It was a lesson well learned at the Constitutional Convention, where Madison had unsuccessfully proposed, among other things, that the president be chosen by the legislative branch rather than by a popular vote channeled through an electoral college, that Congress be given the power to override state laws, and that the membership of both houses of Congress be based on population. Madison would carry with him to the First Congress a disdain for Pyrrhic moral victories, and a pragmatic determination to make the imperfect machine of government work.

Madison, more than any other man, had convinced the conflicted Washington first to attend the convention, and then to accept its chair. Washington would have preferred to remain at Mount Vernon beneath his "vine and fig tree," his favorite euphemism for political disengagement, although he well knew that he could not remain so if the convention were to succeed. Though he shared Madison's anxiety for the country, he feared that he would be accused of selfish ambition if he reentered public life, having so publicly proclaimed his official retirement from it in 1783. Madison, however—he was nothing if not persuasive, everyone agreed—made the case that no other American had the prestige to win nationwide support for a radical overhaul of the hapless Confederation government. Once committed, Washington was unshakable. Hamilton observed of him, "Perhaps the strongest feature in his character was prudence, never acting until every circumstance, every consideration, was maturely weighed; refraining if he saw a doubt, but, when once decided, going through with his purpose whatever obstacles opposed." As Madison had hoped, Washington's presence in Philadelphia helped to balance the discontent of those in the convention who felt that it was going too far in reinventing the government.

Madison's reputation increased during the long campaign for ratification of the Constitution when, as a coauthor of *The Federalist* (with Alexander Hamilton and John Jay), he had laid out a reasoned case for a powerful central government, arguing that it would not weaken but strengthen personal liberties, and explaining to a doubtful public how its machinery would actually function. He boldly challenged the widely held belief that stable republics could work only in miniature societies, such as Greek city-states or homogeneous American communities. "Latent causes of faction"—that is, individual self-interest—he argued, was "sown in the nature of man," and because it was inescapable, it had to be accommodated, not denied. This could best be accomplished in an *extensive* republic whose very diversity would prevent dangerous majorities from riding roughshod over political minorities, where it was less likely that any single party could outnumber and oppress the rest, and that a representative government rather than direct democracy would "refine and enlarge the public views, by passing them through the medium of a chosen body of citizens whose wisdom may best discern the true interest of their country."

Like many political men at the time, Madison believed that the legislature would long remain the most powerful branch of government, and the most likely to suck "all power into its impetuous vortex." To restrain the legislature's greed for power, he maintained that all three branches of government had to be made equally vigorous and endowed with the "means and personal motives to resist encroachments of the others," to prevent an accumulation of legislative power that would inexorably lead to tyranny. Mere "parchment barriers"—that is, well-meaning sentiments with no force to back them up—would not be enough. Dividing Congress itself into two branches vested with different powers was just a first step. The greater challenge was empowering the two weaker branches of government—the executive and judiciary—to resist legislative dictatorship. To this end, the president had been given a veto to protect the independence of the executive branch, while lifetime tenure for members of the Supreme Court would help insulate the judiciary from political interference. "Ambition must be made to counteract ambition," he declared, in a famous formulation. "What is government itself but the greatest of all reflections on human nature? If men were angels, no government would be necessary."

As election results for the new Congress trickled in from the states—there was no fixed day for elections—the results proved vastly more favorable than Washington, Madison, and their fellow supporters of the new Constitution had hoped. Federalists had won overwhelming majorities in both houses of Congress. Americans, in Washington's opinion, had shown good sense, but the future remained fraught with risk. It might not take much to unravel the tentative fabric of a nation that had been rewoven at the Constitutional Convention less than two years earlier. "Some unforeseen mischance," Washington worried, could still "blast [our] enjoyment in the very bud."

The pressure on Washington was immense, and public expectations so high that he could never fully satisfy them, he knew. The president-to-be had received any number of importunate pleas from men such as John Armstrong Jr., a former member of the Continental Congress, who had begged him "to yield your services to the providential voice of God expressed in the voice of your country." (Armstrong may have been one of the less convincing voices, however: In 1783, he had been a central figure in the so-called Newburgh Conspiracy, which toyed with the idea of a military coup against the Congress.) So many conflicting worries tore at Washington, both political and personal: the unrest on the frontier and the financial instability in the states, the resurgence of the Constitution's opponents in Virginia, the planting schedules for his next season's crops of wheat and rye, the challenge of managing the remote lands he owned in the West, the declining health of his eighty-year-old mother, who was dying of cancer at Fredericksburg. And now he was about to shoulder the unprecedented burdens of the presidency. To his neighbor Samuel Vaughn he confessed, as he doubtless did to Madison, "The event which I have long dreaded, I am at last constrained to believe, is now likely to happen. From the moment, when the necessity had become more apparent, & as it were inevitable, I anticipated in a heart filled with distress, the ten thousand embarrassments, perplexities & troubles to which I must again be exposed in the evening of a life, already near consumed in public cares."

What was left of the old Confederation government was scheduled to cease functioning on March 3, and the new Congress to begin on March 4. But continuing wretched weather slowed Madison's northward progress to a crawl. From Baltimore, he wrote Washington the happy news, reported to him by a courier from Georgia, that Federalists had triumphed in that state's elections, too: "All the Candidates I understand are well affected to the Constitution." But Madison's spirits sank a few days later at Philadelphia, when a traveler from New York told him that only a handful of senators and congressmen had arrived there, and that neither New Jersey nor New York had even completed their elections. (The traveler, a planter whom Madison trusted, also delivered the ominous news that British agents were active in the trans-Appalachian Kentucky district of Virginia, agitating against the American government, a development that Madison knew would have to be dealt with.) Much more worried Madison as well during the long, muddy journey to New York: the country's chaotic financial state . . . the angry veterans who everywhere were demanding back pay . . . the divisive debate raging over the site for a permanent federal capital . . . the numerous amendments that roiling popular conventions had demanded be made to the Constitution, which might well undo all the work that Madison had done. He also knew that popular hopes for the new government were unrealistically high. "The people," wrote one Massachusetts voter, "are on tiptoe in their expectation from Congress, we expect more than Angells can do from your Body."

From all over the eleven states that had approved the Constitution, newly elected members of Congress were heading, if glacially, toward New York. None of them knew with confidence whether they could rise to the demands of a new, untested government whose machinery they would have to invent as they went along. "Leaving my domestick peace and hapiness and plungeing into the Ocean of Publick Business, Politicks, and Etiquette is unaccountable even to Myself But the fates will have it so," sighed Senator John Langdon of New Hampshire. Fisher Ames of Boston was so nervous at taking his seat in the House that it seemed like a kind of death. "I am about to leave and renounce this world and go to New York and must so far settle my worldly affairs as to be in a degree prepared for my future state (a state of terror and uncertainty to me)," he confided to a friend. One of Ames's traveling companions, the much more experienced Elbridge Gerry, hardly knew what to expect either. He had been one of only three members of the Constitutional Convention who refused to sign the final document, and the sneering ridicule he had endured ever since left him depressed and discouraged. "You are now launching into the Ocean of Politics, an ocean always turbulent," a supporter gently advised him. "I wish your habits & Experience may preserve you from Seasickness while the rectitude of your mind may lead you to stem the rolling Billows."

New York City, in 1789, occupied only the southern tip of Manhattan Island and still bore the visible ravages of the seven-year British occupation during the Revolutionary War. There was no New Yorker who didn't remember the overcrowding and starvation, the shortages, the streets torn up to build defensive works, the charred swathes of the city leveled by fire, the pathetic tent colonies of refugees, the harsh reprisals against rebels, the winters without firewood when the poor were found dead in their hovels at dawn. Even now, disintegrating forts and redoubts still punctuated the island's rural landscape, while across the East River the bones of American soldiers killed during the 1776 battle for Long Island lay yellowing in plain sight.

As recently as June 1787, a visitor returning from several years in France had found the city still "in a state of prostration and decay." Now, however, the city was roaring back to life. Everywhere, workmen were flattening hills, filling out the shoreline to create a new waterfront, erecting new houses, cutting new streets, constructing new docks. Business was thriving, trade on the rise, and the harbor a forest of tall-masted sailing ships from around the world. Although New York was the nation's second city, with few buildings that rose higher than three stories, for the many members of Congress who hailed from rural areas, it was phantasmagorically cosmopolitan. Its doglegged lanes teemed with Hudson Valley Dutchmen, sailing men from the coast of New England, Jews and Frenchmen, Irishmen and Germans, frontiersmen from the backcountry of western New York, visiting Iroquois tribesmen, free blacks, slaves, and indentured white servants, who—like the enslaved—were forbidden to buy or sell, gamble or marry, or travel more than ten miles from their master's home. The city's newspapers were unfettered and combative. At the Merchant's Coffee House at Wall and Water Streets, one might glimpse the politically potent young lawyers Aaron Burr or Alexander Hamilton amid the crowd of speculators, shipowners, importers, and traders in everything from real estate to slaves. In the surrounding business district, between Broadway and the East River docks, you could find whip makers and wigmakers, refiners of spermaceti and vendors of "nernous essence" for toothache, nurseries selling potted oleander and Arabian jasmine, retailers of tinderboxes, sleigh bells, quills, knee buckles, imported wines and liquors, publishers and printers, dancing masters to teach the latest European steps, and musicians such as the master "klokkenist and componist" Mr. Van Hagen willing to take on students. Even the city gallows was an astonishment, enshrined within a gaudily painted Chinese-style pagoda, next to the whipping post and stocks.

The city's leading physician, the boosterish Samuel Bard, might gush over the city's healthful location, surrounded by luxuriant farmland and blessed with "sweetening and salubrifying air." But many members of Congress were appalled by the ubiquitous filth. The stink of rotting garbage was pervasive, while laundresses scrubbed the city's linen on the shores of the Collect, a body of water near the present-day courthouses, both state and federal, where tanners dumped their chemicals amid floating effluvia that included dead cats and dogs, and rotting offal. Congressman John Page of Virginia disgustedly observed, "The Streets here are badly paved, very dirty & narrow as well as crooked, & filled up with a

Strange Variety of wooden Stone & brick Houses & full of Hogs & mud."
And excrement. The poor simply dumped their chamber pots in the gut-
ters, leaving it to rain and battalions of roaming, rooting hogs to deal with
it. For the wealthy, sanitation (such as it was) devolved upon slaves: long
lines of them could be seen in the dawn light trudging toward the river
with tubs of plutocratic "night soil" on their heads.

Unfazed by such noisome realities, the pious Senator Oliver Ellsworth
of Connecticut found New York reassuringly religion-minded, and well
regulated. There were bans against sawing wood on the sidewalk, planting
trees south of the Collect except in front of churches, and driving water
carts any faster than a walk. Swearing was punishable by a fine of three
shillings or imprisonment in the stocks; churches were plentiful and their
pews were well filled. "And what has added to my pleasure," Ellsworth
wrote to his wife, Abigail, "has been the great decence & appearance of
devotion with which divine service is attended. Instead of gazing, whispering & laughing, most of the Ladies, & many of the Gentlemen kneel
at prayers on . . . benches in their seats with their heads inclined so as to
conceal their faces." Ellsworth apparently never noticed the whorehouses
that jammed the lanes behind the docks just a few minutes' stroll from
his rooming house.

In contrast to the inhabitants of Quakery Philadelphia and straitlaced
Boston, New Yorkers prided themselves on their taste for fashion. Women
wore spectacular dresses luxuriantly displayed over hoops that were flat-
tened fore and aft and stood out two feet on either side. Hairstyles were
architectural confections that rose a foot or more in height and were festooned with lace and flowers. Congressional wives were dazzled by the
array of fabrics available in local stores: lawns, chintzes, calicos, palam-
poors, fustians, dimities, armozeens, taffities, crepes, velvets, bombazeens,
osnaburgs, ticklenburgs, shalloons, fearnaughts, and dozens of others that
were unheard of in the backcountry of New Hampshire or Georgia. Puritanical Yankees were shocked at the bursting bodices of the local women,
which they considered intolerably decadent, not to mention the outrageous behavior of the French ambassador, who affected American homespun clothing but lived openly in his embassy with a mistress who was

also his sister-in-law. Others were offended by New Yorkers' overly refined manners and incessant socializing. "The Tyrant Custom" particularly annoyed the austere Presbyterian sensibilities of Senator William Maclay of Pennsylvania, who sneered at women who accoutered themselves with "a bunch of Bosom and bulk of Cotton that never was warranted by any feminine appearance in nature" and walked bent forward at the middle "as if some disagreeable disorder prevented them from standing erect."

Maclay detested not only New York's inhabitants, congestion, dissipation, and outlandish prices, but even Federal Hall, which he derided as a waste of money, the epitome of New York ostentation, and no better than a "Great Baby House." (This was a play on words: L'Enfant's name meant "child.") "With so many windows and doors, and corners and loop holes . . . all your Honorable Body may play bo-peep, hide and seek, or anything else, for a whole twelve-month in it, without being found out," he wrote anonymously in the *Federal Gazette*. The majority of arriving legislators, however, were amazed at the hall's harmonious redesign and elegant, up-to-date interiors. The facade included an arcade in the Tuscan style, while inside, the lofty vestibule was flagged with marble and led to an atrium roofed with a glass cupola that bathed the first-floor lobby in light. The octagonal House chamber, where many of the most dramatic debates would take place, was widely regarded as a masterpiece. This fifty-by-seventy-foot "representatives' apartment," as it was often called, rose two stories and was amply lit by six tall windows, three on each side, and embellished with fluted, Ionic columns arranged throughout the room. The members' desks and chairs—each covered in blue damask that matched the curtains—formed a semicircle. The smaller upstairs Senate chamber—forty feet square and fifteen feet high—was adorned with graceful pilasters whose capitals had been designed by L'Enfant, and a light blue ceiling from which a sun and thirteen stars radiated over the senators. The oversize chair—some meaningfully referred to it as a "throne"—of the presiding officer, the vice president, was elevated three feet above the floor beneath a draped canopy of crimson damask. Only the House chamber provided galleries for spectators, who flocked in great numbers to hear debates that were regarded as great public entertainment;

the deliberations of the self-consciously elitist Senate would not be open to the public until 1795.

On the evening of March 3, while Madison was still on the miry road from Virginia, the old Confederation was officially "fired out" by thirteen cannon posted at Fort George, at the foot of Broadway. Crowed one newspaper, "The Copartnership of Anarchy and Antifederalism being dissolved by the death of the concerned, the firm ceases to be." At sunrise the next day, eleven guns—one for each of the states that had approved the Constitution—boomed out again across the New York harbor, along with more joyous tolling of bells. "The old government has gently fallen asleep, and the new one is waking into activity," optimistically wrote Representative George Thatcher, who was a member of both. Church bells rang and rang, flags waved, crowds cheered in an atmosphere of uninhibited joy. The fourth of March 1789, predicted Pennsylvania senator and merchant prince Robert Morris, "will no doubt be hereafter Celebrated as a New Era in the Annals of the World."

Morris had crossed the Hudson from New Jersey that morning, just in time to watch the national flag hoisted atop Federal Hall, and to mingle with the rejoicing mobs of citizenry. He had good reason to celebrate. He had done more than most men to bring the new nation into being during the Revolutionary War. As superintendent of finance for the Confederation Congress, he had almost single-handedly saved the revolutionary government from collapse by underwriting its expenses with his personal fortune. As a staunch Federalist he had high hopes for the new government. But he was also a hardheaded businessman and no sentimentalist. That morning on the streets of Manhattan, he saw further than many, if not most, of his euphoric compatriots. No matter how hard Congress struggled to do its duty, he wrote to his wife, Molly, "The Public's expectation seems to be so highly wound up that I think disappointment must inevitably follow after a while. But you know well how impossible it is for Public measures to keep pace with the sanguine desires of the interested, the ignorant, and the inconsiderate parts of the Community."

CHAPTER 2

The Fostering Hand of Government

———— • ————

I never felt greater Mortification in my life to be so long here with the
Eyes of all the World on Us & to do nothing.

—Senator William Maclay, March 1789

The guns boomed again at noon on March 4 to signal the opening of
Congress. Senators and congressmen gathered in the glamorous chambers
that Peter L'Enfant was building for them only to discover to their deep
embarrassment that both houses fell far short of the quorum required to
do business. Only eight senators had shown up, and only thirteen representatives, all but two of them from just three states, Massachusetts,
Connecticut, and Pennsylvania. When James Madison finally reached
New York on March 14, he found that only two more congressmen and
no additional senators had arrived. "When a Quorum will be made up in
either House, rests on vague conjecture," he fumed in a letter to Washington. Without quorums the new government didn't really exist. The ballots
for president and vice president couldn't be counted. No legislation could
take place. Courts couldn't be created. Revenues couldn't be raised. "This
is a very mortifying situation," Fisher Ames wrote to a friend in Massachusetts. "We lose spirit, credit, everything. The public will forget the
government before it is born."

Governor John Sullivan of New Hampshire, who complained that "our Spirit of Electioneering is dirty like the weather of the Season," was just one of many observers who shook their heads in dismay at the political mess. New York's senatorial election was paralyzed by a standoff between the Federalist-controlled state Senate and the Antifederalist Assembly: it would be months before the state had any representation in the Senate. In western Massachusetts, one congressional district was engaged in its *fifth* runoff election, with no end in sight. In South Carolina, a defeated candidate for the Charleston seat was challenging the victor, William Loughton Smith, who had remained safe in England and Europe during the Revolutionary War. And in New Jersey, conflict between two competing slates of delegates threatened to delay the seating of its representatives as well. Reportedly, one Congress member was busy running his gristmill, another was doing spring planting, a third fitting out his fishing vessels. Still others seemed more preoccupied with personal than with public affairs. "One of the Delaware Senators is engaged—in business!" gasped Fisher Ames, adding gloomily, "So much is to be done by so few, and those few are not all competent to do it."

But mostly the missing members blamed bad weather, bad health, bad roads, and bad luck for their absence. Theodorick Bland of Virginia had been "shipwrecked & landwrecked, mired, fatigued with walking &c. &c" and was recovering at George Mason's estate on the Potomac, having completed less than a third of the trip. Representative Samuel Livermore of New Hampshire was stuck at home "seized with a Chollick." Overland travel from Boston meant a six-day journey by sleigh "tumbling from one rock to another riding over the Ice for miles down a river & pushed in a wherry across another," or packed on springless benches in a stagecoach in which shoemakers and statesmen, preachers and peddlers, men and women, all jostled together with egalitarian abandon, through territory that was, though long settled, almost completely unmapped. (The country's first atlas would not be published until 1790 and would describe only about one thousand miles of road between Albany, New York, and Yorktown, Virginia.) When currents, skippers, and weather cooperated, sea travel could be more comfortable, but shipwrecks were not unusual, and drownings were common even on crossings of the Hudson River from New Jersey to Manhattan. When Pennsylvania senator Robert Morris reached the New Jersey shore opposite Manhattan, "the wind blew so hard, the Evening so dark & Fogg so Thick," he wrote to his wife, that he dared not risk a nighttime crossing.

The absent were begged, badgered and cajoled, with only middling success. "What must the world think of us," Charles Thomson, the lame-duck secretary of the Confederation Congress, wrote to laggard Senator George Read of Delaware, who by the third week in March still had not left his home: "As a friend, [I] entreat you to lay aside all lesser concerns & private business and come on immediately. Those who feel for the honor and are solicitous for the happiness of this country are pained to the heart, while those who are averse to the new constitution and those who are un-friendly to the liberty & consequently to the happiness and prosperity of this country, exult at our languor."

What government there was during those pathetic weeks pretty much devolved upon Thomson, who had held his post since 1774 and expected to be named to a post in the new administration. There was also John Jay, who ran the Confederation's Department of Foreign Affairs from his law office, and Henry Knox, who presided over the War Department from rented rooms at a Water Street tavern. The Comte de Moustier was amused by the absurdity of the situation. Americans, he wrote to a su-perior in France, defensively blamed everything on the weather. But, he opined, the members of the new Congress, like their predecessors, "suffer from the general indifference toward public service when it comes to ac-tually doing their part." The new Congress, he felt sure, would prove no more capable of governing than the old one and would surely need foreign protection to survive. If France didn't step in with "guidance," England surely would, he predicted.

Such anxieties nagged relentlessly at the members of Congress as, day after day, they trooped to Federal Hall hoping for the sight of new faces. Meanwhile, they marked time. Wherever they gathered, in taverns and coffeehouses, or during long walks through the fields outside the city, they schemed less about the immediate affairs of state than about the more than two dozen competing sites for the nation's permanent seat of government, from Alexandria, Virginia, to the Bronx. Whatever state won could expect to exert outsize influence over federal patronage, and over the government itself. New Yorkers, having just spent a fortune to renovate Federal Hall, wanted to keep the government right where it was. Virginians dreamed of a capital on the Potomac, Marylanders of Baltimore, Jerseymen of the Delaware River near Trenton. The well-organized Pennsylvanians were fiercely determined to establish the seat of government at "a more Centrical Situation," either adjacent to Philadelphia or on the Susquehanna River. "Pennsylvania will obtain her wishes especially, if we remain to appearance passive, and let the matter be brought on by some of the other States," Representative John Peter Muhlenberg, a Revolutionary War hero and the brother of fellow Representative Frederick Muhlenberg, cautioned. The Philadelphians were certain that if they snagged the temporary capital for their city, with its reliable Federalists, its libraries, printers, and scientific societies, Congress would never want to leave. The caballing Keystoners hatched a plan to call for an immediate adjournment of Congress as soon as the president's election was announced, then to meet again in Philadelphia to proceed to business. But others were well aware of what the Pennsylvanians were up to and were determined to resist. By April, the Pennsylvanians had to face the fact that their numerous rivals had no intention of allowing an adjournment. "You can scarce conceive the rancor and Malevolence that is uttered against Pennsylvania in this place," remarked Pennsylvania senator William Maclay, whose diary is the only detailed record of what took place in the Senate during the First Congress. (In keeping with the Senate's principle that its debates remain closed, senators were explicitly directed not to keep notes. Maclay ignored these instructions.)

On the snowy morning of April 1, the House of Representatives at last mustered a quorum. With the House chamber still under construction, the twenty-nine members on hand crowded into a conference room to begin—four weeks late and still many members short, in an atmosphere redolent of hope and fear, fierce determination and repressed sectional jealousy—to transact the first business of the United States under the Constitution. "The eyes of the people are upon you," a constituent warned George Thatcher of Massachusetts. "We look up to you, and wait for those measures which will bless and rejoice us, or fill us with pain and despair." ("Woe betide you all if you do not make us all compleatly happy," another citizen warned Representative Benjamin Goodhue of Massachusetts.)

The House's first order of business, on April 1, was the election of the corpulent Frederick Muhlenberg of Pennsylvania to the largely ceremonial post of Speaker. William Duer, who as a boy hurried after school to listen to the debates, years later vividly recalled Muhlenberg's powdered head, brown coat, and brass buttons, reminiscing that "his voice and manner were indeed well enough, but yet it seems to me that he wanted both ease and dignity." The job had almost nothing in common with today's powerful, agenda-setting speakership. Muhlenberg's main duties were to ensure decorum and to serve as the initial arbiter for questions involving parliamentary order. In accordance with the rules of procedure, the Speaker rarely participated in debate and was so infrequently permitted to vote, mainly just to break ties, which occurred only five times during the First Congress, that a nasty bit of doggerel had it that

Fred Augustus, God bless his red nose and fat head
Has little more influence than a Speaker of Lead.

The vacuum of institutionalized leadership in the House was what would permit, almost require, Madison to seize the legislative initiative so vigorously in the coming days.

The Speaker was responsible for assigning members to committees, however. These collectively bore no more resemblance to the highly structured system of today than did the speakership. Apart from the Committee on Elections and later Ways and Means, the body's first standing committees, House committees—about 150 were created during the First Congress—were generally appointed ad hoc to review individual pieces of legislation and summarize them. They rarely included more than a few members, carefully selected by Muhlenberg to incorporate differing points of view, and their existence usually expired upon the delivery of their report. The Senate was so small—just twenty members in the spring of 1789, and twenty-six at the close of the First Congress—that committees were often dispensed with altogether and legislation simply discussed by the entire body as a "committee of the whole." (The Senate's first standing committee would not be formed until 1816.)

Four days after Muhlenberg's election, on April 5, Richard Henry Lee of Virginia arrived in New York to make a quorum in the Senate. The celebratory cannon were long silent, the cheering long gone, but at last Congress was able to sit down to work.

Both houses required all members of the federal and state governments, elected and appointed, to take an oath to uphold the Constitution, whatever their politics or sentiments. This might seem merely a bit of political housekeeping, but many Americans, several state governments, the governors of New York, Massachusetts, and Virginia, and a significant minority of members of Congress had once opposed the Constitution, sometimes quite violently. As Congress opened, no one could be sure if these Antifederalists would attempt to subvert the government from within, as a political fifth column, who without such an oath would be free to carry out any sort of political mischief. All those who wished the new government well were relieved when the oaths were made without incident.

The next order of business was the counting of the electoral ballots for president and vice president. As expected, they were unanimous for George Washington. The votes for vice president were another story. They were, in Madison's words, "sufficient to give John Adams the second dignity," but only by a plurality. To Washington's sixty-nine, Adams received just thirty-four, a splintered result that greatly embarrassed a man whose amour propre was easily wounded; the remaining votes were scattered among ten losing candidates, including Foreign Minister John Jay, Gover-

nor George Clinton of New York, Governor John Hancock of Massachusetts, the eminent South Carolina politician John Rutledge, and others.
"Is not my Election to this Office, in the scurvy manner in which it was
done, a curse rather than a Blessing?" Adams demanded, adding that with
respect to his native New England "a greater Insult was never offered
to a People than the Manuvere by which she was horse jockeyed in the
late election of the Vice President." He never forgave Alexander Hamilton, who had helped stage-manage the electoral vote to diminish Adams's
numbers. Hamilton held no office as yet, but he exerted considerable influence among northern Federalists. He harbored no ill feeling toward
Adams, with whom he shared many views, but he doubted that Adams
possessed the personal skills to knit together the still fractious country and
feared that if any votes were withheld from Washington, Adams might
wind up being elected president by a fluke; until the Twelfth Amendment,
in 1804, votes were cast only for president, and the runner-up became vice
president. Hamilton personally asked at least seven northeastern electors
to hold their votes back from Adams, to guarantee Washington's election.

The son of a farmer and church deacon, Adams was born in 1735,
educated at Harvard, a lawyer by training, and already famous as early as
1774 for defending British soldiers for shooting civilians in the so-called
Boston Massacre. He was a voracious and sophisticated reader, deeply
introspective, and given to relentless self-criticism. He was also startlingly
outspoken for an age that prized self-control over self-expression, passionate, quarrelsome, censorious, fiercely independent, and notoriously
thin-skinned, a challenging combination. Of him, biographer Joseph J.
Ellis acutely wrote, "He was riven by insecurity and self-doubt, not in
the sense of doubting his talent or intelligence, but in the sense of requiring incessant assurance that what he knew to be his considerable gifts
would be given to a cause larger than himself." He was an ardent and
superhumanly energetic member of the Continental Congress, where he
was quickly acknowledged as one of its most effective leaders, "the first
man in the House," in the words of Benjamin Rush. Adams early recognized that war with England was inevitable and was thereafter a tireless

advocate for independence, when many other leading Americans equiv-ocated or hoped for a peaceful alternative. In 1776, it was Adams who rose to ringingly proclaim "that these United Colonies are, and of right, ought to be free and independent states . . . and that all political con-nection between them and the State of Great Britain is and ought to be totally dissolved." He authored the Declaration of Rights and Grievances, denying Parliament's authority over the colonies, successfully advocated for republican governments for the states, and chaired the committee charged with drafting the Declaration of Independence, as well as the Board of War and Ordnance—"in effect, a one-man war department," in Ellis's words—during the Revolutionary War. He was probably the most subtle political thinker of the founding generation.

Yet it often seemed that Adams set out deliberately to make himself unpopular, and he usually succeeded. As a diplomat in Paris, his prickli-ness and lack of finesse irritated both Benjamin Franklin and the French. Later, as the first American minister to England, he acquired an enthusi-asm for British forms that would not go down well with the many ardent republicans of the First Congress, where he unhelpfully insisted on refer-ring to the presidency as the "monarchical" branch of government, the Senate as "aristocratical," and the House as "democratical." The Comte de Moustier, who had little fondness for Adams personally and less for his pro-British sentiments, cuttingly reported to the French foreign ministry of the vice president–elect, "Thus it is that small talents mustered and employed with perseverance often elevate an ordinary man, who possesses the art of self-promotion and sometimes the impudence to make use of it for himself above men who are superior to him in talent; in virtue; in merit of all kinds."

However, no other New Englander was more honored and admired in his native region than Adams, and none other had achieved such inter-national renown. Nor had any other New Englander seriously been con-sidered for the vice presidency. (John Hancock, though widely respected, was an Antifederalist and never a serious competitor.) While many Amer-icans, at least initially, considered Adams the perfect "ticket-balancer" for Virginia's George Washington, the new vice presidency was not so well tailored to Adams the man. As David McCullough has put it, "Action had been his métier, advocacy his strength, and the vice presidency offered opportunity for neither." Crowds in every Yankee town through which he passed lined the roadside to cheer him on his journey by coach from Massachusetts to New York. But his shortcomings would do much to mold the lasting disdain of Americans for their country's second-highest office.

Charles Thomson was dispatched posthaste to Virginia to announce to Washington that he was now officially the first president of the United States. Thomson, desperate for a federal job, must have relished the prospect of several days in the company of the great man. He reached Mount Vernon on April 14, having overcome "tempestuous weather, bad roads, and many large rivers," after an eight-day journey from New York. Perhaps standing formally face-to-face with Thomson in Washington's office, Washington delivered a formal statement that, historian Kenneth R. Bowling has wryly written, had been "conveniently waiting in his pocket" for some time: "Whatever may have been my private feelings and sentiments, I believe I cannot give a greater evidence of my sensibility for the honor [the two houses of Congress] have done me by accepting the appointment."

Washington's modesty was calculated, but not insincere. He was by no means sure that he possessed the skill to do what was expected of him—not just to fill, but to *create*, an office that had never before existed, and to tame, if he could, the roiling political seas in which, he feared, the entire national enterprise might easily sink. (Under the Confederation, the chief officer of Congress was known as its "president," but Washington was the first president of the United States as a nation.) For months the prospect of election had worried him. The long delay in the opening of Congress now felt to him like a "reprieve," he wrote to Henry Knox. "I can assure you that my movements to the chair of Government will be accompanied with feelings not unlike those of a culprit who is going to the place of his execution: so unwilling am I, in the evening of a life nearly consumed in public cares, to quit a peaceful abode for an Ocean of difficulties."

His finances depleted by two years of poor crops, he was compelled, humiliatingly, to borrow six hundred pounds to pay for the trip north. A thousand tasks had to be completed before he could leave. Rents had to be collected from tenants, flour casked for shipment, livestock fed, manure sprinkled, tobacco hills allotted to each farm, grass seeds sown, bricks made, slaves dispatched to dig ditches, fill gullies, mend fences, and sow timothy before the next storm dumped more rain onto the soggy land. What lay in store for him in New York was likely to prove much harder, he suspected. The work before him would require infinite prudence, conciliation, and delicacy, as well as firmness. He could only hope and pray that he was up to the task. "I walk on untrodden ground," he later wrote to a British well-wisher, Catherine Macaulay Graham. "There is scarcely any action [I may take] whose motives may not be subject to double interpretation. There is scarcely any part of my conduct which may not hereafter be drawn into precedent." He added, with a sincerity born from deep and anxious introspection, "All see, and most admire, the glare which hovers around the trappings of elevated Office. To me, there is nothing in it, beyond the lustre which may be reflected from its connection with a power of promoting human felicity."

In New York, Fisher Ames was taking stock of his colleagues. The strikingly handsome, Harvard-educated son of a tavern keeper and almanac writer was regarded as a prodigy for having defeated, by just eleven votes, the aging revolutionary Samuel Adams for Boston's seat in the House of Representatives. He would quickly gain a reputation as the House's most elegant orator. Rather to his surprise, Ames felt unawed by luminaries such as Robert Morris, Roger Sherman of Connecticut, and Richard Henry Lee of Virginia, all of whom proved to be appealingly republican in their manners, dress, and speech. But most of his new colleagues, he discovered, fell far short of the "demi-gods and Roman senators" he had anticipated. To a Harvard classmate, he wrote, "I felt chagrined at the yawning listlessness of many here, in regard to the great objects of the government; their liableness to the impression of arguments *ad populum*; their state prejudices; their overrefining spirit in relation to trifles; their Attachment to some very distressing formalities in doing business, and which will be a curse to all despatch and spirit in transacting it. I was sorry to see that the picture I had drawn was so much bigger and fairer than the life." Yet, he conceded, "There are many who have experience, the virtues of the heart, and the habits of business," experienced men, "sober, solid folks," who were not "for the most part" men of intrigue.

Ames was most acutely disappointed in James Madison. "Before I came, I was cautioned against pinning my faith on any man's sleeve. I was afraid of it, for I think I am not apt to resist the influence of those whom I esteem. But I see in Madison, with his great knowledge and merit, so much error, and some of it so very unaccountable, and tending to so much mischief." Madison possessed sound judgment, "which perceives truth with great clearness, and can trace it through the mazes of debate, without losing it," a rare enough talent, and the foundation of his persuasiveness, Ames conceded. "What a man understands clearly, and has viewed in every different point of light, he will explain to the admiration of others, who have not thought of it at all, or but little, and who will pay in praise for the pains he saves them. Upon the whole, he is an useful, respectable, worthy man." Having thus lauded Madison, Ames launched a less flattering parting shot: "Let me add, without meaning to detract, that he is too much attached to his theories, for a politician. He adopts his maxims as he finds them in books, and with too little regard to the actual state of things." Few credited him with the toughness to be an effective leader. To many, he seemed "too meek to govern," too soft-spoken, and lacking "that strength of nerves which will enable him to set at defiance popular and factious clamors." Nevertheless, he immediately plunged the House into urgent and divisive debate over the critical dearth of national revenue.

The Constitution had given Congress the authority to raise revenue, but little guidance on how to do it. Without income, public credit could not be established, and the costs of government could not be met. Although direct taxes were common in several of the states, such taxation by the *federal* government was anathema to citizens who had fought a revolution in no small part against the king's aggressive tax collectors. But without revenue to sustain itself the new government would be no more than a sad joke that would justify the scoffing of Europeans such as Moustier. The most politically viable approach was to levy tariffs on imports and fees on ships, but this posed all kinds of knotty political challenges.

If duties were to be enacted, Madison and his allies knew, it must be done quickly. Otherwise, the government stood to lose a fortune in potential revenue, since the spring shipping season was already under way, and cargo ships were flocking to American ports. Secretary of War Henry Knox estimated that the country was facing a loss of $300,000 unless it could enact import duties on the cargoes arriving in American harbors. This was no abstraction. Members of Congress had only to walk three blocks to the East River waterfront to see the forest of masts rising from some of the eleven hundred seagoing vessels that would enter the port of New York in 1789. The future held even greater promise: the first ship to fly the American flag on the Ganges was even now on its way back to New York, while the recent opening of trade with China unfolded the prospect of vast new Asian markets for exports. Even the Ottoman Empire would soon become a prime market for southern rice, Ralph Izard of South Carolina was telling his fellow senators—if the Barbary pirates could be driven from the Mediterranean, where they were wreaking havoc on American commerce.

On April 9, Madison rose to deliver his first major address to the House of Representatives in its elegant octagonal chamber. From their arc of desks, congressmen leaned forward, straining to hear his tiny voice as he declared that "the union, having recovered from the state of imbecility that heretofore prevented a performance of its duty," now had to act decisively. The plight of the treasury was steadily worsening. "Every gentleman sees the prospect of our harvest [from potential taxes] from the spring importations is daily vanishing; and if [Congress] delay levying and collecting an impost there will be no importations of any consequence on which the law is to operate because, by that time all the spring vessels will have arrived and unloaded."

He proposed four bills. They had two broad goals: to raise revenue, and to encourage nascent American manufactures, commerce, and navigation. The first bill would levy a general 5 percent tariff (or impost), with higher duties on commodities including West Indian molasses, salt, liquors, teas, pepper, sugar, cocoa and coffee, hemp and cordage, silk shoes, tin, brass, wool, rawhide, and many other items. The second would levy a tonnage fee on all ships in which goods were imported, ranging from a modest six cents per ton on ships owned wholly by Americans, to thirty cents per ton on ships belonging to the subjects of countries with which the United States had signed a commercial treaty, to fifty cents per ton on ships owned by citizens of other powers, most significantly Britain, whose ships carried more American trade than all other foreign countries combined. The third bill would establish tariff collection districts at ports of entry and provide for collectors, surveyors, naval officers—the foundation for both the federal bureaucracy and the patronage system. The fourth bill would assume federal control of all lighthouses, beacons, and buoys. Although such revenue sources were familiar in several states, "it is only against their establishment by the general government that the public outcry is raised," observed Moustier, for they required states for the first time to yield jurisdiction over tax collection and parts of their territory to the federal government.

To enact the bills would require all the persuasive power that Madison could muster. Commerce, he declared, "ought to be as free as the policy of nations will permit," in principle. But there had to be exceptions. If the United States left her ports completely free and made no distinction—or "discrimination," in the language of the time—between American- and foreign-owned vessels, American shipping would suffer grievously, to the detriment of the entire country. The imposition of high fees on foreign carriers would, however, bring multiple benefits. It would enable American producers to ship their goods more cheaply, in turn fostering the development of embryonic national industries and protecting the jobs of thousands of workers. The corollary: without "the fostering hand" of government, Madison argued, whole industries would likely perish from cheaper foreign competition.

Madison repeatedly tried to make clear that England was his primary target. (More than one-third of all the ships arriving in New York alone that year would be English owned, and many more were owned by British-American partnerships.) He argued that far too much of the nation's trade was transacted through British merchants and in British ships. "That nation is in possession of a much greater proportion of our trade than she is naturally intitled to," he declared.

Almost as soon as Madison finished speaking, opposing sectional and commercial interests clamorously collided. New Englanders called for heavy duties on all foreign-owned shipping, while southerners, who manufactured little and imported much, rejected any duties at all, asserting that this proposal would hit the South disproportionately hard. One South Carolinian congressman asserted, for instance, that a salt tax would discriminate unfairly against the southern poor since the poor consumed more salted food than the wealthy, and the measure would therefore "operate as a poll tax, the most odious of all taxes." Some New Englanders felt that discrimination against British ships would antagonize their best customers, and perhaps even lead to a commercial war. New Yorkers, the most ardent free traders, protested any form of discrimination against foreign ships, asserting that merchants should be left alone "like the industrious bee to gather from the choicest flower the greatest abundance of commercial sweets."

The bills posed many confusing questions, with implications that reached beyond the simple rules of trade. Could such laws be enforced? Would enforcement be handed over to the states? Would state judges instantly be transformed into *federal* ones, entitled to permanent jobs and salaries? To succeed, the cooperation of merchants was essential—but could they be trusted? Wouldn't high duties spur an epidemic of smuggling and evasion? And what about Rhode Island and North Carolina, which had rejected the Constitution? How could the law be enforced against them? "It is to be feared that it will produce more frauds than money," worried Fisher Ames, who confessed that he was "not an adept in the mysteries of finance." The whole business, he feared, was a "mere experiment," a leap in the dark.

Moralists further complicated the debate. Rum, declared Pennsylvania representative Thomas Fitzsimons, was "not an article of necessity, but on the contrary of luxury, and luxury of a most pernicious kind." He added, "If we could lay the duty so high as to lessen the consumption in any degree the better." James Jackson of Georgia retorted sarcastically that Yankee rum was "five hundred times" worse than any imported rum, and that if certain members really cared about the public welfare, they ought to start by destroying all their own distilleries first. Soon, Fitzsimons reported, the impost "has so intirely occupied us that little else has been thot of."

Debate went on for days over a proposed eight-cent tax on molasses. Members from Massachusetts forcefully insisted that molasses was "a necessary of life" for the poorer class of people, who could never bear the weight of such a high tax. All this was about a lot more than molasses, however. Although they never said it in so many words, the New Englanders were defending Yankee investment in slavery as much as they were the interests of the molasses-eating poor in Salem and Portland. Molasses was the cornerstone of an immensely profitable three-cornered trade that intertwined North Atlantic fisheries, slavery, and rum and bound nominally antislavery New England to both the transatlantic slave trade and to the brutally labor-intensive sugar industry of the West Indies. Cod that was salted and dried hard so that it could survive in tropical heat had long been a staple of the slave diet in the West Indies. New England merchants also traded it along with rum for slaves in West Africa, sold the slaves to planters in the Indies, and purchased molasses, which they carried back to New England to be converted into rum that would be traded for slaves in Africa. In the 1780s, New Englanders also traded vast quantities of the lowest-quality cod directly to the French West Indies, in exchange for molasses and sugar. (When Americans were barred from trade with the British islands from 1780 to 1787, it was claimed that fifteen thousand slaves starved to death in Jamaica alone.) "These circumstances form a material link in our chain of navigation, and upon our success in navigation the most important interests of the United States depend," declared Ames, a professed antislavery man, who nonetheless never faltered as an advocate for the New England shipping industry. If commerce in "summer fish" was injured, "it would carry devastation throughout all the New England states."

Madison appealed to members to transcend their sectional self-interest. "We must consider the general interest of the union," he pleaded, arguing that any system of taxation that was adopted had to be founded on mutual concession. "Let me ask, gentlemen, why these apprehensions for one part of the union more than the other? Are the northern people made of finer clay? Do they respire a clearer air? Do their breasts burn with a more generous ardor for their rights as men, or for their country's happiness and glory? Are they the chosen few? Are all others to be oppressed with accumulated burthens, and they to take their course easy and unrestrained?" Each tax must be seen as part of a larger system. "Let us," he urged, "endeavour to distribute the public burthen with a just and equal hand."

Madison's words fell on listeners who, if sympathetic to his conciliatory appeal, remained so aggressively partisan on behalf of their sections that their interests seemed close to irreconcilable. Months of intermittent but contentious debate still lay ahead before the revenue bill would be hammered into law.

CHAPTER 3

A New Era

The scene was solemn and awful beyond description.

—An eyewitness to Washington's inauguration

Geaorge Washington considered the sluggishness in getting the government up and running to be a national embarrassment. He was determined not to add to it. "As this delay must be very irksome to the attending Members, I am resolved no interruption shall proceed from me that can well be avoided," he assured Madison. The House of Representatives was still debating codfish and molasses when on the afternoon of April 22, Congress learned that Washington had reached the Jersey shore.

Before leaving Virginia, he rode to Fredericksburg to see his dying mother, promising that as soon as he had seen the new government established on a firm footing, he would return to Virginia. She stopped him before he could continue. "You will see me no more," she told him. Washington's relations with her were not warm, and there is no record of any intimacy that now passed between them. But he doubtless knew that what she said was true. Cancer would kill her within the year. Turning his granite face in the direction of New York, he left behind the scenes of his youth, early manhood, and military triumph and began his journey toward the last and most complicated phase of his life.

Washington left Mount Vernon accompanied by his aide David Humphreys, his secretary, Tobias Lear, his enslaved manservant, Billy Lee, and the hopeful Charles Thomson. They crossed the Potomac at Georgetown and headed north toward Baltimore across the rolling hills that some Potomac Valley promoters, Washington among them, hoped might become the site of the nation's permanent capital. He had hoped to travel "in as quiet & peaceable a manner as possible," to conserve his energy. But that was not to be. The entire route was aswarm with cheering, shouting, flag-waving well-wishers throwing flowers at him, holding up their babies, and demanding speeches. Towns that had cannons fired them, veterans marched alongside him for miles, men wept. Banners proclaimed A NEW ERA and BEHOLD THE RISING EMPIRE. Though he slipped the crowds when he could, he agreed when pressed to deliver addresses in Baltimore, Wilmington, and Philadelphia, where twenty thousand people—half the city's population—thronged the cobbled streets shouting, "Long live the father of his people!," and a laurel wreath fit for a Roman emperor was placed on his head. More cheering crowds were waiting for him on the New Jersey bank of the Delaware River, where he had famously crossed during the war. Crisply uniformed cavalry and infantry escorted him to Trenton, between ranks of girls crowned with garlands, who strewed flowers before his feet and sang odes of glory. The *Gazette of the United States* proclaimed that Washington had become virtually divine, standing "upon a scale of eminence that Heaven never before assigned to a mortal."

Finally on the morning of April 23, at Elizabeth, New Jersey, he was met by a committee of both houses of Congress, John Jay, numerous New York officials, and the uniformed rotundity of his Revolutionary War colleague Henry Knox. Dressed in a blue-and-buff suit that recalled his wartime uniform, and seated imperially beneath an awning hung with red curtains, Washington was rowed across the Hudson River in a forty-seven-foot barge manned by thirteen pilots dressed in white garments and black caps, as flag-festooned ships fired cannonades across the harbor. As if inspired by the jubilation, porpoises leaped and dove around the barge. Near Bedloe's Island, the future site of the Statue of Liberty, a boatload of gentlemen and ladies trilled a welcoming ode to the tune of "God Save the King." As Washington neared the Manhattan shore, passed around the Battery, and turned north up the East River to the booming of artillery, huzzahs rose from multitudes of men, women, and children packed "as thick as ears of corn before the harvest." Another observer recalled the successive motion of hats being doffed from the Battery to Murray's Wharf like the rolling of the sea.

The panorama, Washington later wrote, "filled my mind with sensations as painful (considering the reverse of this scene, which may be the case after all my labors to do good) as they are pleasing." It was Washington's first trip back to New York since the end of the war. If any New Yorkers held him personally responsible for losing their city to the British in the catastrophic battle of Long Island, they had clearly forgiven. He was filled with trepidation: all his sacrifices, the years of war and political struggle, the great experiment upon which the nation was about to embark—it might yet collapse into fiasco and come to nothing. An assembly of war veterans met him at Murray's Wharf. At the top of the steps, carpeted in his honor, an officer declared that a guard of honor was ready to take his orders. At this, Washington, turning to the crowd and with a democratic inspiration, declared that he would accept the honor guard, but in truth "the Affections of his fellow citizens was all the Guard he wanted." He rejected the use of a carriage, however, and, preceded by a troop of cavalry, artillery, and uniformed officers, New York governor George Clinton, New York's mayor, assorted clergymen, and "an amazing concourse" of ordinary citizens, strode slowly through streets, hung with silk banners, wreaths of flowers, and branches of evergreen, to the mansion on Cherry Street, near the present-day Brooklyn Bridge, that had been rented for him. Later the skies burst in a torrential downpour, but no one seemed to care. New Yorkers of all classes joyfully roamed the streets admiring the pyramids of candles and other exotic celebratory illuminations that had been mounted in windows everywhere. Massachusetts representative George Thatcher wrote home to his wife, "The streets, houses, doors, windows, stoups, and every eminence of sight was crouded

with Spectators in one moving body. Every mind was agitated with joy &
ready to brake out in Halelujahs & Hosannas."

Not that there weren't dissenters. To at least some republicans, Washington's entire journey seemed like a royal progress that smacked of
monarchical excess and hinted at the elevation of the new president into
a sort of American king. A satirical and sacrilegious caricature that spread
around New York, labeled "the Entry," showed Washington arriving, in
the guise of Jesus, at the American Jerusalem of New York, sitting in
"Billy Lee's" lap and mounted on a donkey led by David Humphreys
wearing devil's horns, and chanting, "The glorious time has come to pass
when David shall conduct an *Ass*." Less nastily, but in its own way no
less significant of the ambivalence toward what some feared were Washington's monarchical pretensions, a member of Congress reported that a
prominent Quaker who had lent assistance to the patriotic struggle, when
told that Washington was approaching his house, replied with Quakerly
disdain for ceremony that he was "perfectly indifferent to the general
commotion at the door" and declined to rise from his dinner table as the
president-elect's procession marched by.

From his perch at the foot of Broadway, the Comte de Moustier observed the president with the clinical eye of a veteran courtier. One of only
three ministers accredited to the American government—the Spanish and
the Dutch were the others—Moustier loomed large in New York's small
but high-toned society. Although an aristocrat, he made a political point
of diplomatically dressing in plain American clothes, "which ought to disconcert every American macaroni, who struts in the fripperies of Europe,"
commented one Yankee of spartan temperament. Moustier was impressed
by Washington, but also puzzled by him: "Benevolence and nobility are
stamped on his countenance, and so happily combined that the one quality easily controls the overconfidence born of the other. His moderation
has yet to be compromised." During the war, Washington had deftly
avoided political damage by deferring—or rather *appearing* to defer—to
the will of others. But this strategy would now be much more difficult in
the exposed role of president, since he was compelled by the Constitution

to shape an ongoing, and perhaps adversarial, relationship with Congress. Washington would not let himself be made a mere "instrument" of Congress, but neither did he seem to want to mold Congress into a tool that would serve him, a strategy that Moustier, who was accustomed to the firm hand of European monarchy, saw as logical for him to pursue. What the future held for the presidency, Moustier declined even to guess.

Amid the jubilation at Washington's arrival, an acrimonious struggle was under way in the Senate over how the president was to be officially addressed. Although the wrangling over punctilio lent itself to mockery, it was far from insignificant. Embedded in its seeming triviality was a subtle struggle over the nature of the office of the president, underscoring the chasm between those who wished the new nation to be governed on a hierarchical model that imitated the kingdoms of Europe, and those determined to subordinate the presidency to Congress. The ensuing debate sapped much of the goodwill with which Vice President Adams had taken office. Unless the president was endowed with "a superior title," asserted Adams, the United States would be subject to "the Contempt, the Scorn and the Derision of all Europe." This eruption marked the debut of Adams's short, turbulent, and ultimately self-destructive turn as the nation's first and only activist vice president until modern times. His only constitutionally explicit duty was to preside over the Senate, but he intended to do it vigorously. He meant to be not a mere bystander to legislation, but the driver of it. Virtually from the moment that he hefted his considerable weight onto the thronelike chair from which he presided, he claimed the authority to set the Senate's agenda. In this role his spiky Yankee personality would not serve him well.

Despite Adams's depth of classical learning and his many years in the public arena, he had little gift for oratory. His fellow Federalist Roger Sherman, an awkward speaker himself, said of Adams, "There cannot be a more striking contrast to beautiful Action" than Adams delivering a speech. "It is Stiffness and Awkwardness itself. Rigid as Starched Linen or Buchram." In the early weeks of the First Congress, Adams would repeatedly intervene in debate, expatiating on almost any subject that came to his mind, including the ambiguities of his own office, comparing it at one point to the paired consuls of ancient Rome and the dual kingship of Sparta. He wondered aloud, probably facetiously, if L'Enfant had deliberately made the presiding officer's chair, on which Adams sat, wide enough to accommodate two men—one, the president, "to have all the power while he held it, and the other to be nothing." Adams told the embarrassed senators, with startling honesty, "I feel great difficulty how to act. I am Vice President, in this I am nothing, but I may be everything, but I am President also of the Senate. When the President comes into the Senate, what shall I be, I cannot be then, no gentlemen I cannot, I cannot—I wish gentlemen to think what I shall be." The kind of philosophizing that might enliven a dinner-table conversation nonplussed the Senate.

After this speech, wrote the unfriendly Pennsylvania senator William Maclay, "as if oppressed with a Sense of his distressed situation, [Adams] threw himself back in his Chair. A Solemn Silence ensued." Maclay found Adams's performance so odd that it was all Maclay could do to keep his emotions under control: "God forgive me, "for it was involuntary, but the profane Muscles of my face were in Tune for laughter." The ever-sober Oliver Ellsworth of Connecticut, whose politics dovetailed with Adams's, finally rose, theatrically took up a copy of the Constitution, ran his thumb over it, and turned its pages for some time. At length he gravely addressed the vice president. "I have looked over the Constitution"—Ellsworth paused for effect—"and I find Sir, it is evident & Clear sir, that wherever the Senate is to be, then Sir you must be at the head of them, but further Sir, (here he looked agast, as if some tremendous Gulph had Yaned before him) I, shall, not, pretend, to, say."

Such patronizing criticism, however politely delivered, hardly behooved a Senate that was as new and untried an institution as the vice presidency, and without a rule book to guide it. Indeed, in several states, it was believed that senators, having been elected by the state legislature, represented those states' governments rather than the public as a whole. In Massachusetts, Pennsylvania, and North Carolina the power to officially "instruct" legislators—that is, control their votes—was specifically enshrined in state constitutions, a potentially crippling rein on senators' work, particularly when it might take weeks for information about upcoming votes to be transmitted from the federal seat of government to a senator's state and require the assembly of the state legislature, or the direction of its governor, to tell the waiting senator what to do.

Nevertheless, scorn for Adams's vanity and vulnerabilities soon percolated through both houses of Congress, where he increasingly became a subject of mockery. Maclay cruelly disdained him as "a monkey in breeches," while Virginia representatives John Page and his friend St. George Tucker amused themselves by exchanging caustic couplets at the vice president's expense. Wrote Page:

In Gravity clad,
He has nought in his Head,
    But Visions of Nobles & Kings,
With Commons below,
    Who respectfully bow,
    And worship the dignified Things.

To this, Tucker replied:

I'll tell in a Trice—
    'Tis Old Daddy Vice
Who carries of Pride an Ass-load;
    Who turns up his Nose
    Wherever he goes
With Vanity swell'd like a Toad.

Adams never saw their doggerel. But he could hardly be unaware of the unsubtle ridicule that members increasingly shared behind his back. It was not an auspicious beginning.

•   •   •

As the inauguration approached, visitors poured into the city, filling taverns, boardinghouses, and private homes. Every one of them was desperate for a glimpse of Washington. "I have seen him!" a young Boston woman breathlessly wrote home. "I never saw a human being that looked so great and noble as he does. I could fall down on my knees before him and bless him." A landlady named Mary Daubing was so overwrought that she experienced a virtually orgasmic collapse: "Her Mind was so overcome by the Expectation of seeing the President that it affected her whole Frame in a very uncommon Manner. It was so painful that tho' she promised herself much Gratification, she wished it over."

On the morning of April 30, packet ships came down the Hudson in clouds, while Manhattan's country roads were thick with travelers hurrying southward through the island's farmlands and craggy hills. Bells pealed solemnly. Parishioners flocked to churches to pray for the nation. Beating drums and the skirl of bagpipes summoned troops of kilted Scottish Highlanders and towering grenadiers dressed in blue coats, yellow vests, and enormous cone-shaped hats. Maclay, togged out in his "best Cloaths," walked to Federal Hall, where he saw "the Croud already great," and climbed the stairs to find John Adams in a tizzy, begging the Senate to advise him as to the proper protocol for receiving the president. "How shall I behave, how shall we receive [him]?" Adams pleaded with a nervous laugh. "Shall it be standing or sitting?" There followed, at Adams's instigation, a hectic, last-minute debate about the customs employed by the House of Commons and the House of Lords when the king of England delivered a speech. Did the king wear robes and crown? Did he sit? Did the Commons stand or sit? Finally Senator Charles Carroll of Maryland got up and exasperatedly declared that it should make no difference to Americans what Englishmen did in Parliament. So engrossing was this absurd debate that the three members delegated to escort the president-elect to his inauguration lost track of the time. Only with difficulty were they made to break off and hasten to the president's residence on Cherry Street.

A little after noon, Washington emerged, looking pensive and strained, hair powdered, modestly dressed in a suit of American-made, brown broadcloth adorned with nothing but plain metal buttons patriotically embossed with the figure of an eagle. At twelve thirty the presidential procession began to move, companies of soldiers in the vanguard, followed by members of Congress in carriages, then Washington in his own coach, and finally by throngs of gay and adoring citizens. "People of every age and description . . . crouded every street and alley where there was a probability of having a peep at this Great Good Person," reported a correspondent for a Newburyport, Massachusetts, newspaper. A few blocks short of Federal Hall, Washington descended from his coach and, removing his hat and bowing left and right, as girls strewed flowers beneath his feet, walked the rest of the way between rows of soldiers into Federal Hall. He passed in silence through its marble-paved and skylighted vestibule, and upstairs to the Senate chamber. There he found the vice president, and the members of the Senate and the House of Representatives, waiting for him.

With some awkwardness, Adams ushered Washington to the presiding officer's elevated chair. Then, almost as soon as Washington had sat down, Adams nervously declared that all was in readiness for Washington to take the oath of office. Rising again, he prepared to speak. However, reported Maclay, "He seemed to have forgot half of what he was to say for he made a dead pause and stood for some time, to appearance, in a vacant mood." Finally he bowed and was led out onto the balcony. At the sight of him, the immense crowd below burst into a wild and noisy frenzy of joy. In accordance with some prior signal, cannons boomed from the Battery and were echoed by every ship in the harbor that had a gun to fire.

At the center of the balcony stood a small table covered with red velvet, upon it a crimson cushion, and on the cushion a large Bible. New York State's highest judicial official, Chancellor Robert R. Livingston, stepped forward to administer the oath of office. (The Supreme Court did not yet exist nor the chief justice—their creation lay among the myriad tasks that Congress had yet to address.) Livingston gestured for silence. The crowd hushed. Washington placed his hand on the Bible and in a barely audible voice intoned, "I solemnly swear to faithfully uphold the duties of the President of the United States and to do all that is in my power to preserve, protect and defend the Constitution of the United States." (Contrary to later tradition, Washington did not add to his oath the words "So help me God," a custom that dates from the late nineteenth century.) One eyewitness later wrote, "The scene was solemn and awful beyond description." To John Randolph of Roanoke, a young Virginian who was attending classes at Columbia University, which had changed its name from King's College five years earlier, it seemed like "a coronation."

Senate secretary Samuel Otis then lifted the Bible to Washington's lips. "It is done," declared Livingston, and turning to the multitude, he waved his hand and in a loud voice exclaimed, "Long live George Washington, President of the United States!" Huzzahs roared from tens of thousands of voices as the news raced in every direction through the city. Washington placed his hand on his heart, bowed to the multitudes, and retreated into the Senate chamber.

After the members of Congress had reassembled, Washington began to read the speech that Madison had drafted for him weeks earlier. "I was looking upon an organ of popular will just beginning to breathe the breath of life," one onlooker recalled almost half a century later. It was obvious that the president, whose mere presence awed every American, was nearly paralyzed by anxiety. In contrast to Humphreys's earlier, overloaded draft, the speech that Madison had shaped was lucid and reassuring. "The magnitude and difficulty of the trust to which the voice of the country called me," Washington told the assembled members of Congress, "could not but overwhelm with despondence, one, who, inheriting inferior endowments from nature and unpractised in the duties of civil administration, ought to be peculiarly conscious of his own deficiencies." The weight of history lay on their collective shoulders, he reminded them. "The destiny of the Republican model of Government" was deeply, perhaps for all time, staked on "the experiment entrusted to the hands of the American people." That is, how they performed in these first sessions of Congress would affect not just themselves, and the voters who had elected them, but untold future generations. Accentuating his willingness to defer to the legislative branch, he observed that while the Constitution had empowered the president to recommend whatever measures he deemed necessary and expedient, it would be "far more congenial with the feelings which actuate me to substitute, in place of a recommendation of particular measures, the tribute that is due to the talents, the rectitude, and the patriotism which adorn the characters selected to devise and adopt them"—the members of Congress. Here he was clearly acknowledging that he recognized Congress as the paramount branch of government. Finally, he declared that he did not plan to accept any salary, even though it was mandated in the Constitution. It was his duty, he said, "that I should renounce every pecuniary compensation." Instead, he would only accept reimbursement for expenditures that he incurred in carrying out his official duties. (This sounded great, but many members of Congress remembered well the huge expenses that Washington had run up as commander in chief, and they now wanted a president who would live within his salaried means; Washington would, with his usual dignity, eventually acquiesce to the generous $25,000 per year that Congress allocated to him.)

The address was firm and almost completely apolitical, in keeping with both Madison's and Washington's belief that the president should rise above partisanship. He mentioned only one specific issue facing Congress by elliptically referring to "an exercise of the occasional power delegated by the Fifth article of the Constitution," in other words, the power of amendment, and "the degree of inquietude" that had led some citizens to object to the Constitution. Through state conventions and legislatures, Americans had proposed almost *two hundred* overlapping amendments, containing dozens of different ideas, setting the stage for an explosive battle that had the potential to overthrow much of the work of the Constitutional Convention. Vague as his remarks were, Washington was signaling that although he would countenance amendments in principle, he would not favor those that would subvert the Constitution or effective government. "I assure myself that whilst you carefully avoid every alteration which might endanger the benefits of a united and effective government, or which ought to await the future lessons of experience," he said, "a reverence for the characteristic rights of freemen, and a regard for the public harmony, will sufficiently influence your deliberations on the question how far the former can be more impregnably fortified, or the latter be safely and advantageously promoted."

Maclay was disappointed less by the content of the speech, upon which he did not comment, than by Washington's physical shakiness. "This great Man was agitated and embarrassed more than ever he was by levelled Cannon or pointed Musket," the Pennsylvania senator confided to his diary. "He trembled, and several times could scarce make out to read, tho it must be supposed that he had often read it before. He put part of the fingers of his left hand into the side of what I think the Taylors call the fall of his Breetches, changing the paper into his left hand. After some time, he then did the same with some of the fingers of his right hand. When he came to the Words *all the World*, he made a flourish with his right hand, which left rather an ungainly impression." Maclay, who adored Washington, was embarrassed for him, wishing that "this first of Men" had simply read his address without his clumsy attempt at oratorical posturing, "for I felt hurt that he was not first in everything."

Fisher Ames, a kinder judge than Maclay, found the inauguration "a very touching scene," and the president's "aspect grave, almost to sadness." To a friend in Boston, he wrote, "It seemed to me an allegory in which virtue was personified." Later in the day, Ames observed Washington more closely and was shocked by how much he seemed aged and tired: "Time has made havoc upon his face."

That evening, the city gave itself up to patriotic abandon. Cannons boomed. Thousands of lanterns appeared in the rigging of ships in the harbor, transforming them into pyramids of stars. At the foot of Broadway rose an enormous illuminated "transparency" of Washington beneath the allegorical figure of Fortitude and flanked by Justice and Wisdom, while the newly opened John Street Theater sported another sumptuous transparency portraying Fame descending from heaven and crowning the president with symbols of immortality. (Transparencies were a popular art form in which color was applied to canvas or thin paper pasted on a framework behind which candles or lanterns provided illumination.)

Washington spent the evening with David Humphreys, Henry Knox, and Robert R. Livingston watching fireworks at the home of the Spanish minister, who had created two magnificent illuminated gardens adorned with statues, colonnades, and triumphal arches overhung by thirteen stars representing, aspirationally, all the states of the new nation: two of the stars were conspicuously opaque, to represent Rhode Island and North Carolina, which had still not ratified the Constitution. At ten o'clock Washington finally headed back toward his Cherry Street home, making his way democratically on foot through jubilant crowds too thick to permit the passage of a coach. What remained was for Congress and the president to invent a government.

CHAPTER 4

Pomp and Quiddling

———◆———

All the World civilized and savage called for titles.

—Richard Henry Lee, May 1789

During an early-spring storm, Elias Boudinot, one of the House of Representatives' most respected members, wrote to his wife back in New Jersey that he would rather spend a day pruning trees in the snow than haggling with his fellow politicians at Federal Hall. He had been a leading candidate for Speaker of the House, but seemed genuinely relieved when he didn't win. Driven by a profound, even religious, sense of duty, he was a rare American who was deeply concerned with the welfare and "elevation" of American Indians, when his contemporaries mostly saw war as the ultimate solution to the "Indian problem." He was also an advocate for the emancipation of slaves, who were still numerous on farms in northern Jersey. Republican politics, for him, was ultimately one more way for him to help bring about the betterment of mankind. So on the floor of the House, on May 19, with a gravity befitting his pious temperament, he proposed the creation of the first cabinet departments and, in effect, the foundation of the modern executive branch.

He urged that, given the government's critical financial plight, a "public financier"—a secretary of the treasury—must quickly be appointed. The interest due on foreign loans incurred during the war, the feebleness of national credit, the swollen domestic debt—taken altogether, the financial crisis the nation faced was overwhelming, he warned. "It will be attended with the most dreadful consequences to let these affairs run into confusion and ruin for want of proper regulations." Boudinot's proposal was just the first shot in what quickly turned into a pitched verbal battle over the nature of the Treasury Department, its powers and responsibilities, and, above all, who would control it.

It instantly kindled opposition from those who, like Elbridge Gerry, though himself a wealthy merchant, feared that a moneyed elite would ruin the country that patriots had fought and suffered heroically to achieve. "The creation of a financier with all the splendor and powers of office" would enjoy "innumerable opportunities for defrauding the revenue, without check or controul" and would doubtless become "a dangerous instrument" in the hands of the president, Gerry argued. What man could be qualified—or trusted—to fill such a powerful office? He doubted that any existed. It would be far safer and wiser to diffuse power in a board of several commissioners who would monitor each other with as much care as they did the public money. Or if the Treasury should have to be placed in the hands of one man, then he should be no more than a sort of chief accountant, whose main duty would be to supply information requested by Congress.

Gerry, one of the three members of the Constitutional Convention who refused to sign the final document, was the most tenacious of all Antifederalist critics in the First Congress. His support for the new government sometimes sounded tentative, at best. "I abhor now as much as ever the corrupt parts of the constitution, but am bound in honor to support a government ratified by the majority until it can be amended, for to oppose it would be to sow the seeds of a civil War & to lay the foundation of a military tyranny," he wrote. However, his doubts were rooted in a complex and individualistic view of the American government. Although he was savaged in the Federalist press for his opposition to the Constitution,

Gerry claimed that he had never rejected the founding document as such, but rather wished to see ratification postponed pending revision. Whether the present system would turn into a monarchy would hinge entirely on alterations that he felt must be made in the Constitution. "Should there be no amendments," he declared, "I am of the opinion that it will verge to a monarchy [and] upon a hereditary establishment."

The Harvard-educated son of a British seaman, the forty-four-year-old Gerry had served in legislative offices since the 1770s, including seven terms in the Continental and Confederation Congresses. Among his New England colleagues, he stood out as something of a paradox, an outspoken republican whose political radicalism contradicted his plutocratic economic interest as a wealthy investor in the West Indian trade. Nervous and high-sttrung in debate, he was often confrontational and sarcastic, a "Grumbletonian," it was said, who seemed to object to everything. Yet he was a deeply principled man, who saw himself as true to the revolutionary republican principles of 1776, and genuinely feared that the new republic was too weak to bear serious internal dissension. Although regarded as a de facto Antifederalist by almost everyone, Gerry "was his own conscience, and no party or factional label adequately fits him," his biographer George A. Billias has written. His primary duty, as he saw it, Gerry told his constituents, was to protect "the *governed* from the rapacity and domination of lawless and insolent ambition."

Following the exchange between Boudinot and Gerry, James Madison proposed the creation of departments of War and Foreign Affairs. No one had emerged, or would, to challenge Henry Knox, Washington's wartime artillery commander, as secretary of war. There was no front-runner for secretary of foreign affairs, but it was generally thought that John Jay, who had served the Confederation in that role for the past several years, was the most likely candidate. Thomas Jefferson, still in France, though planning to come home on leave, was on no one's mind except Washington's. (As the French Revolution swirled around him, Jefferson amused himself by studying the language of the "Mohiccon" Indians, immersing himself in the collected works of the king of Prussia, and reading about the flora of the Carolinas.) Chancellor Livingston had indicated that he wanted the Treasury, but Jay, the young Alexander Hamilton, or, worst of all in the eyes of the small-government men, the arch-Federalist and wheeler-dealer Robert Morris were also presumed candidates. Madison personally felt that Hamilton, with whom he had collaborated on *The Federalist*, was the most qualified for that "species of business," which so few political men fully understood. However, a nasty whispering campaign against Hamilton was already under way: one of Hamilton's many enemies hissed in an unsigned letter to the president that he was nothing more than a self-serving "Judas" who would betray Washington as soon as it suited him.

No one objected to the establishment of executive departments per se: the Constitution had explicitly, if rather vaguely, mentioned that "the principal Officer in each of the Executive Departments"—whose number, names, and powers were left unspecified—was to report to the president; it had also, equally fuzzily, stated that if Congress so chose it could vest the appointment of "inferior officers" in the president alone, or in the courts of law, or in the heads of departments. That was all. The vast undefined space that remained instantly became a battleground. A seemingly modest qualifying phrase in Madison's motion incensed Antifederalists, who regarded the Senate as a coequal part of the executive branch; they charged, with some justice, that Madison would expand the president's power at the expense of the legislative branch. What Madison said was that the secretary of foreign affairs, and by implication any other officials named by the president, were to be appointed "with the advice and consent of the Senate, and removable by the president." Such language did not exist in the Constitution and implied that once a man had been appointed to office, he would then serve at the discretion of the president alone.

The debate that ensued marked the first collision between broad interpreters of the Constitution, Madison among them, and those who insisted that if the Constitution didn't stipulate a power, that power simply didn't exist. In the absence of constitutional direction, some members asserted that Congress had the power to remove executive appointees whenever it wished; others that appointees could be removed only through the formal process of impeachment; others that since the Senate approved appointees, only the Senate could remove them; and still others—including Madison—that removal was the president's business and no one else's.

With just two Antifederalists in the Senate, opposition in that house to the presidential power of removal was feeble. Oliver Ellsworth, a committed Federalist and widely regarded as one of the best lawyers in his native Connecticut, vigorously defended the president's right to fire members of his own department: If he couldn't, what was the point of executive power at all? The enemies of executive power, including some nominal Federalists, put up a sharper fight in the House of Representatives. "What clause is it that gives this power [of removal] in express terms?" demanded Gerry. "I believe there is none such." He further argued that it wasn't the president who appointed his advisers at all, but the Senate through its power of advice and consent. The only acceptable process for removal, added James Jackson of Georgia, was impeachment. "However long it may take to decide in this way it must be done. The body who appointed ought to have the power of removal."

At the bottom of this deepening debate lay a great question, indeed, a whole set of them, with fraught implications for the way the United States was to be governed: Was the president to have independent power? Or was he to be a figurehead, an agent of Congress? Where did the power of government lie? Was the Senate an executive body or a legislative one? How were the powers of the two branches to be reconciled?

Many men, including both small-government men such as Gerry and Federalists such as John Adams, viewed the president as something close to a monarch and his government as a regime that resembled a royal court. After all, they had no other frame of reference since scarcely any other republics—ancient Rome, present-day Holland—existed against which to measure and compare the new machine of republican government that they were inventing. Their imaginations strained, often unsuccessfully, to see Washington as something other than an American version of King George III. At bottom, Gerry considered the whole idea of appointing executive officials as little more than a system of "favorites," a kind of royal court, whose powers must eventually surpass those of the other branches of the government. When it came to appointments, as South Carolina representative William Loughton Smith maintained, the Senate would always be a more trustworthy judge of men than the president, since its members mixed in society and knew public sentiment, "whereas the president lives recluse & converses only with a few favorites, from whom he will generally derive all his information of characters."

It logically followed that if an appointee could be removed only through impeachment by the Senate, he could remain in office indefinitely, as long as he maintained "good behavior"—in other words, any office without a fixed term limit was, in effect, a lifetime appointment. It also seemed to follow that the power over appointments given by the Constitution to the Senate would be rendered pointless if the president was permitted to fire people on his own. "A new president might, by turning out the great officers, bring about a change of the ministry and throw the affairs of the union into disorder," Representative Theodorick Bland of Virginia worried. "Would not this in fact make the president a monarch, and give him absolute power over all the great departments of government?" (The ill-fated Bland, who had been "shipwrecked & landwrecked" on his way to New York two months earlier, was that very day struck down by a paralytic stroke and almost died on the spot; although he eventually returned to Congress, a second stroke would kill him the following year.)

More than a few feared for the republic once Washington passed from the scene. No one dreamed that Washington himself would ever abuse his power. "Things which alarm & give uneasiness if committed by any one else are overlooked when done by him," William Loughton Smith wrote to a friend. Smith feared, however, that the great man's successor would prove "less virtuous and moderate." That successor, everyone suspected, would be John Adams, Washington's heir apparent: "Should Adams obtain the presidency (& I daresay he will in a few years) such is the infatuation of the New England States in his favor, that I suspect he will have it for life. All the great Officers of government will be his dependents, open-mouthed on all occasions against the Senate, should they ever pretend to differ with the President on any constitutional point, clamorous against any member of the other house, who shall presume to thwart him in any design."

A staunch Federalist, the youthful Smith—he was only thirty—descended from a blended line of wealthy South Carolina planters and Boston merchants, whose investments ranged from banking and shipping to the slave trade. Trained as a lawyer and linked by marriage to the most powerful political clan in the state, he had embarked almost effortlessly on a political career, it seemed, then became embroiled in an embarrassing controversy that nearly cost him his congressional seat before he was able to take it. Having sat out the war years as a student in Britain, Smith was regarded by some of his enemies in Charleston as insufficiently patriotic, if not a closet Tory. They would not succeed in having him expelled from Congress, though they tried hard, but a whiff of impropriety clung to him notwithstanding.

Smith sketched out a nightmare scenario of what might ensue if the president were allowed the power to fire his appointees. "These officers from one end of the Continent to the other will form a Phalanx" dependent utterly on the chief executive, "dangerous to any Competitor who may have the folly to be a Candidate for the Presidency. Every engine would be set to work—abuse of the Competitor—panegyrick of the Gentleman in office, bribery, menaces & cabals would all be employed & would undoubtedly succeed." If the Senate didn't crawl before the president, Smith continued, his minions would set to work to undermine its authority completely. "Thus will that useful body be abhorred by the People & lose all its weight in the Government; thus will the Constitutional barrier against the tyrannical incroachments of the Chief Magistrate on the one hand and the intemperate proceedings of the popular branch on the other be pulled down and annihilated, & thus, finally will the whole powers of Government be absorbed by the President and his pretorian Cohort in the H. Of Representatives."

Madison, whose direction of the debate remained firm handed and self-confident, vigorously disagreed. He feared Senate domination far more than he did a tyrannical presidency. The entire Constitution, Madison said, in that whispery, patiently lecturing voice, was rooted in the principle that executive officers should bear full responsibility for their actions, and that anything that weakened that responsibility was contrary to both its spirit and intention. The Constitution had never intended impeachment to be anything more than a kind of "supplemental security measure." The president *must* have the power to fire his appointees—not least because it made him responsible for their conduct and subject to impeachment himself if he failed to "check their excesses." By the same token, if the president was denied that power, a corrupt appointee would be free to "commit crimes" for which he deserved to be removed because the president would have no more power to suspend him than to fire him outright. Moreover, Madison argued, think of the gross inconvenience— and the expense!—that would be caused by keeping the Senate sitting constantly in order to vote on the removal of an appointee; since they might be called on any time, "consequently they could not be a moment absent." The Constitution, he firmly declared, never envisioned a "perpetual Senate."

By this time, a fourth executive department was also under consideration: a Home Department—the apple of Charles Thomson's eye—which would oversee relations between the states and the federal government, Indian affairs, the preservation of government documents, and as-yet-to-be-created patent and copyright offices. It would also report to the president useful ideas for the improvement of manufacturing, agriculture, and commerce. The department could have served a useful function, except that it was widely viewed as a sinecure for Thomson, the longtime secretary of the old Congress. Having toiled heroically at a difficult job, he felt sure that no man was more qualified than he for a senior appointment, and he took it for granted that he would be given one. He was far more experienced than the men Washington finally chose for his cabinet, and Thomson might well have made an excellent presidential assistant. In particular, his opinion that the federal government should actively encourage science, technology, and internal improvements was far in advance of his time, as was his enlightened and humane attitude toward Native Americans, all beliefs that he shared with Washington. (The Delawares, who had adopted Thomson into their tribe, named him Wegh-wu-law-mo-end, or Man-Who-Speaks-the-Truth.)

Thomson fell victim, however, to intense factional rivalries that went back to the 1770s. Many members believed he was a stalking horse for the Philadelphia financier Senator Robert Morris, who was suspected of seeking to build a power base in the executive branch. Morris's enemies scathingly denounced Thomson as a schemer, an "old woman," a mediocrity "past the median of life," or, in Fisher Ames's harsh words, "a smooth, plausible Irishman, but superficial, arrogant, and rapacious." Upon his return to New York with the president-elect, Thomson was shocked to discover that he had not even been invited to Washington's inauguration, a breathtaking slight. And that he was politically dead. The Home Department was the only one of the first four proposed that Congress would reject: its responsibilities would be folded into the Foreign Affairs Department, later to be renamed the State Department. Thomson had by this time written a thousand pages of a projected political history of the Revolution, but soured at his treatment, he burned it. "I should contradict all the histories of the great events of the Revolution," he told friends. "Let the world admire the supposed wisdom and valor of our great men. Perhaps they may adopt the qualities that have been ascribed to them, and thus good may be done. I shall not undeceive future generations." But no one would ever know what he intended to say.

In the Senate, the ongoing debate over titles was growing even more heated. At its center stood the increasingly embattled vice president. Harried by attacks of palsy, resentful at the way his election had been manipulated, frustrated by Americans' political "imbecility," and disgusted by the "avarice of Liberty" that he thought infected his fellow citizens, Adams resented the hours of confinement with senators with whom he sometimes violently disagreed and often disliked. He was fretful and self-destructively combative. Adams saw himself, when he was at his best, as a lonely gladiator battling to "Secure our Liberties equally from a single Tyrant, a Junto of Barons, and a Mob of Madmen." In moments of self-pity, however, which were many, the warrior shrank to a martyr condemned to "a Crown of Thorns." The Comte de Moustier found Adams laughable and wondered if he was "just playing the outrageous American in the interests of the prerogatives of the President."

With his beloved wife, Abigail, Adams had settled into one of the most beautifully situated residences on Manhattan Island, near the present-day entrance to the Holland Tunnel. From their "rather too luxuriant and wild" grounds, the Adamses enjoyed a panorama that encompassed the spires of the city a mile to the south, browsing cattle, and the Hudson River with its daily cavalcade of boats carrying produce from the Hudson Valley's farms "like the cornucopia of Ceres," as Abigail delightfully put it. Abigail was further charmed by an abundance of birds that serenaded her morning and evening and complained to her husband of the hunters who invaded the surrounding area to shoot partridges, pigeons, and woodcocks. She was less thrilled with the servants: "a pretty good Housekeeper a tolerable footman a midling cook, an indifferent steward and a vixen of a House maid."

From this otherwise bucolic perch on the Hudson, like a battery of artillery concealed in the woods, Adams fired off an endless stream of polemical screeds to his vast network of friends, worrying and fulminating about the precarious state of the nation. Adams's anxieties for the United States were sincere and deep. The infant nation seemed so unprepared for survival in the feral world of the great powers that it made him almost physically ill. "Don't babble to me about Patriotism, Zeal, Enthusiasm, Love of Country," he fairly snarled to one friend. "The Corruption of Ambitions and Avarice has more universal possession of the Souls of the Gentlemen of this Country than of the Nobility of any Country in Europe." On what kind of foundation was the government to base its authority? How could it purchase the love and loyalty of a people who seemed so politically naive, contentious, and demanding? "Titles or Marks of Distinction"—he was thinking of the formal "honours" that were bestowed annually by the British crown—"would go a great Way" to create such a foundation, he believed. The only alternative was to govern by military force. "Have we dominion enough over the Minds of the People to do this? Titles would cost much less & be less dangerous to Liberty." So hysterical did he sometimes become on the subject that at one point he wildly predicted "the want of titles" might well lead to social disintegration and civil war and "cost this Country fifty thousand lives and twenty millions of money within twenty years." Americans who remembered the fiery patriot of the 1770s shook their heads. "Is it not [strange] that John Adams the son of a tinker, and the creature of the people should be for titles & dignities & preheminencies, & should despise the Herd & the ill born?" wondered one perplexed citizen.

Adams, the Comte de Moustier reported to the Foreign Ministry in June, "is a declared partisan of a Monarchy." Although Adams claimed to be as much a republican as he ever was, the vice president harbored deep doubts about the viability of popular government and praised both monarchy and aristocracy as "Institutions of admirable Wisdom," predicting (in private) that "America must resort to them as an Asylum against Discord, Seditions, and Civil War, and that at no very distant Period of time." He believed that the Constitution had implicitly created the United States as "a monarchical Republic, or if you will a limited Monarchy." Virtually by definition, however, kingship—no matter what Americans termed it—would be a lifetime office, one which, as Washington's likely successor, Adams one day expected to possess. He feared executive despotism much less than he did the ambition and "Aristocratical Pride" of the Senate, as if that body were a copy of the House of Lords, and the president an independent, beneficent protector of citizens' rights whose essential power lay as much in the magic of regal panoply as it did in the law. By his logic, ensuring that the president could wield kingly power would actually help *defend* the liberty of an "imbecile" public against senatorial usurpation. By this reasoning, Adams's near obsession with pomp and titles made sense.

The titles debate had already percolated outward from Congress through the city's taverns, coffeehouses, newspapers, and beyond, tapping into a tidal shift that was taking place in the way ordinary Americans thought about people of power and privilege. Throughout the United States, talk of liberty and equality was rife. Although some wanted to dub Washington "His Sacred Majesty," pompous titles for public officials were falling into disuse. Ordinary Americans were rapidly adopting the word *mister* as a utilitarian form that cut across traditional social categories, while white servants and workmen were abandoning the class-laden term *master* for the Dutch-derived term *boss.* Legislators risked being labeled monarchists if they favored a regal title for the president. But if they did not bestow a strong title on the head of what was almost universally perceived as the weak executive branch, they risked being damned by others as aristocrats for subverting the authority of the president. (One republican slyly suggested in the press that public men ought to be dubbed with truly descriptive titles, such as "your Turbulence, your Littleness, most Factious, most Stupid, etc. etc. etc.")

Adams tirelessly repeated that Europeans would never take the United States seriously unless its chief executive was endowed with trappings of sovereign grandeur. "A Royal, or at least a Princely Title, will be found indispensably necessary to maintain the Reputation, Authority, and Dignity of the President," he asserted. At a minimum, he considered "His Highness" or "His Most Benign Highness" as the barest acceptable forms of address for the president, although he personally preferred "Majesty" or "His High Mightiness." He scoffed at "Excellency" as demeaning and scathingly dismissed "President" as appropriate for "Fire Companies & of a Cricket Club." Any member of Congress willing to settle for less he considered a "driveling idiot." Adams was willing to allow himself, however, to be modestly addressed merely as "Excellency."

But what of Washington himself? What title did he want? Some members of Congress believed that he would refuse any species of grand title even if it was offered—or forced on him. But he remained silent. "Washington has studied his countrymen carefully, while avoiding the revelation of his own mind," Moustier observed. "The great patience and great power he possesses over himself will serve him well with men who will easily put these qualities to the test." Washington knew that he had the authority to direct foreign policy, but he had no diplomatic establishment to work with, other than John Jay, the lame-duck foreign secretary of the old Confederation Congress, Thomas Jefferson in far-off Paris, and a mere chargé d'affaires in Spain. Nor, apart from the War Department, which continued under General Knox, did any policy-making domestic structure yet exist. The entire executive branch, for all intents and purposes, consisted of a handful of young clerks and secretaries—and Washington himself. Without official counselors, and relying for advice on a few friends, mainly Madison and Knox, Washington had no known agenda beyond the creation of a strong central government. He was doubtless appalled at some of the talk that bubbled from the titles debate: some were saying that the name Washington would itself eventually become a title, to be bestowed on future presidents as the family name Caesar was on the emperors of Rome. Less than a month in office, however, he was far from ready for a test of wills with Congress.

Adams had many critics, but none more relentless than Maclay, who set out single-handedly to block the vice president and his supporters from larding the president with titles. The two men were twins in temperament—rigid, thin-skinned, and socially maladroit—which only exacerbated the deepening rift between them. Although little known outside Pennsylvania, there Maclay was highly respected as a businessman, surveyor, and advocate for the western frontier, which in 1789 began barely a day or two's ride beyond the Susquehanna. A balding, narrow-faced man with a gaze that suggested the severe standards of probity to which, in his eyes, so few of his colleagues rose, he was fiercely democratic, disgusted by pretension and luxury, and pined for the "republican plainness" of Pennsylvania. Unsurprisingly, he found Adams's enthusiasm for "pompous & Lordly distinctions" offensive and ridiculous.

Although elected as a Federalist, Maclay had plebeian instincts that were at odds with those of his more elite colleagues. Apart from his scorn for titles, he opposed what he foresaw as "a most expensive and enormous Machine of a federal Judiciary," "coercive laws for taking Oaths," and other parts of the Federalist agenda. "I believe I have sacrificed every chance of being popular, and every grain of influence in the Senate, by so doing. But be it so. I have the testimony of my own conscience that I am right." Maclay couldn't even get along smoothly with his own Pennsylvania caucus. "I know not how it is, but I cannot get into these Men. There is a Kind of guarded distance on their parts, that seems to preclude sociability. . . . I have been a bird alone," Maclay sighed in his diary.

Maclay may not have been popular, but he was persuasive. His arguments were far more reflective of the sentiments of the mass of Americans than were those of the vice president, who had lived for years in the orbit of European courts. When the patrician Richard Henry Lee of Virginia, Adams's longtime ally, declared on the floor of the Senate that "all the World civilized and savage called for titles," Maclay retorted that "mankind now considered themselves as little bound to imitate the follies of civilized Nations, as the Brutality of Savages." When another senator piously asserted that monarchy was divinely sanctioned by the Bible, Maclay—a hard-shell Presbyterian—declared that the Holy Book was irrelevant to Americans' "horror for Kingly authority." And when the Senate pondered various forms of "Excellency" and "Highness" as titles, he scornfully protested that it was "degrading to our President to place him on a par with any Prince of any Blood in Europe."

Sentiment in the House of Representatives ran strongly against titles. "Does the dignity of a nation consist in the exaltation of one man, and the humiliation of the rest?" expostulated South Carolina representative Thomas Tudor Tucker, one of the House's most vociferous advocates for states' rights. "If so, the most despotic government is the most dignified." Many Federalists thought Adams was going too far. Madison was probably echoing Washington's opinion when, on the floor of Congress, he spoke out against exotic and "impious" titles that seemed to claim "the omnipotence of the deity." He told his fellow members, "I am not afraid of titles because I fear the danger of any power they could confer, but I am against them because they are not very reconcilable with the nature of our government, or the genius of the people."

When the House voted to address the chief executive, in its formal letter of thanks for his inaugural address, simply as "President of the United

States," Adams was shocked. He kept the Senate so snarled that for days it was unable to dispatch its own letter of thanks to Washington. Trivial as this now seems, the dispute exposed a real problem of precedence and protocol. Was the Senate to bow to the will of the "lower house," or the House of Representatives to that of the "upper" one? No one knew. Anxiety on both sides became so severe that Maclay grimly predicted "a rupture with the other House," a crisis that the infant government could ill afford.

On May 9, a Senate titles committee recommended that the president be officially addressed as "His Highness the President of the United States of America and Protector of the rights of the same." Top-heavy and misshapen as this was, a majority of the Senate was willing to accept it. But Adams irritated even those who agreed with him by hectoring them on the need for order and, according to Maclay, "finding fault with everything and everyone" as he pushed aggressively for its immediate adoption and urged the senators to simply ignore the will of the House of Representatives. "What will the Common People of Foreign Countries, what will the Sailors and Soldiers say, George Washington President of the United States, they will despise him *to all eternity*," the vice president peevishly declaimed. In its account of the debate that ensued, Maclay's diary fairly crackles with scorn at Adams's "silly laugh" and "self-conceit." While Maclay was harsher than most of his colleagues, Adams's prestige and influence were withering before his own eyes. South Carolina senator Ralph Izard, whose suggested title of "Excellency" Adams had spurned, took to calling the portly vice president "his Rotundity" behind his back, while others punningly mocked him as "the dangerous vice." The steady shift in senatorial opinion was a triumph for Maclay, who could now write with satisfaction, "Good men take me by the hand."

On May 14, a wet and stormy day, the Senate finally capitulated, declaring somewhat ignominiously that "desirous of preserving harmony with the House of Representatives, where the practice lately observed in presenting a Address to the President was without the addition of Title, [the Senate] think it proper for the present to act in conformity with the practice of the other House." From now on the nation's chief executive would simply be the "President of the United States." Embedded in the Senate's grudging surrender was a tacit acknowledgment that the two houses would share legislative power equally, establishing a precedent that would last—frequently to the frustration of both—to the present day. Madison was also deeply relieved at the outcome. In a coded letter, he wrote to Jefferson, "Had the project succeeded it would have subjected the Presidt. to a severe dilemma and given a deep wound to our infant government." Maclay wrote an epitaph to what he called this "Idolatrous Business," telling his diary, "May I never hear Motion or debate on Thee more."

Although Washington never publicly criticized the vice president's behavior, his confidence in Adams plunged. He would remain on the margins of Washington's administration, never really part of the executive branch, and the presiding officer of a legislative chamber many of whose members held him, at best, in scant regard. After a month of fulmination, fearmongering, badgering, and bullying, he had alienated friends, undermined public confidence in his political skill, and turned himself into a laughingstock. During these precedent-setting first weeks of the Congress, he had established a lasting template for vice-presidential inconsequence.

Meanwhile, Madison's nimble fingers seemed to be everywhere. He had written the core text of Washington's inaugural address to the houses of Congress. He *then* wrote the letter that the House of Representatives sent to the president thanking him for the address. He *also* wrote the *president's* return letters thanking both houses for their compliments. "Your affectionate address produces emotions which I know not how to express," Washington—that is, Madison—wrote. "I feel that my past endeavors in the service of my country are far Overpaid by its goodness: and I fear much that my future ones may not fulfill your kind anticipation." It has been said that the ubiquitous Madison was, in effect, in dialogue with himself.

CHAPTER 5

A Very Perplexing Business

———— ◆ ————

A permanent revenue is permanent power.

—Fisher Ames, May 1789

The debate over the "very perplexing business" of the national revenues ground on. Every day brought new delays and frustrations. Even Madison, a painstaking parliamentarian if ever there was one, complained to Edmund Randolph, "In every step the difficulties arising from novelty are severely experienced." Those who expected government to act speedily and decisively were frustrated. "We correct spelling, or erase 'may' and insert 'shall,' and quiddle in a manner which provokes me," complained Fisher Ames. "A great clumsy machine is applied to the slightest and most delicate operations." But even the conservative Robert Morris understood that inefficiency was built into, and essential to, republican government. The great machine was clumsy by design. A generation older than the impatient Ames, Morris observed, "There are a great many to speak in the Public Debates and they seem fond of exercising their rights." However, he added, "I have so often seen good Consequences arise from Public debate and discussion that I am not amongst the number of those who complain of the delay."

On the whole, Madison was not unhappy with the course of the debate so far. He wrote to Jefferson that the House's deliberations had been "marked with great moderation and liberality," adding optimistically that they should "disappoint the wishes and predictions of many who have opposed the Government." French minister Moustier, on the other hand, watched with bemused detachment as what he patronizingly called "the American areopagus"—its political elite—a gaggle of stumbling amateurs, in his opinion, groped forward through a wilderness in which none of them knew the way. "The current Congress is more a school, where politics is studied tentatively, rather than a formally complete political assembly," he reported to Paris. After three months of existence, "the federal treasury is empty, debts are accumulating, and in the end the Americans will realize the absurdity, especially in matters of revenue, of wanting to make perfect laws."

Northeastern businessmen were predicting doom if a heavy impost was enacted. Moralists warned that high taxes would lead to smuggling on an epidemic scale; even honest merchants would be tempted to break the law. Declared Fisher Ames, "Once a system [of smuggling] is formed, the persons engaged in it will not stop at molasses alone, they will include every other article in an illicit trade, so that it is impossible to know the extent of the evil, or provide a remedy." This was rather apocalyptic, but the potential for crippling resistance to taxes was significant. Each state had its own tax regime, or none at all. Some explicitly barred state officials from enforcing federal laws, while alien Rhode Island and North Carolina were potential havens for smugglers of every conceivable commodity. British ships were already packing into American ports, unloading whole mountains of goods, while Congress argued. Yes, the risk of commercial "depravity" existed, Madison admitted exasperatedly, but the government had no choice but to impose taxes of some kind, since it had no income.

Undeterred, Ames continued to hammer away against what New Englanders considered the excessive taxation of rum and molasses. When he spoke, characteristically with his head slightly raised and his chin thrust out, men listened. Perhaps the most gifted orator in the House, it was said of him that his words "dropped upon you as the rain upon the thirsty ground." Although he often tried to rise above sectional concerns and had both the intellect and the moral depth to do it, such aspirations were at war with his loyalty to New England's commercial interests. Frequently bored with the desultory pace of debate, Ames waxed eloquent when it came to molasses. Without the molasses trade, he said, the fishery would collapse. "They are so intimately connected that the weapon which wounds the one will stab the other." Along with nearly all the New Englanders, Ames ardently supported federal action—"interference," as he put it—to protect commerce and manufacturing. "The proposed duty is indescribably odious in this place—and positively it will never be collected, unless it is done at the point of the sword!" threatened one Mainer.

Rebutting those who defended the heavy taxation of molasses as a principled assault on the evils of demon rum, Ames declared, "We are not to consider ourselves while here as at church or school, to listen to the harangues of speculative piety; we are to talk of the political interest committed to our charge. The present Constitution was dictated by commercial necessity more than any other cause." If anyone imagined that a tax would turn drinkers from rum to allegedly milder malt liquors, "they must have more romantic notions of legislative influence than experience justifies." To this, he then added a passionately populist argument. A tax on molasses was like a tax on bread. "No decent family can do without something by way of sweetening," he pleaded, adding ominously that a molasses tax would undermine the republic itself. "Mothers will tell their children when they solicit their daily and accustomed nutriment that the new laws forbid them the use of it, and they will grow up in a detestation of the hand which proscribes their innocent food." Children would turn against the government and sow the seeds of anarchy and revolution! Although molasses was the most common sweetener in New England, Ames was really defending the interests of the shipping industry.

Ames begged Congress not to be swayed: "Money is power, a permanent revenue is permanent power, and the credit that it would give [is] a safeguard to the government." Never would the zeal for government be as great as it was now, he reasoned. Factions would inevitably arise, and opposition to taxes inexorably grow. It was therefore imperative to act immediately, for the opportunity would all too soon slip away. "I am sick of fluctuating counsels, of governing by expedients," he pleaded. "Let us have stability and system."

Into the midst of the seemingly endless haggling over rates that made no one happy, George Thatcher hurled a metaphorical bomb: If imported rum and molasses were to be taxed, then why not tax imported slaves at, say, $50 a head? The iconoclastic Thatcher, from Massachusetts's Maine district, was one of the House's more vivid personalities. Because he shunned organized religion, he was accused by his enemies of being an atheist, "unprincipled, light, frothy and even boyish in [his] conduct." Descended from early settlers on Cape Cod, Thatcher hailed from a long line of local politicians, and had studied law at Harvard. His notably dry humor was often in evidence during the First Federal Congress. During one debate, when a colleague proposed minting a coin embossed with the eagle, Thatcher suggested placing a goose on it instead, and putting goslings on the smaller denominations. When challenged to a duel by the bill's offended sponsor, he demurred, offering instead to tack an image of himself on a barn door and allowing his challenger to blaze away at it to his heart's content.

Satirical as Thatcher's proposal sounded, he was as close to an abolitionist as then existed in Congress, and insofar as he intended to provoke southern slaveowners, he succeeded. A tax of $50 per slave, he drily went on, would be no more onerous than what southerners wished to impose on New England's most cherished imports. The mere mention of slavery, however, produced a figurative—and perhaps literal—gasp from Thatcher's colleagues. Madison, offended but diplomatic as always, rose to say that he would not comment upon Thatcher's "language," though by mentioning it was implicitly condemning it.

Thatcher's suggestion was mainly a rhetorical turn to make southerners think twice about the heavy taxes they supported on commodities important to New England. But on May 13, Josiah Parker of Virginia, a former Revolutionary War officer who openly opposed slavery on both moral and economic grounds, proposed a tax of $10 on every slave imported into the United States in an effort to discourage the slave trade. Declaring that it was time to "wipe off the stigma" of slavery that stained America, he became the first national legislator in American history to formally introduce an antislavery motion in Congress. While Parker's moral objection to slavery was unquestionable, he was also in tune with sentiments of many practical men in Virginia, where, as in Maryland, traditional tobacco cultivation was giving way to crops that required less intensive labor, resulting in a market glut of slaves and disenchantment with slavery itself. (In mid-May, a friend reported to James Madison that prices were so depressed in Williamsburg that "Negroes sell at the auctions of sheriffs for 1/5 of their value.")

The reaction to Parker and Thatcher from Deep South members was fierce and immediate. While tidewater masters sought to disencumber themselves of their human "excess," the demand for slaves—and with it the political power of slavery—was growing dynamically in South Carolina and Georgia as new upcountry lands were opened for settlement. It might be the "fashion of the day" to favor the liberty of slaves, erupted the ever-excitable James Jackson of Georgia, who loved slavery as passionately as he did white men's liberty, but, he said, it should be obvious to all that they were better off enslaved in America, where they had a master to provide them with support and comfort, than free amid the rampant barbarism of Africa. "What are they to do if they are discharged?" he demanded incredulously. "Work for a living? Experience has shewn us that they will not." Freed, they simply turned to villainy. Everyone knew that. Virginia already had enough slaves, he sniffed. She didn't need to import any more. But Georgia and South Carolina did. "Gentlemen ought to let their neighbors get supplied before they imposed such a burthen upon the importation." He pleaded, have some consideration for others—that is, for slavemasters. Don't "charge us for every comfort and enjoyment of life, and at the same time take away the means of procuring them." Turning, rhetorically at least, to the northern members, he declared that if any motion to tax slaves were ever introduced again, it ought to include "the white slaves as well as black," who he alleged were exported from the jails of Europe to serve as indentured servants in northern homes and shops, and whose contracts were bought and sold as readily as any slaves in the South.

Madison did his diplomatic best to deflect, in the end successfully, what threatened to become a dangerously inflamed confrontation. There was, he said, nothing unconstitutional about Parker's proposal, as some had suggested, but national unity must not be sacrificed to sectional rivalry. Although Madison was genuinely troubled, in principle, by "considering the human race as a species of property," he would do nothing to weaken slavery in practice. His "antislavery" idealism, such as it was, aimed itself not against slavery but rather against the transatlantic slave *trade*. "It is to be hoped that by expressing a national disapprobation of this trade we may destroy it, and save ourselves from reproaches, and our posterity the imbecility ever attendant on a country filled with slaves," he feelingly told his fellow congressmen. In the long run, he added, it was even in the interest of South Carolina and Georgia, because every shipload of slaves they received weakened them by rendering them less safe, since in case of foreign invasion slaves would be the means of inviting attack, as they had been during the Revolutionary War, when the British offered freedom to runaways, and thousands responded. But putting an end to this commerce was not the same thing as putting an end to slavery itself. And he didn't mention that a permanent termination of the slave trade would significantly increase the value of Virginia's "excess stock."

In the end, Parker withdrew his motion and the crisis passed. This was not the last that members of Congress would hear about slavery, however. It was merely an overture. Slavery's sharp edge would soon again cut into the deliberations of the First Congress, climaxing in 1790 with the first lobbying campaign in American political history, and threats of secession.

By mid-May, life for members of Congress had taken on a steady, if demanding, rhythm. Their workday began with committee meetings, usually followed at 11:00 a.m. by formal sessions of the House and the Senate, and ended between 3:00 p.m. and 4:00 p.m. Already irritated by the slow pace of work, members often labored manfully to make themselves heard over the clatter and roar of the city that percolated into Federal Hall from the street, where barking dogs, squealing pigs, bleating goats, and tolling bells warred against the cries of itinerant milkmen, chimney sweeps, knife grinders, lamp menders, woodchoppers, yeast makers, mattress stuffers, and cartmen touting clean Rockaway beach sand for strewing on muddy floors. "Such a noise!" groused one member. Having no staffs or offices, the members usually caucused after hours at a boardinghouse or in one of the city's taverns over meals of venison, oysters, terrapin, or roast bear washed down with punch, port, or Madeira, or such popular quaffs as mimbo, brewed with rum and loaf sugar, calibogus, a mixture of rum and beer, pumpkin-flavored beer, or an appalling concoction of rum, blackstrap molasses, and herbs that was so smelly that fish were hung alongside it to overpower its aroma.

Of the time that was left to the members, hours of every day were usually spent writing letters. Senator Oliver Ellsworth of Connecticut advised his young daughter Abigail to mind her studies: "You must shut yourself up, a part of every day & study Geography & read the Spectators or other books & also do something at Arithmatick. You will rule your letters till you have accustomed yourself to write straight." George Thatcher, with his epicurean zest for life, urged his wife, Sarah, not to succumb to loneliness. "These dull & gloomy feelings ought never to be indulged in by a woman—Their indulgence is almost as pernicious as drinking drams, chewing tobacco, taking snuff &c. in men. Gloomy women make gloomy children—And gloomy men always destroy the happiness of his dear wife." Nearly every member was expected to personally answer floods of inquiries from constituents, such as this fairly typical one from John Leland to Madison, probably the busiest member of Congress: "It would inform my Mind to have an Account of all our National Debts; to what Powers they are due, and at what per Cent; and likewise of our internal debt. And it would give me further Satisfaction to know whether the Duties arising from Commerce are sufficient (without a direct Tax) for supporting the federal Government, and the Payment of our Interest upon Debts." As an afterthought, Leland added, "If I could see all the laws I should be glad, altho' in Person I have little Use for them."

On days off, congressmen enjoyed excursions into the countryside to tour Manhattan's Revolutionary War battle sites, enjoy an hour's ease at a tea garden near suburban Greenwich Village, or visit one or another of the experimental farms where gentleman agriculturalists were happy to show off new crop varieties and innovative farm machinery. (Washington was especially interested in a device that he saw on a farm near present-day Union Square that measured the force a plow required for use in any given type of soil.) Some members doubtless also found a different mode of relaxation in the city's more than three hundred taverns and grog shops, or the whorehouses near Collect Pond, amid the tanneries and sailors' haunts that spread northward behind the East River docks.

In the gay whirl of soirees, dowagers and debutantes encased in hooped panoplies of exotic color—batswing and bottle green, "mouse's ear," "London smoke," garnet, mulberry, "drake's head," and "changeable pearl"—sipped claret, nibbled blancmange, and stepped to the latest dances imported from Europe. There was almost constant entertaining. "The Americans make a big deal of dinners and they think that men in office have not merit and are deficient in their duties if they do not give frequent and sumptuous feasts," Moustier somewhat patronizingly commented. Presiding over this world was Lucy Knox, the ample, extravagant wife of the war secretary, who affected a military style in her ballroom dress and was said, when she cruised across a dance floor, to resemble a frigate under sail. Puritans such as Maclay were disgusted by New Yorkers' frivolities and fopperies, but they pretty much carped alone.

The lodestar of New York's social whirl was the austere figure of the president. Washington's silence about congressional debates reflected his reluctance to interfere in its deliberations, along with a deeper uncertainty about what it meant to be "presidential." Back in March, he had written to Madison, "It is my wish & intention to conform to the public desire and expectation, with respect to the style proper for the Chief Magistrate to live in." But "it might be well to know what these are before he enters upon it." The presidency was still a work in progress. What kind of life was he supposed to live? Whom was he to model himself on? A king? A state governor? A county magistrate? A tidewater gentleman? How were others to behave toward him? There was no template. He knew that everything he did, from his mode of dress, to his physical bearing, to his pattern of speech was likely to define presidential behavior for ages to come. He also had an instinct for patriotic simplicity—serving only native cheese, porter, and other foods in his Mount Vernon home, or taking the oath of office in a suit of Yankee homespun, for example—that stood in sharp contrast to John Adams's Anglophilia. Washington's ethical standards were also unimpeachable. Besieged by unctuous job-seekers begging for "lucrative offices," as one put it, Washington rejected most out of hand. To a neighbor seeking a job for his son, Washington replied that favoritism would lead to endless jealousies and potentially "fatal consequences" for the nation, not to mention the ruin of his own reputation. But he also initiated the practice of consulting members of Congress on prospective appointees for their home districts, turning what might have evolved into a scheme of executive power-building into a collaborative process.

He knew it would be impossible to craft a presidential identity that would please everyone. "But to mark out and follow one [line of conduct] will meet general approbation," he wrote to Madison, in May. "The true medium must lye in pursuing such a course as will allow [the president] time for all the official duties of his station. This should be the primary object. The next, to avoid as much as may be the charge of superciliousness, and seclusion from information by too much reserve and too great a withdrawal of himself from company on the one hand, and the inconveniences as well as reduction of respectability by too free an intercourse and too much familiarity on the other." This was not just a theoretical problem, but a practical and pressing one. Visitors appeared at any hour. "I was unable to attend to any business whatsoever," he complained to a friend in Virginia. "Gentlemen, consulting their own convenience rather than mine, were calling from the time I rose from breakfast—often before—until I sat down to dinner. This, as I resolved not to neglect my public duties, reduced me to the choice of one of these alternatives, either to refuse them altogether, or to appropriate a time for the reception of them." Were he free to "give indulgence to my inclinations," he would most prefer simply to be left alone. But he was committed, as a matter of republican principle, to give everyone free access, "as consists with that respect which is due to the chair of government."

Among those to whom Washington turned for advice was his former aide-de-camp Alexander Hamilton. Hamilton, who as yet held no office in the administration, clearly gave the matter detailed thought. In his response to the president may be seen the elitist and incipiently authoritarian tendencies that would reveal themselves more fully in later years. He advised "a pretty high tone in the demeanour of the Executive," although "the notions of equality" that pervaded the young nation made this a delicate challenge. He suggested holding a formal levee, or reception, once a week, with the president to remain just half an hour, no more, and only to "converse cursorily on indifferent subjects." The president should return no visits and accept no invitations, although he might provide "formal entertainments" on special occasions, such as the anniversary of his inauguration. On levee days, the president might also hold "family dinners," to which he should invite no more than six or eight guests, limited to members of Congress and individuals of comparable stature, but "the President [ought] never to remain long at table." Hamilton further recommended that members of the Senate, which he evidently regarded as the more significant and respectable branch of Congress, be granted individual access to the president on matters of public administration, but that members of the House of Representatives should not. "I think the discrimination will be proper & may be hazarded," he advised.

Republicans were disappointed by the president's seclusion, and even more so by the debut of the extraordinary new state coach, a canary-yellow confection shaped like a half-pumpkin, drawn by six white horses and ornamented with cupids brandishing flowery festoons. Maclay, who was determined to win the seat of government away from New York, worried increasingly that his hero had fallen under the influence of "the Pompous People of New York."

The four-story Georgian mansion that had been rented for the president on Cherry Street lay on the outskirts of the city. There he maintained a busy household staffed by a mixed force of hired white and enslaved black servants dressed resplendently in handsome liveries, cocked hats, gloves, and gleaming shoes. After passing armed sentries posted in boxes outside the front door, guests arriving for the levees would find reception rooms appointed with fine furniture, plate, and china, floors covered with rich Turkish carpets, with paintings and family heirlooms that Martha Washington had brought with her from Mount Vernon. These starchy events suggested something like a royal audience, which is probably what Hamilton had in mind. Guests were first mustered in an anteroom. Eventually the door to an inner room was ceremoniously flung open, and Washington's aide Major David Humphreys appeared, sonorously intoning, "The president of the United States!" Inside, Washington would be seen posed statuesquely in a black velvet coat and breeches, holding a cocked hat in one hand, and resting his other hand on the steel hilt of his sword. Beginning on his right, the president passed regally from one guest to the next, granting each a moment's attention and then moving on. Prestigious as these affairs were, no one liked them, from Revolutionary veterans who complained that former Loyalists were allowed to enjoy the president's patronage, to prominent citizens who found them stifling and stilted.

Martha Washington suffered most of all. Martha had never wanted to leave Mount Vernon, which she loved, and she found life in New York oppressive and claustrophobic. For her, the presidential protocol was a gilded cage from which she could not escape. "There is certain bounds which I must not depart from—and as I cannot doe as I like I am obstinate and stay at home a great deal," she complained to a friend. Apart from her own formal levees, she barely socialized. "I lead a very dull life here and know nothing that passes in the town. I never goe to any publick place,—indeed I think I am more like a state prisoner than anything else."

Martha's unhappiness was but one of the sacrifices that George Washington the man made to invent George Washington the president. Despite the grumbling of republicans, one of his signal accomplishments in that seminal year of 1789 was to create the aura of charismatic power that, if perhaps somewhat tattered, still enfolds the presidency, intertwining regal pomp with democratic modesty in a distinctly American style. Although the presidential levees smacked of European pretension, Washington was seen often riding in the city accompanied by a few aides, wrote many of his letters in his own hand, and maintained a daily routine more typical of a soldier than a head of state. He was usually up and dressed at five o'clock in the morning, looked over his house and stables, and issued orders for the day's work. He then took exercise by riding for a few hours through the fields outside the city. After his return, he worked in his office and saw visitors, dined at 2:00 p.m., then retired to his office at 5:00 p.m., where he remained until his bedtime at 9:00 p.m. Yet an indefinable aura of mystery hung about him. "Nobody has ever been more impenetrable than General Washington," Louis-Guillaume Otto, who would replace the Comte de Moustier as French minister in 1790, later reflected. "The mystery which envelops him makes his demeanor so icy that with the exception of the days of public audience his house is deserted and it can be said that he enjoys all the advantages possible excepting the comforts of friendship. It is certain that the constraint in which he lives, either by choice or necessity, can leave him no other joys than those of a satisfied ambition; but even this flower is not without thorns."

CHAPTER 6

A Great and Delicate Subject

————•————

*Poor Madison got so Cursedly frightened in Virginia, that I believe
he has dreamed of amendments ever since.*

—Robert Morris, August 1789

By midmorning on June 8, the air had become oppressive and sultry,
adding a foretaste of New York's muggy summer weather to the discomfort of congressmen dressed in heavy broadcloth, snug vests, and linen
neckcloths. Although the House chamber's tall windows helped the circulation of air, the atmosphere inside was dense from the combined effects of the heat and the sweaty bodies of the members and spectators
who had packed in to hear James Madison at last broach "that Great and
Delicate Subject" of amending the Constitution. Few knew just what he
intended to say. "Whether he means merely a tub to the whale or will
suffer himself to be so far frightened with the antifederalism of his own
state as to attempt to lop off essentials I do not know," Representative
George Clymer of Pennsylvania wrote to a friend as he waited for Madison to begin, referring to a traditional ploy of panicky mariners, who,
when menaced by a whale, would commonly throw a wooden tub into the
water in hope of distracting him.

Madison had two goals: to win the support of Antifederalists, and to fend off amendments that would fatally injure the Constitution. With a sheaf of scribbled notes in his hand, he rose. Members strained to hear as he frankly admitted that a number of serious objections had been leveled against the Constitution. A small minority, he observed, challenged its basic structure because they believed it usurped the powers of state governments. Many more found fault with it because it failed to safeguard basic freedoms that Americans prized. He now promised, with strained syntax that perhaps reflected his ambivalence about what he was setting out to do, that "if the Constitution can be made better in the view of its most sanguine supporters by making some alterations in it, we shall not act the part of wise men not to do it." A moderate "revisal" might be acceptable since, he conceded, "if all power is subject to abuse, then it is possible the abuse of the powers of the general government may be guarded against in a more secure manner."

In the French embassy at the foot of Broadway, the Comte de Moustier was wondering what Madison was really up to. A product of the French court, and a skeptic by nature, he assumed that Madison and the Federalists must be playing a courtier's game of some kind, and that his "principal, but hidden" motive was actually to "retouch" the Constitution to shift more power to the presidency. "If this is the secret aim of the framers, they will only get there through detours and routes that draw away the attention of the public, which must be made to think that everything is being done solely for its benefit," Moustier wrote to his government in Paris—a regime that would itself within weeks begin to sink into the bloody maelstrom of the French Revolution.

Madison's speech was less an embodiment of political intrigue than it was the culmination of a long political journey. Everyone knew that Madison had adamantly opposed altering the Constitution in any way. The whole question of amendment had seemed settled at the Constitutional Convention, where George Mason and Elbridge Gerry had begged for the inclusion of a bill of rights, but had been outvoted. But much of the country lacked trust in a strong central government that to many smacked

of Britain's all-too-recent tyrannical rule. Squalls of opposition threatened
to sink the Constitution entirely during its unsteady voyage toward ratification by the states. Although only North Carolina and Rhode Island had
failed to ratify, in other states the votes had been achingly close. Moreover,
several state ratifying conventions had offered a dizzying farrago of more
than two hundred often-overlapping proposals. Many of them demanded
bedrock changes, such as guaranteeing the permanent dominance of the
legislative branch; a rebalancing of power to favor state governments; lim-
itations on the jurisdiction of federal courts; federal commissions empowered to override unpopular Supreme Court decisions; term limits for the
president and members of Congress; restriction of the president's powers
of pardon and military authority; restraints on the power of Congress to
raise revenue, oversee federal elections, govern the federal seat of government, and pass commercial laws; and imposing a two-thirds or three-
fourths vote of both houses of Congress to approve treaties.

New York's convention had called for an amendment declaring that the
powers of government may "be reassumed by the People whenever it shall
become necessary to their Happiness"—a virtual recipe for anarchy—
along with a clarion call for the permanent enshrinement of states' rights
in an amendment that would require federal officials to swear an oath not
to violate the rights and constitutions of the *states*. A proposed amendment
requiring both houses of Congress to keep their doors open to the public
wasn't quite as mundane as it seemed: unlike the House of Representatives, the Senate closed its sessions to outsiders, offending citizens who
regarded such secrecy as an ominous sign of aristocratic tendencies. Still
other amendments stipulated the size of congressional districts, barred
creation of a standing army, and banned direct taxation by the federal
government. Although the term *bill of rights* would be loosely bandied
about during the debate that was about to begin, some state conventions
had never mentioned personal freedoms at all. Most troubling, in Madison's view, was the demand made by several conventions to reinstate the
restrictive language of the Articles of Confederation: that all powers not
expressly delegated to the national government automatically be reserved

to the states. Such a measure, one of Madison's allies opined, would hobble the government "with Fetters of Iron."

Several things had converted Madison into an apostle for amendment: North Carolina's continued refusal to ratify the Constitution without amendment, and the shock of his own failed hopes for election to the Senate by the Virginia legislature, followed by his uphill campaign for the House against the Antifederalist (and future president) James Monroe. During weeks of sleet, snow, and freezing temperatures that left some of his constituents frostbitten, Madison had repeatedly, if a bit desperately, declared "that I always conceived the constitution might be improved," and that now its ratification "leaves me free to espouse such amendments." Pennsylvania's Robert Morris put Madison's change of heart tartly: "Poor Madison got so Cursedly frightened in Virginia, that I believe he has dreamed of amendments ever since."

Madison's evolution doubtless was also influenced by his friend and mentor Thomas Jefferson, with whom he corresponded frequently and at length. Although close in many respects, the two men differed significantly on the proper balance between federal power and popular will. Madison was uneasy with majority rule and popular movements, while Jefferson breezily allowed that "a little rebellion now and then is a good thing." However, from his perch across the Atlantic, far from the withering debates over ratification, Jefferson had repeatedly urged Madison to support the guarantee of rights that "the people are entitled to against every government on earth, general or particular." Such a bill might cramp government's work in the short run, it was true, but "the inconveniencies of the want of a Declaration [were] permanent, afflicting & irreparable." (Madison also had the support of the president, who in his inaugural address had bestowed his elliptical blessing on the principle of amendment, although Washington himself had been guided by *Madison*, who had written the address.)

Madison never expected the Constitution to be cast as if it were a bronze idol, a sort of American baal, immutable for all time. "Is it not the glory of the people of America that they have not suffered a blind veneration for antiquity, for customs, or for names to overrule the suggestions of their own good sense, the knowledge of their own situation, and the lessons of their own experience?" he challenged. Instead, his defense of the Constitution was essentially pragmatic. It rested on appeals to experience, not authority; on a hardheaded justification of specific constitutional provisions. But the real merits and defects of the Constitution, he underscored, were "such as will not be ascertained until an actual trial shall have pointed them out."

The challenge now facing Madison revealed his political instincts at their strategic best. He knew that if he didn't seize the initiative, the Constitution's enemies surely would. Therefore some "conciliatory sacrifices" by Federalists would have to be made to blunt the opposition "by detaching the deluded opponents from their designing leaders." Madison believed that if he did not propose the amendments, they would come within three days from the Antifederalist side. It was better that the amendments should "appear to be the free gift of the friends of the Constitution" than to have been "extorted" from them by its enemies. Finally and most important, he predicted, "It will kill the opposition everywhere, and by putting an end to the disaffection to the Govt itself, enable the administration to venture on measures not otherwise safe."

Antifederalists understood perfectly well what was afoot. "Their object is unquestionably to break the party by divisions," Senator William Grayson of Virginia reported to his patron, Patrick Henry, Madison's most relentless enemy in his home state. Grayson had arrived in New York with a painful case of gout and diarrhea, and he was in no mood to be pushed around by "Little Jemmy" Madison and his Federalist cronies. "After this I presume many of the most sanguine expect to go on coolly in sapping the independence of the State legislatures," he caustically told Henry.

Having promised amendments, Madison now had to deliver. He had whittled the scores of proposals down radically, pruning away the trivial and the politically unpalatable, combining some, rewriting others, and totally ignoring those that failed to fit his agenda. He would countenance no "alterations" that undermined the presidency—already the "weaker" branch of government—in any way, he told his colleagues. Rather, his proposals targeted Congress itself, "for it is the most powerful [branch], and most likely to be abused." Some members—here he was talking tough to his fellow Federalists—asserted that a bill of rights was unnecessary because many states had already enacted their own bills of that sort. This was a poor argument, he said, since some states had no such bills at all, and others had enacted "absolutely improper" bills that actually *limited* citizens' rights in the name of protecting them.

Once the protection of rights was incorporated into the Constitution, he went on, "They will be an impenetrable bulwark against every assumption of power." He may have had in mind Jefferson's prescient prediction that a bill of rights would reveal its true value in the future, when it would someday be discovered as a powerful tool that the as-yet-unformed national judiciary could deploy against miscarriages of justice by both the federal government and the states. Madison then proposed a preamble for the Constitution that deliberately echoed the Declaration of Independence—which Jefferson had mostly written—asserting that "all power derived from the people," that government existed to be "exercised for the benefit of the people, which consists in the enjoyment of life and liberty," the right to acquire and use property, "and generally of pursuing and obtaining happiness and safety." Madison added, significantly, that "the people have an indubitable, unalienable, and indefeasible right to reform or change their government, whenever it is found adverse or inadequate to the purposes of its institution." All this had a radical edge that worried some of Madison's more conservative colleagues and would likely have opened vast areas of American life to federal supervision. He also wanted the amendments inserted—"ingrafted" like new cuttings, he said, with a planter's felicitous turn of phrase—into the body of the Constitution itself, where they would remain forever part of the great document.

Madison then turned to his other amendments. He proposed that the number of representatives not exceed the proportion of one for every thirty thousand persons, and that each state be guaranteed at least two representatives; that members of Congress be barred from increasing their salary until after an intervening election; that a minimum limit be placed on the amount of damages that might be sought in federal courts; and that jury trials be held reasonably close to the place where the alleged crime was committed. Only then did Madison finally (and rather cursorily) address personal freedoms, calling for the inclusion of language to protect freedom of conscience, speech, press, petition, assembly, the right to bear arms, prevent unreasonable searches and seizures, establish rights of the accused in judicial proceedings, and allow religious objectors to avoid military service. Next, he advanced what was arguably the most far-reaching of his amendments, which he declared "of equal if not greater importance" than all the others: an explicit statement that not only the federal government but also the *states* had no power to violate the rights of conscience, freedom of the press, or trial by jury, declaring that there was "more danger of those powers being abused by the state governments than by the government of the United States." Also controversial, he proposed an amendment underscoring the separation of powers among the branches of the federal government, and including a statement that "the powers not delegated by this constitution, nor prohibited by it to the states, are reserved to the states respectively." This addressed—but deftly evaded—the cornerstone demand by Antifederalists that all powers except those *expressly* granted to the federal government be retained by the states.

If Madison imagined that his amendments would enjoy speedy approval, he was sorely mistaken. To Fisher Ames, who considered amendments completely unnecessary, it sounded as if Madison had merely "hunted up all the grievances and complaints of newspapers—all the articles of Conventions—and the small talk of their debates," while Roger Sherman of Connecticut, a brilliant but clumsy speaker and as stiff as starched linen, one of the House's Federalist lions, suggested that "taking up the subject of amendments at this time would alarm more persons than would have their apprehensions quieted thereby." The Constitution was probably imperfect, Sherman conceded, but what in the world wasn't? "I do not expect any perfection on this side of the grave in the works of man." Fiery James Jackson of Georgia dismissed the entire batch of amendments as "a mere *ignis fatuus*"—fool's fire—"amusing by appearances, and leading often to dangerous conclusions." Indeed, he added, some states that had so-called bills of rights exhibited some of the worst abuse of individual rights in the country. Jackson then embarked on one of the most ornate metaphors launched during the debate, comparing the Constitution to a newly built ship that hadn't yet put to sea. "She is now laying in the dock—we have had no tryal as yet; we do not know how she may steer—what force of a helm she carries. Upon experimentation she may prove faultless, or her defects may be very obvious. In this state, will the prudent merchant attempt alterations? Will he employ two thousand workmen to tear off the planking and take asunder the frame?"

After Madison's nominal allies had done with him, the Antifederalists took their turn, complaining that Madison had ignored the structural amendments that had been demanded by several of the states, including his native Virginia. Along with them, Samuel Livermore of New Hampshire, an antiadministration Federalist, accused Madison of picking only the amendments that he liked from among the vast number that had been proposed—unless, Livermore cuttingly added, Madison supposed that he was superior in wisdom and abilities to all the states and their conventions combined. Elbridge Gerry, long a strident advocate for extreme structural overhaul, startled his colleagues by now coming out *against* Madison's proposals. Gerry considered other matters more urgent, declaring that "the salvation of the country depended upon its establishment, amended or not." He also maintained that *all* the amendments proposed by the states should be considered, not just Madison's paltry selection from them. A skilled political infighter, Gerry realized that if the Virginian got his way now, the Antifederalists would probably never succeed in building a majority for the radical revisions that they wanted. Gerry was not afraid of a fight, but he wanted to be ready for it.

Many southern Federalists saw something much more particular to worry about. South Carolina, warned Congressman William Loughton Smith, should be "extremely cautious" about any "innovation" that was proposed for the Constitution. Smith had succeeded in deflecting those who had questioned his loyalty and challenged his election and was becoming one of the most active members of the House, as well as one of its staunchest defenders of slavery. As the document stood, it posed no threat to "our State-rights," Smith confided to a friend, but if "ingenious men & able orators" succeeded in giving it a different shape, it was impossible to say what further alterations might be wrought upon it over time. Once begun, where would the process of amendment stop? It might eventually fix its sights on South Carolina's most cherished economic institution. "Our State is weak in the Union—it certainly is—we have no [other] state to support our peculiar rights, particu[larl]y that of holding Slavery. The other States are all agst. us; but while the Constitn. remains unaltered, they can't touch our negroes for 20 years & perhaps not constitutionally after that time." Although a few representatives from slave states occasionally professed a desire to see an end to slavery, Smith was exaggerating South Carolina's isolation. For the great majority of slave-state lawmakers, any suggestion that all men were by nature equally free and independent, as Madison dared to proclaim in his preamble, and possessed rights that government was bound to respect, threatened the basis of slavery.

In short, to Madison's dismay, no one wanted to talk about amendments. They clamored that his grab bag of "alterations" was, if not a total waste of time, then premature. Far more pressing business was at hand. What about the escalating Indian attacks in the Southeast? "Georgia is now in the greatest distress," cried a correspondent of the *New-York Daily Advertiser.* "Urge Congress to do something soon, or the state is lost." And the federal land offices that were supposed to be established to direct settlement west of the Alleghenies—what about them? Thomas Scott of Pennsylvania warned that millions of people would be crossing the mountains in the years to come, and it would hardly be in the national interest "to have that country settled by an unprincipled banditti." What about the establishment of courts? What about a system of customs houses to collect the nation's anticipated revenues? "The people are waiting with anxiety for the operation of the Government," pleaded John Vining of Delaware, a Federalist stalwart. "Have they passed a revenue law? Is not the daily revenue escaping us? Let us not perplex ourselves by introducing one weighty and important question after another, till some decisions are made." The amendments, to Madison's chagrin, would have to wait.

Madison had hoped and expected that the revenue bills would be passed in time to tax the spring imports. But that opportunity was now long gone, given Congress's late start, as well as "so many local Interests—& so many Prejudices—to be reconciled," sighed Pennsylvania representative Thomas Hartley, a Revolutionary veteran and ardent Federalist. A cacophony of competing interests combined to bring debate to a crawl. Daniel Carroll of Maryland, a prosperous merchant and landowner, and scion of one of the most prominent Catholic families in the country, whose district included a large glassworks, called for—and got—protection for glassmaking. Roger Sherman insisted that imported tobacco be sufficiently taxed to discourage competition with Connecticut-grown tobacco. Benjamin Goodhue, who represented the shoe-manufacturing town of Lynn, Massachustts, called for high duties on shoes, galoshes, and slippers. Aedanus Burke of South Carolina wanted a stiff duty on hemp, while Virginians argued for one on coal, which was a burgeoning industry in their state. Tempers grew raw. The Irish-born Thomas Fitzsimons of Pennsylvania—a close associate of Robert Morris's, and one of the floor managers of the impost bill in the House—sneered at the "tenacity of the Massachusetts people who have shown a littleness injurious to their reputation," while Fisher Ames privately disparaged the Pennsylvanian as an "artful" character "whose face, manner and sentiments concur to produce caution, if not apprehension and disgust." All in all, it was "a very perplexing business," as Senator Paine Wingate of New Hampshire put it.

When the revenue bills were finally sent to the Senate in mid-May, senators continued to rehash many of the arguments that their House colleagues had been nagging at for weeks. "Members, both from the North, and still more particularly from the South, were ever in a flame when any articles were brought forward that were in any considerable use among them," Maclay diarized. The patrician South Carolina senator Pierce Butler "flamed away and threatened a dissolution of the Union with regard to his State, *as sure as God was in the firmament*," and attacked the entire impost bill as "solely calculated to oppress S. Carolina" because the proposed duties would weigh more heavily than he thought they should on his state. Meanwhile, the tall, slender Richard Henry Lee of Virginia—"certainly ambitious and vainglorious," Maclay commented, but "a man of a clear head and great experience"—drew laughs when he challenged Pennsylvanians' efforts to protect their local sugar industry, declaring that "the loaf Sugar of America was bad it was lime and other vile composition, he had broke a Spoon in trying to dissolve and separate it," adding in "so tremulous an accent and so forlorn an aspect as would have excited even Stoics to laughter." The customarily humorless Maclay reported that Lee went on to say, "I must go on breaking my spoons, and three Millions of People must be taxed to support half a Dozen People in Philada."

In the House, Madison had successfully argued for a system of duties that favored nations with which the United States had treaties of friendship, most specifically France, and pointedly retaliated against England for her refusal to negotiate a commercial treaty with the United States and for barring American ships from Britain's Caribbean ports. However, northern mercantile interests deeply invested in trade with Britain maintained that such positive discrimination on behalf of France was little more than sentimentalism disguised as policy, since French ships carried a far smaller proportion of the transatlantic trade. Why irritate trading partners—namely England, Spain, and Portugal—that had not yet inked treaties with the United States, but who might well do so if Americans didn't needlessly insult them? The United States might as well "declare commercial War" against the British, Caleb Strong of Massachusetts fulminated. Maclay, a stalwart friend of France's, retorted that "if Commercial Treaties were of any Use at all, Nations in Treaty should stand on better Terms than those Who had kept at a Sulky distance," but he stood virtually alone. The political geometry of the Senate was quite different. Northern mercantile interests were much more heavily represented than they were in the House. By a large margin, the Senate voted to abolish discrimination, and to keep protectionist duties high across the board. The House then acquiesced to the Senate's overwhelmingly expressed will, prompting expressions of unadulterated joy among the New Englanders. Crowed Fisher Ames, "The Senate, God bless them, as if designated by Providence to keep rash and frolicsome brats out of the fire, have demolished the absurd, impolitic, mad discrimination."

When the amended bills returned to the House, they were "so Prund, & Mutilated" that they were barely recognizable. Although some in the House were swayed by the Senate's arguments, the majority refused to budge. The result was another test of wills between the two houses of Congress. Everyone knew that the outcome, whatever it was, would set a precedent and could potentially establish one or the other house of Congress as its dominant body. Some representatives were so tired of the subject that they were ready to capitulate to the Senate. Others were prepared to fight to the bitter end. To head off a confrontation that might seriously damage the government, cooler heads called for the creation of the first joint conference committee in American history—such joint committees are commonplace today—to try to iron out the differences between the two houses.

Meanwhile, on June 16, the House paused in its frustrating debate over revenues to vote on the creation of the Department of Foreign Affairs, the first of what would eventually become four cabinet offices, along with War, Treasury, and the Attorney General, laying the foundation of the executive branch of the federal government. In the lobbies of Federal Hall, in the taverns and rooming houses of the city, and on street corners, everyone, it seemed, was talking about who would fill the new top-level jobs that Congress was creating. Livingston was still hungry for the Treasury Department, while others were promoting Timothy Pickering

of Pennsylvania, or the New York Antifederalist Samuel Osgood. However, reported Madison, "Hamilton is most talked of." Although it was
still supposed that the Anglophile John Jay could have the Department
of Foreign Affairs if he wanted it, it was rumored that he would prefer to
be named chief justice of the Supreme Court, instead. If that happened,
the president might offer Foreign Affairs to the passionately pro-French
Thomas Jefferson, who was still serving as minister to the court in Paris.
As one of the most experienced men available to the administration, Jefferson would certainly be offered *something*. But what did he want? Neither Washington nor Madison—"being *unacquainted with your mind*," as
Madison put it in a letter to Jefferson—had any idea.

The nagging question of the president's right to remove his appointees
still remained, however. Could he or could he not fire them? "No question has been so warmly agitated," reported one Maryland congressman.
For Madison, the answer was crucial. He feared that if department heads
were completely dependent on the will of the Senate, a faction there might
support them against the president, paralyze the executive, and cripple
public business.

Articulating the worst fears of those who thought that the country
could ill afford to allow the president the power to hire and fire executive
officers at whim, the hatchet-faced firebrand James Jackson of Georgia
declared with colorful hyperbole that such a power would "blast all those
delightful buds of happiness which the establishment of the new constitution flattered us would expand and ripen into fruition." Born in England,
the thirty-one-year-old Jackson had come to the United States at the age
of fifteen, where he was taken in as the ward of a prominent Savannah
family and, in 1776, it was said, became "the first Boy [in Georgia] who
bore arms against" the British. By the time he was twenty-four, he commanded his own brigade in the Georgia militia and had fought on several
of the bloodiest southern battlefields of the war. He had also fought at
least two duels, in one of them killing his opponent, and earning a reputation as a political brawler, as well as a fiery republican. Although he
revered Washington as "the greatest man alive," he had been instrumental

in defeating the efforts to lard the president with lavish titles, for fear of setting a precedent should "a worse Character fill his Station" in future. Jackson was universally considered the First Congress's most flamboyant (if often heedless) orator, and so loud of voice that the senators upstairs were at least once forced to shut their windows to block out his rant.

Speaking, probably, with the blustery physicality for which he was well known, he cited historical precedents reaching back to ancient Greece, Carthage, and "the Jewish theocracy," declaring that Americans rightly "dread the accumulation of power in the hands of the president." No one imagined that the glorious Washington himself posed a threat to liberty. "But the time may come when venality will subtilely insinuate and infuse itself through the system, and corrupt the whole constitution destroying its beauty, consuming its spirits, and subverting its frame." The president was already the commander in chief of the army. Imagine a president in some future time who also enjoyed the power of controlling the head of the Treasury Department: he would clutch the nation's purse strings in his hands, "and you only fill the strong box, and collect the money of the empire, for his use," thus handing him the power "to lay prostrate the liberties of America."

James Madison was virtually Jackson's opposite as a speaker: dispassionate, didactic, and soft-spoken. He reiterated that a strong presidency was imperative, and that an executive dependent on the Senate to approve all his hiring and firing of aides would soon be left helpless. Dictatorship in America was *impossible*: given that it took the votes of millions to elect a president, it was inconceivable that any "vicious character" could ever be raised to that station. However, if the Senate seized the power to remove the president's appointees, they would quickly realize that their job security depended not on the man who had selected them but on the *legislature*; they would become, in essence, agents of the Senate. Once Congress created an office and the president filled it, "the legislative power ceases," Madison asserted. He had repeated the same principle countless times, and he was still acknowledged to be the Constitution's leading interpreter even by most of those who disagreed with him. What he said carried considerably more weight than the harangue of the overwrought militia general from Georgia.

The House then voted decisively, 30–20, to give the president what Madison wanted. Hard-core Federalists were elated. "My whole heart has been engaged in this debate," reported Ames. "Indeed it has ached. In this debate a stroke was aimed at the vitals of government." But the Antifederalist stroke had missed its mark. The Senate would not act on the bill for another month, but Madison was deeply relieved. He had won another victory for a strong presidency.

CHAPTER 7

Vile Politicks

———•—•———

Our successors will have an easier task.

—James Madison, June 1789

T he president played no part in any of these debates. Members of Congress were forever wondering what Washington was really thinking, what Washington really intended, whether he had plans of his own or was a mere tool in the hands of others. "He has been very cautious hitherto, or rather inactive," remarked Maclay with his inimitable gift for the cutting turn of phrase, "or shall I say like a Pupil in the hands of his Governor, or a Child in the Arms of his Nurse." Maclay was referring to Madison, who he suspected exerted a Svengali-like power over the chief executive. "Alas Poor Washington if You are taken in this Snare, how will the Gold become dim?" he lamented.

Maclay underrated the president's ability to think for himself. As a matter of principle, Washington was scrupulous about even the appearance of interfering with the legislative process. But that was not the only reason for his sudden disappearance from the political and social scene. The president, many feared, was on his deathbed. In an age when many Americans died young, the fifty-seven-year-old Washington's robust health was legendary. He had survived the war without a scratch. But overwork and exhaustion in the weeks after the inauguration had driven him close to collapse. Then, in mid-June, he was suddenly struck down by a mysterious ailment. Some whispered of anthrax. It was widely rumored that he was too ill to continue in office, and that he would resign any day. Washington was actually suffering from a huge, infected carbuncle, "a Bile on his Seat, which had been so inflamed by his riding on horse-back as to grow into an Imposthume as large as my two fists," reported William Loughton Smith of South Carolina. The levees ceased. Visitors were turned away from the presidential mansion. New York mayor James Duane ordered Cherry Street blocked with a chain to stop noisy traffic from disturbing the president's rest and ordered straw to be spread on the sidewalk to muffle the tread of passing feet.

Beyond lancing the boil, doctors could do little. Antibiotics were un-known, and even the simplest operations were potentially life-threatening. (Quacks were abundant: one popular New York physician, Elisha Perkins, advocated the use of metal scraps resembling horseshoe nails known as Perkins's Metal Tractors, which he claimed possessed curative properties for any ailment from ague to tuberculosis when rubbed over the afflicted area.) Washington's physician, the eminent Dr. Samuel Bard, adopted a draconian approach. He summoned an assistant and ordered, "Cut away. Deep—deeper—deeper still. Don't be afraid. You will see how well he bears it!" Washington, always stoic, accepted the possibility that he would never recover. "Do not flatter me with vain expectations," he told Bard. "I am not afraid to die, and therefore can bear the worst." If he did, the in-creasingly unpopular John Adams would automatically become president, a prospect that made many members of Congress gasp with apprehension. Washington's death would have prompted a constitutional crisis that the nation, fortunately, would not have to face for another fifty-two years, until the death in office of William Henry Harrison in 1841.

The House again took up the revenue bills on June 26. While the con-ference committee had failed to craft a formal compromise, the debate cranked into motion with a distinct air of weariness. A consensus was developing that the high duties originally voted by the House were excessive and that lower ones would probably generate more revenue because citizens would be less likely to evade them by smuggling. "Our own citizens, possessing superior advantages for that business, would more probably evade those laws than strangers," Representative Josiah Parker of Virginia, a major planter and slaveowner, though an opponent of the international slave trade, drily reminded his colleagues.

Thomas Fitzsimons of Pennsylvania warned that if the House continued to resist the Senate's version, the entire bill would be lost: "I leave you to answer for the consequences, to your constituents, and to the world." The House would now either lose the bill completely, or it would have to compromise. The choice was blunt. Even Elbridge Gerry, usually adamant against any perceived federal encroachment, was an economic realist, who had served several years on the wartime treasury board: he knew that government couldn't function without income. He reminded his colleagues that delay had already cost at least hundreds of thousands of dollars in lost revenue, and he pointed out that the government had to come up with $6 million to meet its expenses for 1789, and another $9 million for 1790. "Where the money is to come from I know not, but come it must," he exasperatedly barked. Unless Congress took action immediately, he charged, "We must therefore abandon the hopes of supporting our public credit, or lay on burthens which will make the political colts to caper & kick."

In the end, on July 4, the House gave way. There would be no war of precedence between the two houses of Congress. (Although the Senate was already being called the "upper house," it was not for any reason of institutional superiority: it was literally just *upstairs*.) The heatedly debated molasses tax was reduced to a palatable two and a half cents, the tax on distilled spirits to a level acceptable to everyone, and the tonnage tax on American-owned ships was similarly slashed to just six cents per ton, and on foreign vessels, from whatever nation, to fifty cents per ton. Even the South Carolinians surrendered. "Upon the whole [the bills] are as favorable to the Southern Interests as we could have expected," reported William Loughton Smith, who confessed that he had "become a Convert among many others," rationalizing that "had we not cried out so lustily, the New-England delegates were disposed to make [the duties] much higher."

Madison was not happy. He had tenaciously argued for higher duties on British vessels, and he had lost. British influence had clearly swelled in the United States, while gratitude toward France had withered. Madison rather mean-spiritedly blamed the outcome on New York City itself, a political punching bag even then, which, he claimed, was "steeped in Anglicism" dominated by "Tory" business interests. But he was a pragmatist. He would not remain embittered. He chose to take a long and hopeful view, remembering that during the debate there had been far less conflict between the northern and the southern states than he had feared, and that members from the same state or region found themselves on opposing sides of questions as often as they did on the same side. He wrote hopefully to Jefferson, "Our successors will have an easier task. And by degrees the way will become smooth short and certain."

The revenue bills would not solve all the nation's financial problems: they would scarcely dent the mountain of debt that hung over the government and would do little to placate the nation's foreign and domestic creditors. But at least the government would have income: salaries could be paid, bills met. Still more far-reaching, Congress had demonstrated that it was able to reconcile divergent sectional interests and to ameliorate conflict between the two houses. Men who had raged at perceived slights to their states had yielded, if grudgingly, to a notion of common interest. Indeed, throughout the debate, attendance by the members had been high—a demonstration of their commitment—and negotiations over the bills had, on the whole, been good-tempered, and the atmosphere surprisingly free of "intrigue, cabal, management, or cunning," Fisher Ames approvingly observed.

(Two related bills would be passed later in the month. The Coasting Act would describe federal forms for registering and clearing all vessels plying American coastal waters, and the Collection Act would establish a system of more than one hundred customs collectors and other port officers to ensure that the duties would actually be paid. "It is a novel thing in America, and on the enlarged scale on which we are obliged to attempt it, it is a most difficult undertaking," Representative Richard Bland Lee wrote to a cousin in Virginia. He was speaking of this first step in the creation of what would eventually become the mighty federal bureaucracy.)

After the passage of the revenue bills, Congress shut its doors early to enable members to join the city's rollicking Independence Day celebrations. Bands played, flags fluttered, fireworks were shot off. In the sort of hieratic ceremony so beloved by Americans of the early republic, pompous congratulations from city officials and assorted clubs and guilds were formally delivered to the Speaker of the House, Vice President Adams, and—to the immense relief of the public and Congress alike—to the president himself, in his first wobbly public appearance since he had been prostrated by the monstrous "imposthume." Somehow he mustered the strength to don his blue-and-buff general's uniform and posed monumentally in the doorway of his residence as a parade of soldiers swung by, accompanied by bands and artillery. It would be weeks yet before he was able to shoulder his former workload and the burdens of presidential hospitality. But the crisis had passed. Washington would live.

Later, without the president in attendance, members of Congress, the vice president, army veterans, and local luminaries, including "a splendid assembly of ladies," gathered in St. Paul's Chapel, a short walk from Federal Hall, for a celebratory service. This was capped by a soaring eulogy for the deceased Revolutionary War general Nathanael Greene, delivered by the rising talent—everyone knew he was destined to play a role in the new government—Alexander Hamilton. Married to the daughter of former general (and soon-to-be-named New York senator) Philip Schuyler, founder of New York's first bank, wealthy, charismatic, and handsome, Hamilton was approaching the apogee of his career. It seemed he could do nothing wrong. Then, at St. Paul's, he did. In praising Greene's well-trained regular troops, he slighted local militias as "the mimicry of sol-diership." Then, adding injury to insult, Hamilton—who was a founder of the New York Manumission Society and had been impressed by the bravery of black troops he commanded during the war—observed that the American campaign had been made more difficult than necessary because it had confronted not just the British army but also "a numerous body of slaves bound by all the laws of injured humanity to hate their masters." In other words, not only had runaway slaves turned against their former owners, but they were morally justified in doing so. (During the war, perhaps as many as one hundred thousand slaves had defected to the crown; South Carolina alone hemorrhaged twenty-five thousand, about one-third of its African-American population.) Southern congressmen in the audience were shocked and offended at the airing of such incendiary sentiments in public. Since Hamilton was not yet a member of the gov-ernment, they could do nothing but smolder. But they would not forget.

Washington's recovery was in the minds of senators when they recon-vened to complete their debate on the establishment of the Department of Foreign Affairs. Oliver Ellsworth lost no time in exploiting fear about Washington's survival to punch up support for the bill. Depriving the president of the power to control his appointees would be a kind of moral assassination, he theatrically declared with red-rimmed eyes, mournfully declaiming, "It is Sacrilege to touch an Hair of his head, and we may as well lay the President's head on a block, and strike it off with one blow." The Senate vote was scheduled for July 16.

Senators and representatives huddled in knots on the stairs in deep, last-minute confabulation—Ames with Morris, Charles Carroll with Strong, then Paterson with Carroll. Adams seemed to be everywhere, talking animatedly to everyone in what Maclay disapprovingly called the "court party." As soon as Adams gaveled the Senate to order, Ellsworth's taciturn ally William Paterson of New Jersey rose. "After he had warmed himself with his own discourse, as the Indians do with their War Song," Maclay commented, Paterson pointed out that not a word in the Constitution granted the Senate the right to remove executive officials. (As students at Princeton, Paterson and Ellsworth were fellow members of a fraternity quaintly named the Well Meaning Club, and Paterson had later served as tutor in law to Aaron Burr.) Paterson was followed by another reliable Federalist, George Read of Delaware, a "fatiguing" but persuasive speaker who, Maclay remarked, "was swinging on his legs for an Hour" before he, too, declared himself in favor of the president's right to fire his appointees. After Read, several more senators formally withdrew their earlier opposition to the measure. "Recantation was in fashion," sneered Maclay, who spoke at length for restraining executive power. He was infuriated to see Adams, his nemesis, deliberately trying to rankle him by "snuffling up his Nose, kicking his heels, or talking & Sniggering" the whole time that Maclay had the floor.

Despite the intense lobbying beforehand, when the votes were cast, they split evenly: ten for retaining the president's power, and ten against. Adams, "with great joy cried out *it is not a Vote!*" before he had even declared the totals, then added his own vote on behalf of securing the president's power, which he doubtless assumed would one day be his own. It was the first instance of a tie-breaking vote cast by a vice president in American history. Afterward, the Virginia Antifederalist William Grayson claimed the floor, ominously rumbling that "consolidation is the object of the New Government, and the first attempt will be to destroy the Senate, as they are the Representatives of the State legislatures."

But it was done. The Department of Foreign Affairs, later to be renamed the State Department, had come into being, and the president was now assured of the power to fire his advisers at his discretion. The advocates of strong government, the "court party," had set another precedent that would resonate through American history. They had established a firm foundation for the decisive and autonomous presidency that would evolve in time to come.

Even as it was wrangling over presidential power, the Senate was inventing the federal justice system. Under the Articles of Confederation, the national government exercised legal jurisdiction over only three spheres: crimes committed on the high seas, boundary disputes between states, and competing western land grants by different states. Suspicion of courts was a deeply embedded Anglo-American tradition. In colonial times, courts were essentially political agents of the royal governors, cogs in the machinery of British repression, dependent on "the eccentric impulses of whimsical, capricious, designing men," as Thomas Jefferson put it. Americans harbored an even deeper dislike for lawyers in general, many of whom had been Tories and fled for their lives during the Revolutionary War. Those who remained didn't fare much better in public opinion; in 1786, residents of Braintree, Massachusetts—John Adams's hometown, no less—voted en masse to "crush . . . that order of Gentlemen denominated Lawyers."

Following independence, state legislatures filled the legal vacuum, codifying laws and writing statutes to replace unwritten common law—an often-haphazard process undertaken by self-interested legislators and unreliable state courts with an alleged propensity to "vicious" misbehavior. Meanwhile, jury duty was generally evaded by the richer sort and left "to poor, uninformed men, many of whom are unacquainted with the English language," while the prospect of a court summons made ordinary Americans groan with despair. Growled one citizen, "We see numbers of helpless men in the depth of winter and fiercest weather camping out in the woods, during the sitting of the courts, who are dragged from home through mere timidity and indigence, being unable to pay the fine" for nonappearance when they were called for jury duty.

The judiciary system that was created by the First Congress would touch the lives of Americans more than almost any other legislation that it enacted. The Constitution empowered Congress to create a Supreme Court and "such inferior Courts as the Congress may from time to time ordain." New judicial machinery had to be invented, and speedily. But how would it work? How many Supreme Court justices should there be? Were the state courts to be divorced from the new system or included in it? Would federal courts dare to review state laws? Could state courts review federal courts' decisions? What would happen if a state tried a case that belonged in federal court? Could judges serve simultaneously as state and federal judges? If so, if a judge was impeached by his state, would he still remain on the federal bench? The possibility of serious confrontation between the federal and state governments was enormous. Antifederalists feared with some reason that the new court system could pose a fatal threat to states' rights. As Connecticut lieutenant governor Oliver Wolcott Sr. put it, in June, "I think that some of the Governors of these States do not wish to have it beleived that they have any earthly Supirior."

The bill's primary author was the prodigiously hardworking Senator Oliver Ellsworth, among the staunchest of Yankee Federalists, who believed that a government that lacked coercive power was no real government at all. "A perfect uniformity must be observed thro' the whole union or jealousy and unrighteousness will take place," he asserted, "and for a uniformity one judiciary must pervade the whole." One of the most experienced members of Congress, the forty-four-year-old Ellsworth was a highly regarded litigator and judge and had served both in the Continental Congress and as a delegate to the Constitutional Convention, where he was a vigorous advocate for the interests of small states. Ellsworth served on no fewer than *eighty* committees in the First Congress, more than any other member, and had chaired the committee that reviewed the amendments that Madison had just proposed in the House of Representatives. Although most regarded him as "a man of remarkable clearness of reasoning," Ellsworth was not universally well liked. Maclay derided him in the privacy of his diary as a man "governed by conveniency or cabal," meaning that he was skilled at the retail politics that was necessary to actually get things done (unlike the isolated and frustrated Maclay).

After much "Intrigate & Laborious Work," the bill was ready in late April. It provided for a Supreme Court consisting of a chief justice and five associate justices, who would meet twice a year at the seat of government, and the division of the country into thirteen judicial districts, each with its own "inferior" federal court, US attorney, and federal marshal. In a major innovation, the creation of three regional circuit courts consisting of a district judge and two traveling members of the Supreme Court, would also meet twice annually to hear appeals from the district courts and thus "carry Law to [the people's] Homes, Courts to their Doors," as William Paterson put it. While the district courts would rule mostly on maritime cases, minor crimes, and revenue collection, the circuit courts would serve as national trial courts in cases involving major federal crimes, out-of-state or foreign citizens, and appeals from the district courts. In lawsuits where the amount in question was more than $500 and the litigants were from different states, the out-of-state litigants had the option to take their cases away from the often-biased state courts to the (presumably) more neutral federal ones. Finally, the bill would create the office of the attorney general—"to prosecute and conduct all suits in the Supreme Court."

Maritime issues loomed especially large in Ellsworth's concerns. Because virtually all the government's income—87 percent of it between 1789 and 1800—would derive from import duties, federal enforcement was vital. Without it, smuggling would run unchecked and revenue would evaporate. In addition, since the United States had no navy, the country depended in wartime on officially commissioned but privately owned raiders who were allowed to sell prize cargoes for profit. (During the Revolutionary War, American privateers had captured some two thousand British vessels, and cargoes estimated to be worth 18 million pounds, a fabulous sum.) Federal courts would regulate privateering by validating captured prizes and ensuring that privateers didn't treat their commissions as a license to commit outright piracy.

The bill spurred vigorous debate. Edmund Randolph of Virginia, who in a few months would become the first attorney general, protested in a letter to Madison that six Supreme Court justices were too few "to make headway against eleven state judiciaries, always disposed to warfare." A vocal minority argued that no federal judges were needed at all, while hard-shell Federalists were appalled at the suggestion that federal cases might be left to the "foreign and hostile jurisdiction" of the states. Others warned that it would be a big mistake to allow a federal district judge to participate in circuit-court deliberations since he would doubtless have already formed his opinion in the trial held in his own court and was not likely to relinquish it. Still others warned that the system, which was estimated to cost between $50,000 and $60,000 annually, was far too expensive for the nation's underfunded, debt-ridden government and would "Create Jealousies, and uneasiness among the people." Vividly illustrating the point, insulted New Hampshirites complained that their state had been lumped in the same district as Maine, then still part of Massachusetts, implying that it was "inferior to any other state in the Union."

But no one hated the bill more than Maclay, who felt that Ellsworth was bullying the Senate with "elaborate harangues" and stifling debate. "This Vile Bill is a child of his, and he defends it with the care of a parent," seethed the Pennsylvanian, who regarded the bill as little more than a self-enrichment scheme by a coterie of "Cloven-footed" lawyers. Maclay was having a hard time all around. He felt unpopular and isolated, and his knees were so swollen from rheumatism that he could hardly walk. "I stay here wrangling vile politicks, where all is Snip Snap, and Contradiction," he complained to his diary. Combined with his lingering disgust at pompous titles, and his disdain for Adams's "caballing," he was beginning to despair for the whole federal enterprise. "My mind revolts in many instances against the Constitution of the United States," he rather startlingly confessed. "Indeed I am afraid it will turn out the Vilest of all Traps that ever was set to ensnare the freedom of an unsuspecting people." In particular, Maclay's libertarian streak rebelled at the granting to federal judges of "inquisitorial power" that permitted them to "extort evidence from any Person" by requiring him to testify against his will, a practice no different in its essence from the horrible medieval custom of extracting confessions from "the Carcass of the Wretched Culprit by Torture," he charged. But Maclay's attempts at amendment were in vain. "I have been pushed at from both right and left by them, and not a Man to second me," he lamented.

Meanwhile, Ellsworth assured doubters that although the new courts would step in if a state dared "make a law which the Constitution does not authorize," they would never "meddle" in states' internal affairs. A fierce debater, Ellsworth "hung like a Cat to Every particle" of the bill, arguing, cajoling, inspiring, and when necessary employing his usual courtroom theatrics to sway the undecided. The nub of controversy lay in the sections of the bill that allowed federal courts to overturn state laws if they conflicted with national treaties, federal statutes, or the Constitution. Although some in the South worried that federal judges might someday rule against slavery, a greater number feared the more immediate danger of federal interference with state-court decisions that forestalled payment of debts to foreign—especially British—creditors. Debt posed a particularly knotty problem. The United States had an exceptionally poor record of repaying debts, both public and private. During the war, thousands of British creditors had been left holding sometimes substantial American debt. The Treaty of Paris, which ended the war, stipulated that creditors on both sides should "meet with no lawful impediment to the recovery of the full value" of their debts. However, many debtors, with the connivance of their legislatures, especially in the South, still refused to pay their debts.

American financial unreliability had created serious foreign-policy problems by further weakening the country's already dismal credit abroad. If Congress permitted creditors to sue for claims as small as a few hundred dollars each, it would open the possibility that defendants—and voters— would be dragged into distant federal courts to answer British claims. Ellsworth was thus torn between the moral and political need to meet the nation's treaty commitments, and widespread popular resistance to paying creditors anything. The solution he came up with was not entirely principled, but it was elegant. The bill stipulated that claims for sums less than $500 would be barred from federal courts, a convenient figure since few claims were larger than that. (Many of the debts in question were small by modern standards, but not insignificant in an age when most Americans had incomes of just a few hundred dollars per year.) For all practical purposes, the vast majority of small British creditors would have to abandon their claims as hopeless. Voilà!

For the judiciary to work it had to be accepted by the distrustful public. For that to occur, it would have to be adopted by substantial majorities in both houses of Congress. A close vote in either house would lend credence to the warnings of the bill's enemies, such as Senator Pierce Butler of South Carolina, who raged apocalyptically that the bill was "a wanton Exercise of power," and that its inescapable effect would be "to destroy, to Cut up at the Root the State Judiciaries, to Anhialate their whole system of Jurisprudence & but finaly to Swallow up every distinguishing mark of a Distinct Government." Like the protests of Maclay—who detested Butler as an arrogant windbag, but now found himself fighting in the same foxhole—Butler's bluster fell on largely deaf ears. After eighteen days of debate, Ellsworth's bill passed mostly intact on July 17, aided by Congress's apparent readiness to approve amendments to the Constitution that would protect citizens' rights to jury trials. Only six senators voted against the judiciary bill, the two Antifederalist Virginians, and four Federalists, including Maclay, who wrote despairingly in his diary, "It certainly is a Vile law System, calculated for Expence, and with a design to draw by degrees all law business into the federal Courts."

In September, the bill would be approved by the House of Representatives, with rather limp support from James Madison, who considered it too complicated and too expensive. "The most that can be said in its favor," he griped to North Carolina governor Samuel Johnston, with an almost audible sigh, "is that it is the first essay, and in practice will be [merely] an experiment." It proved to be a more enduring one than Madison ever imagined, laying the foundation for a system of federal courts that by the twenty-first century would employ thousands of judges, lawyers, and other staff and encompass twelve circuits and ninety-four districts, and a Supreme Court whose power to challenge both federal and state laws would raise its stature to equal that of the legislative and executive branches.

Ellsworth's reassurances that the federal government would never meddle with the states' internal affairs were disingenuous. The bill's full impact would not be felt for many years, even generations, to come. But combined with the rights that were being codified in the first amendments to the Constitution, it would one day become a great and dynamic engine that would carry justice into every community and transform American society to its roots. The federal judiciary created by Ellsworth's bill would establish a significant role for federal jurisprudence that trumped state power and would, in a future that was dimly sensed but deeply feared by slavery's defenders, eventually help to tear down the South's peculiar institution and its racist underpinnings.

As the season advanced and New York's scalding midsummer heat bore down, members escaped whenever they could to the open country which began just a short walk north of Federal Hall, where the city's lanes petered out into market gardens, orchards, and meadows so thick with briars that cattle sometimes got lost in them. The nautically inclined could hire a boat to row them across the Hudson for a climb up the towering Palisades of New Jersey, or across the harbor to the village of Brooklyn for a ramble among the tidy Dutch farms of Long Island, where slaves raised crops for the city's markets. (Passengers paid a fare of twopence; it cost an additional one shilling sixpence for those traveling with an ox.) Excursionists with more time to spare could rent a horse for twenty-five cents per hour—shockingly exorbitant, Maclay thought—to ride up the rocky spine of Manhattan Island to the Revolutionary War battle sites at Murray Hill, Bloomingdale, McGowan's Pass, and Fort Washington, ten miles to the north.

For those of a solitary bent, the generously supplied shelves of the New York Society Library offered a collection of 818 volumes, the largest in the United States outside Philadelphia. "I am never without a book, or my pen in my hands—And there not being a Congress I spend about ten & twelve hours a day in reading and writing," Representative George Thatcher of Massachusetts reported to his wife. Although Alexander Hamilton signed out the steamy-sounding *Amours of Count Palviano and Eleanora*, and others enjoyed novels such as *The Fair Syrian* and *The Platonic Guardian*, works of history, travel, and biography were the most popular among members of Congress. The most frequently checked out were Captain Cook's *Voyages*, Gibbon's newly published *Decline and Fall of the Roman Empire*, and Johnson's *Lives of the Poets*. "Classical history," as the twentieth-century historians Frank Monaghan and Marvin Lowenthal put it, "was the requisite of a gentleman and the ammunition dump of a patriot with a gift for oratory." There were also booksellers galore: a few minutes' walk from Federal Hall, Robert Hodge was announcing the publication of what he declared to be the first American novel, *The Power of Sympathy, or the Triumph of Nature*, while Thomas Allen was advertising for sale the first volume of the new *Encyclopaedia Britannica*.

Everyone devoured newspapers, many of which published copious daily accounts of the debates in Congress. Federalists favored the *Daily Advertiser*, published by a protégé of John Jay's, while the pious might read the *Packet*, which weighed in with relish on religious and sectarian disputes. Members of high society scoured John Fenno's *Gazette of the United States*, whose "columns read like a fulsome court gazette in a third-class German principality." There was always the *Hutchins Almanac*, a compact but encyclopedic book that spared its readers the political news but provided them with a cornucopia of presumably useful information on such subjects as the dangers of alcohol, eclipses of the moon, approaching comets, planting sunflowers, the recent bellyache epidemic in Jamaica, and advice for the lovelorn.

Members enjoyed chamber music concerts presented by the Musical Society, cricket matches, an exhibition of "natural curiosities," which included a sloth, a crocodile, a tame tiger, and assorted snakes, and a waxworks on Water Street, where they marveled at lifelike representations of George Washington, the king and queen of England, and the Episcopal bishop of New York, along with a variety of biblical scenes. A showman named Joseph Decker enthralled audiences nightly with a mysterious "speaking figure" suspended by a ribbon from the center of a Grecian temple, which when asked questions about itself would whisperingly answer them "with delicacy." In early August, as the debate over amendments raged, Decker further astonished everyone by ascending in a balloon from the old fort at the foot of Broadway and sailing over the city until he finally alighted in the Harlem River nine miles away.

Since the opening of the red-painted John Street Theater in April, members had also been able to enjoy the thespian delights of the alluring Mrs. Henry—"a perfect fairy of a woman"—who wore hoops of such circumference that she had to be lifted sideways out of her carriage and lived scandalously with her two sisters and Mr. Henry, also an actor, "in matrimonial alliance of more or less irregularity." She and her company performed nightly in plays ranging from Sheridan's risqué *School for Scandal* and Shakespeare's *Merry Wives of Windsor*, through such less memorable productions as *The Careless Husband*, *Who's the Dupe?*, and *Poor Paddy's Whole History*. A farce called *Darby's Return* was said to be one of the few things that ever made George Washington laugh.

The apogee of the theatrical season was reached in July when, as the members of Congress battled over codfish, rum, tariffs, and states' rights, Federal Hall itself starred, somewhat bizarrely, in the John Street Theater's pantomime rendering of *Robinson Crusoe*. In its finale, actors dressed as Indians orotundly declaimed Shakespearean-sounding prose as a figure representing the patriotic "genius of Columbia" appeared among them and prophesied that "he will clear the mist that mantles o'er their minds; and show them in vision what shall come to pass" by revealing the glorious American future in the form of a painted image of Federal Hall, where, "Columbia" proclaimed to swelling music:

There shall the noblest spirits of this western world,
With one accord, one soul of freedom animating all,
In union firm, deliberate for the common good,
And lose the private in the public cause. . . .

CHAPTER 8

Propositions of a Doubtful Nature

———— • ————

The Constitution of the United States interferes too much already.

—Thomas Tudor Tucker, August 1789

Considering the gravity that the Constitution's first ten amendments have now acquired, Congress's debate over "that Great and Delicate subject" was remarkably short, snappish, and driven by the politics of the moment rather than by appeals to lofty ideals. When Congress finally got around to it during a steamy week in August, a few members spoke of the rights of man. But more indicated that they thought the whole debate was simply a frivolous exercise. Representative Samuel Livermore of New Hampshire dismissed Madison's amendments as "a mere musketo bite," for which the public, he predicted, "will not give a pinch of snuff." The imperious Senator Pierce Butler of South Carolina dismissed them scornfully as "a few milk-and-water amendments, such as liberty of conscience, a free press, and one or two general things already well secured."

For James Madison, however, this was the climax of a long, painstaking campaign to build support for amendments. He had started back in the winter by winning over George Washington, who, like Madison, was initially opposed to altering the Constitution. Then, with Washington's assent, Madison wove into the president's inaugural address a clause reminding Congress of its "duty" to consider amendments. Next, in the House's formal reply to Washington—which Madison *also* composed— he incorporated a promise to address the issue of amendments with "all the attention demanded by its importance." As the constitutional historian Paul Finkelman has observed, by having Washington ask Congress to act, Madison was shrewdly getting the president to officially endorse amendments without appearing heavy-handed. And by writing a speech in which Washington deferred to Congress to work out the details, Madison was taking little political risk since he was already the leading figure in Congress.

Madison allotted just a single week of floor time to the proposed amendments. The debate was hurried, even at times perfunctory, and centered on concerns that are now largely forgotten—the size of congressional districts, for instance. There was no inspiring rhetoric, no lofty philosophical consideration of human freedoms. Indeed, the real debate was not so much over the content of the amendments, but whether any amendments would be allowed at all. While the Antifederalists paid lip service to civil rights, what they really wanted were structural amendments barring federal taxation, imposing term limits on elected officials, asserting states' rights, clarifying delegated powers, and requiring supermajorities for revenue measures.

Madison was in a hurry because he knew that his window of opportunity was narrow. He knew that allowing the scores of proposed amendments to go to the floor would bring all other business to a halt and create legislative chaos. He made clear that he intended to keep the debate moving briskly forward. To those who charged him with ramming his amendments through too fast, he retorted that the ones he brought to the floor were precisely those most desired by constituents. As Livermore and Butler noted, they were also the least controversial. "While I approve of these amendments," Madison said, "I should oppose the consideration at this time of such as are likely to change the principles of the government, or that are of a doubtful nature; because I apprehend there is little prospect of obtaining the consent of two-thirds of both houses of Congress, and three-fourths of the state legislatures, to ratify propositions of this kind." He added, with characteristic pragmatism, that he would act "as a friend to what is obtainable."

Convincing Congress to *enact* the amendments would now require parliamentary agility, diplomacy, and decisiveness, qualities Madison enjoyed in abundance. Even so, the outcome was not entirely certain. Between Federalists who wanted no amendments at all, Antifederalists who felt that Madison's proposals didn't go far enough, and those who complained that more important work was to be done, the opposition was substantial. To complicate matters, the language that members used to discuss what they were doing was often confusing; sometimes they spoke of enacting "amendments" and at other times of merely making "alterations" or simply "changes." Only rarely did they refer to the proposals at hand as a "bill of rights." Madison worried that if he delayed any longer, the already impatient members would never get around to the amendments at all. He would have to keep debate brief, ruthlessly "exclude every proposition of a doubtful & unimportant nature," and be willing to compromise even against his own grain. He also understood that he would have to treat the House's Antifederalists respectfully; if he humiliated them, he might never win over their followers.

On July 21, Madison again tried to move his amendments to the floor and was again rebuffed. Instead, the amendments were dropped in the pro-Federalist lap of a select, ad hoc committee that included one member from each of the eleven states then in the Union—among them Madison himself—and chaired by Madison's Delaware ally, the well-liked John Vining. The committee's most forceful member was the crusty Connecticut conservative Roger Sherman. Throughout the spring of 1789, it had been Sherman, not Madison, who represented the mainstream of Federalist thinking. For months, he had maintained that amendments were not only unnecessary but dangerous, arguing that they would "obstruct the wheels of government, and throw everything into confusion." He vigorously opposed the popular idea of term limits, declaring that it would both abridge the freedom of voters to elect whom they wanted and undermine the commitment of officials to the offices to which they had been elected. "Nothing renders government more unstable than a frequent change of the persons that administer it," he wrote in an open letter, in 1788. He also believed that it was much too soon to "tamper" with the Constitution, whose shortcomings, if it had any, could surely be dealt with by conventional lawmaking. "Experience will shew best if it is deficient or not."

John Adams, a personal friend of Sherman's, admired him as "an old Puritan, as honest as an Angell," though adversaries found him "as cunning as the devil," and so intellectually quick that gaining advantage over him was like trying "to catch an Eel by the tail." Yet he was so deeply religious that he objected to Congress's scheduling a meeting on a Sunday. Having started out as a mere shoemaker with little formal education, he rose to become a respected jurist, the mayor of New Haven, a successful land speculator, and a major benefactor of Yale University. In 1789, he was one of the most experienced political men in the country, having served in the Continental Congress, on its treasury board, and on the committee charged with drafting the Declaration of Independence. At the Constitutional Convention, he was the principal author of the Great Compromise, which granted small states equal representation with large ones in the Senate while providing that members of the House be elected according to population, as larger states wished. At sixty-eight, his bony face, deep-set, wary eyes, and tight mouth suggested his austere Calvinist personality, if not his still-boundless energy. His oratory was ragged at best, striking more aristocratic members as odd, laced with "vulgarisms" and "that strange New England cant," as one southerner put it. (As Sherman wrestled manfully over amendments, he was suffering a private agony that he did his best to conceal from his colleagues: his family was coming apart. His eldest son, John, was an alcoholic, in debt, and constantly begging him for money. His second son, William, a divorced bankrupt, stood accused of defrauding his regiment during the Revolutionary War and died suddenly in 1789. His third son, Isaac, although praised for his wartime service, also proved a failure at business and was struggling to make a living as a surveyor in frontier Georgia.)

By midsummer, something had changed Sherman's gristly Yankee mind. He had decided that Madison's proposals were probably harmless. Most likely, Madison had played his ace in the hole: a not-quite-secret private letter from George Washington—undoubtedly written at Madison's instigation—that the president told him he could use to help sway the hesitant. "I see nothing exceptionable in the proposed amendments," Washington wrote. "Some of them, in my opinion, are importantly necessary, others, though in themselves not very essential, are necessary to quiet the fears of some respectable characters and well meaning Men. Upon the whole, not foreseeing any evil consequences that can result from their adoption, they have my wishes for a favorable reception in both houses." As pallid an endorsement as this was, it was enough to move key Federalists from dismissive opposition to at least grumbling resignation. No one wanted to challenge the explicit wishes of a man whose will was still beyond overt challenge.

When Vining's committee reported back its recommendations, Madison's "alterations" had been reshuffled, tightened, and reconfigured into a more coherent list of nineteen. These ranged from the pedestrian—renumbering Article 7 of the Constitution as Article 8, for example—to the profound. Madison's list of basic rights—to speak, publish, assemble, petition the government for redress of grievances, receive a speedy trial, and confront one's accusers—remained, as did the provisions against search and seizure, double jeopardy, self-incrimination, excessive bail, and the quartering of troops in private homes. His most provocative amendment, which would extend the courts' protection of civil rights against the power of oppressive state laws, also remained.

Throughout the debate that ensued, there would be surprisingly little consideration of the freedoms that modern Americans most cherish as legal bastions of civil rights. Proposed amendments protecting the freedoms of speech, press, assembly, petition, and religion; barring the quartering of soldiers in private homes and unreasonable search and seizure; prohibiting self-incrimination and ensuring due process; guaranteeing speedy trial and the assistance of counsel; banning cruel and unusual punishments— all would be approved after no more than the most cursory floor debate, almost none of it substantive. (If there was more in-depth discussion of them in committee, there is no record of it.) Federalists regarded most of these as so self-evident that they had no compelling reason to address them at length, while the Antifederalists made clear by what they *did* fight for that they were more interested in advancing the cause of states' rights than in articulating individual freedoms.

There were a few surprises. Madison's clarion call for unbounded freedom of conscience had been sharply compressed to accommodate the wishes of more conservative religionists. His original language had powerfully stated, "The civil rights of none shall be abridged on account of religious belief or worship, nor shall any national religion be established, nor shall the full and equal rights of conscience be in any manner or on any pretext infringed." The committee narrowed this to "No religion shall be established by law, nor shall the equal rights of conscience be infringed." After some debate, it would be tweaked again to read, with more clarity, "Congress shall make no law establishing religion or prohibiting the free exercise thereof, nor shall the rights of conscience be infringed."

A pointed, if brief, exchange was prompted by the language that was proposed for the protection of religious freedom. Roger Sherman declared that no such provision was needed at all since Congress had no authority to establish a religion even if it wanted to. To this, Daniel Carroll, the House's most prominent Catholic, replied that the amendment would do more to conciliate the people to the new government than any other that had been proposed. He was not alone, he supposed, in his uneasy feeling that protection for minority sects was inadequately protected by the Constitution as it now stood. "Rights of conscience," Carroll concluded, were "peculiarly delicate" and could suffer grievously from even "the gentlest touch of the government hand."

Benjamin Huntington of Connecticut countered that the amendment threatened "the cause of religion" itself. In New England, arguably the most religiously conservative region of the country, ministers depended for their livelihood on contributions from their parishioners, which was enforced by local law. Suppose a citizen failed to pay his tithe? Could he no longer be compelled to pay what was due? If such an amendment had to be adopted, Huntington warned, it ought at least to be rewritten so as not to "patronise those who professed no religion all."

To mollify Huntington, Madison suggested inserting the word *national* before *religion*.

At this, Elbridge Gerry leapt to his feet. The very use of the word *national* would imply a "consolidated" union and a diminishment of state powers, he protested.

Madison withdrew his motion, assuring Gerry that he hadn't by any means meant to imply that *national* implied "a national government." One can almost hear him sigh with resignation across the centuries.

What the amendment's words meant ought to be clear, Madison said: Congress could not enforce the legal observance of any religion nor compel anyone to worship God in any way contrary to his conscience. Whether the words were necessary or not wasn't the point, however. Several state conventions had demanded them because they feared that the Constitution's "necessary and proper" clause permitted that body to establish a religion, if it so chose. The amendment would lay their fears to rest. In other words, this was all about politics, not theology.

To Madison's disappointment, his preamble, a ringing endorsement of the people's "indubitable, inalienable, and indefeasible" right "to reform or change their government, whenever it be found adverse or inadequate to the purposes of its institution"—that is, by implication to overthrow it—had been erased and replaced with a lukewarm assertion that government was "intended for the benefit of the people." Further irritating Madison, Sherman indicated that he wanted the amendments tacked on at the end of the Constitution, where, in his opinion, they would do less harm than they would if they were woven into its fabric, as the Virginian wanted.

Sherman held that any change in the Constitution as it had originally been written would, in effect, *repeal* the Constitution as it had been ratified by the states and thereby create a *new* Constitution that had not been approved by any of them. He combatively declared, "We might as well endeavor to mix brass, iron and clay, as to incorporate such heterogeneous articles." Sherman was supported by James Jackson of Georgia. "If we repeal this Constitution we shall perhaps the next year have to make another—and in that way the people will never be able to know whether they have a permanent constitution or not," Jackson roared, sniffing that Congress had no business demeaning the Constitution by patching it up "with various stuffs resembling Joseph's coat of many colors."

To the astonishment of some, Eldridge Gerry lent his support to Madison, arguing that putting the amendments at the end of the Constitution would weaken respect for them and confuse the public. "I presume the title of our first amendment will be a supplement to the Constitution of the U.S.," he facetiously griped, "the next a supplement to the supplement, and so on, until we have supplements annexed five times in five years, wrapping up the Constitution in a maze of perplexity." If the original text was to be treated as something "sacred," untouchable and unalterable, he asked, what was the point of amendments at all?

In a last-ditch effort to change Sherman's mind, Madison pleaded that if the amendments were treated as a mere "supplement" it would be too difficult for citizens to figure out what part of the Constitution they referred to as they accumulated over time, someday doubtless filling a volume so huge that ordinary citizens wouldn't know where to find anything in it. The whole document, he predicted, would become hopelessly "complex and obscure." But even with Gerry's support, Madison could do the math. Sherman had enough committed Federalist votes to thwart the Virginian.

Several members took exception to the suggested prohibition against cruel and unusual punishment. "Because it may be thought cruel, will you therefore never hang anybody?" Livermore demanded. "Villains often deserve whipping, and perhaps having their ears cut off; but are we in future to be prevented from inflicting these punishments because they are cruel?"

Theodore Sedgwick of Massachusetts attacked the proposed right to public assembly, scoffing that it was "beneath the dignity" of the House to insert such "minutiae" in the Constitution, and asserting that Congress might as well declare "that a man should have a right to wear his hat if he pleased, that he might get up when he pleased, and go to bed when he thought proper." To this, John Page of Virginia, a wealthy planter with republican leanings, retorted that under British rule Quakers had been ordered to pull off their hats when they appeared "before the face of authority," just as they had been prevented from assembling lawfully; if the people could be deprived of the right of free assembly, they could be deprived of every other right.

Vining's committee also revised Madison's militia amendment— which had proposed an absolute individual right to bear arms—to make clear that the amendment applied specifically to an organized, officially sanctioned body: "A well-regulated militia, composed of the body of the people, being the best security of a free State, the right of the people to keep and bear arms shall not be infringed." The intent was to make clear that in a country that was deeply suspicious of a permanent military establishment, nationalized state militias were to serve as the front line of defense against foreign invasion. (To Americans, mention of a standing army evoked swaggering redcoats bullying them in the streets and molesting them in their homes, and the more distant abuses of Oliver Cromwell's troops in mid-seventeenth-century England.) Many construed the amendment's language more broadly, in ways familiar to modern Americans. As one Massachusetts man put it, Congress was dutybound to ensure "the right to keep arms for Common and Extrodenery Occasions Such as to Secure ourselves against the wild Beast and allso to amuse us by fowling," as well as "our Defense against a Common Enemey . . . for it is impossible to Support a Standing armey large Enough to Guard our Lenghey Sea Coast." Antifederalists, in particular, maintained that the Constitution had already concentrated too much military power in the national government, and that behind the amendment lurked a sinister Federalist plan to create exactly the kind of national army that they feared. Gerry, for one, saw militias as an essential bulwark against a federal government that might someday run amok. "Whenever government mean to invade the rights and liberties of the people, they always attempt to destroy the militia, in order to raise an army upon their ruins," he warned.

One of the fiercest points of contention didn't concern rights at all, but congressional districts. In 1789, before the first census, the population of congressional districts varied from ninety-six thousand in George Thatcher's Maine district to just sixteen thousand in James Jackson's Georgia district and was further skewed in the South by the abundance of slaves, who, under the three-fifths rule, were counted for the purposes of representation, but could not claim any of the rights that the members of Congress were debating. In some southern districts, once slaves, women and children, and propertyless whites were subtracted, the actual number of voters was as low as three thousand. The committee proposed to set each district's size at thirty thousand inhabitants. Although this might seem a mere technical issue, it threatened to pit populist republicans against elite Federalists, many of whom feared that increasing the number of congressmen would lead to paralysis and instability. Fisher Ames, for example, charged that "small" districts (of thirty thousand) would create such an "enormous mass" of legislators that serious deliberations would become impossible. "In proportion as you encrease the number of reps the body degenerates," he lectured. "Men of inferior abilities will undoubtedly creep in." In addition, size would "engender parties, delay the public business," and breed hostility to the government. To save the country from these perils, he proposed increasing the size of districts to *forty* thousand inhabitants, an immense leap by the standards of 1789. To this, James Jackson complained that by Ames's reasoning legislation by just two or three men must be better than that of a body of sixty or one hundred, though the American people might not like it very much.

The outnumbered Antifederalists fired off fusillades of their own amendments in a rearguard action that they hoped would at least demonstrate to their constituents that they had put up a good fight. Waving copies of structural amendments that had been urged by various state conventions but ignored by Madison, the hot-tempered Aedanus Burke of South Carolina snorted that the Virginian's proposals were "little better than whip-syllabub, frothy and full of wind, formed only to please the palate," and demanded explicit civilian control of the military, and a prohibition against standing armies in time of peace. "The antifederals in our House have thrown difficulties in the way of Amendmts merely because they can't carry alterations which wod overturn the Governmt," fumed the Federalist William Loughton Smith, also of South Carolina, who feared that amendments could eventually lead to federal interference with slavery. He warned Edward Rutledge, "If it is in the power of a few ingenious men & able orators to new-model the powers of the government by construction and implication & give it a different shape from the one it had when we adopted it, there's no saying to what lengths these alterations may be gradually carried in time."

The Antifederalist counterattack was led by Bermuda-born Thomas Tudor Tucker, yet another notably temperamental South Carolina slave-owner and planter, and one of the House's most belligerent advocates of states' rights. An austere and stony-faced man with a beaked nose and a sour distrust of the Constitution, Tucker bombarded the House with new would-be amendments that would strip the federal government of the power to set criteria for federal elections, replace lower federal courts with limited maritime tribunals, eliminate the president's role as commander in chief, and impose term limits on federal offices: a maximum of two terms for president, six years for representatives, and annual election of senators, with none being allowed to serve more than five years in a sequence. Tucker also moved to strike out Madison's proposal to extend the federal protection of basic freedoms against encroachment by state governments. This, declared Tucker, amounted to an intolerable intrusion upon the sacred rights of states. "The Constitution of the United States interferes too much already," he proclaimed. "Leave the state governments to themselves."

Tucker also proposed an amendment popular with Antifederalists that would deny the federal government the power to tax citizens directly. Gerry, speaking in support of this, denounced the federal government's "rapacity" and predicted civil war and "the annihilation of the state governments" if they surrendered their financial independence. Imagine, he fairly gasped, "what umbrage it must give every individual to have two sets of collectors and tax-gatherers surrounding their doors": it was a recipe for a "sowered populace" and "perpetual discord." To this, Tucker added that it would take far too much time to invent a fair system of taxation that could operate through all the states and suggested that Congress simply ask for donations from the states in the form of "requisitions," as it had (often to little effect) under the Articles of Confederation.

In defense of the federal government's basic right to raise its own revenue when it needed to do so, James Jackson retorted—this might have been one of the occasions when the senators shut their windows—that some "requisitions" made years earlier under the Confederation were *still* unpaid. What would ever compel unwilling states to pay their share? "This plan of requisitions," he warned, "will excite jealousies, insurrections, and civil war, dissolve the Union, and expose us to the contempt and invasion of foreign powers"—and, more important to Jackson, to attack by the Indians on Georgia's frontier. Without the power of raising money, how could any country secure itself against foreign invasion? It was impossible! "We shall be rent asunder by intestine commotion or interior assault, and when that period arrives we may bid adieu to all the blessings we have purchased at the price of our fortunes, and the blood of our worthiest heroes."

Gerry also stridently supported the Antifederalist proposal to bar the federal government from setting the criteria for federal elections, which, he argued, ought to be left to the states to decide. "Why are gentlemen desirous of retaining this power?" he demanded. Was their hidden motive to "establish a government of an arbitrary kind"? What might be next—an article abolishing the secret ballot, which would in turn oblige men to vote publicly "for a man or the friend of a man to whom he was under obligations"? Or ordering elections at remote polling places where only the candidates' friends would attend? "Gentlemen will tell me that these things are not to be apprehended," he warned. "But if they say that the government has the power of doing them, they have no right to say the government will never exercise such powers, because it is presumable that they will administer the Constitution at one time or another with all its powers, and whenever that time arises, farewell to the rights of the people."

Nothing generated more heated debate, however, than Thomas Tudor Tucker's attempt to amend the Constitution to give citizens a right to "instruct"—really, to *order*—their congressmen how to vote. This idea, which had been advanced by several state conventions, reflected a popular fear that representatives would be brainwashed by their colleagues or the culture of the capital and forget about the voters who had elected them. Antifederalists rallied vigorously behind Tucker's proposal. "Our constituents have not only a right to instruct, but to *bind* this legislature," declared Gerry, who believed that government was by its very nature oppressive, and that its abuses could be checked only by the raw will of the people.

These arguments were not about rights in the abstract. The shadow of Shays's Rebellion loomed like that of an ogre over the memories of New Englanders in particular, feeding the fears of those who believed that too much democracy would inexorably lead to chaos. When Representative Theodore Sedgwick, for one, protested against including a constitutional right of free assembly, he was doubtless thinking of what had happened just three years earlier, when the "assembled" Shaysites demanding debt relief had taken over the courts where he practiced in western Massachusetts, menaced his neighbors, abused his law clerk, and invaded his own home at Stockbridge. Although the forty-three-year-old Sedgwick had been an early patriot and served with distinction in a variety of military and political roles during the Revolutionary War, he was a comparatively conservative Federalist in a state that harbored strong Antifederalist strains and was unenthusiastic about amendments of any sort, despite having been explicitly instructed by the Massachusetts ratification convention to support them.

Sedgwick and his fellow Federalists maintained that while the voters in a town meeting might be within their rights to tell their elected officials what to do, the United States was a lot more complex than a mere hamlet. Members of Congress would be paralyzed if they had to obey "instructions" imposed by their constituents; compromise would become impossible, and active government would collapse. "All that a man would have to do would be to produce his instructions and lay them on the table, and let them speak for him," Roger Sherman sarcastically commented. The job of every elected representative was to serve the people at large, not just the loudest faction of them, he argued. If a representative's "instructions" happened to coincide with his own ideas, they were unnecessary, and "if they were contrary to his convictions, he was bound by every principle of justice to ignore them."

Madison had held himself aloof through most of the debate. But he now cut to the heart of the matter. This supposed right of instruction was a "doubtful" idea at best. (For the ever-reserved Madison, this counted as scathing disapproval.) Who were "the people" anyway? What self-appointed group of citizens had the power to nullify a law enacted by the Congress of the entire nation? "Is every small district the People? And do the inhabitants of this district express the voice of the People, when they are not a thousandth part, and although their instructions may contradict the sense of the whole people besides? Have the people in detached assemblies the right to violate the Constitution or controul the actions of the whole sovereign power? This would be setting up an hundred sovereignties to the place of one." By the time Madison was done, the absurdity of the Antifederalist position had been fully exposed, and even Gerry was left acknowledging that "instructions" couldn't be allowed to nullify federal law or violate any representative's oath of office.

CHAPTER 9

Paper Guarantees

——— · ◆ · ———

The weather was excessive hot, & the blood warm.

—William Smith of Maryland, August 1789

On August 18, Thomas Tudor Tucker launched his most significant assault on the Constitution. He proposed a one-word change in the proposed Eighteenth (and future Tenth) Amendment, which stated, "The powers not delegated by this Constitution, nor prohibited by it to the States, are reserved to the States respectively." He proposed to insert the seemingly innocuous word *expressly* between *not* and *delegated.* Tucker and his fellow Antifederalists wanted the national government to be explicitly and absolutely restricted only to such actions and powers as were spelled out in the Constitution, restoring the relationship between the federal and the state governments closer to what had existed under the Articles of Confederation, when the balance of power had tilted decisively in favor of the states. By so conspicuously omitting the word *expressly*, Madison had subtly shifted the balance of power toward the central government. Upon this single word thus pivoted the fundamental difference between Federalism and Antifederalism, between hard-line states' rights and cautious centralism, between a rigidly narrow interpretation of the Constitution and a more evolutionary one.

When Tucker's proposal came up for a vote, it failed. Three days later, Gerry tried again. Despite the importance of what was at stake, the debate over Gerry's proposal, like Tucker's, was probably measured in minutes, certainly not in hours. Gerry demanded a recorded vote: he lost it resoundingly by 32–17. Immediately afterward, Roger Sherman strengthened the last clause to make it read: "The powers not delegated to the United States by the Constitution, nor prohibited by it to the states, are reserved to the states respectively, or to the people." Just what those powers were, and what the practical and political consequences of protecting them might be, was left perilously undefined. Sherman's motion was adopted without debate, fundamentally (if ambiguously) shaping the relationship between the national and the state governments for generations to come, and paving the way for a flexible reading of the Constitution that would enable its future interpreters to respond in creative ways to problems that were unimagined in 1789.

By now, everyone was worn out and on edge. There had been more "ill-humour and rudeness displayed [in a single day] than has existed since the meeting of Congress," exclaimed one southern congressman. Madison seemed near the end of his rope, complaining that "the work has been extremely difficult and fatiguing." The heat was close to intolerable. It was said that six or eight people had dropped dead in the street from heatstroke, or from drinking too much cold water. "I feard lest the Excessive heat would be Too much for you in N. York," a distraught Pamela Sedgwick wrote to her husband. "I had formed Sanguine hopes that you would most certainly be at home [by now] . . . but I fear I shall not see you until the latter part of September A mortifying Circumstance this—but I must call in potions to my Aid." The battlefield excursions, the hikes in New Jersey, the strolls through the Manhattan dells, the escapes to the Greenwich tea gardens—none of it seemed to help much. As Representative William Smith of Maryland put it, "The weather was excessive hot, & the blood warm." Tempers flared. Calls for order went unheeded. There was even rumbling talk of duels among irritated members. Speaker Muhlenberg of Pennsylvania opined, "Such is the present Temper of the House that I think the sooner we close the Session the better." But that was not to be. The wheels of Congress would continue to grind on for another month, and they would grind slowly.

To everyone's relief, President Washington had made a full recovery from his illness and was once again his rather inscrutable, occasionally irascible self. The chain that barred noisy traffic in front of his residence had been taken away. Visitors were once again received. The official levees and receptions resumed. While invitations to dine at the Washingtons' home were coveted, it wasn't a lot of fun. (French minister Moustier, who greatly admired Washington, found him "infinitely cold.") Typically, the president and his wife, Martha, sat opposite each other at the middle of the table, often in complete silence. One evening, the lonely William Maclay found himself dining there with several other senators, the John Jays, and members of the Adams family, including Maclay's nemesis, the vice president. The food was the best Maclay had ever eaten. Soup was followed by fish, the fish by an assortment of roasted and boiled meats and fowls, and that by apple pies, puddings, ice creams, gelatins, watermelons, muskmelons, peaches, and nuts. After the tablecloth had been removed, Washington filled a wineglass and formally drank a health to each member of the company, after which each guest did the same. "Such a buz of health sir and health Madam, & thank You sir and thank You Madam never had I heard before," Maclay reported. Apart from all the ritual toasting, however, "there was a dead Silence." At last Mrs. Washington withdrew with the ladies, "but the same Stillness remained," until the president at last offered a labored story about a New England preacher who had lost his hat and wig while crossing the Bronx River. When Washington smiled, indicating that the story was meant to be humorous, everyone politely laughed. After this, the president ventured a sentence or two "on some common Subject," John Jay told a slightly off-color joke about the Duchess of Devonshire, and Adams's son-in-law annoyed Maclay by misquoting Virgil, while the president—who probably knew no Virgil at all—fidgeted with a fork by tapping it on the edge of the table. After this painful interlude had gone on for some time, when Washington retired upstairs with the rest of the guests, Maclay gratefully made his escape and headed for his rooming house.

The president's renewed vigor was on full display on August 5, when he strode into the Senate to demand an accounting for its refusal to approve his appointment of the federal naval officer in Savannah. After the debate over executive appointments back in June, Washington had assumed that he could name anyone he wanted to the new federal posts that had to be created in accordance with the revenue acts, and that the Senate—charged by the Constitution with the duty of advice and consent—would respectfully go along with his choices. He had, after all, consulted in most if not every case with local congressmen before making appointments. To the Savannah post he had named the capable, well-connected president of the Georgia Executive Council, Benjamin Fishbourne, a protégé of the Revolutionary War general Anthony Wayne. To Washington's astonishment, Fishbourne was rejected without explanation. No other candidate he had proposed had been turned down.

Determined to get to the bottom of it, Washington set out for the Senate and startled the assembled members by appearing in the door of the chamber unannounced. A visit from the president was unprecedented, and without protocol. Flustered, John Adams immediately hopped up from his great chair and offered it to Washington, who bluntly demanded to know why the Senate had shot down his appointee. "After long minutes of embarrassed silence," Senator James Gunn of Georgia rose and admitted that he had objected to Fishbourne, and that his colleagues in the Senate had gone along with his wishes.

The story behind this was long and serpentine. Years earlier, Fishbourne, or rather his patron General Wayne, had somehow offended Gunn, who had also served under Wayne during the war. Now thirty-six, Gunn was a notoriously lazy legislator who had ignored his elections to both Georgia's Executive Council and to the Confederation Congress. He was, on the other hand, an enthusiastic duelist, who in 1785 challenged former general Nathanael Greene in an "affair of honor." (Greene essentially ignored him.) Fishbourne and James Jackson, now a congressman, had at that time been charged with delivering Gunn's challenge to Greene. Although Greene declined, this had somehow led to a contretemps between Fishbourne and Gunn. This duel, too, was halted before anyone was hurt, but Gunn continued to hold a grudge against Fishbourne, and when his name came up for confirmation by the Senate, Gunn "urged nothing of any consequence but personal invective and abuse," it was reported. (Wayne later interpreted Fishbourne's rejection, probably correctly, as a "false, Malignant, and invidious" attack on himself.)

Most members of Congress were probably unaware of this background. Gunn now declared, with Washington present, that "he would have it distinctly understood to be the sense of the Senate that no explanation of their motives or proceedings was ever due or would ever be given to any President of the United States." But since Washington had asked, Gunn would tell. This was pretty close to an insult to the presidency. Just what the president said in response to this is unknown. However, as one senator reported, Washington, who was generally a model of restraint, "shewed great want of temper." Stalking out of the chamber, he announced to his secretary, Tobias Lear, that he was sorry he had ever gone to the Senate at all.

In itself, the incident was minor. However, in this ever-innovating Congress, even the trivial became precedent. Gunn had turned what should simply have been a matter of presidential preference into a matter of honor. This pebble in the pond of the Senate's deliberations continued to ripple through the centuries to become the virtually unbreachable custom of senatorial courtesy, that is, the ability of any senator to block the executive appointment of an individual he opposes from his state or for any federal office in his state.

Washington again tempted fate—or at least the Senate's jealousy of its prerogatives—on August 22, when he marched into its chamber, accompanied by Secretary of War Knox, to obtain the Senate's support for negotiating a treaty that was being prepared for several southern Indian tribes, most notably the Creeks, who inhabited a wide swath of western Georgia and the future state of Alabama. The Constitution required the president to seek such "advice and consent" for all treaties with foreign powers, which Indian tribes then were. But no rules existed to tell the president how to ask for the Senate's consideration, or the Senate how to provide it. Washington provided the senators with a set of questions: Were Georgia's treaties with the Creeks fair and equitable? If not, should federal commissioners attempt to obtain a cession of land in return for compensation in goods and money? If the Creeks failed to respond, should the United States issue an ultimatum? It was clear that the president expected the Senate's "advice and consent" to be little more than a formality.

Vice President Adams attempted to read a plaintive letter from frightened settlers on the North Carolina frontier, but the clatter of carriages on the cobblestones outside Federal Hall was so deafening that no one but those closest to him could hear. Maclay, for one, "could tell it was something about Indians, but was not the master of one Sentence of it." A clerk was dispatched to shut the windows, lessening the noise but adding to the already stifling heat. Adams then reread the letter. When he finished, he rather peremptorily demanded, "Do you advise and consent?"

There was a dead pause. It seemed evident that both Washington and Adams expected the Senate's assent without debate. The silence lengthened.

Finally, Maclay reluctantly rose. "It appeared to me that if I did not, no other one would, and we should have these advices and consents ravish'd in a degree from Us," he confided to his diary. The subject was completely new to the Senate, he said. Members hardly knew what they were being asked to approve. It was lengthy and complex and would take time to digest. Moreover, felt Maclay, "I saw no chance of a fair investigation of the subjects while the President of the U.S. sat there with his Secretary at War, to support his Opinions and overawe the timid."

Washington made it abundantly obvious that he did not like the turn that things were taking. He glowered at the brash Pennsylvanian with "an aspect of Stern displeasure." Doubtless straining to rein in his temper, Washington agreed that the provisions of proposed negotiations might be read, along with several more letters from southern settlers. Finally, after a brief debate, and irritable exchanges between the vice president and several senators, the Senate voted to postpone the entire matter for several days while, at Maclay's suggestion, the proposals were referred to a committee for further consideration.

As soon as Maclay sat down, Washington "started up in a Violent fret," the Pennsylvanian reported. "This defeats every purpose of my coming here," he exclaimed. But he could do nothing about the delay. The Senate, he was coming to understand, was not his to command. Looking deeply disgruntled, the president finally strode out with "sullen dignity," but no approval.

Following upon the Senate's unceremonious rejection of Washington's nominee for collector of the port of Savannah, this new episode further inflamed his sense of violation of both presidential and personal dignity. Upon exiting Federal Hall, Washington was widely reported to have declared that "he would be damned if he ever went there again."

The Senate, after due deliberation, would approve Washington's plans and, by so doing, would set the stage for the most colorful event of the First Congress, the arrival in New York a year later of an exotically befeathered Indian delegation to sign the final document. Of arguably more lasting importance, yet another precedent had been established. The in-built but, until now, largely invisible stresses between the executive and legislative branches of the government were beginning to come into focus. Not until Woodrow Wilson would a president again personally cross the Senate's threshold to explain or defend a treaty, or to beg for its consent. Although Maclay continued to adore Washington as a man, he had begun to feel that "the first Character in the World," at least in his capacity as president, "wishes to tread on the Necks of the Senate." Apparently, Maclay sadly ruminated, Washington wished the Senate not to think for itself, but to take his word for everything, and to "bear down our deliberations with his personal Authority & Presence," leaving senators nothing to do but to rubber-stamp his wishes. "This will not do with Americans."

•   •   •

Two days after Washington's latest abortive trip to Federal Hall, the seventeen amendments approved by the House of Representatives—they were adopted in individual votes, mostly by margins of three or four to one—were carried upstairs to the Senate chamber by the clerk of the House. They received a distinctly unenthusiastic reception. According to Maclay, they were treated "contemptuously" by several of the more prominent Federalist members. Among these was Robert Morris, who was far more preoccupied with trying to secure the nation's permanent capital in Pennsylvania than he was with reforming the Constitution. Complaining disgustedly of "the Waste of precious time" being devoted to "the Nonsense they call Amendments," Morris admitted that he hadn't seriously thought about any of them or bothered to discuss them with his fellow senators. He sneered, "I Condemn the attempt by the Lump."

Unfortunately, little is known about the texture of the debate that ensued, since the body met in secret and the voluble diarist Maclay was stuck in bed with gout for all but the first day of debate, when Oliver Ellsworth tangled himself in such lawyerly knots that he drove his fellow members to laughter. "For a While he was listened to, but he wraught himself so deep in his niceties and distinctions as to be absolutely incomprehensible," Maclay smugly recorded. Since only two Antifederalists were in the Senate, the two Virginians—Richard Henry Lee and William Grayson—the field was left largely to the Federalists. "We might as well have attempted to move Mount Atlas upon our shoulders," Lee gloomily reported to Patrick Henry. Lee was particularly mortified that one Federalist had actually suggested, though unsuccessfully, deleting the freedoms of speech and press altogether, on the grounds that they tended to encourage "licentiousness." The Senate further compressed the proposed amendments into twelve. Of these, Amendments Three through Twelve were recognizable as what would eventually become familiar to Americans as the Bill of Rights. The First Amendment, which had consumed much of the House's time a few weeks earlier, set the size of congressional districts at thirty thousand; the second regulated congressional pay raises by stating that they could not take effect until after the next election, to prevent members from enriching themselves immediately at the public expense. That amendment would be defeated but would eventually become the Twenty-Seventh Amendment, in 1992.

The Senate also made various text changes. It slightly, if fuzzily, amplified the clause dealing with the separation of church and state by replacing the word "religion" with "articles of faith or a mode of worship," but deleted the proposed exemption of conscientious objectors from military service. The Senate trimmed away the provision that federal trials be held close to the scene of a crime, as well as the requirement that a minimum value of property be at issue to warrant an appeal to federal court. The Senate version of the militia amendment further underscored the legislators' clear original intention, by deleting the elastic phrase "composed of the body of the people." While the senators continued to see the militia as the first line of national defense against foreign enemies, they made it even clearer that this did not mean a force composed of the *mass* of "the people," but one limited to men sanctioned by the state.

The Senate deleted Madison's separation-of-powers amendment, which would have rigidly barred each branch from exercising powers given to another branch. This would have tossed a potential monkey wrench into the constitutional machinery, since the Constitution had appointed the vice president a quasi legislator in his role as presiding officer of the Senate, and given Congress judicial authority in the case of impeachment. More significant, the Senate slashed his amendment that barred state abuse of civil rights. It would be almost eighty years before the Reconstruction-era Fourteenth Amendment required states to honor basic rights, and it would be well into the twentieth century before the federal government effectively used that amendment to support the demands of the modern civil rights movement.

The House agreed to most of the Senate's changes. A conference committee reconciled the few remaining differences, but proposed two changes that nudged amendments back toward the stronger versions passed previously by the House. The committee revised what became the First Amendment to state more forcefully, "Congress shall make no law respecting an establishment of religion, or prohibiting the free exercise thereof." And in what became the Sixth Amendment, the committee restored the requirement that federal trials would take place before "an impartial jury of the district wherein the crime shall have been committed."

"After exhausting themselves as well as the patience of their brethren," the Antifederalists finally gave up what little hope they retained of pushing through stronger amendments. They had occasionally poached the support of a few wobbly Federalists, but they had lost every significant vote by lopsided margins. The least threatening amendments would now—after Roger Sherman's tweaking and massaging—become part of the Constitution. No amendment that threatened to undermine the government or change its basic structure had been adopted. Madison would soon feel confident enough to tell Washington that "the late opponents are entirely at rest, and more likely to censure a further opposition to the Govt as now Administered than the Government itself." Public support for a second, revisionist Constitutional Convention had seeped away, as Madison had predicted it would. Elbridge Gerry's reputation had plummeted still further. "He certainly does not comprehend the great National System . . . and will assuredly find himself lost amidst Rocks & sands," that is, politically shipwrecked, remarked Abigail Adams, who had once admired him, but now despaired of him.

Madison was physically drained. His legislative skills had been tested more severely than before, and he was disappointed by what Congress had done to his handiwork. For once, he even seemed overwhelmed by the challenges of republican government. "The difficulty of uniting the minds of men accustomed to think and act differently can only be conceived by those who have witnessed it," he wearily confessed. And to New Hampshire senator Paine Wingate, he petulantly proclaimed himself so discouraged with the rump remainder of his amendments that he would "rather have none than those agreed to by the Senate." For a man rarely given to revealing his feelings, these were strong words. But his strategy had nonetheless succeeded brilliantly, and he had emerged from the debate politically strengthened. Not the least of his achievements was winning over Roger Sherman, who had begun as an enemy of amendments and had wound up piloting them safely to port. Sherman exacted his price, however: the amendments would forever remain appendages to the Constitution, though far more consequential ones than Sherman supposed. (It is possible though unprovable that Madison surrendered his radical preamble as part of a quid pro quo for Sherman's support.)

The collective mood was less one of triumph than of sheer exhaustion. No one in Congress regarded passage of the amendments as much more than an exercise in political housekeeping. Relief was felt at having staved off the Antifederalist assault on the Constitution more than any sense of exaltation at enriching the Constitution with freedoms that had been left inadequately unprotected. Theodore Sedgwick was disgusted by the whole debate, writing to his wife, Pamela, that the business "argues a frivolity of character very inconsistent with national dignity." Other Federalists feared that "the expectations of further amendments might unsettle the minds of the people," and that the poisonous seeds of social disorder had been sown. Meanwhile, Antifederalists grimly saw their defeat as a giant step in the direction of despotism. Disgusted at what Madison had accomplished, the Pennsylvania political essayist Samuel Bryan declared that Madison "had rendered Machiavelli piddling by comparison." Richard Henry Lee dismissed the result as "mutilated and enfeebled," telling Patrick Henry, "The english language has been carefully culled to find words feeble in their Nature or doubtful in their meaning." Permitting amendments to be written after the Constitution had already been ratified had turned out to be a strategic mistake of the first order, having proved, as Lee put it, "little better than putting oneself to death" with an expectation that "the doctor, who wished our destruction, would afterwards restore us to life." Thomas Jefferson, still in Paris, was more sanguine at the outcome, but unenthusiastic, telling Madison, "I like it as far as it goes; but I should have been for going further."

It would be left to the courts and future generations to interpret and give force to the minimalist language of the amendments. Virtually no members of Congress imagined that they had just passed a set of measures that would become, in their own right, part of the sacred canon of American democracy. The members were practical, impatient, and tired politicians, many of whom had regarded the whole debate as at best a distraction from things that mattered: the national revenue, the protection of codfish and molasses, the establishment of courts, defining (or enlarging) presidential power, and agreeing on a permanent capital. The rights that the amendments described would be nothing more than paper guarantees until the judiciary discovered them: in 1789, they were for the most part only aspirational and unenforceable. A great deal more had been left to future interpretation by a court system that was itself just a work in progress and would eventually have to decide just what powers had been reserved to "the people" or still belonged to the States or to the federal government. Few powers had been enumerated. Plenty of room remained for dispute, confusion, and reinterpretation by later advocates of states' rights, civil rights, federal power, and radical libertarianism, and by citizens of all stripes who would find support for their aspirations in the creative ambiguity of the amendments and the Constitution.

Three-quarters of the states were required to ratify. Although nine states would ratify all the amendments within ten months, it was more than two years before the eleventh state ratified ten of them, making them law. The final order of the amendments was completely arbitrary. It had no correlation with what the members had deemed most or least important. Indeed, the First Amendment, as it is known today, became so only by default, when the two preceding amendments—on congressional apportionment and compensation for members—failed to achieve ratification by enough states. (The math for ratification changed as more states were admitted: North Carolina in November 1789, Rhode Island in May 1790, Vermont in March 1791, and Kentucky in June 1792.) Almost no one at the time referred to the amendments collectively as a "bill of rights." Madison matter-of-factly referred to them as the "plan of amendments." Three states—Massachusetts, Connecticut, and Georgia—would not officially ratify even the ten amendments until the sesquicentennial of the debate, in 1939. Nor would the Bill of Rights acquire the sacred aura that surrounds it today until well into the twentieth century, a development that owes less to the foresight of the Founding Fathers than to the determination of morally aroused citizens and the willingness of the modern judiciary to challenge discriminatory and oppressive state legislation. As late as 1880, a Supreme Court justice could declare that the federal Constitution "unlike most modern ones, does not contain any formal declaration or bill of rights."

While the Senate was debating amendments, the House returned to the long-delayed judiciary bill. Its enemies went at it with vigor, led by Samuel Livermore of New Hampshire, a gouty, fifty-seven-year-old lawyer with a bulbous nose, a swatch of thinning, white hair, and a cantakerous tendency to undercut his fellow Federalists. He had earlier denounced the judiciary bill as a "monster" and now declared that it would create an "obnoxious" and "new fangled" system that would swallow up state courts and crush the country beneath the onerous "burthens" of judges' salaries and court costs. "The country didn't even *need* federal courts," he insisted. The states could perfectly well administer the Constitution without them. The bill would not only "lead to an entire new system of [federal] jurisprudence" but the "disgusting" prospect of a second system of courts operating within the states.

Picking up on Livermore's warning, his ally the chronically ill Michael Jenifer Stone of Maryland—"The air—The Water—and the Scents of [New York City] have made War upon my weakly Frame," he complained—launched on behalf of his states' rights convictions one of the most splendid metaphors of the entire debate, declaring that no nation could survive the terrifying chaos of two different court systems operating in the same place at the same time: it would, he warned, be like the very planets "rolling in their orbits," colliding with each other in violation of their divinely assigned roles. States were "complete republics" in themselves, he intoned, enjoying sovereign power that must not be interfered with. Weren't *all* crimes really committed against *states* anyway? If a man raised a rebel army in New York, for instance, didn't that constitute a rebellion against a *state*? It had nothing to do with the federal government. With this bill the federal government was claiming powers that it had no right to. He declared, "I am for this government moving as silent as death, that the people should not perceive the least alteration for the worse in their situation."

Theodore Sedgwick protested that if Livermore's motion carried, it would rob government of one of its most elementary duties—the delivery of justice. "If this is destroyed, your constitution is but the shadow of a government." Madison added that it should be obvious to everyone that state courts couldn't be trusted to execute federal laws. What if a state government proved hostile to the federal government and refused to take responsibility for national business? What redress would there be for aggrieved citizens? Most state judges were so dependent on their state legislatures for their appointment and salaries, Madison concluded, that if Livermore's recipe was followed, it "would throw us back into all the embarrassments which characterized our former situation" under the Articles of Confederation.

Surprisingly, however, perhaps the most significant riposte to Livermore came not from among the Federalists, who everyone knew had the strength to enact the bill with plenty of votes to spare, but from the House's arch Antifederalist. Elbridge Gerry's incessant opposition had made him unpopular among his colleagues, a sentiment that was only strengthened by his labored speech-making, "broken and interrupted with many a heck & hem & repetition of ofs & ands." Gerry had apparently decided, at long last, to make clear that despite his incessant rodomontades against federal power, he was ultimately committed to the Constitution and the new national enterprise. The Constitution, after all, was but a "political experiment," he believed. Whether the experiments worked or led to some other, as-yet-unforseen systems were "secrets that can only be unfolded by time." Gerry was a realist. He knew that he and his small band of allies had lost the battle over the judiciary bill, just as they had lost the battle over amendments and the battle over executive power. He had fought hard and hopelessly against impossible odds and had been subjected to unending scorn and ridicule for his trouble. Now he was telling his few friends in Congress, as well as the broader Antifederalist movement, that they had lost, and that it was time to move on. The Constitution had been ratified. No matter what he felt, a majority of Americans clearly supported it and wanted it put into effect. "We must suppose they understood what would be the operation of the system of government they adopted with such avidity," he declared in his halting fashion, with what one supposes must have sounded like glum resignation. "We are to administer this constitution, and therefore we are bound to establish these courts, let [come] what will be the consequence."

CHAPTER 10

A Centre Without Parallel

——— ·•· ———

Negro Slaves will be your Servants by day—musquitoes your centi-
nels by night, and bilious fevers your companions every Summer &
fall.

—Benjamin Rush, March 1789

Few questions, perhaps none, agitated Congress more than where to
plant the country's capital. During the years of the Confederation, the seat
of government had nomadically wandered from Philadelphia to Princeton to Annapolis to Trenton and finally New York City, satisfying few
and irritating many, who chafed at the inconvenience, expense, squalid
accommodations, and venal innkeepers. The Constitution mandated the
establishment of a seat of government, but few, very few, could agree on
where it ought to be. By the late summer of 1789, it was a potentially explosive conundrum. Failure to solve it "will lay a foundation for animosities that no government can prevent or heal," the *Pennsylvania Gazette*
had warned in March.

Apart from the practical necessity of having a place for the several
branches of the new government to meet, the capital-to-be was also seen
by many as a potentially transcendent symbol that would, they hoped,

knit the diverse and divergent parts of the nation together emotionally, and even spiritually, in ages to come. For the moment, that mystical role was filled by the charismatic George Washington. But Washington would not live forever; his recent illness had underscored his mortality. "While we had a Washington and his virtues to cement and guard the union, it might be safe," reflected Representative John Vining of Delaware, "but when he should leave us, who would inherit his virtues, and possess his influence? Who would remain to embrace and draw to a centre those hearts which the authority of his virtues alone kept in union?"

More than thirty sites had been proposed since 1783, from New York's Hudson Valley to Virginia. Trenton, New Jersey; Alexandria and Norfolk, Virginia; Georgetown, Baltimore, Hancock, and Williamsport in Maryland; Wilmington and Newark in Delaware; the Pennsylvania towns of Carlisle, Lancaster, York, Reading, and most vociferously the Philadelphia suburbs—all proclaimed their various advantages: an excellent port, location on a river or a post road, healthful air, pleasant landscape, well-stocked libraries, cheap food, good fishing, and plentiful firewood. Others had proposed what Americans now know as the South Bronx, Marietta in the remote, trans-Appalachian Ohio Country, or that Congress shuttle back and forth between sites, prompting one annoyed citizen to explode at legislators "who talk of moving from place to place with as much indifference as a set of strolling players." Even Newport, Rhode Island, a favorite summer residence for wealthy southerners, had its advocates, though perhaps only tongue in cheek, since it was not yet even part of the United States. Speculators were already raffling off building lots in the optimistically christened town of Columbia, on the Susquehanna River, in anticipation of its selection. New York City had spared no expense to make Congress feel comfortable, but the Pennsylvanians were fanatic in their opposition to staying there. They, along with southerners, had taken to calling Federal Hall "the Trap," asserting that its magnificence would tempt susceptible congressmen into remaining forever.

The notion of a government seat intended to stand for the ages troubled at least some thoughtful Americans, who could not conceive of the vast territorial and demographic growth that lay in store in generations to come. "For two or three hundred years to come," Representative George Thatcher opined, the center of population would likely remain in the mid-Atlantic. How could Congress decide where to situate a capital that would be convenient for centuries? Would the country even remain a single nation under one government or be divided into separate and distinct confederations? The future "can only be compared to the glimmering rays of a glow-worm in the blackest night," he reflected. Yet, it seemed wiser to base judgment on the hope that the nation would remain united than upon the unhappy alternative.

Many agreed, at least in principle, that this federal city or town should be more or less centrally located, "that the heart should be so placed as to propel the blood to the extremities, with the most equable and gentle motion," as Fisher Ames gracefully put it, preferably in a place—in the words of Timothy Pickering—that enjoyed a "salubrious" climate "where southern constitutions may be benefited & northern ones not injured," a plentiful food supply, close to sources of financial capital, and safe from "a sudden stroke from an enemy by land or water." But what did that actually mean? Near the center of population? The geographical center? The center of wealth? Wouldn't a central seat of government drain all the revenue from the rural hinterlands and impoverish them? Since the country was steadily moving westward, what was the center in 1789 might be far from it twenty-five years hence. Expansionists argued that the capital ought to be somewhere close to the Applachian Mountains, while easterners urged a site near the coast, preferably a port, which pretty much boiled down to Georgetown, Baltimore, New York, or somewhere near Philadelphia, since the Pennsylvania ratification convention had barred the state from granting Congress *permanent* jurisdiction over Philadelphia itself. Businessmen argued that a large city would bolster commerce. Others asserted that the quietude of "some small village" would enable members to ponder matters of national importance at leisure. Meanwhile, Philadelphians insisted that their city was the best *temporary* seat of all because it harbored no more than a handful of Antifederalist enemies of the Constitution; deploying a lovely Franklinesque image, Benjamin Rush asserted,

"Like Electrified Clouds our *plus* will unite with their *minus*, & a federal equilibrium will be produced which shall pervade the whole continent." Meanwhile, Virginians touted the Potomac River Valley, which, if not the fenny wilderness of later legend, failed to enthuse many members of Congress except those who lived there and to the south of it.

Since the early 1780s, Virginians had dreamed of a great commercial city on the Potomac to rival Philadelphia and New York. The most optimistic among them, including Washington, Jefferson, and Madison, saw the river as the most practical and profitable corridor of trade between the Atlantic Ocean and the fast-settling territories as far west as the Great Lakes and the upper Mississippi. In 1784, with Jefferson's vocal support, Madison had convinced the Virginia legislature to levy an annual tax of $25,000 to begin clearing and canalizing the river for commercial traffic, a project that was well under way as Congress launched its debate. Not until early 1789 did anyone seriously propose the gently rolling six-hundred-thousand-acre plain between the Anacostia River and the small river port of Georgetown, Maryland, as the site of the future national capital, which would secure the seat of government for the slave-holding South, give southerners an advantage in hiring for federal jobs, and permanently attract both immigrants and commerce to the region. By autumn, a cottage industry of local speculators was comparing the supposed imperial grandeur of the mid-Potomac to the Thames, the Seine, and the Rhine, and gushing that the industrial might of the valley would one day clothe the world, from the natives of Siberia to the English aristocracy. That was only the half of it. So naturally impregnable was the setting, enthused one promoter, John O'Connor, that it could shelter the capital from "the Cannons of the Universe," and the Anacostia River could host ten thousand ships the size of Noah's ark. As a prospective capital, it was unmatched—"a centre without parallel on the terraqueous globe." At least some southerners thought that a Potomac capital would eventually draw Pennsylvania into the southern orbit, that the site would be "worth millions" to that region and "convert it into a field which Speculation will enrich and adorn."

The rival campaigns for the seat of government reached a feverish pitch. For months, Pennsylvania's delegation had schemed to win it for their state. By early September a new and politically viable site had come into play: Columbia, about seventy miles west of Philadelphia, and fifty miles north of Baltimore, on a gentle bluff overlooking the rocky channel of the Susquehanna River and a panorama of thinly settled countryside to the west. Scoffers sardonically mocked the locals for imagining that their wisp of a hamlet was destined to become the hub of the universe. Pennsylvania's congressional delegation was in a hurry, fearing with good reason that the longer Congress remained in New York, the harder it would be to pry it loose from the city's louche seductions. Not only was New York "British hearted," but it was a virtual sump of European corruption, warned the hyperbolic Benjamin Rush, who was a chauvinistic advocate for placing the capital adjacent to his native Philadelphia. "Think of the influence of the light tea parties—Music parties—&c. &c. upon the manners of the rulers of a great republic."

No other issue that had come before Congress had produced the same frenzy of backroom bartering and vote trading. The battle was joined on August 27, when Thomas Scott of Pennsylvania, a huge, rough-hewn Federalist from the state's backcountry, rose in the House to urge that "a permanent seat for the government ought to be fixed as near the centre of wealth, population and extent of territory, as shall be consistent with the convenience of the Atlantic navigation, having also a due regard to the circumstances of *the Western country*." While these criteria might have applied to a number of places, Scott was talking about the Susquehanna.

All kinds of deals and combinations were bruited in the halls and stairwells, taverns and rooming houses, during rambles in the Manhattan countryside, and strolls along the Battery. "A permanent residential fever prevails in those States where there is any probability that Congress may finally rest," exclaimed one Yankee. Fisher Ames, who had come to Congress expecting deliberations as high-minded (he supposed) as those of the ancient Athenians, decried "this vile, unreasonable business" of feverish vote swapping, but nonetheless threw his weight and his eloquence into the battle. New Englanders and New Yorkers, who preferred a maritime capital, offered their support to the Susquehanna—*if* the Pennsylvanians would vote to retain New York as the temporary seat of government. Few northerners wanted to bestow the capital on Virginia, which was already the largest and most populous state, while southerners feared Pennsylvania, with its menacing legions of antislavery Quakers and free blacks; to many of them, continuing the seat of government in New York City, where slaveowning was actually on the *rise*, seemed the lesser evil. Madison, ever loyal to the Potomac interest, forcefully intervened and sequestered himself with the Pennsylvanians, who thereupon told the New Yorkers that they would have to suspend their negotiations. New Jersey members were said to be playing a deep game, hoping that if the Susquehanna failed, the capital would come to Trenton. (Snarled one Pennsylvanian, the Jersey members "lie by to mar every project alike that is not to carry Congress to the Delaware.") "The real designs of the members are nearly impenetrable," sighed Fisher Ames.

The Pennsylvanians had long agreed to vote as a bloc, but the more certain it seemed that they had secured the seat of government, the more that bloc began to crack. While several of the state's ten-member delegation were wedded to the Susquehanna, others, led by the powerful Robert Morris, were intently looking for a way to capture the seat of government for the Philadelphia suburbs of Germantown or Morrisville on the Delaware. On September 6, the Pennsylvanians reached what they thought was a smart deal with a group of southerners to establish the temporary seat at Philadelphia and the permanent one on the Potomac. (Like the New Yorkers, many Pennsylvanians hoped that once they had captured Congress for their state, it would never actually leave.) The New Englanders then allied with the New Yorkers to "break this intrigue," as Ames termed it, and threw their votes collectively to the Susquehanna. The Pennsylvanians then acquiesced to the Susquehanna as well, and to remaining in New York until the new capital was ready. Now the Virginians begged for delay: Madison was "sore & offended" that the Yankees and "Yorkers" had privately been caucusing with the Pennsylvanians, although this was precisely what the Virginians had been doing with the Pennsylvanians a few days earlier.

At times, the arguments became so confusing that members wrangled irritably over just what the "seat of government" was anyway. Was it where the two houses of Congress met? Or was it where the public offices were established? Or where the president resided? Or where the Supreme Court sat? Were these necessarily the same? Nonetheless, the debate proved exceptionally entertaining to the public, who crowded the halls and elevated visitors' gallery—the "palladium of liberty," as it was known—and annoyed the congressmen below by loudly cracking nuts with their teeth and treading on the shells.

On September 4, Madison laid out his case for the Potomac. As always, he was cogent. Many states, he pointed out, were wisely moving their capitals from "eccentric positions" to more central ones: Virginia from Williamsburg to Richmond, South Carolina from Charleston to Columbia, Georgia from Savannah to Augusta. New York and Massachusetts seemed about to do the same. The West had to be taken seriously indeed, since "dangers will be most apt to assail that quarter of the union," as "an astonishing mass of people" steadily filled its virgin reaches. Whether they became integrated into the United States or "separated into an alien, a jealous and hostile people" might well depend on their access to the nation's capital. Imagine, he warned, "instead of peace and friendship, we shall have rivalship and enmity; instead of being a great people, invulnerable on all sides, and without the necessity of those military establishments which other nations require, we shall be driven into the same expensive and dangerous means of defense." Happily there was an alternative. The Potomac, he confidently declared, "is the great highway of communication between the Atlantic and the western country," to which it provided far better access than did the Susquehanna. Granted, the present center of population was most likely in Pennsylvania. "But are we chusing a seat of government for the present moment only?" Look toward the future, he urged: the nation's demographic center would undoubtedly move *southward* in years to come and thus recede ever farther from the Susquehanna, perhaps even "beyond the Potowmack." Madison was calculatedly vague about where on the Potomac he would put the government, but he at one time suggested a distance of 250 miles upriver, which would place it in the vicinity of Hancock, with its resonant New England name, where Maryland is at its narrowest, and significantly farther west than Columbia, Pennsylvania.

Alexandria congressman Richard Bland Lee, at twenty-eight one of the youngest members of Congress and a Madison ally, argued further that only a Potomac site could safeguard "perpetual union and domestic tranquillity." Embedded in this was a not-so-veiled threat: thwart the will of the South at your peril. Northern Federalists had had their way on nearly every major issue that had come before Congress—if they now claimed the nation's seat of government for the North, it would further confirm the predictions of those southerners who had opposed the Constitution. "One part of the Union would be depressed and trampled on, to benefit and exalt the other," Lee declared, adding fiercely that if they felt disregarded yet again, "it would be an alarming circumstance to the people of the southern states." The logical outcome, he said, must be secession. How the question was resolved would determine "whether this government is to exist for ages, or be dispersed among contending winds."

The antislavery Theodore Sedgwick of Massachusetts protested the absurdity, in his view, of including the South's ever-swelling population of slaves in its efforts to claim the center of population for the South. "Would any gentleman pretend that men who were merely the slaves of the country, men who had no rights to protect, being deprived of them all, should be taken into view in determining the center of government? If they were considered, gentlemen might as well estimate the black cattle of New England." Sedgwick was pointing out southerners' hypocrisy, but he was not simply being glib. On the subject of slavery, he was as radical as any man in the United States. In 1780, his courtroom defense of an enslaved woman named Mumbet, who had fled to his hometown of Stockbridge from New York State, established the precedent that ended slavery in Massachusetts, a legal benchmark that pointed the way toward gradual emancipation in the northern states. Mumbet later joined Sedgwick's household as its effective majordomo and personally defended it against the Shaysite attack in 1786. (Mumbet was well known in Stockbridge for insisting that she be treated by whites as an equal; her no less assertive great-grandson would be W. E. B. Du Bois.)

Sedgwick scoffed at the notion of placing the capital on the Potomac, saying its climate was well known to New Englanders as "destructive to northern constitutions" and that "vast numbers of eastern adventurers had found their graves there." Benjamin Rush, who was also an abolitionist, expressed northern resistance to a southern capital even more starkly in a letter to John Adams: failing to attach the government to Philadelphia would mean being dragged to the banks of the Potomac, "where Negro Slaves will be your Servants by day—musquitoes your centinels by night, and bilious fevers your companions every Summer & fall—and pleurisies, every Spring."

At last the beast in the garden had gotten loose, the unspoken and un-acknowledged subject that arguably more than any other had the power to threaten the stability of the Union: human slavery. A few months earlier, Madison had marveled at how much less conflict he'd found between the northern and southern states than he had expected. That golden moment was past. The fissure between South and North had finally cracked open. Fear of confrontation and disunion began to percolate outward among Americans, who feared for the integrity of the country. Thomas Dwight wrote to Sedgwick that until now Congress had managed to "conceal" that "odious distinction between Northern and Southern interest." Now it was out, and the consequences could not be good. "Will it not cre-ate a party spirit which will be carried into all other measures?" worried Dwight.

To the delight of Pennsylvania's westerners, the House voted to place the seat of government at "some convenient place" on the east bank of the Susquehanna by a decisive vote of 32–19. Three appointed commissioners were to select the best site, purchase land, and within four years complete the construction of buildings for the federal government. In the mean-time, Congress would remain quartered in New York. At this, Pennsylva-nia's rivals panicked. Richard Bland Lee of Virginia moved to "amend" the resolution by substituting for the Susquehanna the "North bank of the river Potowmack." This motion was defeated. John Vining then proposed, with an equal lack of success, replacing the Susquehanna with Wilmington, Delaware. Next, Elias Boudinot of New Jersey sought to replace the buffeted Susquehanna with a fuzzier formulation—"Potowmack, Susquehannah, or Delaware"—but this too failed. The notion of a Potomac capital now appeared to be dead.

The Susquehanna bill required the approval of the Senate, of course. Here things began to go wrong for the Pennsylvanians. The state's two senators were divided. The Susquehanna's leading advocate was the gout-stricken and irritable William Maclay, who detested New York as too sophisticated, too elitist, too expensive, and too sick-making. "I will not be perfectly contented while Congress remains in this place, and I never had a series of worse health than since I came here," he complained. "One of my knees is now swelled a third above the common Size." Having surveyed the Susquehanna's banks and served as a state commissioner responsible for clearing obstructions from its bed, he knew the river intimately and tirelessly maintained that it was the most practical route to the west, via a confusing congeries of backcountry rivers—the Juniata, Poplar Run, the Conemaugh, the Kiskiminetas, and the Allegheny—to Pittsburgh, the someday-to-be metropolis of the trans-Allegheny region, the Ohio River, and the Great Lakes. (The Potomac's promoters, including George Washington, not to be outdone in geographical legerdemain, were pushing their own only slightly less tortuous route to the Ohio.)

Meanwhile, the gregarious Robert Morris had quietly (and not so quietly) been laboring to win support for placing the seat of government near Philadelphia. Expansive in his appetites as well as his ambitions, his life had thus far been remarkable. Although republicans considered him devious, which he could be, his friend John Adams praised him for his "masterly understanding, an open temper, and an honest heart," which was also true. Born in Liverpool and orphaned early—his father was killed in a bizarre accident when wadding from a cannon fired in honor of one of

154 THE FIRST CONGRESS

his merchant ships struck and killed him—the young Morris was raised by a Philadelphia merchant who took him into his trading firm, where he proved a quick study and was soon investing in everything from Carolina indigo to New England rum, frontier lands, and slaves. In 1762, he imported the largest shipment of Africans to arrive in Philadelphia: "premium stock" from the Gold Coast, as the *Pennsylvania Gazette* reported at the time, all with "natural good Dispositions, and being better capable of hard Labour." Morris's credentials as a patriot were unimpeachable: he had served the Continental Congress in multiple capacities during the Revolutionary War, and afterward as its superintendent of finance. When Congress failed to pay its bills, he supported the patriot government with his own line of credit. But an unapologetic elitist, he had advocated for lifetime appointment to the Senate and had little regard for the political aspirations of the "lower orders."

More than almost any other man, apart from George Washington, Morris would try to make the federal metropolis a reality, bridging the idealistic hopes of the founders with the embryonic American faith in big money. He now set out to derail the plan to put it on the Susquehanna. "There has been a Violent Schism between him and the Pennsylvania delegation, or at least a part of them," Maclay reported. Early in the session, Maclay had tried to maintain friendship with Morris and had swallowed his hurt when the Philadelphia plutocrat snubbed him. His bitterness now boiled out. "Thus barefacedly to drive away Congress from the State rather than a few Barrels of flour should pass by the Philadelphia market in descending the Susquehannah, and rather than the Inhabitants of that River should enjoy the natural advantages of opening the navigation of it," Maclay smoldered. "I think it is probable these vile arts will prevail."

Morris's trump was a donation of $100,000 from the state of Pennsylvania to erect new buildings for the federal government in the Philadelphia suburb of Germantown. But he couldn't quite close the deal. "I have been exceedingly plagued with the question of 'Permanent Residence,'" he complained to his friend Gouverneur Morris of New York. "We have been playing hide and seek on the banks of Potomac, Susquehannah, Conegocheague, &c. &c." (This last tongue-twisting stream, spelled in various ways, joins the Potomac at Williamsport, Maryland.) But he remained undaunted. "I have been the prime mover in this affair, and shall continue so, until it is decided one way or the other."

Certain that the Pennsylvanians would never oppose a permanent location anywhere in the state, and equally sure that many northerners weren't firmly committed to the Susquehanna, he now tirelessly lobbied Yankee senators to throw their weight behind the Delaware, arguing that a Susquehanna site would be no benefit to the profitable flow of commerce. Reported Maclay, Morris "flamed away in favor of Germantown, running backwards and forwards like a boy, taking out one senator after another to them," swearing that if the state of Pennsylvania failed to find the money, he would raise it himself—a promise that no one doubted he was capable of fulfilling. He promised the New Yorkers that if they voted for Germantown, he would round up enough votes to ensure that the temporary seat of government remained in New York City at least until 1793, even if the new capital was ready sooner. Then, on September 24, he administered the coup de grâce to the Susquehanna by moving to delete it from the bill and replace it with a blank, in the expectation that he could get it filled with Germantown.

Maclay's diary is the only source for that day's cascading votes and confusing parliamentary thrusts and counterthrusts. But the stunning outcome is beyond dispute. Maclay himself first moved unsuccessfully that Morris's proposal be ruled out of order. Next, the Virginians proposed filling the blank with the Potomac. Another motion called for planting the seat of government on the Susquehanna in *Maryland*. Morris then reiterated his offer to provide $100,000 if the capital went to Germantown. When the votes were finally tallied on Morris's original motion, it appeared that he had triumphed: the Susquehanna was struck out. Feeling the momentum in his favor, Morris immediately proposed inserting Germantown in the blank. Maclay, whose footwork was far less skilled than Morris's, knew that he had been decisively outmaneuvered. He was so livid with frustration that he voted against Morris's motion, leaving the Senate evenly divided, nine to nine. The fate of the Susquehanna—and, though it was not immediately obvious, Pennsylvania—now rested with John Adams. As the vice president, he held the tie-breaking vote.

Maclay probably disliked Adams more than any other man in the chamber. In temperament, the two blunt-spoken, sharp-edged, irritable men had much in common. But they couldn't abide each other. Adams regarded the Pennsylvanian as an uncooperative troublemaker, while Maclay considered the vice president as no more dignified than "a Monkey just put into Breeches." According to Maclay, Adams first flattered the Virginians by "extolling" the Potomac. He next made some disparaging remarks about Maclay's beloved Susquehanna. Following that, Adams said that he would personally prefer that Congress alternate between New York and Philadelphia. At last he reached his climax. Pennsylvania's—or rather Morris's—promise of $100,000 was the clincher. His vote would go to Germantown. "Thus fell our hopes," wrote the heartbroken Maclay.

Morris was one of the deftest political animals in either house. But he was outfoxed by James Madison when the House took up the Senate bill a few days later. Even some of the Virginians had by now resigned themselves to the unappealing prospect of a northern government seat. But Madison, the master parliamentarian, suspected that if he could somehow cripple the bill as it stood, he might still be able to maneuver the prospective federal city to the Potomac. If Virginia played its cards cleverly, it might just get the southern capital that it dreamed of. He came up with a ploy so subtle, so seemingly inconsequential, that few members probably realized what he was up to.

Pennsylvania had generously donated land at Germantown for the new capital, Madison acknowledged. But what law, he asked, would govern that tract while the federal town was being constructed? Logically, it ought to be Pennsylvania law, at least until the federal government could determine what code of its own to apply. This was just common sense. No one could object to amending the bill to say so, could they? And no one did. Madison's parliamentary technicality was a brilliant stroke.

The Pennsylvanians had been decisively sandbagged. The amendment required that the whole bill now be returned to the Senate—which immediately voted by a majority of one vote to postpone it to the next session of Congress. Morris insisted that "as sure as fate" Germantown would become the new capital, while the Susquehanna's overconfident partisans felt sure that once Congress returned, they would easily recruit the votes they needed. But the whole process would have to begin again, and its outcome was far from assured. Madison had once again gotten his way, this time not by statesmanship, but by sly parliamentary maneuver. Wrote Fisher Ames, "And thus the house that jack built is vanished in smoke."

The first session finally came to a sputtering end. Everyone was exhausted after six months of slogging labor, and in a hurry to get home before the autumn weather turned the roads to mush and the seas to stormy cauldrons. In private, one heard plenty of irritable carping about the caliber of the members of both houses. "You might search in vain for the flashes of Demosthenes, or for the splendid illumination of Cicero," sighed John Adams. A disillusioned William Maclay confided to his diary that he had come to New York "expecting every man to act the part of a God," but had instead found "rough and rude manners, Glaring folly, and the basest selfishness apparent in almost every public transaction." Fisher Ames, who had in the spring derided "the yawning listlessness" of his colleagues and "their overrefining spirit in relation to trifles," did not revise his opinion upward.

More seriously, dangerous political fissures had deepened. In May, optimists had expressed relief that much less conflict between the northern and southern states was evident than they had expected. By September, they couldn't be so sure. The Antifederalists, who had repeatedly been defeated, as well as some southern Federalists, were left feeling marginalized and bitter. The harsh debate over the seat of government, William Grayson reported to Patrick Henry, had "left very strong impressions on the minds of the Southern gentlemen; they suppose with too much reason that the same kind of bargaining which took effect with respect to the Susquehannah may also take effect in other great National matters which may be very oppressive to a defenseless naked Minority." By this he of course meant the agricultural, slaveholding South. Grayson's bitterness was echoed by South Carolina senator Pierce Butler, who complained to the North Carolina jurist James Iredell, "Never was a man more egregiously disappointed than I am. I came here full of hopes that the greatest liberality would be exercised; that the consideration of the *whole*, and the general good, would take place of every other object; but here I find men scrambling for partial advantages, State interests and in short, a train of those narrow, impolitic measures that must, after a while, shake the Union to its very foundation. . . . I wish you to come into the confederacy," Butler begged, "as the only chance the Southern interest has to preserve a balance of power." Senators William Grayson and Richard Henry Lee, in a formal letter to the Virginia House of Delegates, warned that what they deemed to be overwhelming federal power would sound the death knell of what remained of American freedom: "It is impossible for us not to be apprehensive for Civil Liberty when we know no instance in the Records of history that shew a people ruled in freedom when subject to an undivided Government and inhabiting a territory so extensive as that of the United States."

To be sure, much work was left undone. The monthlong effort to establish a seat of government had ended in failure. More ominously, that daunting mountain of state and national war debt still loomed, crippling the nation's ability to borrow. Somehow the government would have to find a way to pay for it. By most every measure, however, the session's legislative record was impressive; few, if any, later Congresses would come close to matching it. The machine of government had begun to work.

Twelve amendments to the Constitution had been passed to reassure the incensed partisans of liberty, as Antifederalists tended to see themselves, thwarting their efforts to weaken the Constitution. Although Antifederalists continued to charge that the amendments were "so mutilated & gutted" that they were valueless, their pressure on the Federalists had produced both an unintended personal triumph for James Madison, who had deftly distilled scores of multifarious proposals into a compact group that could actually be passed by an indifferent Congress, and, eventually, a more universal triumph for Americans of later ages, who would assert human rights in ways that were unimagined by the members of the First Congress.

An ongoing revenue stream for the federal government had been created by imposing tariffs on merchandise and ships entering American ports, with an embryonic national bureaucracy of "collectors," "naval officers" (who, confusingly, were actually civilians), and "surveyors" to make the system work, providing the government's primary source of income until the enactment of the income tax in the twentieth century. (The jobs were political plums, and their holders soon established the lasting bureaucratic penchant for turf warfare; the naval officer at Boston, one James Lovell, was soon complaining that the port was infested with "Intrigue," and that a cabal led by the local collector had invented "a sort of Hermaphrodite" office—part naval officer and part controller—that had reduced poor Lovell to the level of a mere "Lacquie.")

Federal judicial districts had been laid out and circuit courts created. The Supreme Court had been established by the Constitution. With the Senate's almost instantaneous assent, George Washington appointed as the high court's first chief justice the universally respected John Jay, one of the most experienced political men of the founders' generation. A pivotal figure in bringing about New York's ratification of the Constitution, he had threatened that New York City would secede from the state if upstate Antifederalists failed to come around. Under Jay, the Supreme Court could be counted upon to protect the central government against rearguard challenges by the Antifederalist opposition.

The Senate also passed the first list of federal crimes, including treason, counterfeiting, murder on federal property, and piracy. Critics who carped that the judiciary bill wore "so monstrous an appearance" that it would never work in practice would soon be proved wrong, as respect for the new federal judiciary took hold. Although the Punishment of Crimes

Act still required a House vote, it would quickly be reintroduced and approved at the start of the second session, in January. (At least one of the bill's provisions might leave modern Americans feeling a bit queasy: it authorized murderers to be sentenced to dissection after execution and imposed both harsh fines and prison terms for anyone attempting to rescue a body from such a fate.)

Congress had also established several executive departments and approved the president's superlative appointees. They were a youthful group. Chief Justice Jay was forty-four. Portly Henry Knox, who was carried over as secretary of war, the only member of the Confederation government to be retained, was thirty-nine. Attorney General Edmund Randolph—who was essentially a consultant, with no office or staff and a retainer of $1,500, half as much as other executive officers—was thirty-six. Thomas Jefferson, Washington's second choice for secretary of state after Jay expressed his preference for the Supreme Court, was forty-six. (Jefferson wouldn't learn of his appointment for weeks, and no one in New York knew if he was still in Paris or had left for home.) Alexander Hamilton was the boldest appointment of all. At thirty-four, Hamilton was arrestingly handsome, slender, with blue eyes shading toward violet, reddish-blond hair, and, in the words of a contemporary, "a resolute, frank, soldierly appearance." His "application is as indefatigable as his Genius is extensive," enthused one well-wisher. Washington had discussed the Treasury appointment with his old friend Robert Morris, and had perhaps offered him the secretary's job. Morris recommended Hamilton instead. "He knows everything, sir," Morris is said to have assured the president. "To a mind like his nothing comes amiss." Hamilton knew better than anyone else what he was up against. He wrote to his wartime friend the Marquis de Lafayette, "In undertaking the task, I hazard much, but I thought it an occasion that called upon me to hazard."

Not the least of the session's achievements was that it had continued to function despite so many personal, local, and ideological rivalries and conflicts that, had members exhibited less self-control and commitment to their divergent ideas of the public good, it might easily have transformed political conflict into crippling crisis. In short, the machine of government had begun to work.

The session had also been good for George Washington. From a man whose hands had shaken as he took the oath of office six months earlier, and who had embarked, heroically or foolhardily he didn't know, "on untrodden ground," not knowing what the outcome of his journey in the political wilderness might be, the sense of relief was palpable. The politically wounded might be lying about him, but he knew that a great victory had been won. "It was indeed next to a Miracle that there should have been so much unanimity, in points of such importance, among such a number of citizens, so widely scattered and so different in their habits in many respects, as the Americans were," he wrote to a British well-wisher, Catherine Macaulay Graham. "So far as we have gone with the new Government (and it is completely organized and in operation) we have had greater reason than the most sanguine could expect to be satisfied with its success." Washington was no wordsmith, but his sense of pride and relief was intense. Washington had proved to everyone his mettle as president, that their faith in him had not been misplaced. His personal behavior—aloof but visible, soldierly yet humble—was beyond reproach, and his reputation for superhuman fortitude had been further gilded by his near-fatal illness and slow, painful recovery. He had set a model for the presidency that everyone accepted. Correspondence by members of Congress reveals almost no hint of criticism, much less mockery, of the president.

The vice president was another story. He was, French minister Moustier remarked, "nowhere near as important a personage as Mr. Adams would like to make him; all the efforts he has made in this regard have only served to render him ridiculous." If Washington had bestowed a sort of chilly republican grandeur to the invented presidency, Adams had shrunk his office into annoying insignificance. Some days—particularly when he was compelled to cast a tie-breaking vote—self-pity seemed to gush from his pores. "Every unpopular point is invariably left to me to determine so that I must be the scape goat, to bear all their sins, without a possibility of acquiring any share in the honor of any of their popular deeds," he fairly whined. But he was also entirely correct in his assessment. Was there anyone else in Congress, he asked, who in the service of the people daily "ran the gauntlet among halters, axes, libels, Daggers, cannon balls, and pistol bullets as I have done?"

CHAPTER 11

Interlude I

———•———

We must pay it; it follows as close as the shadow follows its substance.

—William Loughton Smith

Lew York soon began hemorrhaging senators and congressmen. Madison, never robust, was physically spent after the draining months of heroic parliamentary labor. After postponing his departure from New York for ten days in hope that Jefferson would show up, he finally turned south toward Montpelier, his Virginia estate, but collapsed in Philadelphia, where he was forced to remain for two weeks to recuperate. Fisher Ames staggered into Boston on October 6 with scarcely the "breath or spirits to hold a pen," feverish after days of "shivering, starving & nodding for want of sleep." Elbridge Gerry reached Boston in even worse shape, almost blind from an eye infection, and bone-rattled from the journey over Connecticut's corrugated roads, with his trunk and all his personal papers having been stolen. William Loughton Smith of South Carolina set out across the Hudson River in a rowboat that was nearly overturned by a sudden squall, but fortunately righted itself with no loss other than one passenger's new hat. (The man angrily complained that it had cost no less than thirty shillings and was moreover made of fur. Smith punned, "It is *fur* enough by this time, for you'll never see it again.")

George Washington, instead of returning to Mount Vernon, embarked on a grand tour of the northern states that might have daunted a much younger man, not to mention one just barely recovered from the effects of the "imposthume." He explained to his sister Betty Washington Lewis that he wanted to recover his health after the "long and tedeous complaint" that had afflicted him. He also just wanted to get out of town, away from the crowds, the importuning office seekers, and the pressure of politics. On the road, he intended "to acquire knowledge of the face of the Country the growth and Agriculture thereof and the temper and disposition of the Inhabitants toward the new government." This was thus to be a sort of executive inspection tour that would also carry the single most vital symbol of the new federal government—himself—into the hinterland, where it would help to assure the nation's citizens that the new government was well and truly launched.

Before he departed, declaring it to be "the duty of all nations to acknowledge the providence of an Almighty God, to obey his will, to be grateful for his benefits, and to humbly implore his protection and favor," he called for a national day of thanksgiving for November 26, the first such proclamation in American history. Although Washington almost never spoke about his personal faith, his words were redolent of a deep if somewhat amorphous piety. The president, like most southerners of his class, had been raised in the Anglican (now Episcopal) Church. It is doubtful that he believed in the divinity and resurrection of Christ, and he certainly did not consider the US government based on the Christian religion, but he did have faith in the existence of a "great and glorious Being" who had extended his "signal and manifold mercies" over the American struggle for independence.

On the morning of October 15 he set off in his coach up Manhattan Island, beneath a wet and leaden sky, accompanied by six servants and slaves; his secretary, Tobias Lear; and his military aide, Major William Jackson. They continued through intermittent showers across what would one day be known as the Bronx but was then still a bucolic part of Westchester County. With a farmer's eye, Washington observed that although the road was rough and stony, "the Land [was] strong, well covered with grass and a luxurient Crop of Indian Corn intermixed with Pompions [pumpkins]." He also noted in his diary that he had passed four droves of beef cattle heading for the city's dinner tables, a flock of sheep, floods of geese, and any number of "large but rather long-legged" pigs.

Across the state line in Connecticut, the roads deteriorated, pitching over precipitous hills where the president's coach teetered precariously on boulder-strewn slopes. Later, safe in the flatland, Washington was pleased to see farmers industriously harvesting and pressing apples for cider. Stopping to chat with them, he noted approvingly when they said their wheat fields yielded up to twenty-five bushels per acre. At Stratford, on the seventeenth, he was pleased to discover that the new local textile mill had already turned out four hundred bolts of cloth. At Milford, he admired "a handsome Cascade over the Tumbling dam," at New Haven a linen mill and a bottle factory, and, at Wallingford, mulberry orchards where silkworms produced "exceedingly good" silk for the local textile industry. At Wethersfield, he visited the woolen factory that had woven the suit he had worn on Inauguration Day. At Middletown, on the Connecticut River, he noted that the depth of water was, at ten feet, four feet deeper than at Hartford, and that at Springfield, Massachusetts, the powder magazine was "in excellent order."

But almost everywhere he was met by bevies of local dignitaries, windy speechifying, celebratory odes, and militia displays, like those at Leicester, Massachusetts, where a company of snappily dressed artillerymen saluted him with a cannonade of thirteen guns on his arrival and departure from the town. Finally, on October 24, he reached Cambridge, just outside Boston, where he was formally received by a delegation from the state government, including the old patriot Lieutenant Governor Samuel Adams, and members of the state's executive council. This stately cavalcade then proceeded into Boston, where more dignitaries, delegations of citizens flying the banners of their trades and professions, and a "vast concourse" of ordinary men and women lustily cheered the president. To his evident chagrin, he was then subjected to a rendition of a specially composed "Ode to Columbia's Favorite Son: Great Washington, the Hero's Come"—just the sort of florid stuff Washington hated—performed by a select group of singers. "Every muscle of his face appeared agitated," an eyewitness reported.

In the midst of all this, Washington couldn't fail to notice the absence of Governor John Hancock, a strident Antifederalist, who pleaded incapacity due to an attack of gout. Whether or not this was true, Washington treated it as a slight to the presidency and an implicit declaration of Hancock's ambivalence toward federal authority. Washington rejected Hancock's invitation to visit him in the governor's mansion—a gesture that the president felt would imply the subservience of federal to state authority—and refused to meet him at all until, gout or no gout, Hancock presented himself for a formal call. The governor quickly capitulated and came the next day to Washington's lodgings to contritely sip tea and apologize for his "indisposition."

A flu epidemic surging up the East Coast hit Boston while Washington was there and, when he fell victim to it, would ever after be dubbed "the President's cough." Despite his illness, which included a painful inflammation of his eye, and the soggy weather, Washington embarked on a characteristically vigorous tour of local factories, including a textile operation where he observed children spinning flax for cloth in ten-hour shifts. "They are the daughters of decayed families, and are girls of Character," he approvingly reported. Later, at Harvard College in Cambridge, he marveled at an elegant orrery, a mechanism for showing the revolutions of the planets, and the college library, one of the largest in the United States.

Washington pointedly spurned the opportunity to visit Rhode Island, whose legislators refused to call a convention to ratify the Constitution. Some even fantasized that several larger states were ready to revolt against the federal government and looked to them for leadership. For months, influential members of Congress had pleaded with Rhode Islanders to join the Union, to no avail. "What security against external force can your people have?" Fisher Ames demanded of a correspondent in Rhode Island.

"The sea is open to the Fleets of foreign Nations, and an imaginary Line divides you from your neighbors. Either the States will be friendly, or they will not. Suppose them hostile, encroaching Neighbors, what will protect your State?" Local Federalists were frustrated to the point of apoplexy. The state, in the words of one, had become "the Botany Bay of America; the receptacle of the seditious, the disaffected, and the bankrupts of other states, an Augean stable, whose accumulated filth will take some modern Hercules at least thirty years to clear away."

Instead of dignifying the recalcitrant Rhode Islanders by his presence, Washington next traveled from Boston to Salem, where, one witness remarked, he was subjected to yet another "ditty" in his honor and, looking "as if he could bear no more," fled into the house where he was staying to escape it. After this, he went on to the shoe-manufacturing town of Lynn, where perhaps the president felt relieved to be once again surrounded by silent workers and their humming machinery, then on to Marblehead— dear to his heart, perhaps, because men from there had saved the remnants of his army after their disastrous defeat in the Battle of Long Island, in 1776. Then on to New Hampshire, and ultimately to Kittery, Maine (still part of Massachusetts), for doubtless stimulating discussions about local lumber, fish, and potash industries.

With winter in the offing—heavy snows deterred him from visiting Vermont, not yet a state—Washington at last turned his coach southward. Despite increasingly wet weather and meandering roads in Massachusetts, which "in every part of this State are amazingly crooked, to suit the convenience of every Man's fields & the directions you receive from the People [are] equally blind & ignorant," as Washington irritatedly jotted in his diary, he managed to average a remarkable thirty miles a day. En route, he had hoped to visit his old companion-in-arms General Israel Putnam at his home in Connecticut, but without reliable guides couldn't find him "without deranging my plan" and regretfully continued on. He was further annoyed the next day, a Sunday, when he learned that it was "contrary to Law & disagreeable to the People of this State" to travel on the Sabbath, and he was compelled to waste the day going twice to a church where he was subjected to "very lame discourses" by the local minister. He finally arrived at New York on November 13, after a month on the road, where—to his dismay, perhaps—he found Martha Washington entertaining a large company of guests at the Cherry Street mansion.

Road-weary as he must have been, Washington afterward crowed that he had never had a better time in his life. The harvests of wheat, the "encrease of Commerce" visible in every port, the variety of new manufactures being produced in New England factories, all impressed him as nothing short of "astonishing." The countryside seemed almost everywhere to have recovered from the ravages of war, and the people, he felt sure, were "delighted with a government instituted by themselves." New England was not only secure, it was thriving. "The ill-boding Politicians who prognosticated that America would never enjoy any fruits from her Independence & that She would be obliged to have recourse to a foreign Power for protection," he was certain, had been proven wrong.

While others traveled, Alexander Hamilton toiled. He faced not only the organization of the largest department of government, but also the daunting challenge of stabilizing the country's chaotic finances. He set to it all with what his biographer Ron Chernow describes as "torrid" energy. Treasury employed thirty-nine clerks in New York, plus dozens of revenue collectors and inspectors in ports from Portland to Savannah, dwarfing the State Department's staff of five and the War Department's four. Hamilton had to invent bookkeeping and auditing systems, create a system of seagoing monitors—the genesis of the US Coast Guard—to suppress smuggling, erect lighthouses and buoys to secure the coastline for commercial shipping, and issue trustworthy paper money to facilitate business. But with revenue at a trickle, his first, supremely urgent duty was to raise money just to keep the government running: his second day on the job, he arranged a $50,000 loan from the Bank of New York.

Most important, two weeks after he took office, the House of Representatives asked Hamilton to prepare a report on the reestablishment of public credit, giving him until January to complete it, before Congress reassembled. "No other moment in American history could have allowed such scope for Hamilton's abundant talents," writes Chernow. "Hamilton was that rare revolutionary: a master administrator and as competent a public servant as American politics would ever produce." Certainly, as a creative economic thinker he was unsurpassed among his contemporaries. In contrast to Madison, Jefferson, and other patrician founders, Hamilton, a West Indian immigrant, was bound neither to inherited land nor to any particular state and was thus, as historian Thomas K. McCraw puts it, both more national in his outlook and "better able to appreciate the intrinsic rootlessness of money—and how its mobility could serve the public good." His approach to the nation's financial crisis would be both forceful and creative: although Hamilton admired the theories of Adam Smith, he believed that a country as weak as the United States was in 1789 still needed the "fostering care" of government, especially in fiscal policy.

Hamilton was a genuine intellectual, who thought deeply about the problems of national defense, industrial development, taxation, and above all financial policy. Few of his contemporaries knew anything about the emerging study of economics. As Representative Jeremiah Wadsworth of Connecticut expressed it in a public letter that autumn, "The people of this country were as new in the arts of finance as those of war." Hamilton knew that if he was to succeed in reshaping the financial landscape of the United States—and he intended to do that—he would have to radically change the attitude of Americans, for whom borrowing connoted wild speculation and moral failure, and prolonged debt was anathema. As the Philadelphia reformer Benjamin Rush, a man of exemplary morals and austere habits, put it, public credit—that is, borrowing—"is to nations what private Credit & loan offices are to individuals. It begets debt—extravagance—vice—& bankruptcy."

The United States was essentially bankrupt. Unless the country restored its credit, Hamilton knew, it could not survive. No one even knew just how much the country owed, or exactly to whom, or whether state war debts ought even to be counted as part of the national debt. At least $12 million in overdue loans was owed to French and Dutch bankers, with interest mounting daily, and millions more in worthless paper currency that had been issued without hard-currency backing, along with vast quantities of depreciated pay certificates and other securities that had been issued to soldiers and wartime suppliers, who had in turn sold them to speculators for a pittance in the belief that the government would never redeem them. "When the country had drained the last drop of service it could screw out of the poor soldiers, they were turned adrift like old worn-out horses, and nothing said about land to pasture them upon," a Yankee veteran, Joseph Martin, bitterly wrote. "No one ever took the least care about it, except a pack of speculators, who were driving about the country like so many evil spirits, endeavoring to pluck the last feather from the soldiers." Back in 1783, dozens of Pennsylvania and Maryland troops with fixed bayonets demanding back pay had confronted the Pennsylvania executive council, scaring the panicked Confederation Congress out of Philadelphia, and leaving a lasting fear of armed and angry masses. When veterans and speculators alike now clamored to be paid off, politicians paid attention.

Several states that had suffered from heavy fighting during the war were in financial free fall. Massachusetts, for instance, owed $5 million, coupled with annual interest payments of $300,000, while South Carolina owed almost $3.5 million, with $240,000 due in annual interest. These were fantastic sums by the standards of the time. Other states that had come close to paying off their debts wanted no responsibility for those that hadn't. Politically, any solution to the debt crisis bore directly on the increasingly sensitive problem of states' rights: whichever level of government paid the debt would likely possess the major taxing power and the allegiance of the people. Opponents thus saw a federal takeover of state debts as an unconstitutional threat to state sovereignty, if not a prelude to the outright extinction of the states themselves. It was all a bewildering rat's nest that had defied solution for years. To this was added Hamilton's concern for national security. He well knew from his own wartime experience that if the United States could not defend itself, it could not survive. National defense meant the establishment of a credible navy and larger army than the weak and overstretched forces that now lay scattered along the western frontier. That, too, would require far more money than the infant republic now had. Almost every member of Congress agreed that the country had little alternative to paying the mounting interest on its debts. "We must pay it; it follows as close as the shadow follows its substance," as Representative William Loughton Smith wrote. Further procrastination would "be mischievous and destructive of the general welfare," warned Representative Theodore Sedgwick. "Nay, I do not know but it will tend to the destruction of the government itself, by destroying that energy on which all is to depend."

Working through the shortening days of autumn at a simple pinewood table amid growing mountains of files, Hamilton gradually conceived a supremely bold scheme to transform the financial landscape of the United States. "In considering plans for the increase of our Revenues, the difficulty lies not so much in the want of objects as in the prejudices which may be feared with regard to almost every object," he wrote worryingly to Madison, whom he still regarded as an ally, a misapprehension from which he would soon be disabused. "The Question is very much, What further taxes will be least unpopular?" He knew, as fellow Federalist Representative Jeremiah Wadsworth of Connecticut would put it in a widely read article, that it would be both "wicked and impolitic" to smother already tax-averse Americans with burdensome new levies. But there was no need for that: he knew that Britain was shouldering a heavier national debt than any other nation, but had deftly converted it into a strength by enticing lenders to advance more money—and thereby strengthen the government and national stability—in order to protect the funds they had already invested. He further knew that the French Revolution, the decline of the Dutch republic, and the onerous indebtedness of other European nations had increased the attractiveness of the United States as a place for continental investors to park capital.

Hamilton was essentially self-taught in what the historian John E. Ferling termed "the boggy landscape of finance." Hamilton's early life was anything but privileged. Raised by his unwed mother on the Caribbean island of St. Croix, as a boy he learned in a local trading firm the rudiments of bookkeeping, the unstable value of currency, and the use of credit. Even then, ambition burned hot in him. At twelve, he wrote to a friend, "I contemn the grov'ling and condition of a clerk . . . and would willingly risk my life tho' not my Character to exalt my station." A wealthy benefactor sent him to King's College (later Columbia University) in New York. There, fired by the spirit of revolution, he threw himself into the patriotic struggle. He fought bravely as an artilleryman at the battles of Trenton and Princeton and later served for four years "with incandescent brilliance," as Thomas McCraw has written, as George Washington's personal aide-de-camp. In 1781, he stormed the British breastworks at Yorktown at the head of a partly African-American regiment, which helped to cement his views on emancipation, which were well in advance of all but the Quakers of his time. Revolutionary though he may have been, he had no fondness for the messiness of democracy. He had urged that the president and senators hold their offices for life to counterbalance the "turbulent and changing" masses, who, he declared at the Constitutional Convention, "seldom judge or determine right."

During the war, he devoured the works of Adam Smith, Jacques Necker, and other European financial thinkers and began to see how the power of money could be used to build a modern nation-state. Even as he polished his report for Congress, he charged his sister-in-law Angelica Church to send him from London "by the first ships every well written book that [she could] procure on the subject of finance." Besides realizing how imperative it was for the United States to pay its debts, he also began to see that creative capitalism could be made to serve as a tool both to drive the nation's economic development and to weld the states into a stronger union. He regarded businessmen as a key pillar of support for the new government—"its most interested and affectionate nurses," as his ally Benjamin Lincoln put it: tying them firmly to the new government was imperative. Banks, the chief instrument of credit, "have proved to be the happiest engines that ever were invented for advancing trade," Hamilton wrote. Debt could, he also realized, be translated into political power.

In 1784, at the age of twenty-nine, Hamilton had helped to found the Bank of New York, the second commercial bank in the United States, and by the end of the decade, when he penned many of the essays that became *The Federalist Papers*, he was recognized as one of the leading financial minds in the country. After wedding the daughter of the grandee Philip Schuyler, Hamilton gained entrée into the salons of New York's most powerful families. By the time of his appointment as treasury secretary, he ranked as one of New York's leading power brokers. During the presidential election, he had secretly (and needlessly) convinced several northeastern electors to withhold their votes from John Adams, to ensure that his electoral votes did not surpass or equal George Washington's. Then, in early 1789, Hamilton had attempted to oust New York's Antifederalist governor, George Clinton, who he feared might be tempted to subvert the new national government. A few months later, he blatantly and this time successfully lobbied for the selection of his friend Rufus King, a Massachusetts transplant, for one of New York's Senate seats against the candidate favored by the aristocratic Livingston family, converting them almost overnight from allies to opponents. (New York's other senator was Hamilton's father-in-law, Philip Schuyler.) As ruthless as Hamilton might be in the political arena, he was impervious to corruption, refusing to accept any kind of outside income while he served as secretary—a remarkably principled stand in a free and easy age. His enemies were plentiful and unforgiving. One anonymous letter writer warned the president of "the artful machinations and designs" of his former aide-de-camp, "who (like Judas Iscariott) would for the gratification of boundless Ambition, betray his Lord, and Master," and who "can readily assume any shape, to suit his nefarious purposes."

Such ludicrous accusations aside, Hamilton was a natural executive and possessed an irrepressible instinct for power. During his first months as treasury secretary, as if he hadn't enough to do already, he seized the initiative in foreign policy in an episode that would have severely embarrassed the administration had it become public. An outspoken Anglophile, Hamilton sought to nudge the United States closer to Britain, a policy favored by a number of leading Federalists, including Adams, Jay, Fisher

Ames, and Philip Schuyler, but stoutly opposed by those, such as Madison and Jefferson, who felt profound gratitude to France for its support in the Revolutionary War. In the autumn of 1789, Hamilton began meeting secretly with George Beckwith, a former British army officer and a not-so-secret agent of the crown, who was sent to New York to quietly test the political sentiments in the United States. Although official relations between the two countries were frosty and complicated by several knotty boundary issues, commerce between them was robust and growing. After their first meeting, Beckwith reported to his masters that Hamilton had told him, "I have always preferred a connexion with you, to that of any other country, *we think in English*, and we have a similarity of prejudices and predilections." More concretely, they discussed a possible commercial treaty, issues bearing on the navigation of the Mississippi River, American intentions toward Canada, and even the possibility of a naval alliance. These back-channel meetings played a part in the ultimately fruitless dispatch of Gouverneur Morris as a special envoy to England. However, they were indicative of the deep rift that was opening between the friends of Britain and those of France, which would shape American foreign policy throughout the decade and into the next century.

The putative secretary of state had no clue that he had been appointed by the president until he stepped ashore in Norfolk, Virginia, on November 23. Jefferson's voyage had been remarkably fast, a mere twenty-six days "from land to land," as he put it, and except for the first few days, when he and his companions—his daughters Patsy and Polly and their enslaved relatives James and Sally Hemings—were all seasick, they were blessed by fine autumnal weather. At the Virginia capes they were met by thick fog and stiff winds, but the captain, "a bold and judicious seaman," forged ahead and, though nearly colliding with an outbound brig, brought the ship safely to port. The only mishap occurred an hour after Jefferson's party had disembarked, when a fire broke out in steerage and burst through the cabins, but somehow left Jefferson's baggage unharmed. On his arrival, he wrote to John Jay—who, as far as Jefferson knew, was still in charge of foreign affairs—announcing that he planned to return to France once he had taken care of pressing business at Monticello. There was much to do: his farms had deteriorated during his six years' absence, and even the mansion, one of his life's great works, had begun to suffer from neglect.

Jefferson was startled to see himself proclaimed in the newspapers and by local officials as the secretary of state. Once he saw the president's letter of appointment, which reached him in Norfolk, he recognized that it would be difficult to refuse. But he was determined to postpone his decision as long as he could. As much as he had missed Monticello—he savored the moment when he would again at last "plunge into the forests of Albemarle"—he missed Paris more, with its banquet of scintillating intellects, books, paintings, and fine wines, not to mention the luxurious life of the Hôtel de Langeac, where he (or rather his slaves and servants) had kept house. And of course there was the Revolution, which swirled through the city and country, overturning the old order, and in Jefferson's eyes seemed to promise the ultimate triumph of the rights of man that he celebrated. As he traveled homeward across Virginia, lingering to visit friends along the way, he fairly brimmed over with "favorable accounts" of the tumultuous events he had witnessed.

He finally reached Monticello two days before Christmas. (Then a two-story building, Monticello then looked quite different from its modern appearance: Jefferson would eventually remove the upper floor and replace it with the now iconic dome.) Later legend had it that Jefferson's jubilant slaves unhitched the horses from his carriage and pulled it up the mountain by hand, weeping tears of joy and kissing him as they carried him bodily into the great house. Whether or not this happened—by the mid-nineteenth century memories were thin, and such a scene lent itself to the imperatives of proslavery propaganda—Jefferson's slaves may well have been relieved to have him back after years of management by agents and overseers. Many had been leased out to other masters and were likely worried that their long-absent master's debts might mean slave sales and the permanent breakup of families. "They were cheering out of hope for themselves and their families within the very limited framework allotted to them, not necessarily for their unlimited love for the man who owned them," writes Jefferson biographer Annette Gordon-Reed.

There was much to be done: accounts to be put in order, plans for the tobacco crop to be determined, wagons to be organized to carry his trunks and foodstuffs from Richmond—a case of hats, shoes, four loaves of sugar, twenty-three pounds of cheese, tea, chocolate, coffee, three bottles of mustard, six codfish, and more. Perhaps he would manage to squeeze in a few games of tennis; his friend Edmund Randolph, he learned, had just sent him a pair of racquets, along with two bundles of "Elegant and Correct" maps, which were also certain to absorb the polymath attention of his copious mind.

Not until December 15 did Jefferson finally respond to the president's offer of appointment to the Department of State, and then it was with grave ambivalence. "When I contemplate the extent of that office, embracing as it does the principal mass of domestic administration, together with the foreign, I cannot be insensible to my inequality to it," he diplomatically wrote. In other words, it seemed like too much work, or at least too much work on things that didn't interest him. (Congress had shoehorned into the State Department a farrago of responsibilities that didn't seem to fit anywhere else—the patent office, the mint, the national census, copyrights, territorial affairs, land offices, and the archives—most of which would have been handled by the stillborn Home Department.) "I should enter on it with gloomy forebodings from the criticisms and censures of a public just indeed in their intentions, but sometimes misinformed and misled," he added. "I cannot but foresee the possibility that this may end disagreeably." He would much have preferred to return to France: "As far as my fears, my hopes, or my inclination might enter into this question, I confess they would not lead me to prefer a change." But he was willing to accept whatever the president desired, he fairly sighed. If he was compelled to become secretary of state, his only comfort, he wrote to George Washington, would "be to work under your eye, my only shelter the authority of your name." That is, he would expect heavy political cover from the president. In any event, he would not be prepared to leave Virginia until March, two months after Congress reconvened. Until then, the government would have to get along without him. Not even his friend James Madison, who rode over from Montpelier to see him just after Christmas, could make him budge.

"I was sorry to find him so little biased in favor of the domestic service allotted to him," Madison wrote to Washington. Madison had tried to convince Jefferson that the domestic responsibilities assigned to the State Department were too "trifling" to warrant a department of their own. But if the burden of them still proved too much for Jefferson, Madison had assured his friend, then "he will be relieved by a necessary division of it." Jefferson, he was saying, we must have you at all costs.

The close of the first session had suspended the rancorous debate over the nation's seat of government. But the partisans of a Potomac capital had been far from idle. They realized that if they were to overcome Pennsylvania, they had to win the support of Americans outside the South. In the autumn they launched what may have been the country's first nationwide public relations blitz. Their claims were founded for the most part on a widely circulated essay that appeared in a Baltimore newspaper in January 1789, by George Walker, a Georgetown businessman who tirelessly devoted himself to promotion of the Potomac's commercial potential. Writing anonymously as "A Citizen of the World," he proclaimed the river to be uniquely, indeed perfectly, situated for the creation of a world-class metropolis: it lay equidistant between the North and South, it could easily be defended against foreign invasion (so he imagined), and it would appeal to foreign investors who sought convenient access to the interior of the continent. "Thus a connexion and energy would be given to commerce and manufactures, the arts and sciences, civilization and elegant refinement, hitherto unknown in America," he enthused. Walker was also the first person to suggest placing the federal city-to-be between Rock Creek and the Eastern Branch of the Potomac, today known as the Anacostia River. Soon, he predicted, "A great city would be raised up as if by magic."

Walker's glorious vision captivated like-minded enthusiasts. Soon newspapers, broadsides, and pamphlets from around the region were declaring grandiosely that mighty industries that grew up with the capital city would someday "clothe and cherish the perishing sufferers in the wilds of Siberia, as well as the pampered Alderman on the English Exchange." And that was only the half of it. The new city was also destined to become the nation's gateway to the vast, undeveloped territories of the interior, as emigrants flocked through it, drawn by the beckoning lure of the West. Magic wasn't all: the ante was upped further when, in December, Virginia and Maryland jointly promised $192,000 for the construction of government buildings at a site to be selected anywhere on the Maryland side of the Potomac.

The southern party would also soon be fortified by the addition of North Carolina, which had finally ratified the Constitution in November, by a better than two-to-one majority. Residents of the coastal counties, where most of that state's trade was concentrated, had been "in a gr[e]at Pain on the Idea of being shut out from the Union," as one North Carolina Federalist put it, while embattled residents of the western districts wanted federal protection from the Indians, and—probably most important—Antifederalist resistance had been undercut by Congress's passage of the first amendments. Federalists were further heartened by the mood of conciliation demonstrated by the Constitution's opponents. The imminent arrival of North Carolina's five new representatives and two senators would mean that many more votes for a Potomac capital and, fellow southerners rejoiced, for the protection of slavery.

In New York City, the new year began with a combination of solemn thanksgiving and boozy abandon. Shops and offices shut, while churches opened for divine service, and families spent the day visiting and welcoming guests, to whom they typically offered a traditional local delicacy, "New Year's cookie"—a thick, crisp molded wafer imprinted with secular or religious designs—and tureens of "cherry bounce," a potent concoction made with fresh cherries, sugar, and rum or brandy. Abigail Adams sniffed that the common people were all too ready "to take rather too freely of the good things of this Life." In other words, they got drunk. "Finding two of my Servants not all together qualified for Business I remonstrated to them, but they excused it Saying it was New Year." But the evening was glorious. Bundling themselves against the cold, the Adamses drove across the fields of lower Manhattan to the president's mansion to attend the official holiday levee. Among women brilliantly dressed in great hooped skirts and festooned with diamonds, Abigail was nostalgically reminded of the ceremoniousness of the British court. As touchy about protocol as her husband, she appreciated the president's eviction of several women from the choice spot at Martha Washington's right hand in order to make room for her. For the Adamses, it counted as a social triumph.

In the days that followed, members of Congress began returning to the city, with the usual complaints about intolerable roads, bone-rattling coaches, and sick-making sea journeys. Representative Alexander White of northern Virginia was amused to read in the newspapers that he had drowned crossing the Hackensack River in New Jersey in a rainstorm. ("The ladies all alarmed—but no damage done.") Madison, however, was absent. Severe dysentery had struck him, forcing him to miss the opening of Congress while he recovered in Georgetown until, as he reported to his father, "[I] regained my flesh." Soon New York was all abustle. "Never since the war was so much activity seen here," exclaimed the new French minister, Louis-Guillaume Otto. The next session, he predicted, would be more important than the first, and more delicate, for "it will decide about the purse and the sword."

On January 8, 1790, promptly at 11:00 a.m., the president left his residence and settled himself in his canary-colored coach. Preceded by David Humphreys and the uniformed Major Jackson, both mounted on white chargers, his several other secretaries in the open presidential carriage, and Chief Justice Jay, Henry Knox, and Alexander Hamilton in their respective vehicles, the executive entourage progressed to Federal Hall. There the doorkeepers of the House and Senate escorted Washington upstairs to the Senate chamber, where the assembled members of both houses rose to greet him.

French minister Otto, in the audience that day, was pleasantly surprised by Washington's "happy mixture of authority and modesty." To his superiors in Paris he wrote, "While playing the role of the King of

England he mingles in the crowd of his fellow citizens and appears to give them advice rather than orders, to propose doubts to them rather than principles, to indicate to them the road to public prosperity rather than to want to lead them there himself." This apt observation would probably have pleased the president himself.

Washington began the first State of the Union speech in American history by welcoming North Carolina into the fold of states, and by extolling what he termed the "general and increasing good will towards the government." This wasn't boilerplate. The enactment of amendments had stalled the Antifederalist surge everywhere but Rhode Island, cooling public anger, and winning conditional support for the Constitution. Washington went on to commend Congress for what it had accomplished during the first session, particularly in light of "the novelty and difficulty of the work" it had undertaken.

Looking forward to the session that was about to begin, he focused, as so many future presidents would, on national security: "Providing for the common defense will merit particular regard. To be prepared for war is one of the most effectual means of preserving peace." Americans, who had virtually no army at all, had to face the need to gird themselves for their defense to deter future enemies. "A free people ought not only to be armed but disciplined, to which end a uniform and well-digested plan is requisite." Indeed, a "proper establishment" of troops was "indispensable." He was calling for a permanent military establishment, something that was anathema to citizens who regarded a standing army as a hallmark of tyranny. To underscore his point, Washington reminded his listeners that the "pacifick measures" that had been attempted with "certain hostile tribes of Indians" had failed to bear fruit, and that it was imperative to provide military security for the southern and western frontiers, "and, if necessary, to punish aggressors."

Washington next called for the speedy adoption of a smooth procedure for naturalization of immigrants to facilitate the transformation of foreigners into citizens, the establishment of a postal system, and for national uniformity in currency and in weights and measures. He further urged Congress to encourage new and useful inventions, and to actively foster American science and literature, either by subsidizing established institutions or creating a national university. Federal support for education, he declared, would contribute to the Constitution in numerous ways: "by teaching the people themselves to know, and to value their own rights; to discern and provide against invasions of them; to distinguish between oppression and the necessary exercise of lawful authority; between burthens proceeding from a disregard to their convenience, and those resulting from the inevitable exigencies of society; to discriminate the spirit of liberty from that of licentiousness . . . [and] an inviolable respect to the laws." Washington was calling for public subsidies for public works, a major national investment in higher education, and a broad agenda of enlightened, activist government.

Near the end of his remarks, seemingly almost as an afterthought, the president mentioned one other subject, "support of the publick credit," which he termed "a matter of high importance to the national honour and prosperity." He blandly expressed his confidence that Congress would devise a plan "as will be truly consistent with the end." The reason for his reticence was not immediately clear. But he well knew what Alexander Hamilton had been working on for the past two months, and he conspicuously declined to stake his name and his prestige on what was fast becoming the most controversial issue facing Congress, a problem so difficult that it would dominate the deliberations of Congress for months to come and threaten to shatter the still-frail national consensus that the first session of Congress had struggled so hard to preserve.

CHAPTER 12

The Labyrinth of Finance

————•+•————

Public credit, and confidence in the government being firmly estab-lished, private credit and confidence will as naturally result as vege-tation does from the approach of the sun.

—Charles Pettit, January 1790

Mid-January was bitterly cold, with crisp, clear days alternating with bouts of freezing rain, snow, and slushy thaws. New Yorkers were talking about plans to finally demolish the remains of Fort George, the crumbling eyesore at the foot of Broadway, and about the "extraordinary spirit of fanaticism prevailing" among local Methodists, which some feared would "spread like the influenza." In the city court, the law took its gloomy course: Thomas Night was to be hanged for highway robbery, Anne Tibu-rona (alias Anne Bunyan, alias Anne Drummond) had just been sentenced to two months in jail for bigamy, and John Alexander had received twenty lashes for horse stealing. Meanwhile, members of the city's taste-making elite were pleased to learn that copies of the popular comic opera *Patrick in Prussia, or Love in a Camp* were now for sale for one shilling and six at McGill's printery, that an exceptionally skillful Scottish cabinetmaker named Duncan Phyfe had recently opened a workshop near Federal Hall, and that the Water Street textile merchant John Delafield had just got in a new shipment of shalloons, velveteens, and printed Indian dimities suitable for fashionable waistcoats.

In the newspapers, there was good news from Virginia, where the House of Delegates had overcome Antifederalist opposition to approve the constitutional amendments proposed by Congress. Hopeful reports came from rejectionist Rhode Island, where another state convention was being called to reconsider ratification. On January 14, the *New-York Daily Advertiser* carried a bulletin from Maryland, where one hundred citizens, most of them Quakers, had submitted a petition to the state's General Assembly, calling for the abolition of slavery, and an end to the "disgraceful commerce" of the slave trade. Few New Yorkers seemed to be aware that delegations of Quakers were gathering with antislavery petitions and preparing for a lobbying campaign, which would soon rattle Congress and agitate the nation. "Finances are now the grand Topick here," reported one politically well-connected observer.

Alexander Hamilton was at a high pitch of anxiety. On the snowy afternoon of January 14, at Federal Hall, his past three months of intense labor would come to a climax. He would have preferred to deliver his "Report on Public Credit" to Congress in person. The intricate document had much that would need to be explained. He wanted to be there to answer the many difficult questions that were sure to come. But unfriendly members of Congress had made it clear that his presence would be regarded as an invasion by the executive branch of Congress's constitutionally sacrosanct preserve. Instead, his report would be read aloud by the clerk of the House of Representatives, John Beckley, a former mayor of Richmond and a noted calligrapher, a talent that was doubtless of some use in deciphering the fifty-one handwritten pages of Hamilton's prose.

Few members of Congress knew what to expect. "What his plans are is kept a secret," Representative Benjamin Goodhue of Massachusetts, a Federalist, wrote to a friend. "This will open a field of a very extensive, interesting, perplexing, and as I conceive of a most difficult nature." Although Goodhue personally supported the treasury secretary, he added, "I make no doubt his plan may strike the minds of many Gentlemen with disgust at its first promulgation."

Hamilton's report began with a primer on what he termed the "plain and undeniable truths" of finance. Even wealthy nations had to borrow money. In a new country such as the United States, "which is possessed of little active wealth," the need for reliable credit was all the more urgent. "To be able to borrow upon good terms, it is essential that the credit of a nation should be well established. For when the credit of a country is in any way questionable, it never fails to give an extravagant premium, in one shape or another, upon all the loans it has occasion to make." Hamilton was saying, if your credit is bad, it will cost you more to borrow. If the United States could not borrow on favorable terms, "the individual and aggregate prosperity of the citizens of the United States, their character as a people [and] the cause of good government," all must suffer. How was the nation's credit to be guaranteed? By good faith, and by punctually honoring contracts. "States, like individuals, who observe their engagements, are respected and trusted, while the reverse is the fate of those who pursue an opposite conduct."

Good credit was more than a moral obligation. "It was," Hamilton reminded Congress, "the price of liberty. The faith of America has been repeatedly pledged for it." Thus far, however, the nation had failed to keep its promises. The time for excuses was long past. The nation's obligations had to be met "to promote the encreasing respectability of the American name; to answer the calls of justice; to restore landed property to its due value; to furnish new resources both to agriculture and commerce; to cement more closely the union of the states; to add to their security against foreign attack; to establish public order on the basis of an upright and liberal policy."

Then came the numbers. Hamilton estimated the par value of the combined federal and state Revolutionary War debt at $79 million, a monstrously large figure. Of this, Hamilton calculated the foreign debt at $12 million in principal, plus $10 million in overdue interest, and estimated the combined, more complex domestic debt at about $29 million in principal, plus some $25 million in interest. (The actual total may have been closer to $74 million, but it was still a chokingly large sum.) For the foreseeable future, Hamilton projected federal income at a mere $2.8 million annually, from which the government's running expenses would have to be subtracted. (The resulting ratio of debt to income would be 26.4 to 1, "by far the highest in American history," according to Thomas McCraw.) To address the debt, Hamilton proposed not levying heavy taxes—the conventional course—but refinancing it by borrowing *more* money, an expedient that horrified many members of Congress and other Americans, who regarded debt as a sin.

Hamilton then explained one of his most provocative ideas: that debt could be used as a creative force. As the interest on debt was paid, the debt's value would increase, adding to the creditors' assets, because the borrower—in this case the United States—was proving the trustworthiness of its commitment. The national debt could then become a commodity that could profitably be bought and sold in the financial marketplace. Creditors would support national stability, in their own self-interest, while the shared debt would help bind the states more closely together, and at the same time create an alliance with the banks that would make possible dynamic economic growth for all. Debt would, in effect, become a substitute for money. In turn, the nation's economy could be stimulated because more capital would be circulating to invest in manufacturing, commerce, and agriculture.

Hamilton went further. He proposed that most of the war debts of the states be *assumed* by the federal government—that is, folded into the federal debt—and that the Treasury issue its own new securities to replace the old ones. This would dramatically strengthen the federal government, but it would antagonize the defenders of states' rights, Hamilton well knew. He further proposed that creditors be paid the full face value of the old securities that they already held. This, too, would produce ferocious opposition, and not only from the Antifederalists. Many patriotic Americans utterly loathed financial speculators as a species and reserved a special malice for those who stood to reap a fortune if Hamilton's program was enacted. As one horrified Mainer demanded of Representative Thatcher, "How can it be right that the poor and perhaps Bleeding Soldiers which sold his Notes of one hundred pounds for Ten should now be obliged to Swett Even Blood to pay the Ninety he was Cheated out of by Some Viliane who in the war was afrad to Turn out and Stand a Mark for the Enemey to shoot at?"

Hamilton had yet one more idea up his sleeve. Nearly all the government's outstanding loans were set at 6 percent. Hamilton would reduce the rate to 4 percent, mainly by the sale of federal land to replace the missing 2 percent. In this he hoped that creditors would "chearfully concur," since they ought to be glad to get 4 percent of something rather than 6 percent of nothing that they were getting now. This would mean a massive reduction in the amount of money the government would have to pay out over the coming decades.

Critics would charge that Hamilton's plans would cast the nation into a hopeless spiral of unending debt from which it would never recover. In fact, although he regarded the refinancing of the present debt as "a national blessing," he regarded permanent debt as "a position inviting to prodigality, and liable to dangerous abuse." He therefore advised that "the creation of debt should always be accompanied with the means of extinguishment." A certain portion of the government's annual receipts from import duties ought therefore to be set aside as a sinking fund—a cash reserve—that could be drawn on in times of crisis. This, he declared, was "the true secret for rendering public credit immortal."

The report was a tour de force. Although Hamilton's ideas were not wholly original—they were based partly on precedents established by Robert Morris when he was the superintendent of finance for the Confederation Congress—his synthesis of diverse theories, and his pragmatic application of them to the nation's pressing financial crisis, was brilliant. No American had ever advanced such a comprehensive and ambitious economic plan. Its outcome was far from foreordained, however. The treasury secretary believed that the economy would burgeon dynamically, but whether the government would actually take in as much revenue as he projected was uncertain. If the economy failed to grow, there wouldn't be enough money to pay the interest on the national debt, much less run the federal government. (In 1789, the government had just $0.162 million in revenues, and in 1790 it would take in a still-modest $1.6 million.)

To much of the public, it seemed that their legislators were lost "in the labyrinth of Finance," as one confused Yankee put it. A befuddled Marylander similarly wrote his congressman, "I confess that I do not comprehend the magick of the funding systems sufficiently to know why, like a charm, they should more than everything else conciliate the public confidence." Most members of Congress weren't much clearer about what Hamilton intended. Representative Jeremiah Wadsworth of Connecticut, who *supported* Hamilton's plan, confessed, "Finance is of a nature so complicated that to comprehend it requires more real physical skill and mathematical knowledge than I am possessed of. We have been so little accustomed to system, and have lived so long at loose, that we are scared out of our wits at the sight of a long financeering report."

Once they took in the full implications of Hamilton's plan, most Federalists were well pleased by it. William Bradford Jr., the attorney general of Pennsylvania and son-in-law of Elias Boudinot, optimistically predicted that it would once and for all "cut up by the roots all those jealousies & heart-burnings which have taken place between the different states." Fisher Ames thought it "a masterly performance." So did Robert Morris, who crowed, "Credit, public Credit particularly, is a *Jewell* so invaluable as to exceed all price." Morris also saw nothing unethical in exploiting his information by immediately dispatching an agent to buy up as many discounted securities as he could before their prices rose.

Others saw great danger in Hamilton's plan. Wild rumors abounded. Some claimed that the treasury secretary was secretly conspiring with certain state governors and contractors; others that a cabal of army quartermasters intended to issue more securities in their own names and would become fabulously rich when they were redeemed; still others that speculators had already drained the Bank of New York of specie and were buying whole

townships and counties, where they would set themselves up as an aristocracy. "I sicken every time I contemplate the European Vices that the Secretary's gambling report will necessarily introduce into our infant republic,"
Benjamin Rush wrote Madison. Rush feverishly predicted that rewarding
speculators "will rank hereafter with the Slavery of the Africans by our
Southern states, and with the ravages committed by Great Britain upon
property & life in America during the late War." The Antifederalist Richard
Henry Lee of Virginia considered Hamilton's "political tricks" abominable
to a free people and warned that his scheme would lead only to unending
debt "encouraged by wanton expeditions, wars & useless expences."

The fiercest attack on the funding plan came from James Jackson of
Georgia. To packed galleries, he complained that in the two weeks since
Hamilton's report had been issued, speculators "as rapacious as wolves"
had swarmed out of New York to sweep up securities from unsuspecting
citizens. "My soul rises indignant at the avaricious and immoral turpitude
which so vile a conduct displays," he declared. As overwrought as Jackson
could often be, this time he wasn't too far off the mark. Assistant Secretary of the Treasury William Duer, like many other insiders, was buying
as many securities as he could on the sly, while the newly named Representative Hugh Williamson of North Carolina was writing to a friend
back home urging him "to buy up all you can" of old securities, promising
that he would "dispose of them here as fast as you can send them on."

The volatile Jackson, who would continue to play a forceful role in the
funding debate, had arrived late in New York after a "violent passage" by
ship from Savannah and was still settling in. Despite his swaggering and
bullying on the floor of Congress, his private letters reveal a surprisingly
warm and uxorious man, complaining of his bachelor state, with its "cold
Climate & Beds," and adding that "most People can console themselves
on these occasions with temporary comforts. I have not yet been able to
conquer the foolish ideas of the strict ties of matrimonial connections nor
do I wish it." In other words, he missed his wife, Mary, and five children,
and shunned whoring with his pals. Such sentimentality, however, was
rarely, if ever, on display in the House.

Jackson now predicted that utter national ruin would result if Hamilton's plan—"a dangerous leap in the dark"—was adopted. "Though our present debt be but a few millions, in the course of a single century they may be multiplied to an extent we dare not think of." Like an "*ignis fatuus*," a false flame, the secretary's scheme "will deceive us, and lead us and our posterity into a wilderness of politics from which we shall never be able to extricate ourselves." He then made a passionate plea for the healthful influence of direct taxation, which he asserted would have a halcyon effect on both personal and national character. "For my part, I would rather have direct taxes imposed at once, which in the course of a few years should annihilate the principle of our debt." Jackson blamed the fever of speculation squarely on what he insisted was the corrupting influence of New York City—a theme that he and others would soon renew with particular verbal savagery when debate over the permanent seat of the federal government was renewed. "I wish to God that we had been on the banks of the Susquehanna or Potomack, or any place in the woods, and out of the neighborhood of a populous city," where the government's deliberations could have been kept private, he declaimed. Jackson's sentiments were echoed in the Senate by Maclay, whose puritanism rebelled at the notion of institutionalized debt.

It quickly became clear that the initial battle over debt would focus on the highly charged issue of "discrimination," as everyone termed it: that is, whether to pay the current holders of securities at face value, or to disfavor them—to *discriminate* against them—by reimbursing only what they had paid for the certificates, and to pay to the securities' original recipients the difference between the face value and whatever fraction of that amount they had sold them for. This was not simply a matter of logic and law. An emotive patriotic mythology had grown up around the securities. "Look at the gallant veteran, who nobly led your martial bands in the hour of extreme danger," pleaded Jackson. "See him deprived of those limbs which he sacrificed in your service! And behold his virtuous and tender wife, sustaining him and his children in a wilderness, lonely, exposed to the arms of savages, where he and his family have been driven" by speculators who had drained from him his last pittance.

In fact, no one knew just how many securities were issued, how many former soldiers had sold theirs to speculators or, with any detail, for what price. Nor did many remember just how the securities had become so widely disseminated. Congress had initially made the securities nontransferable; it had never envisioned any further payment to veterans. Soldiers themselves had demanded the right to sell them after the end of the war, in hope of recouping something from instruments that then seemed utterly worthless. That didn't stop Representative Thomas Scott of Pennsylvania from scathingly likening veterans who had bought up others' securities to whores who "have since wedded to Mrs. Speculator, by which they have lost all title to the honorable appellation of a soldier."

Opponents of discrimination were equally vehement. Fisher Ames reminded his colleagues that failing to pay the current holders full value would be a blatant breach of contract: they had bought the securities in good faith precisely because they hoped to make a profit on them. If the securities' profitability could be undone on a political whim, however well intentioned, it would shrink or even wipe out their value. "Must every transaction that took place during the course of the last war be ripped up?" he demanded. "If this is the case, what kind of rights will the people have in their property? What security will they derive from a new promise?" None: "The public faith will be destroyed, our future credit a mere vapor." Speculation, others pointed out, was a violation of neither moral nor political law. "A love of property is a political virtue; remove this motive and civilized society will be destroyed," declared Jeremiah Wadsworth. "A power to alienate property is one of the rights of man, which government ought not to invade." At bottom, the debate was not just about the pros and cons of discrimination, but about the American future, and about what kind of nation the United States was going to be, one in which capitalism would be embraced as a driving engine of federal policy, or whether it would be trumped by a rejection of creative finance and a largely mythical vision of self-sufficient agrarian innocence.

For weeks, as debate raged around Hamilton's plan, James Madison said almost nothing. When at last he rose to speak on February 11, nearly a month after John Beckley had delivered the "Report on Public Credit," expectations were high. Many took it for granted that he would assume leadership of the increasingly emotional debate as he had during the first session, and that he would use his persuasive gifts to lead the warring parties to an amicable compromise. Like Jackson, Madison had also come late to the session, not arriving until the third week of January, and suffering from a painful attack of piles, which had made his journey north a hellish feat of endurance.

The problem of funding was difficult, Madison admitted. He had tried "to view it under all its aspects, and analyze it into all its principles," and had thus far "chused rather to be a hearer than a speaker." But now, because of "the turn which the arguments had taken"—he probably meant the violence of emotion that increasingly threatened to overwhelm reason—he felt that he had to speak. What he said next shocked his friends, Hamilton most of all. Madison had, he declared, "never been a proselyte to the doctrine that public debts are public benefits." He "considered them, on the contrary, as evils which ought to be removed as fast as honor and justice would permit." He rejected the entire foundation of Hamilton's plan, and the belief that debt could and should be exploited as a tool of activist government. "A Public Debt is a Public curse, and in a Representative Government a greater [curse] than in any other," he wrote to Richard Henry Lee.

He also wholeheartedly embraced discrimination, declaring with uncharacteristic emotion that "the sufferings of the military part of the creditors can never be forgotten, while sympathy is an American virtue." Earlier, in tune with Hamilton, whom he considered a friendly colleague rather than a close friend, Madison had put himself on record as a supporter of paying face value to all the holders of government securities. Now, dramatically abandoning that ground, he claimed that there was "something radically immoral" about stripping the value of the securities from "the gallant earners of them." He also strongly suspected that many of the securities had been acquired fraudulently, which he felt morally negated the claims of their present holders.

Yet, he conceded, the government did have an undeniable duty to discharge its debt to its creditors: "No logic, no magic, could dissolve this obligation." Three things could be done, he said: pay both categories of claimants in full, reject one or the other, or work out a compromise between them. To pay both was beyond the country's resources. On the other hand, "to reject wholly the claims of either is equally inadmissible." National stability demanded that contracts be respected, while "human nature recoiled" at the idea of making the original holders "the sole victims" of national policy. Therefore, the only option was obviously compromise. "Let it be a liberal one in favor of the present holders; let them have the highest price which has prevailed in the market," he said, in a seeming concession to investors. But this still meant just a fraction of the securities' face value. Meanwhile, the difference between the face value and the current market price would be paid by the government to the original "sufferers." Said Madison, "This will not do perfect justice; but it will do more real justice, and perform more of the public faith, than any other expedient proposed. The original sufferers will not be fully indemnified, but they will receive from their country a tribute due to their merits, which, if it does not entirely heal their wounds, will assuage the pain of them." It was not a great speech. But it was a quintessentially Madisonian attempt to square the political circle.

Some liked it. An anonymous veteran, writing in the *Massachusetts Centinel*, praised Madison, "who, fearless of the wreathing of bloodsuckers will step forward and boldly vindicate the rights of the widow and orphan, the original creditor, and The War-Worn Soldier." And another anonymous fan poetized:

A Madison above the rest,
Pouring from his narrow chest,
More than Greek or Roman sense,
Floods of Truth and Eloquence.

The reactions of most Federalists, however, ranged from disgust to pity. One sneering letter writer to the *New-York Daily Advertiser* dismissed

Madison's proposal as "Hocus Pocus Humbug," while Representative Thomas Fitzsimons of Pennsylvania scathingly remarked, "Tho Mr. Madison has done honor to his feelings as a man, he has forfeited all character, & that of a legislator by advocating the measure." Another member of the Pennsylvania delegation, Thomas Hartley, was impressed by the elegance of Madison's delivery, but thought that "it had more the Scent of the Chamber Lamp than generally appears in his Productions—in short that it was not founded upon practical life." Indeed, discrimination as Madison envisioned it posed a massive logistical problem that he left unaddressed. Tens of thousands of securities had been sold and resold any number of times. Records were scant, and the infant federal government possessed no one trained to investigate, sort out, and evaluate competing claims. To do so would entail an investment of resources far beyond the government's abilities, not to mention many years of difficult work.

Madison was taking a considerable risk. Up to now, in the eyes of many, he had enjoyed the enviable role of a sort of American philosopher prince above workaday politics, almost miraculously able to get what he wanted from Congress without offending anyone. The honeymoon, which had begun to pall during the autumn debate over the federal capital, was clearly over. Business-oriented Federalists now decided that Madison, whatever his virtues as a thinker, knew little about finance. Although he had read Adam Smith and understood Hamilton's thinking, he was repelled by the Treasury Secretary's affection for a "British" system that would, Madison feared, lead to the creation of a new aristocracy of money men. Madison was also evidently more concerned about his reelection than about crafting viable policy and had yielded his principles to appeal to his voters in Virginia. The unfolding debate would prove to be a watershed, inexorably reshaping Madison's role in Congress, his relationship with Alexander Hamilton, and his politically potent intimacy with George Washington.

CHAPTER 13

A Gross National Iniquity

When we entered into this confederacy, we did it from political, not moral motives, and I do not think my constituents want to learn morals from the petitioners.

—William Loughton Smith, February 1790

J anuary bled into an equally slushy and flu-ridden February. Bundled in their boardinghouses and the frosty corridors of Federal Hall, members of Congress ruminated gloomily about the desperate pleas for help that had been received from American sailors held by the Barbary pirates, and the dispiriting news from Rhode Island, which still refused to ratify the Constitution—"Blasting our Sanguwine Expectations," as John Adams exasperatedly put it—provoking some to threaten an embargo, or even the dispatch of troops to bring the defiant state to heel. Gathered in front of the fire in their favorite taverns, they chatted about President Washington's move from the distant Cherry Street house to the grander and more comfortable Macomb mansion at the foot of Broadway, swapped rumors about the imminent demise of the ailing Senator William Grayson of Virginia, or complained about the maddening state of the federal archive, where it could take weeks of wading through the chaos of old papers to find a single document, now that their longtime keeper, Charles Thomson, had retired.

On February 2, the Supreme Court convened for the first time at the Royal Exchange Building on Broad Street, a few steps from Federal Hall. Symbolically, the moment was pregnant with promise for the republic, this birth of a new national institution whose future power, admittedly, still existed only in the mind's eye of a few farsighted Americans. Impressively bewigged and swathed in their robes of office, Chief Justice Jay and three associate justices—William Cushing of Massachusetts, James Wilson of Pennsylvania, and John Blair of Virginia—sat augustly before a throng of spectators and waited for something to happen. Nothing did. They had no cases to consider. After a week of inactivity, they adjourned until September, and everyone went home. But no one seemed to mind too much. The real action was up the street at Federal Hall.

More pressing matters were on members' minds. Secretary of War Knox's "Report on the Militia" had provoked considerable agitation. It was the government's first attempt to create a system of national defense without resorting to the politically unpalatable expedient of a standing army. Knox, a classics-minded former Boston bookseller who had risen to become George Washington's chief of artillery, proposed that all able-bodied white men be organized into grand "corps": an Advanced Corps of those from eighteen to twenty, a Main Corps of those from twenty-one to forty-five, and a Reserved Corps for those forty-six and older. These three corps would in turn be subdivided into "legions" of three thousand men each, modeled on those of the ancient Roman republic. Men in the youngest group would be called up for training one month out of each year. They would eventually graduate to the Main Corps, which would be the first line of defense and would be supplemented when necessary by veterans from the Reserved Corps.

Public opposition to Knox's scheme was intense. In Salem, Massachusetts, citizens threatened to burn him in effigy, along with copies of his plan. Critics raged that it would take thousands of northern white men away from their work, while in the South blacks—who performed comparable labor—would be excluded, to the profit of their masters. Others protested that the young draftees would "acquire such a habit of Idelness that it will be allmost imposeable to Eradicate it, & make them Service-able as before, & will have attendancy to Corrupt there Moralls," and that the expense of maintaining troops in peacetime would be insupportable for a government that was already insolvent. Benjamin Rush, who though a Presbyterian was influenced by Quaker pacifism, denounced the whole idea of a military, declaring that it seemed to "consider man as created not to cultivate the earth [but] to wear a regimental coat—& to kill or be killed," and suggested that if just half the money that Knox was asking for was spent building schools and teaching young people morality, it would banish war forever from the United States.

Controversy also arose over the proposed census, the nation's first. Members complained that the plan—which would enumerate all white inhabitants of the United States, other "free persons" (except Indians, who paid no taxes), and slaves—was too ambitious, too detailed, and subdi-vided the population into "classes too minute," including every imaginable profession from merchants and landowners to stocking weavers and hat-makers. Besides that, New Hampshire representative Samuel Livermore warned, Americans would resent federal agents invading their privacy and suspect that the government was secretly trying to assess their ability to pay taxes. In the census's defense, rejoined Madison, didn't members want to know when Congress debated bills bearing on agriculture, commerce, manufacturing, and the various trades how many citizens were actually engaged in such activities, and what proportion of the population they were, so that when Congress made policy "they might rest their argu-ments on facts, instead of assertions and conjectures"?

The naturalization bill also prompted a short, sharp debate that fore-shadowed the nation's persistent ambivalence about immigration, which for generations to come would pit nativist anxieties against those who believed that America was a transformative engine that would remake foreigners into a new kind of republican. What should be required to be-come a citizen? members asked each other. Was a simple oath of allegiance enough? Should there be some kind of residence requirement? Should new immigrants be allowed to vote? Should naturalization be uniform throughout the country, or should it be left to the states to set their own rules? What about people who left the country and stayed away—should they lose their citizenship? Wouldn't foreign merchants and ships' captains become Americans simply to avoid the duties levied on their vessels? (Such seamen were "but leeches—they stick to us until they get their fill of our best blood, and then they fall off and leave us," Representative Aedanus Burke of South Carolina fulminated.) Theodore Sedgwick of Massachusetts, though liberal on the subject of race, was a nativist on immigration, fearing that the United States was in danger of being "overrun with the outcasts of Europe," and urged that none but "reputable and worthy characters" be admitted.

In answer to such fears, Representative John Page of Virginia—one of the largest slaveowners in the state, but often conciliatory on national issues—replied, "We shall be inconsistent with ourselves if, after boasting of having opened an asylum for the oppressed of all nations, and established a government which is the admiration of the world, we make the terms of admission to the full enjoyment of that asylum and government so hard as is now proposed. It is nothing to us whether Jews, or Roman Catholics, settle amongst us; whether subjects of kings or citizens of free states wish to reside in the United States, they will find it their interest to be good citizens; and neither their religious or political opinions can injure us, if we have good laws, well executed."

When James Jackson suggested with his customary splenetic vigor that grand juries ought to be impaneled to judge the worth of each immigrant, Page responded with a cutting irony that, for once, seemed to silence the Georgian, himself an immigrant. "We must [then] add an inquisition," Page said, and since it would probably not be sufficient to ensure "immaculate citizens," then a bureaucracy of censors ought to be added, to banish the immoral who were already citizens. "Indeed, I fear, if we go on as is proposed now, in the infancy of our republic, we shall in time require a test of faith and politics of every person who shall come into these states."

·   ·   ·

The militia, the census, citizenship: these were contentious issues, but few doubted that what disagreements existed could be reconciled through gentlemanly negotiation. Slavery was another matter. In mid-February, it burst like an unwanted guest at a dinner party onto the floor of Congress. What followed was the bluntest public defense yet heard in an open forum of slavery as an essential and eternal component of the nation's political, economic, and social fabric.

On February 6, eleven Philadelphia Quakers appeared in New York to begin the first systematic lobbying campaign in American history. They were led by sixty-three-year-old John Pemberton, a Quaker minister and brother of James Pemberton, vice president of the prolixly named Pennsylvania Society for Promoting the Abolition of Slavery, for the Relief of Free Negroes Unlawfully Held in Bondage, & for Improving the Condition of the African Race, usually known simply as the Pennsylvania Abolition Society. Joined by their local coreligionists, they "way-laid" members in the lobby of Congress and "assailed" them in their homes and boardinghouses, on street corners, and in the taverns where they dined, begging their support for a trinity of antislavery petitions that within days would provoke one of the most incendiary battles of the First Congress. They distributed as they went a blizzard of antislavery pamphlets: essays by the famous British abolitionist Thomas Clarkson, copies of recent English legislation, an excerpt from Thomas Jefferson's *Notes on the State of Virginia*, and a shocking, fact-based diagram showing the deadly overcrowding on a typical slave ship, where mortality sometimes reached 50 percent.

Five days later, on February 11, Pennsylvania representative Thomas Fitzsimons, a Catholic, formally presented the first of the Quaker petitions. Drafted by the Philadelphia Yearly Meeting, which represented Quakers in several of the middle states, it called upon Congress "with a sense of religious duty" to put an end to "the gross national iniquity of trafficking in the persons of fellow-men," and "the inhuman tyranny and blood guiltiness inseparable from it." Representative John Laurance, a non-Quaker Protestant and a member of the New York Manumission Society, then introduced a petition from the Quakers' New York Yearly Meeting begging Congress to prohibit slave ships from fitting out in the state's ports, a measure that the state legislature had recently declined to address, claiming that such commerce was the responsibility of the federal government. The petitions didn't make much initial impression on the half-filled House chamber. "Few appeared to give much attention; more was given to conversation and News papers," John Pemberton disappointedly reported that afternoon.

The next morning, House Speaker Frederick Muhlenburg introduced the third petition, from the nonsectarian but Quaker-dominated Pennsylvania Abolition Society. It was signed by Benjamin Franklin, now eighty-four years old, the society's president. "From a persuasion that equal liberty was originally the Portion, & is still the Birthright of all men, [we are] bound to use all justifiable measures to loosen the bonds of Slavery & promote a general enjoyment of the blessings of Freedom," the petition declared. It begged Congress "to countenance the Restoration of liberty to those unhappy Men, who alone in this land of Freedom [are] degraded into perpetual Bondage." It further, and most provocatively, called upon Congress to interpret its powers so broadly that it could rid the United States of slavery's curse. The language was dispassionate, but its meaning was clear: it was calling for a national commitment to emancipation. It landed like a bombshell. Criticism of the slave *trade* might be irritating, but it was marginally respectable. To members from the lower South, talking openly about abolition was racial treason.

Franklin remained in Philadelphia, but his name on the petition guaranteed that it could not be ignored. Hamilton's financial plan was temporarily pushed aside, as Congress surrendered to the subject it least wanted to discuss. Franklin's long life reached back to an era when bondage was common even in his native New England and went largely unquestioned and unjudged. As early as 1729, he had published Quaker tracts against slavery, even though he continued to own slaves himself and well into middle age openly expressed physical distaste for blacks, asking, "Why increase the sons of Africa by planting them in America, where we have so fair an opportunity, by excluding all blacks and tawneys, of increasing the lovely white and red?" He eventually came to believe that blacks' natural abilities were equal to whites', and to regard slavery as "an atrocious debasement of human nature." He had come to the Constitutional Convention with a proposal for the inclusion of a condemnation of slavery and the slave trade, but quickly realized that even his immense prestige could not win its passage without destroying southern support for the Constitution. Now he was dying, and he wanted to put slavery onto the national agenda while he still could.

The Quakers' labors had been crowned with success in Pennsylvania, which had a decade earlier voted to end slavery in that state by 1799. But the Quakers were now in a far more challenging arena. The Constitution had left the federal government hostage to the inflexible imperatives of slavery: the three-fifths compromise that allowed each slave state to count that proportion of its enslaved population toward its congressional representation was a logical monstrosity, but it palliated southern anxieties by writing the protection of slavery into the nation's founding document. Antislavery delegates to the Constitutional Convention had reasoned, or at least rationalized, that since slavery was already on its way toward peaceful extinction, as many then hoped, it was wiser to leave it alone than to risk losing the southern states to the new federal union.

Quakers' opposition to slavery was rooted in both a palpable fear of sin and hellfire, and the belief that a universal "divine light" was manifest in the soul of every person, female and male, white and black, and that to claim ownership of another human being was therefore not only a moral but a spiritual crime. "The Colour of a man avails nothing in Matters of Right and Equity: Negroes are our fellow creatures," John Woolman of New Jersey, whose influential midcentury preaching maintained that no slaveowning Friend could hope to gain salvation, had written in words that were quite radical for their time.

Beginning in the 1760s, almost every Quaker meeting from Pennsylvania to New England had appointed committees to persuade slave-owning Friends to free their human property. Manumission was a process rather than a single event. Even in the north, it might take years for the members of a given meeting to free all their slaves. In southern states, it would take decades. Sin and redemption apart, most Quakers shared views that were racist by modern standards: they permitted few blacks to join the Society of Friends, and most believed, as James Pemberton did, that racial intermarriage would "reverse the order of Divine Providence who in his wisdom inscrutable to us has been pleased to form distinction of Colour." They were also gradualists who believed that slavery should be ended only by institutional action, not by disruptive popular agitation. Antislavery attitudes inspired by idealistic notions of the secular rights of man percolated more slowly through northern communities; slavery, though on the wane, was still woven into the fabric of many families' lives. Nominally antislavery senator Oliver Ellsworth of Connecticut, for instance, was even now casually negotiating for the purchase of "a negro girl," whom he would not take "as a slave for life," but would plan to free at the age of twenty-five.

The reaction of slaveholders to the Quaker petitions was explosive. Reported John Pemberton, "The southern members seem very averse to a prohibition of this wicked traffic." This was quintessential Quaker understatement. For hours on end, slavery's defenders—mainly the Georgians and South Carolinians—held the floor, haranguing their colleagues in what was in effect a filibuster, although the term would not come into use for many more years. They accused the Quakers of "intemperate and unwarrantable meddling," of "an intolerant spirit of persecution" against the slave states, of disloyalty, cowardice during the Revolutionary War, and the promotion of "Insurrections & bloodshed & persecution."

Abraham Baldwin, a former Yale minister from Connecticut, now living in Georgia and committed to slavery, declared that the petitions were unconstitutional and no more worthy of respect than ones that "prayed us to establish an order of nobility or a national religion." Thomas Tudor

Tucker of South Carolina declared the petitions would merely buoy slaves with false hopes, "and as they could not reason on the subject, as more enlightened men would, they might be led to do what they would be punished for," warning that a general emancipation "would never be submitted to by the southern states without a civil war." To this, his fellow Carolinian William Loughton Smith truculently added, "When we entered into this confederacy, we did it from political, not moral motives, and I do not think my constituents want to learn morals from the petitioners."

James Jackson declared that if the Quakers were so eager to free the Negroes, they ought to step forward and buy them in the open. If not, they ought to shut up and mind their own business. Religion "from Genesis to Revelations" had approved of slavery, along with every government on earth including "the purest sons of freedom in the Grecian republics, the citizens of Athens and Lacedaemon," and the feudal system. Who were the Quakers to lecture to anyone? Did they write the Constitution? Did they fight for independence? (This was a telling blow: as pacifists, Quakers generally stood aside during the war, and some—including the Pemberton brothers—had been interned as crown loyalists.) Was Congress now, at *their* instigation, to injure southern, slaveowning patriots who had risked their lives and fortunes on behalf of liberty?

In response, the usually caustic Elbridge Gerry of Massachusetts, who was as staunch an enemy of slavery as he was a defender of states' rights, warmly confessed that when he thought about the slave trade, he couldn't help but visualize his own children and friends subjected to the same unspeakable miseries as helpless Africans. The Quakers' cause was the cause of humanity itself, he said, and he wished "with them, to see measures pursued by every nation to wipe off the indelible stain which the slave trade had brought upon all who were concerned in it." Indeed, Congress was well within its rights to purchase every slave in the southern states and then free them, and to pay for it by the sale of public lands in the West. Gerry had just broached the only policy that might peacefully have freed the nation's slaves and forestalled civil war, but it fell upon deaf ears.

Thomas Scott, the frontiersman from western Pennsylvania and president of his county's abolition society, added, "I look upon the slave trade as one of the most abominable things on earth. I do not know how far I might go if I was one of the judges of the United States, and those people were to come before me and claim their emancipation, but I am sure I would go as far as I could." To this, Jackson retorted that if Scott were a federal judge who dared to emancipate slaves who came before him, "I believe his judgment would be of short duration in Georgia," adding threateningly, "perhaps even the existence of such a judge might be in danger."

After two days' debate, Representative William Loughton Smith of South Carolina smugly wrote to Edward Rutledge, a fellow slaveowner, "We had a great deal of warm debate about these cursed negro petitions, & I think we so effectually tired the members out & embarrassed them that they will not be in a hurry to bring the subject on again." This was an overly optimistic assessment.

The three petitions were finally referred to a select committee headed by Representative Abiel Foster of New Hampshire, who was also a Congregationalist minister. (New Hampshire was ending slavery, but would be found by the 1790 census still to have 158 slaves within its borders.) The committee was intended to include members from each state. However, every southern state except Virginia refused to participate. When the committee began its deliberations on February 15, several Quakers showed up at Federal Hall to further urge Congress to "open the Eyes of the People" to the iniquity and injustice of the slave trade. They reiterated their by-now-familiar concern that out-of-state slave ships were freely re-fitting in New York Harbor and introduced additional information on the *reenslavement* of freed blacks in both North Carolina and Virginia. Was it not Congress's duty, they asked, to frame regulations addressing "the condition of the oppress'd Africans," in order "by proper and wise gradations [to] advance them nearer to an equality with their fellow men & render them in time more fit for a state of freedom"?

The notes from this hearing, the earliest surviving record of oral testimony before a congressional committee, were made by one of the more extraordinary personalities to make his way, sometimes blunderingly, through the annals of the First Congress. At forty-five, Warner Mifflin stood more than six feet tall and fairly oozed shame and remorse for his years as a wealthy slaveholding Quaker farmer in Delaware. When, on February 16, nearly all the other Pennsylvania Quakers left the city, Mifflin remained, along with John Pemberton. Despite a bad cold he became a hulking gadfly, day after day circulating among the proslavery members of Congress, pleading, cajoling, and (in their view) making himself an insufferable nuisance on behalf of the preposterous notion of black freedom.

On February 26, an overwrought Mifflin "stalked" into William Loughton Smith's parlor, as the genteel Smith put it, and for two hours they "endeavored to convert each other in vain." Although neither man left a detailed account of their no doubt blustery encounter, Mifflin later wrote to Smith, probably reiterating the gist of what he had said in person. "I wish thee well—and would not injure thee knowingly more than I would myself," Mifflin said, assuring Smith that he had no intention of "corrupting" his servants, or making them "dissatisfied in their condition." Mifflin confessed that he had personally received a "prejudiced education in favor of negro holding" and would never have given up his own slaves "if I could have conceived that I might have got to heaven and have kept them." But he had come to believe that, as a slaveowner, "the main avenues to that kingdom, would have been effectually shut against me." God mandated, he said, that a Christian must love God and his neighbor as himself. It was inescapable that a man who loved his neighbor as himself could not hold that neighbor as chattel property. Not only had he emancipated his own slaves, but also those belonging to an estate of which he was the executor. But this transcended the personal, he emphasized. "I do much desire also, to remove in the Lord's way and time the guilt from our nation: for this cause my concern is great, to stop, as much as can be done with competency, the wicked, barbarous, and devilish trade to Africa for slaves. Did ever the people of Africa injure us in any sense? Then why should we desire to so grievously afflict them?" In an era that highly valued stoic self-restraint, Mifflin's sense of insupportable guilt fairly palpitated. "Oh horrible, horrible indeed! Thus I feel; how can I help it? It is disagreeable to me to have those sensations—I cannot help them—and so am constrained to plead with others."

When Smith finally tired of this weepy giant, he sent Mifflin to see his father-in-law, South Carolina senator Ralph Izard, another firebrand on the subject of slavery, who lived a couple of doors up Broadway, opposite Bowling Green. An hour later, when Smith himself went to Izard's home, he found the two men "in close debate attacking each other with Texts of Scripture." The aristocratic senator Pierce Butler of South Carolina was also there, and Smith smugly reported, "We all fell foul of friend Mifflin who was glad to make a retreat."

The Quakers had expected stronger support for their petitions in the Senate, but they were again disappointed. John Adams read the petitions to the chamber on February 15, but he did so, William Maclay reported, "with rather a sneer," seeming to indicate that he was performing an official but highly distasteful function. (Although Adams loathed slavery, he had little use for Quakers, who had reprimanded him during the war for allegedly discriminating against their sect, or for Benjamin Franklin, whom he detested after Franklin had repeatedly upstaged him during their diplomatic tour in France.) There is no detailed record of the Senate debate. But according to William Maclay, the senators from South Carolina and Georgia were so fiery—Pierce Butler launched a personal attack on Franklin, while Izard denounced the Quakers as a gang of "fanaticks &ca."—that little was said in opposition to them.

James Madison, meanwhile, was keeping a low profile. Three things were starkly clear to him: that slavery contradicted the Revolution's founding commitment to human equality, that southerners (including his own constituents) would resist yielding control over their slaves to a national government where antislavery men held any influence, and that political combat over slavery would likely explode the two-year-old constitutional compact. His present goal was to push the slavery question off Congress's agenda because he believed that it would lead to the destruction of either the planter class, to which he belonged, or the nation itself. Unlike hotheads such as Jackson and Burke, Madison did not claim that debate about slavery was unconstitutional, but he wanted to ensure that no matter what members might say, its opponents could actually *do* nothing about slavery—and that they knew it. In this, Madison embodied what Joseph Ellis has aptly termed "the Virginia straddle," an evasiveness about slavery that "talked northern but thought southern." Writes Ellis, "Any effort to locate the core of Madison's position on slavery, therefore, misses the point, which is that there was no core, except perhaps the conviction that the whole subject was taboo." The son of the largest slaveowner in Orange County, Madison had lived comfortably among slaves his entire life. Intellectually at least, slavery gnawed at him. Any government that claimed to be democratic, he opined, must "in proportion as slavery prevails in a State be aristocratic in fact." Like many Virginians of his class, he opposed the slave *trade* as cruel and immoral and at times seemed to embrace something superficially resembling abolition, mainly in his lifelong support for the resettlement of freed slaves in Africa; such colonization, he remarked, "might prove a great encouragement to manumission in the Southern parts of the U.S. and even afford the best hope yet presented of putting an end to slavery." However, he shared Thomas Jefferson's conviction that color prejudice was so fundamental that racial integration was not just impractical but unimaginable. And Madison did nothing to challenge slavery as an institution, to inhibit its territorial expansion, or to nudge his fellow southerners toward acceptance of the kind of gradual emancipation that was taking place in the North. (Whatever his abstract thoughts about slavery, in 1788 he had obligingly hunted up a "Negro boy" for a French acquaintance who wanted one to pair with a "girl" she already owned, "in order that they may breed.")

He regarded the Quaker petitions as impolitic at best, and a serious distraction from the all-important battle over Hamilton's funding plan. Madison first tried to quiet his ranting colleagues, reminding them that nothing in the petitions threatened the importation of slaves for the next

New York's bustling streets teemed with immigrants, Yankee merchants, and both free and enslaved blacks. It would soon surpass Philadelphia as the republic's largest city.

Federal Hall was deemed the finest building in America after its redesign by Peter L'Enfant. Southern members of Congress called it "the Trap," fearing that its magnificence would deter Congress from moving the national capital out of New York City.

Washington sought to balance the majesty of the presidency with the accessibility that he believed appropriate for the leader of the new nation. The enslaved manservant hovering behind him suggests the shadow of slavery that loomed over the early republic.

The First Congress was already in session when George Washington arrived in New York. He was celebrated as a near demigod whose election as president inspired public confidence in the untried new government.

Although he was only thirty-eight years old when the First Congress met, James Madison was already widely regarded as the foremost authority on the Constitution. For much of the First Congress, the Virginian served as virtual prime minister for the president.

As the presiding officer of the Senate, Vice President John Adams's popularity plummeted during the First Congress. His ill-considered intrusions into floor debates led to accusations that he harbored monarchical tendencies, and he left the vice presidency permanently weakened.

The Manhattan landscape was still bucolic in 1789. During the first two sessions of the First Congress, Adams and his wife, Abigail, rented this rustic estate located near the present-day entrance to the Holland Tunnel.

Irascible senator William Maclay of Pennsylvania kept the only private diary to record the proceedings of the Senate. His acute, often caustic observations remained unknown for almost a century.

Adams called Oliver Ellsworth the Senate's "firmest pillar" of the administration. Legislation he wrote during the First Congress created the federal court system.

Largely self-taught, and a shoemaker in his early life, Roger Sherman rose to become one of the most brilliant jurists of his time. He and Ellsworth—both from Connecticut—were pivotal figures in the great compromise that created the nation's bicameral Congress.

Representative Elbridge Gerry of Massachusetts was the most articulate Antifederalist in the House of Representatives. He had voted against the Constitution and played an active and provocative role in the First Congress.

Senator Robert Morris of Pennsylvania was a large man of large appetites. He was one of the few members of Congress with experience in finance, and he was a tireless advocate for locating the nation's new capital in Pennsylvania.

Representative James Jackson of Georgia, a former Indian fighter, was among the most zealous defenders of slavery and other southern interests. His harangues were so loud that senators in the chamber above shut their windows to block out his voice.

Secretary of the Treasury Alexander Hamilton gradually replaced James Madison as the president's closest adviser. His proposals to address the national debt crisis and establish a national bank were among the most contentious issues to face the First Congress.

Thomas Jefferson would have preferred to return to Paris as the American ambassador, but instead he reluctantly agreed to accept appointment as secretary of state. His growing rivalry with Hamilton would lay the foundation for national political parties later in the decade.

Cong^{ss} Embark^d on board the Ship Constitution of America bound to Conogocheque by way of Philadelphia.

Satirists mocked proposals to establish the "federal city" somewhere in the near wilderness of the upper Potomac River Valley. Of the Conococheague, a site near the narrow waist of Maryland, it was said that the name alone was so uncivilized that it would make maidens blush.

Many members feared that if the national capital was even temporarily placed in Philadelphia it would never leave. Southerners, in particular, felt that Philadelphia's sedate streets belied the menacing influence of the city's antislavery Quakers.

eighteen years, at which time the further importation of slaves would constitutionally be prohibited; much less did the petitions threaten the institution of slavery itself. "Gentlemen need not be alarmed," he soothed. Privately, he confided that he found the bullying bluster of Jackson and his friends "shamefully indecent." They would have been smarter "to let the affair proceed with as little noise as possible," he confided to Edmund Randolph, so that the petitions could be disposed of with the least public notice. But the chance for that was now lost.

With the Quaker petitions now dispatched to committee, Madison returned to the fight for debt discrimination with undiminished ardor. Once again, he invoked the pathetic plight of the alleged legions of ragged veterans deprived of their just reward for valiant service. Suppose, he challenged his fellow members of the House, you had been "one of that band who had established the liberties of his country," and in lieu of the silver and gold you had been promised for your sacrifice, you wound up with "a piece of paper" that you had been forced to sell for a tenth of its value to someone who stood to make many times that amount in profit. Was it not shocking "that this exorbitant accumulation of gain was made at the expence of the most meritorious part of the community?" How could Congress possibly now *not* vote to discriminate against the speculators and on behalf of "the gallant earners"?

But Madison's persuasive powers failed to dent the core of Hamilton's central argument: that the nation's credit and its economic stability depended on the security of investments. On February 22 the House decisively rejected Madison's attempt to substitute language calling for discrimination by a crushing majority of 36–13. Hamilton had gained his most important legislative victory so far, and Madison had suffered a painful defeat. Disheartened, he consoled himself after the fact that "the idea is much better relished I find in the Country at large than it was in this city."

The more emotional Benjamin Rush declared the defeat of discrimination to be a moral catastrophe. "I feel disposed to wish that my name was

blotted out from having contributed a single mite towards the American revolution," he flamingly wrote Madison upon hearing the news. "We have effected a deliverance from the national injustice of Great Britain, to be *subjugated* by a mighty Act of national injustice by the United States." Hamilton's plan, Rush predicted, would now lay the foundations of an American aristocracy of wealth and serve as "a lasting monument of the efficacy of idleness—speculation and fraud," as well as a "dark warning" to nations attempting to lift themselves up out of despotism, for it established the principle "that revolutions like party Spirit are the rage of *many* for the benefit of a *few*." Representative Peter Muhlenberg, the brother of the Speaker and another advocate for discrimination, sarcastically proposed that John Trumbull, who had made himself famous by painting the Founding Fathers in the heroic mode, undertake a new series of canvases showing a speculator driving a coach-and-four over a fallen American soldier, an impoverished veteran selling his watch and shoe buckles to pay the interest due on a loan, and a major who'd sold his securities for one-tenth of their value dying in jail of a broken heart.

Madison had by now made clear that he believed "funding in any shape to be an evil." However, he was a realist, and timid as he might seem, he was a tenacious parliamentary warrior: he had lost a battle, but the struggle to reshape Hamilton's larger program had just begun. His standing thus slid further among Federalists, who regarded him as an apostate from nationalist principles. He "hangs heavy on us," Fisher Ames commented disgustedly. "If he is a friend, he is more troublesome than a declared foe. He is so much a Virginian; so afraid that the mob will cry out, *crucify him*; sees Patrick Henry's shade at his bedside every night." Theodore Sedgwick wondered, had Madison become a convert to *anti-federalism*? Or was he simply motivated "by the mean and base motive of popularity" with his constituents? Or did he mean "to put himself at the head of the discontented in America?" Only time would tell, Sedgwick wrote to his wife, Pamela.

Hardly had the smoke cleared from the discrimination battlefield when, on February 23, the House plunged into an even more contentious

struggle over the proposed federal assumption of the states' debts, an issue that cut to the bone of the nation's identity. This time, the battle lines were less clear and—with the arrival of the North Carolinians—virtually equal in size: a loose alliance of doctrinaire Antifederalists, members from states that had already paid their debts, advocates of an across-the-board default on the debt, befuddled temporizers, and enemies of speculation in any form squared off against the representatives from beleaguered debtor states and orthodox Federalists who viewed the national debt, as Hamilton did, as a creative tool to strengthen the central government. Although he knew that he had Washington's support, "it is a sentiment I have not made known here," in keeping with the president's determination to avoid any hint of executive interference with Congress, Hamilton confided to a friend in Virginia. The president knew better than almost anyone else that the most beleaguered states would likely have abandoned the war for independence had they not believed that their sacrifices would be repaid later on. But Washington remained silent.

In his "Report on Public Credit," Hamilton had argued that unless the federal government took sole responsibility for the debts, each state would be left to deal individually with its own debt and would have to compete with the other states and the national government itself for the same limited number of investors, at a congeries of different interest rates—a recipe for "mutual jealousy and opposition," if not unremitting hostility. To this, forty-two-year-old representative Michael Jenifer Stone, a slaveowning Federalist planter from Port Tobacco, Maryland—his plantation's name, ironically, was Equality—warned ominously that Congress would be taking a "vast and dangerous leap blindfold" if it dared to endorse Hamilton's plan. Chronically ill—Stone was rumored to be suffering from "the Effects of *Love*," that is, venereal disease—his attendance at Federal Hall was patchy, but when he had the energy to speak, his oratory was often vivid and cogent.

A system that gave Congress power over state revenues would doubtless "draw us close together," Stone agreed. But was that what Americans wanted? And would the Constitution permit it? What right had Congress to saddle the Union with a new debt of such magnitude, and then levy new taxes to pay it? If the states were foolish enough to acquiesce to such a scheme, they would be committing constitutional suicide. "After this, might it not be found convenient to destroy the state governments altogether?" he asked. There would surely be even worse to come. Soon it might seem "inconvenient" to hold such frequent elections, and the "doctrine of conveniency" would extend terms of office to seven years, or ten years. "The most convenient would be to elect a man for life, and suffer the legislature, afterward, to fill up the vacancies." The people, then, "will labor undisturbed with the cares of government. Nay, for a people who have parted with their liberty, the most convenient government is an arbitrary one." Assumption of debt, Stone was saying, was the next step on the path to dictatorship.

Opinion on assumption seemed fairly evenly divided. Opposition would come mainly from Virginia, Maryland, and—it was anticipated, once her delegates arrived—North Carolina, which had all paid off their debts. Pennsylvania, Massachussetts, Connecticut, and South Carolina were strongly for it, along with elements of the New York, New Hampshire, and New Jersey delegations. Massachusetts and South Carolina—which had suffered worst from wartime depredations—stood to benefit most. (Together, they accounted for about 40 percent of the total debt.) Virginians, Madison among them, meanwhile, argued that any further assessments on their state would be unjust, as did "poor little Delaware," which stood to be saddled with somewhere between $200,000 and $300,000 in new assessments, protested that state's pudgy, usually amiable senator Richard Bassett.

Verbal rocks were thrown in every direction. Why, demanded Stone, should Maryland, which had paid her debts, be obliged to contribute toward South Carolina's? To compare Maryland to South Carolina was intolerable, retorted Aedanus Burke. The Irish-born Burke, a wealthy judge who had opposed ratification of the Constitution, was notorious for his insulting manners and penchant for "blunders, vulgarisms, and Hibernianisms." A fierce proponent of republican equality among white men, he was also one of the House's most unyielding defenders of slavery. The war had left Maryland completely unscarred, Burke seethed, while South Carolina's debts had been undertaken in the common defense. "There is not a road in the state but has witnessed the ravages of war: the skeletons of houses to this day point out to the traveler the route of the British army," while her citizens had been exposed to every kind of violence, their capital taken, men, women, and children murdered in cold blood by the Indians and the Tories. Was it so surprising, he hurled at Stone, "that she is not able to make exertions with other states?" Stone drily replied that Maryland had nevertheless paid her debts, while South Carolina had not.

On March 1, Madison suggested a compromise: that the state debts be "contemplated" as they stood at the end of the war, in 1783. This quaint locution meant that if the debts of any states were to be assumed by the federal government, as Hamilton wished, then those states that had already paid off all or most of their debt would be reimbursed for their earlier outlays. To assume the debts of some states but not others "cannot fail of giving umbrage to a great proportion of the citizens of the United States," he maintained, because the revenues collected to pay those debts would naturally flow to the central government, while "the distant states" would receive no benefit from it. However, if his proposal was adopted, he said, the revenues would stay in the states where they were collected. This of course would totally negate Hamilton's political goal of using debt to bind the states more tightly together by sharing responsibility for the unpaid debts.

The strongest support for assumption came from business-oriented New Yorkers and New Englanders. Feelings in western Massachusetts, the epicenter of Shays's Rebellion, were particularly alarmist. Unless the federal government committed itself to assumption, the *Stockbridge Western Star* predicted, the overtaxed inhabitants of Massachusetts would flee en masse to neighboring New York, which had no debt and vast tracts of fertile and uncultivated land. Hamilton's Federalist allies were joined by none other than Elbridge Gerry, who offered a tortuous but helpful states' rights defense of the treasury secretary's plan. Wedded though Gerry was to the republican ideal of small government, he was also a wealthy businessman with far-flung investments in international shipping, which depended in no small degree on foreign credit. He dismissed Madison's proposal out of hand, making it clear that he considered the Virginian ignorant of elementary financial principles. Madison's motion, Gerry declared, would increase the debts of the states "to an enormous height" and "embarrass us in making provision for the payment of the interest on a capital so much accumulated." In other words, the country couldn't afford it.

Gerry then declared that to him no difference existed between the federal and state debts: they had all been incurred in the common defense, and it was the nation's duty to make good on them. Those who held that consolidation of the debt would inflate the federal government and "depress" the states had it wrong. If that were true, he said, he would oppose assumption as vigorously as anyone. Failure to assume state debts would actually *undermine* the autonomy of the states. Why was that? Because if Congress rejected assumption, it would wind up creating two hostile competing forces: federal creditors on one hand, and on the other state creditors, who would oppose every measure of the federal government that they supposed would favor the center at the expense of the states. "It will sow discord among the citizens of the union," he predicted, and in the end subvert the operation of the state and federal governments alike.

By early March, assumption appeared to have strong support in the Senate, but at best only a tenuous majority in the House. The atmosphere in Federal Hall had reached a high pitch of tension. "A constant and painful attention has been necessary to keep the majority united," worried Theodore Sedgwick. Added the French chargé d'affaires, who was soon to be appointed minister, "Parties form and become embittered. Dispassionate arguments give way to personalities, and it is difficult to regain the calmness and the moderation which had formerly characterized the deliberations of Congress." With the anticipated arrival of North Carolina's five-member delegation to the House, who were known to oppose assumption, the odds against it would soon become steeper. Hamilton had reason to worry.

CHAPTER 14

The Trumpet of Sedition

———— •◆• ————

Human fears too much prevail.

—John Pemberton, March 1790

The souring atmosphere wasn't helped by the outbreak of flu that swarmed through Congress, along with the crepuscular skies that kept New York's unpaved streets mired in snow, slush, and mud. Both William Maclay and William Smith of Maryland complained of "violent head Ache, & Sore throat," while Sedgwick was down with "vertiginous complaints" and had sixteen ounces of blood drawn, after which, he tried to reassure his wife, he felt "quite relieved." Theodorick Bland had so far escaped the flu but was half-crippled from an attack of gout, which, he groaned, had "exerted its utmost violence on my hands feet Knees and Elbows," a plight made only worse by the miserable weather. The stoical Robert Morris, although one of the wealthiest men in Congress, was tramping through the icy muck in "wore Out" shoes and begged his wife, in Philadelphia, to send him a new pair posthaste.

The special committee's draft report on the Quaker petitions did little to improve the general mood. The report's most substantive article explicitly denied Congress any right to emancipate slaves, or to interfere with the slave trade before 1808, as stipulated by the Constitution. This was just what the Georgians and Carolinians wanted, but they were incensed to see that it also declared a tax on imported slaves—a provision that northerners believed would inhibit the slave trade—encouraged states to revise their laws to promote the improved treatment and "happiness" of slaves, enabled the government to prohibit foreigners from building or servicing slave ships in American ports, and—worst of all—boldly declared that "in all cases to which the authority of Congress extends they shall exercise it for the humane objects of the Quaker memorialists, so far as they can be promoted on the principles of justice, humanity, and good policy." This sounded worrisomely like a moral capitulation to the Quakers' presumption that something was wrong with slavery.

When the House again took up the petitions on March 16, the proslavery forces immediately went on the offensive. James Jackson once more led the attack. His full-throated diatribe, which extended over several days, was intended less to persuade than to bully the Quakers' friends into silence. He quoted scripture: Colossians, Corinthians, Titus, Peter, the Old Testament, the Mosaic laws. He cited the customs of the Egyptians, the Phoenicians, the Babylonians, the Greeks, and the Romans, who sold their own children by law. He was pragmatic: slavery might arguably be an "evil habit," but nothing could be done about it—only black slaves were physically conditioned to cultivate the torrid regions of South Carolina and Georgia, so there was no alternative to them. He was patriotic: Congress didn't want to deprive the nation of the revenue that it derived from those slave-cultivated lands, did it? He was anthropological: Africans were congenitally incapable of mastering freedom, having "imbibed despotism with their mother's milk." If ever they were freed, they would either have to be deported wholesale, or incorporated into white society—an intolerable prospect. "However fond the Quakers may be of this mixture and of giving their daughters to negroes' sons, and receiving the negro daughters for their sons," he sarcastically charged, "there will be those who will not approve of the breed." The attempted colonization of freed blacks in Africa by the British had already proved an unmitigated disaster, while the notion of exiling them to the North American frontier was equally harebrained, since surely "some king would rise among them, and make the rest slaves. Or they would be made slaves of the Indians." Slavery was now woven into the fabric of the nation: to attempt to unravel it now would shred the fragile national consensus. The Quakers were blowing "the trumpet of sedition"! If they loved Negroes so much, "let them go to Africa. There they may marry and be given in marriage, and have a motley race of their own."

To this, Aedanus Burke of South Carolina added his opinion that "our domestics" led far happier and more secure lives in southern slavery than ever they had in Africa, living now "at ease and in great plenty," with comfortable houses, good clothing, and the ministrations of devoted doctors. Emancipation would not only be "impolitic and mischievous to the public interest," but would perpetrate a terrible cruelty on the Negroes themselves. William Loughton Smith of South Carolina warned that southerners would never tamely suffer their property to be "torn from them" by people who claimed to possess some supposed moral superiority. Did slavery even *have* a moral dimension? "If it be a moral evil, it is like many others which exist in all civilized countries and which the world quietly submits to," he scoffed. And the slave trade—was it really as terrible as its critics alleged? Hardly. "All voyages must be attended with inconveniencies, and those from Africa to America not more than others. As to the slaves' confinement on board, it was no more than necessary. As to the space allotted them, it was more than was allowed to soldiers in a camp."

The Quakers had surely hoped, naively, for some kind of support from some of the government's leading men who were known to be unfriendly to slavery. President Washington, who despite his ownership of slaves was moving steadily toward an embrace of abolitionism—less than three years earlier he had privately declared it to be "among my first wishes to see some plan adopted by the legislature by which slavery in this country may be abolished by slow, sure, & imperceptible degrees"—judiciously avoided the whole issue and made it clear that he wished the Quakers had never shown up with their "very mal-apropos" petitions. Alexander

Hamilton, a founder of the New York Manumission Society, and well known as an enemy of slavery, mutely stood by, fearing that if the debate became any more inflammatory, he would lose whatever chance he had of winning southern votes for his funding plan.

Fears of sectional fissure weren't entirely groundless. Rumors that Congress was about to vote a general emancipation swept Virginia, leading to general alarm among slaveowners, and the panicked sale of slaves for trifling sums, compounding widespread dissension among those already embittered against the government by the proposed assumption of state debts. Reports from Charleston said that the petitions had caused "as great an uproar amongst the slaveholders as St. Paul's preaching did among the silver-smiths at Ephesus."

In Congress, the Quakers' nominal friends responded feebly to the South's rhetorical assaults. "Human fears too much prevail," John Pemberton wrote to his brother James. "They fear that the Southern delegates will rise in a flame, & so temporise." The usually philanthropic Elias Boudinot of New Jersey hastened to assure the southerners that he, for one, could not support "so extravagant a conduct" as wholesale emancipation, for "it would be inhumanity itself to turn these unhappy people loose to murder each other or to perish for want of the necessaries of life." And John Vining, known fondly to his admirers as "the pet of Delaware," where he represented many Quaker constituents, asserted that the issue at hand was no more than a mere *technical* question—the "operation of the Constitution upon an abstract question of commerce." Although it might be an immutable truth, he allowed, "that all men are born equal," and that freedom was therefore an inalienable right that could be neither sold nor purchased, the petitions wouldn't actually free "a particle of property."

Fisher Ames, likely speaking for other New Englanders, as he was increasingly to do, expressed polite regret that so much time had been consumed by the petitions and declared himself opposed to "the idea of the House going into a declaration of abstract proposition." James Jackson then apologized, vaguely, for his earlier behavior and formally complimented Ames on his "conduct." It appeared that a tacit agreement had been reached, perhaps with Madison's subtle mediation. "It was a matter of scratch me and I will scratch thee," wrote Pemberton, with something as close to disgust as the ever-restrained Quaker would permit himself. He speculated that at least several northern men had agreed to swap their votes against the petitions in return for southern support on assumption of debts. "The funding system is so much their darling that they want to obtain the favor of those from Carolina and Georgia."

Southerners were just as "disgusted" with the Quakers as northerners professed to be with the South's toleration of slavery, William Loughton Smith declared on the floor of the House. Deploying the kind of salacious innuendo that became slavery's defenders' stock-in-trade, he leeringly accused the Quakers of both hypocrisy and secret sexual license, conflating them with the separate sect known as Shakers—he called them "Shaking Quakers"—who claimed to practice celibacy, "yet, in consequence of their shakings and concussions, you may see them with a numerous offspring about them." Repugnant as Quaker customs were, he said, by adopting the Constitution "we made a compromise on both sides. We took each other with our mutual bad habits and respective evils, for better for worse; the northern states adopted us with our slaves, we adopted them with their Quakers."

The mere presence of the Quakers in the elevated visitors' gallery seemed to bring out the meanest streak in their enemies. Jackson glared menacingly up at them when he spoke. Others complained that their refusal to remove their hats during the chaplain's invocation was an insult to Congress. With their black suits and wide-brimmed, black hats, Smith sneered, they were "like evil spirits hovering over our heads." Through all this, the weary Pemberton wrote, the Quakers sat silently, "as composed and resigned as we could expect to be under our long detention," watching, listening, and praying, to "shew ourselves & to remind them we are waiting upon them."

Back in February, Madison had hoped to shunt the petitions quietly into oblivion. That hope was dashed when the Georgians and Carolinians re-

acted to the petitions with rhetorical apoplexy. Now he decided to leverage their barely veiled threats of secession as a tool to produce a precedent
that would permanently clarify the constitutional power of Congress to
legislate on slavery. In the twenty-first century, this would have required
a ruling by the Supreme Court. But in March 1790 the Supreme Court
was still a work in progress, devoid of experience, and without the power
of judicial review that would become the cornerstone of its constitutional
authority in later times. If the congressional door on emancipation was to
be permanently nailed shut, as Madison wished, Congress would have to
do it. It did.

By the time the House completed its debate, even the most watery hu-
manitarian sentiment had been sluiced away. The reference to "justice, humanity, and good policy" was gone without a trace. So was the right to tax
the importation of slaves, and the encouragement to states to legislate better treatment for slaves. Even the authority to bar foreigners from fitting
out slave ships in American ports was gone. Instead of laying a foundation
for future antislavery legislation, the House firmly endorsed the status quo
and the protection of slavery. All power to legislate on slavery, the report
declared, resided with the states alone. Abiel Foster of New Hampshire
later revealed that he had cast the deciding vote in favor of the clause that
affirmed Congress's inability to emancipate slaves, he said, "with a view to
make the report set easy with the Georgia and Carolina men, &c."

There was a final skirmish. Southerners, hoping to erase every vestige
of the Quakers' hateful petitions, objected to allowing the committee's
report to be recorded in the House journal. Madison, victorious on the
issue that mattered, could now afford to be magnanimous. He proposed
inserting the committee's report in the journal, a courtesy to the cowed
North and a concession with no adverse consequences to his southern
friends since, as historian William C. di Giacomantonio has written, it
"effectively buried them in an unmarked grave."

The Quakers' campaign had no practical effect but was not without
significance. It palpably deepened southerners' suspicion of the North,
which would soon manifest itself with renewed toxicity in the coming

debate over the establishment of the federal capital. It also created an unofficial "gag rule," which in the 1830s would explicitly bar any discussion of slavery in Congress. Still more lasting was the coalescence of a proslavery polemic so well wrought that—refined, polished, and endlessly reiterated—it would be used in debates for the next seventy years, until it finally led to the secession and civil war that the Southerners of 1790 so loudly threatened. "Our early and violent opposition had This good effect—it convinced the house that So. Car. & Georgia look with a jealous eye on any measure in which the negroes are at all concerned," William Loughton Smith triumphantly proclaimed. "We assured them that whenever Congress should directly or indirectly attempt any measure leveled at our particular rights in this respect, they must expect a revolt in those States, which [would] never submit to it, & that the most violent opposition would be given to every step which might appear to interfere in any manner with our negro property."

The Quakers had been naive: they had trusted too much in their modest powers of persuasion to sway men who were contemptuous of everything they represented. However, they had elevated the constitutional right of petition, which up to now had served mainly to convey personal grievances, into a political weapon that nineteenth-century abolitionists would wield with significant propagandistic effect in their campaign against the slave power in Congress. But in the end the Quakers left New York with nothing but head colds and the mockery of their enemies ringing in their ears. "It was a singular favor our friends escaped without having their bones broken & also from being drowned," John Pemberton drily remarked.

After the chastened Quakers started for home, George Washington wrote to a friend in Virginia, with palpable relief and ill-founded optimism, "The slave business has at last [been] put to rest and will scarce awake."

As the debate ended, Benjamin Franklin loosed a Parthian shot at the proslavery forces in their moment of triumph. He bitingly mocked their hypocrisy in a savage satire, literally written on his deathbed, putting

James Jackson's most fiery speech into the mouth of a fictional Barbary Arab, one Sidi Mehemet Ibrahim, who asserted that without the continued kidnapping and enslavement of white Christians, the Algerian economy would collapse. In this, Franklin was evoking the much-publicized plight of scores of American seamen who were being held, some of them for years, by the so-called Barbary pirates in ports along the North African coast, mainly Algiers. The inability of the United States to protect its merchant ships was the most painful demonstration of its helplessness on the high seas, a shaming embarrassment that no American was unaware of. "If we forbear to make Slaves of their People, who in this hot Climate are to cultivate our Lands? Who are to perform the common Labours of our City, and in our Families? Must we not then be our own slaves?" Unless fresh supplies of white slaves could be obtained, "our Lands will become of no value for want of Cultivation," and the Algerian economy would be ruined. "And for what? To gratify the whims of a whimsical Sect, who would have us not only forbear making more Slaves, but even to manumit those we have." Freeing their white slaves would be an injustice, since they would inevitably become a burden on Algerian society, for "Men long accustom'd to Slavery will not work for a Livelihood when not compell'd." In captivity, on the other hand, they were fed, clothed, and lodged at no expense to themselves and blessed by exposure to the splendorous sunlight of true religion—Islam. Opined Ibrahim, "Sending the Slaves home would be sending them out of Light into Darkness." With his forwarding of the Pennsylvania Abolition Society petition to Congress, Franklin had in his last political act attempted, unsuccessfully, to force slavery onto the national agenda before it became permanently embedded in the national fabric. Within a month, he was dead.

On March 21, Thomas Jefferson at last arrived to shoulder his duties as the country's first secretary of state, "after as laborious a journey as I ever went through" on the road from Virginia. His acceptance had come after five months of courtship by both the president and his protégé James Madison, who had personally driven to Monticello at Christmas to press

Jefferson yet again to join the administration in New York. (As late as January 24, Madison had written to Jefferson that "a universal anxiety is expressed for your acceptance.") Jefferson had made his lack of enthusiasm obvious. He wanted to go back to Paris. Short of that, he preferred to stay home and enjoy his squire's privileges at Monticello. But the president wanted him in New York. "To have gone back [to France] would have exposed me to the danger of giving disgust, and I value no office enough for that," he admitted to his former deputy in Paris, William Short.

Much had to be done before he could set out. Countless letters had to be written: his Paris lease had to be broken, servants there paid off and discharged, horses and carriages sold, paintings, wines, marble busts and pedestals, venetian blinds, rolls of French wallpaper, and gourmet foodstuffs—macaroni, Parmesan cheese, Marseilles figs, raisins, almonds, mustard, oil, and anchovies—prepared for shipping. His books had to be individually wrapped, and his collections of "philosophical instruments" stowed in the drawers of commodes, to be dispatched to New York along with his furniture. Meanwhile, at Monticello, stocks of wheat and tobacco had to be baled and sold, debts paid, slaves seen to, and a collection of plants from the greenhouses—magnolia, liriodendron, calycanthus, sassafras—packed in moss and sent off to a friend in France.

Jefferson finally started off on March 1, a few days after marrying his eighteen-year-old daughter, Martha, to the aristocratic Thomas Mann Randolph Jr., and dispatching twelve-year-old Polly to the care of her aunt Elizabeth Wayles Eppes, writing her en route to see that the easily bored Polly read ten pages a day in *Don Quixote*. In snow-blown Alexandria, he declared to a gathering of citizens that republican government was the only form "not eternally at open or secret war with the rights of mankind," and that the infant United States already served as a beacon to peoples everywhere, "pointing out the way to struggling nations who wish, like us, to emerge from their tyrannies."

He had left Monticello with the two enslaved Hemings brothers, Robert and James, in his two-horse phaeton, a light, open carriage. But the snowfall at Alexandria convinced him to ship the phaeton to New York by sea, and to himself "bump it" the rest of the way by public stage, on roads so bad that he was rarely able to travel faster than three miles an hour during daylight, and just one mile per hour at night. Recurrence of his chronic migraines added to his discomfort. He rested one day at Baltimore, then another at Philadelphia to see the dying Franklin. Robert Hemings, who had gone on ahead, secured lodgings for Jefferson at the City Tavern in New York, and then at a boardinghouse on King Street, until Jefferson and the Hemingses were settled into a house on Maiden Lane, in June, around the corner from Madison's lodgings.

The unmatchably urbane secretary of state was quickly seized as a prize by New York's social elite. "Mr. Jefferson is here, and adds much to the social circle," Abigail Adams reported to her sister. He was hardly a stranger to sophisticated life. But the city's driving commercialism and the hard Federalist cant of its politics appalled him. (He would later write to Benjamin Rush, "I view great cities as pestilential to the morals, the health and the liberties of man.") At dinner tables, he often found himself "the only advocate on the republican side of the question," hardly what he had expected from the patriots he'd left behind in 1784. "Politics were the chief topic, and a preference of kingly, over republican government was evidently the favorite sentiment." He was equally disgusted by the "mimickry of royal forms and ceremonies" that he witnessed at Federal Hall, and by the expression of aristocratic sentiments by highly placed members of the government.

Jefferson had returned from France with his reputation unscarred by the ideological warfare that had accompanied the writing of the Constitution and the sometimes bitter state-by-state campaign for its ratification. But he was not yet what a later age would call a political "player." He was not a member of Congress, the real engine of government. And he was a late addition to an administration that had already been functioning for a year, heading a department that employed only three men besides himself. His responsibilities were time-consuming and far-flung. Apart from distracting domestic concerns such as copyrights and the oversight of land offices, he was responsible for crafting policies to succor the American sailors rotting in Algiers, when there was no money to pay their ransom, and the encroachment of British settlers in Massachusetts's Maine district—Jefferson had to find a reliable map to determine just where the boundary was supposed to run.

Most pressing of all his responsibilities was the slow-motion management—it took months to exchange letters with William Short in Paris—of the all-important American relationship with France as it spun in its revolutionary maelstrom. Just days after taking office, Jefferson learned that the French royal family had been brought from Versailles to Paris, that soldiers of the royal bodyguard had been killed, and that martial law had been declared in the capital. As they got to know Jefferson's true views, Federalists would be shocked by his enthusiasm for the increasingly bloody revolution that was unfolding across the ocean. "I like a little rebellion now and then," he had jauntily informed Madison, who somewhat more cautiously shared Jefferson's pro-French sentiments. "It is like a storm in the atmosphere." Jefferson's fondness for revolution remained confined to white people. Although he professed distaste for slavery and believed that it corrupted the morals of whites, he had never freed a slave and believed that Negroes were by nature "inferior to the whites in the endowments both of body and mind," emitted a "strong and disagreeable odor," lacked delicate sentiments, were incapable of complex thought, felt less pain than whites, and probably mated with orangutans, views that he had expressed in his influential *Notes on the State of Virginia* of 1781, which two congressmen had approvingly cited in their defense of slavery during the House debate on the Quaker petitions.

William Maclay, though he also shared some of Jefferson's radical opinions, was unimpressed upon meeting him for the first time that spring, finding him dressed in clothes too small for his lanky frame, and exhibiting a "loose shackling air" and a "vacant look" instead of the "firm collected deportment which I expected would dignify the presence of a Secretary or Minister." Never the lightest of spirits, Maclay was more miserable than ever that cold and soggy spring. After the months of legislative toil, he missed his family, was racked by rheumatism, and then laid low by the flu. He suffered from nightmares of women passing by him in flights, of a man plunging to his death from the roof of a sawmill, of a dead child, and woke up drained and confused. Even his attempts at relaxation seemed to conspire against him. In mid-April, he joined a riding party that set out for the picturesque Harlem flats, but an icy wind suddenly blew up and drove them back to the city, prompting him to gloomily reflect, "Like most other human expectations, Our hopes vanished in disappointment." His mood darkened further when he was taken on an excursion to watch the agonizing slaughter of two enormous bullocks, a sight so cruel that it haunted him for days. To make the beef white, the animals' necks were stretched with a rope, while their jugular veins were repeatedly sliced open and drained, before they were finally killed. "Oh, Man, what a monster thou art," he sighed to his diary. But the political paralysis at Federal Hall depressed him most of all: "The Very Goddess of Slowness seems to have possessed Congress."

Although the Quaker petitions had officially been consigned to the congressional scrap heap, the episode left behind it a residue of southern resentment that bled corrosively into the funding debate. Washington's neighbor David Stuart reported from Virginia that public opinion had only just begun to recover "from the fever which the Slave business had occasioned" when the new battle over the assumption of state debts soured it again. Before the Quakers' arrival, William Loughton Smith of South Carolina had counted a majority of five or six for assumption, which he supported. That edge had now evaporated. He blamed what he feared to be the imminent collapse of the entire funding plan specifically on fallout from the debate from the petition campaign. Accusing the Quakers of "intemperate and bigotted zeal," he declared, "It was a mortifying thing to see an attempt made to deprive us of our property so soon after we had established a government for the express purpose of protecting it." Along with other key southerners, Smith now felt seriously alienated from the Pennsylvanians, who had defended the Quakers, and now—adding outrage to insult—demanded the nation's future seat of government for their state. Not only assumption, but the entire funding package hung in the balance as Congress stalled and wrangled. Madison, the leading enemy of assumption, gloated that it was losing ground daily and predicted that it would ultimately be defeated, though the decision would likely turn on just one or two votes.

The price of congressional paralysis fell most heavily on already economically depressed Massachusetts, which was deeply in debt and dependent on maritime trade. Moaned one Boston merchant, "Our Fishery is discourag'd & is lessened One hundred sail this Spring," while the harbors were "crouded with British Shipping," and American shippers begged for freight. Madison was excoriated by northerners, who blamed him personally for blocking assumption. His behavior, seethed one, "disgusted many of his best friends," while Theodore Sedgwick, a leading advocate for assumption, accused the Virginian of irresponsibly retailing "unfounded facts, monstrous premises, and inconclusive deductions" in his effort to cripple or kill Hamilton's plan. Lamented another prominent northerner, "He becomes more and more a Southern Partizan, & loses his assumed candor and moderation."

With neither Madison nor Hamilton able to command enough votes to prevail, the debate ground on through week after rainy week, as the muddy lanes of New York seemed to mimic the quagmire in which the legislators found themselves. The same arguments were rehashed over and over. Assumption's opponents insisted that the states ought to be responsible for their own debts, that it was too difficult to separate debts contracted for the Union from the states' other debts, that assumption was unjust to the states that had already paid what they owed, and that, in any case, funding was unconstitutional because it was not explicitly mandated in the founding document.

Assumption's supporters countered that since the debts had been contracted for the benefit of the entire country, it was the duty of the federal government to pay them, that no more money could be squeezed from the already overburdened taxpayers of the afflicted states, that assumption would bind creditors more tightly to the federal government, that the nation's resources would soon be sufficient to pay off both interest on the debt and the principal. To those who claimed that the funding plan was unconstitutional, Representative Roger Sherman of Connecticut retorted that the Constitution was always intended to be elastic and expansive, and that "the novelty of it is no just objection against adopting it—if the measure be just."

Beneath these by-now-familiar arguments lay half-submerged, like a treacherous reef, the insistent claims of states' rights, which would continue to challenge the supremacy of the Federalist vision for the next seventy years. Representative Alexander White of Virginia, for one, declared with rhetorical astonishment that assumption's advocates were utterly mistaken to speak of the "interests of the Union" as if it were something apart from the states that composed it, while Virginia's still influential former governor, Patrick Henry, hinted that secession might be the only remedy if Congress overreached itself by daring to approve assumption. No one could predict how it would all end. Declared the anxious Federalist congressman John Vining, "I feel as if I were on a precipice surrounded with imminent dangers, and where a single false step might prove fatal."

On April 12, assumption was defeated in the committee of the whole by a margin of two votes. Hamilton left no record of his reaction to this defeat, but his friends, who likely shared his feelings, were stunned. Maclay, who went downstairs to the House chamber to watch the vote, reported that the dazed Sedgwick grabbed his hat and stumbled out of the chamber, returning later with his face streaked with tears, Gerry looked like a cadaver, Boudinot's mouth drooped like a horseshoe, "Fitzsimons reddened like Scarlet," and Clymer's "neck & Breast consented to gesticulations resembling those of a Turkey or Goose, nearly strangled in the Act of deglutition." Maclay's glee was premature, however. The battle was far from over.

CHAPTER 15

Cabals, Meetings, Plots, and Counterplots

————•————

Ye noddies, how noozled, perplex'd and bamboozled,
Are ye of Potowmack, are ye of Potowmack?

While the assumption debate staggered along in ever-tightening circles, Congress was simultaneously engaged in fierce but equally inconclusive bargaining over the future seat of government. "This question about Residence has been the Demon of the present, and it ever will prove a haunting Ghost till it is laid by fixing a permanent seat," opined George Thatcher, who supposed that another century would pass before the question was solved. Both issues were entwined in a Gordian knot whose strands hobbled the passage of any but the most pedestrian legislation through Congress. The government's future residence, it was now apparent, was actually *two* separate but interlinked questions: the designation of a permanent capital, and of a temporary one while the permanent site was developed. Similarly, Hamilton's funding plan as a whole was hamstrung by the seemingly intractable problem of assumption.

Establishing the seat of government was more than a matter of finding a convenient patch of real estate. After years of nomadic administration under the Articles of Confederation, the Constitution had mandated the establishment of a permanent capital not only for the sake of stability but also to embody what most Americans recognized as the first great physical symbol of national unity—a district that would belong not to any one state, but to the entire nation. It was also widely believed that the federal city, wherever it was sited, was destined to become the nation's greatest metropolis, whose wealth would radiate out through the surrounding region. To Richard Henry Lee of Virginia, for one, it seemed obvious that a great mass of citizens would be drawn to the place where "the pecuniary business of the nation" was transacted, since the excise receipts from all the states would be concentrated and spent there, he believed.

Opinion had now pretty well settled on only a handful of options: to remain indefinitely in New York City, or to move to one of Philadelphia's outlying suburbs in Pennsylvania or New Jersey, to Baltimore, or to the Potomac or the Susquehanna. Night after night, revolving klatches of members caucused in New York's boardinghouses and taverns, swapping prospective compromises, cynical deals, and rumors. New Englanders huddled with New Yorkers, New Yorkers with Carolinians, and the Pennsylvanians with almost everyone. Remarked Madison, "The business of the seat of Government is become a labyrinth." Virginia and Maryland, it was whispered, would agree to adjourn to Philadelphia for the next session if the Pennsylvanians threw their weight against assumption. The New Yorkers were prepared to abandon their seemingly ironclad commitment to assumption in return for the capital.

Sectional animosities grew more intense by the week. Lamented Pennsylvania representative Thomas Fitzsimons, the thwarted floor manager for assumption in the House, "The Irritation is so great that it would be Vain to hope for any Union of Sentiment on any other question." Massachusetts distrusted Virginia, and Virginia New York; Georgia was envious of South Carolina, and South Carolina of Pennsylvania. Pennsylvanians feared that South Carolina, Massachusetts, and New York would gang up to prevent the removal of Congress from New York and its swarms of "Tories, antifederalists, and aristocratical Whigs," while distrustful Virginians such as the influential tidewater politician Henry Lee held out little hope for the Union unless the seat of government was secured for the South. Unless the government's "ministerial functions" were co-opted for the South, he advised Madison, "a monopoly will take place from the northern hives in this, as in everything else in their power. To disunite is dreadful to my mind, but dreadful as it is, I consider it a lesser evil than union on the present conditions, I had rather myself submit to all the hazards of war & risk the loss of everything dear to me in life, than to live under the rule of a fixed insolent northern majority."

Behind Madison loomed the publicly silent figure of the president. While the two men diverged sharply on the issue of assumption, their common interest in developing the Potomac Valley was long-standing. As one of the largest owners of trans-Appalachian real estate in the United States, Washington understood that the nation's future would be shaped profoundly by the great tidal flow of western settlement. He was also the most prominent devotee of what came to be called Potomac Fever, that hyperbolic enthusiasm for grandiose development that virally infected speculators and landowners up and down the valley. "It is the River, more than any other, in my opinion, which must, in the natural progress of things, connect by its inland navigation the Atlantic States with the vast region which is populating (beyond all conception) to the Westward of it," Washington would write in 1791. "It is designated by law for the seat of Empire; and must, from its extensive course through a rich and populous country become, in time, the grand Emporium of North America." Washington had proposed an elaborate route that would link by means of portages the Ohio River, the west fork of the Monongahela, the Castleman River, Wills Creek, the North Branch, the Cheat, the North Branch of the Potomac, and ultimately the Atlantic Ocean. Unlikely as such a route seems today, it made a kind of sense in an age when roads were rare and nearly all long-distance travel and commercial shipping took place by water.

Before he became president, Washington had predicted that development of the Potomac Valley would produce "the greatest returns of any speculation I know of in the world." At his instigation, like-minded landowners had, in 1784, incorporated the Potowmack Navigation Company, whose members included many of the wealthiest men on the river. In 1790, Washington held company stock that may have been worth as much as $1 million in present-day terms, three-quarters of it given to him gratis by the State of Virginia. Washington had also served as the company's president and had encouraged many of his political friends to invest in land around Georgetown, which would dramatically multiply in value if the national capital was established anywhere in the vicinity. Although Washington did not advertise his bias, it was no secret. Wrote Maclay, "It is in fact the Interest of the President of the United States that pushes the Potowmack, by means of Jefferson, Madison, Carroll and others."

The mood in Congress wasn't helped by the unfriendliness toward Hamilton harbored by many southern members, who found his opposition to slavery distasteful and suspected him of bias against the South generally. Southerners recalled that on the previous July 4, while eulogizing General Nathanael Greene, Hamilton had passingly blamed Virginia's "embarrassments" during the Revolutionary War on the defection of thousands of her slaves, including several of Thomas Jefferson's. Others in the audience also felt that he had also insulted the militiamen who had fought under Greene by belittling their discipline. Now, almost nine months later, in a flailing diatribe against the funding plan, Aedanus Burke of South Carolina suddenly resurrected Hamilton's remark—or a half-remembered version of it—claiming that Hamilton had deliberately slandered his state (which he had not) with words so like "a dagger in my breast" that Burke had been too keenly hurt to react at the time. Turning toward the visitors' gallery, supposing that Hamilton might be there, he "threw the lie in Hamilton's face," as he put it. Although the chair gaveled Burke down, publicly calling a man a liar was unpardonable among "men of the blade," as Maclay put it. For several days, a duel seemed inevitable: it was averted only by the desperate intercession of several members of Congress. This was more than a matter of personal honor: it would have been a national catastrophe. Had Hamilton been killed, his funding plan would likely have collapsed, with unknowable consequences for the financial organization of the United States. Fortunately, to everyone's relief, Burke was prevailed upon to do the necessary thing, and a week after he had hurled his insult, he agreed to retract what he had said once Hamilton had circulated a letter disavowing any intended insult to the touchy Carolinians.

As late as mid-April Madison doubted that the Potomac would prevail. Although he had strong support in the Virginia and Maryland delegations, he could not count on the rest of the southern members, since several were known to be averse to further aggrandizing Virginia's power in the Union. He also knew that no compromise could be achieved without the agreement of Pennsylvania, whose size, wealth, senators, and ten representatives could not be ignored. The only way to sway the Pennsylvanians, he surmised, was to leverage their virtually feral hostility to leaving the seat of government in the grip of their New York rivals.

In the House, Pennsylvania's team was captained by the able if ethically flexible Thomas Fitzsimons—a Philadelphia merchant of glaring eye "whose face, manner, and sentiments concur to produce caution, if not apprehension and disgust," as Fisher Ames rather cruelly wrote of him. In the Senate, the hard-charging Robert Morris worked in tandem with the difficult Maclay, who wanted to plant the capital on the Susquehanna, far from southern slavery and away from the corrupting influences of the big city. Morris, like Washington, regarded his private designs and the public interest as conveniently congruent. Having bought up real estate in the prospective sites near Philadelphia, he stood to make a great deal of money if any of them was selected.

Morris's worldwide shipping ventures and vast land speculations had made him one of the wealthiest men in America, at least on paper. But his reputation as a wheeling-and-dealing opportunist and "moneyman" antagonized planters and populists alike. "He will absolutely say anything," wrote Maclay, who often felt upstaged by the more dynamic Philadelphian. "Nor can I believe that he has a particle of Principle in his composition." (During Congress's first session, Morris had blindsided Maclay by derailing the establishment of the capital on the Susquehanna in his failed attempt to place it at Trenton, New Jersey, or Germantown, Pennsylvania.) Morris's once-sterling reputation as a patriot had also suffered. Although as the wartime superintendent of finance he had pledged his own fortune to pay the wages of the Continental Army, his enemies accused him of profiteering by siphoning public money into his own coffers, and by 1790 many Americans remembered only that, as George Thatcher put it, "His fortune carried an odor of dishonesty about it."

Morris was not without heart, however. His frequent letters to his wife, Mary, and their children were deeply affectionate, and, as he had himself been orphaned at an early age, his generosity to needy children was unbounded. In April, in a fairly typical exchange, he expressed great relief to Mary that she had managed to find a good home for a certain "poor Miserable Foundling," who had suffered from brutal parents. He supported a brother and at least one illegitimate daughter of his own, as well as a school in Philadelphia run by an immigrant who had left England to raise her own illegitimate daughter in America.

The tension among members was acute. Representative George Clymer of Pennsylvania fairly exploded at the "incessant disputation" and "tedious procrastination" that "we have both here in their highest perfection." Added William Smith of Maryland, "It is truly distressing to be detailed here so long & do so little good." Public disgust with the paralysis at Federal Hall—and by extension with the new government itself—was also reaching an ominous pitch. "Everything seems conducted by Party, Intrigue & Cabal," exclaimed Adams's friend John Trumbull, a frequent observer of the deadlocked deliberations; if things continued this way, he feared, "we may bid adieu to the hopes of a Foederal Government." (Ignoring the countless hours spent in committees, public opinion was also inflamed by reports that members of Congress, who officially sat for only four hours a day, enjoyed the then-princely salary of $2 per diem.)

Competing proposals filled the air. Morris at one point claimed to have achieved a compromise with the New Englanders and Jersey men that would place the capital at Trenton, which fell under Philadelphia's economic and political influence. At this, Maclay drew himself up in his most supercilious fashion and informed Morris that as a matter of principle he would have no part in any compromise, warning Morris that to bargain with the "Eastern men"—as New Englanders were often termed—would lose him the support of Maryland and everything south of it. Maclay added loftily, "We must be able to declare upon honour that we have no bargain."

When Morris pragmatically replied, "Leave all that to me," Maclay rejoined, "No, sir, I will make no bargain. If it is but suspected that we have a bargain we are ruined."

Morris must have been ready to scream. He knew, if Maclay did not, that without a horse-trading bargain there could be no solution at all.

By May 24, Trenton had faded and Morris was again on the Senate floor, proposing that Congress meet for its next session in Philadelphia. Three times the Senate divided 12–12, with Vice President Adams casting his tie-breaking vote to deny the Pennsylvanians what they wanted.

The House proved more amenable. Despite Elbridge Gerry's protest that the bill would turn the government into "a mere shuttlecock," to be knocked back and forth from place to place, as it had been under the Articles of Confederation, his colleagues disagreed and voted by a generous majority of sixteen votes to leave New York for the Quaker city.

When the news reached Pennsylvania, Philadelphians were "half mad with joy," reported one correspondent to the *New-York Daily Advertiser.* "Some are brushing away the cobwebs from their parlour windows; others projecting galleries in the state-house, another set proposing bell ringings, &c. &c &c. Our landlords, remarkably severe and avaricious, are only watching some such opportunity to squeeze exorbitant rents from the industrious tenant."

Their rejoicing was premature. At Federal Hall, uncertainty still reigned. "For this whole week we have warred with the influence of New York," Maclay wearily noted on June 5, as the weather grew steadily hotter, matching the rising temperature inside the hall. In addition, he groaned, Hamilton's funding bill, "the accursed thing which I fear future generations will hate is come up to Us." As much as he distrusted Morris, when the Philadelphian inexplicably disappeared for a day, allegedly on personal business, Maclay worried that Hamilton had co-opted him with some kind of secret bargain and peeled him away from his fellow Pennsylvanians. "I could almost curse [him] for having left me at such a time," Maclay seethed.

The feverish atmosphere was not merely rhetorical. For much of the spring, an exceptionally virulent strain of the flu had been sweeping through New York, felling the president, Secretary of State Jefferson, countless ordinary citizens, and members of Congress. "The plaguy Influenza Cough sticks faster than a blister," gasped Richard Henry Lee, who like many of his colleagues was unable to function for days. Washington temporarily went deaf and was so debilitated that many feared once again that he wouldn't survive to finish his term. But his seemingly indestructible constitution eventually rebounded, and he decamped for the open fields of what is now Brooklyn to regain his strength riding in the fresh air. Not so poor Representative Theodorick Bland of Virginia, who on June 1 was found dead in his lodgings, having finally been brought down by the flu after months of suffering from something he cryptically termed "gout in my head." He was the first member of Congress to die while performing his duties and was ceremoniously interred at Trinity Church, within sight of Federal Hall. His state funeral, the nation's first, was attended by every ambulatory member of Congress.

The debate, when it resumed, with members wearing black ribbons in Bland's honor, was harsher than ever. "It was nothing but Snip Snap & Contradiction," Maclay exclaimed. Parliamentary maneuvering grew even more byzantine. Eleven senators who were deemed "friends" of Philadelphia agreed to vote as a bloc against anyplace else that was suggested as a permanent seat of government. Then when Lee proposed that the issue of the permanent residence be postponed in order to take up the House's resolution to hold the next session at Philadelphia, southern enemies of Pennsylvania erupted. "Izard flamed and Butler bounced & both seemed to rage with madness," Maclay recorded. "All was hurry and confusion."

The southerners sent for the ailing Samuel Johnston of North Carolina, who was hauled into the Senate chamber in a sedan chair, wearing his nightcap and attended by two doctors. William Few of Georgia, who was also ill, somehow dragged himself into the chamber on his own feet. When at last a vote could be taken, Lee's resolution was defeated. A motion was next made to declare the Potomac the permanent seat, but this was easily defeated, as were Baltimore and Wilmington after it.

The imminent arrival of the newly elected delegation from Rhode Island threatened to complicate matters still further. Defiant Antifederalists had continued to hold the balance of power there, until Congress finally lost patience and abandoned persuasion in favor of force to bring the tiny holdout into the Union. The Senate voted to break off all land and water communication with Rhode Island by July 1, on pain of seizing all ships, wagons, and merchandise en route to the recalcitrant state and its Antifederalist renegades, along with severe fines and six months' imprisonment for anyone who defied the law. (Maclay, appalled, considered such bullying a "tyrant's" method, "meant to be Used the same Way That a Robber does a dagger or a Highwayman a pistol.") Panicked Federalist businessmen in Providence, Newport, and other commercial towns threatened to secede from the state and join the Union on their own. Finally on May 29, "in the greatest consternation," the state's ratification convention approved the Constitution, by a hair-thin majority of two votes. Even so, intense resistance remained among state legislators to swearing loyalty to the United States. "They did not chuse to have the Oath crowded down their throats," wrote one observer. "However they finally yielded, and all the members of both houses swallowed it." The forces arrayed against each other in New York assumed that both Rhode Island's new senators—Joseph Stanton, "an obstinate Anti to the last," and the more "ingenious" Theodore Foster—would oppose both assumption and the removal of Congress to Philadelphia.

As the days dragged by, once-pressing issues—Indian treaties, regulation of the coastal trade, fee schedules for the federal courts—received short shrift from Congress. Should post offices in thinly populated rural communities be farmed out to bidders, since they could never be maintained except at a loss? Should Friedrich von Steuben be granted a lifetime annuity of $2,700 per year in gratitude for bringing his Prussian drillmaster's discipline to wartime patriot volunteers? Should the court of admiralty for New Hampshire be relocated from Portsmouth to Exeter? The judiciary laws be extended to North Carolina? Arrears in pay be granted to the aging officers and men of Virginia and Carolina regiments? Debates on these and a score of other issues were perfunctory at best. When Congress paused to appoint a committee to create a library, the cynical scoffed. "It is indeed laughable to see that illustrious body, in the midst of the greatest national questions, attending to the purchase of books for their *amusement* or *instruction*. Is it not sufficient that we already pay them [a salary] but we must allow them a considerable sum for tuition and books?" growled one self-described "republican." With virtually no debate, however, Congress did pass a different piece of legislation whose import resonates resoundingly into the present day: the nation's first copyright act. Introduced by the literary-minded Elias Boudinot of New Jersey, it called "for the encouragement of learning by securing the copies of maps, charts, books and other writings, to the authors and proprietors" for fourteen years, renewable to a total of twenty-eight years, and imposing a fine of fifty cents per page on pirated editions.

Beyond the claustrophobic confines of Federal Hall, life went on. On May 12, New Yorkers were treated to the "grotesque scene" of the recently formed social and patriotic organization that dubbed itself the Sons of St. Tammany parading noisily through the city's lanes in Indian getups and painted faces. Remarked the puzzled Maclay, "There seems to be some kind of Scheme laid of erecting some kind of Order or Society Under this denomination, but it does not seem Well digested as Yet." (Named after a legendary chief named Tamanend, the society had about 250 members in 1790; as Tammany Hall, it would eventually become the dominant political force in New York politics well into the twentieth century.) Lurid stories frequently shouldered aside the political news, such as the scandalous suicide of a Georgian named Telfair, who slit his throat with a razor and whose enslaved companion was found clinging to the dead man's body and only with difficulty was prevented "from committing Violence on himself," and the fate of seagoing murderer Thomas Bird, who had killed his captain off the African coast. Bird wrote personally to George Washington begging for clemency. When the president asked Chief Justice Jay if there "would be prudence, justice or policy in extending mercy to the Convict," Jay's answer was a terse "No." Bird's public hanging resulted from the first capital conviction by a federal court under the Constitution.

Little of this seemed to penetrate the mind of the president, whose attention and anxieties remained fixed on Federal Hall from his new quarters at Bowling Green. "Jealousies & distrusts are spread most impolitickly far & wide," he wrote to his fellow Potomac landowner David Stuart, who was also Martha Washington's son-in-law, and as close to a confidant as the president possessed. "The questions of Assumption—Residence—and other matters have been agitated with a warmth & intemperance, with prolixity & threats, which it is to be feared has lessened the dignity of that body." Yet he took a patient and remarkably democratic view of the unseemly congressional wrangling. There would always be political conflict, he ruminated. "Can it well be otherwise in a country so extensive, so diversified in its interests? And will not these different interests naturally produce in an assembly of Representatives who are to Legislate for, and to assimilate & reconcile them to the general welfare, long, warm & animated debates? Most undoubtedly. The misfortune is that the enemies of the Government—always more active than its friends, and always on the watch to give it a stroke—neglect no opportunity to aim one."

CHAPTER 16

A Southern Position

————•◆•————

I feel ashamed of the body to which I belong.

—Benjamin Goodhue, June 1790

By June, the Pennsylvanians were losing their once-smug self-confidence, having realized that they didn't have enough votes to snare the permanent capital for themselves. Although they presented a united front, their bargaining power was diluted by their internal division over assumption, with some members of the delegation supporting it and others opposed. But they were also well aware that no other faction was strong enough to get its way without their support. So they continued to dicker. "The New Yorkers are alarmed again," reported Representative Thomas Hartley. "They offer to give the Permanent Residence to Pennsylvania—Temporary Residence at New York for only two years—but this is all deception—we must go on steadily with the Virginians—Temporary is all we can aim at, at present."

The New Englanders were particularly frustrated. Assumption seemed to be reeling out of their grasp as the residence question pushed itself forward. "There is such caballing and disgracefully mixing National with local questions that I am heart sick of our situation," wrote

Benjamin Goodhue. "I feel ashamed of the body to which I belong." On June 10, the Senate moved to tack assumption to the funding bill. But Morris and his allies refused to go along, lest the funding bill itself be lost as a result. "Their declaration is plain proof that Philadelphia stands in the way of the state debts," fumed Fisher Ames. "It is barely possible for any business to be more perplexed & entangled than this has been. We are sold by the Pennsylvanians, and the assumption with it. This despicable Grog shop contest, whether the taverns of N. York or Philadelphia shall get the custom of Congress, keeps us in discord & covers us all with disgrace."

The sense that the republic's fate hung in the balance (as well as a desire for free entertainment) brought spectators crowding into the House chamber to witness what everyone recognized was one of the great dramas of the First Congress. Not all of them treated the spectacle with the gravity that members considered their due, offering a competing cacophony to the soaring and plummeting oratory below: the incessant cracking of nuts. "Those who are fond of almonds, walnuts and brown hullers will be so good as to have them cracked at home every morning, so that when they make their exhibition in the gallery they may proceed to eating, as the platoon firing of teeth against the corps of nut shells prevents the spectators from hearing some of the best speakers in the house," complained one local newspaper. Once they'd eaten their fill, the *New-York Daily Gazette* advised, they should please pocket the shells "as the noise of pedestrial troops proudly crushing them to atomi produces the most inharmonious sounds that could possibly be invented."

Almost daily, new alliances formed, broke apart, and re-formed in a different way. In the House, the Virginians and the Marylanders, who had long lobbied for a site on the Potomac, now voted decisively *against* just that, in line with their coalescing accord with the Pennsylvanians, asserting that before any decision was made on a permanent site, Congress should first relocate temporarily to Philadelphia, "with all the hurry and dispatch that could have taken place had the salvation of the United States been at hazard," as George Thatcher sarcastically put it. Then, just a day later, it was successfully moved by a different faction to strike Philadelphia out of an identical motion and insert *Baltimore* instead, taking Madison by surprise. Some of the Potomac's partisans were close to giving up in frustration. "Machinations may be formed to defeat totally [our] object: either absolutely—or by a compromise which may establish the permanent seat of government in a station very unfriendly to the Southern Interests," Richard Bland Lee worried.

Madison dismissed the vote for Baltimore as a ploy. Although he was by no means confident he could achieve what he wanted, he skillfully positioned his Virginians to make the most of any opportunity that presented itself. "The Potowmac stands a bad chance," he confessed to James Monroe—with whom Madison remained on good terms, despite their competition for the House seat that Madison won—as late as June 17, "and yet it is not impossible that in the vicissitudes of the business it may turn up in some form or other." The shape of possible compromise already cohering in his mind, he added, "The assumption still hangs over us. I suspect that it will yet be unavoidable to admit the evil in some qualified shape."

By now, virtually the entire government had been engulfed by the surf of proposals that rose, crested, receded, and surfaced again with new and unexpected force day after day. Even the most astute foreign observer in the United States, French minister Otto, found the debates in Federal Hall an incomprehensible rat's nest of confusion. "The intrigues, the cabals, the underhanded and insidious dealings of a factious and turbulent spirit are even much more frequent in this republic than in the most absolute monarchy where they are concentrated in the palace without infecting the mass of the nation," he exclaimed to the foreign ministry in Paris. "Today they agree on a principle; tomorrow they reject it. . . . The individual members vote obstinately sometimes for and sometimes against the same question. It is surprising to see that almost at the same time a measure can appear good and bad, just and unjust."

Just when paralysis seemed about to set in once again, things began to happen with startling speed. On June 11, Hamilton made an indirect approach to the Pennsylvanians through his newly appointed assistant secretary, Tench Coxe, who was well known to the members of Pennsylvania's delegation. Coxe's initial target, surprisingly, was the irascible Maclay. Coxe told him that Hamilton would provide enough northern votes to plant the government on the Susquehanna if the Pennsylvanians would vote for assumption. Though Maclay's dream was suddenly in his grasp once again, true to form he expressed shock at the mere hint of a quid pro quo. "I contained my indignation at this proposal, with much difficulty, within the bounds of decency," Maclay huffily wrote in his diary. "I gave him such looks and answers as put an end to this business."

Coxe next tried Morris. Cannier than Maclay, Morris asked Coxe to tell Hamilton that at a certain hour the next morning he would be strolling along the Battery, then an earthwork that stretched several blocks along the tip of Manhattan Island and was ironically enough being converted into a public promenade as part of the city's beautification plan to induce Congress to remain in the city. If Hamilton was serious, Morris was willing to meet him there face-to-face, as if they had met by chance. They must have made a striking pair: the rather blowsy, obese Morris, and the handsome, dapper, diminutive Hamilton, heads bent close in intense conversation. As they walked, oblivious of the salty stink of the harbor, the seaport's forest of masts lay spread before them like a winter-bare wilderness undulating on the waves, and beyond them the low, green shore of still-rural Brooklyn. Closer by, they could see the ruins of Fort George, at the foot of Broadway, which workmen were demolishing to make room for the mansion that optimistic New Yorkers intended as a permanent dwelling for future presidents.

Although the two men were years apart in age—Hamilton was only thirty-four and Morris a ripe fifty-six—they had much in common. Both were immigrants as well as committed Federalists and hardheaded men of finance. Thus far, they had been unyielding partisans on behalf of their adopted cities. Hamilton now explained to Morris that in return for one vote in the Senate and five in the House, he would trade enough votes to put the permanent seat of government at either Germantown or Trenton, with the temporary residence remaining in New York for a fixed number of years.

Morris reported the news first to Maclay, saying that he would consult the rest of the Pennsylvania delegation.

"You need not consult me," Maclay snapped back.

Maclay thought Hamilton was playing Morris for a sucker. "Never had a man a greater propensity for bargaining than Mr. Morris," Maclay wrote later in his diary. "Hamilton knows this, and is laboring to make a Tool of him." Leaving the temporary government seat in New York in return for Hamilton's promise to erect the permanent one *somewhere* in Pennsylvania *sometime* in the future was no more than a stratagem to give the Yorkers time to "fortify & entrench themselves" so that the capital could never be pried loose. Maclay might have been right, but this was precisely how many other members of Congress felt about Philadelphia.

However, Hamilton's initiative fizzled. Less than twenty-four hours later, Morris received an apologetic note from the treasury secretary, admitting that he didn't have the votes he promised after all. His friends wouldn't hear of it, he confessed.

A day later, Morris received an even more intriguing proposition from Thomas Jefferson: the temporary residence at Philadelphia for fifteen years, in return for the permanent seat at Georgetown. Having been abroad for much of the past decade, Jefferson enjoyed goodwill among the members of Congress, and was well positioned to serve as an interlocutor for Madison and the president. He recognized that unless a compromise formula was found, "there will be no funding bill agreed to, [and] our credit will burst and vanish," he wrote to James Monroe. Although Jefferson viscerally detested assumption, he confessed, "I see the necessity of yielding for this time to the cries of the creditors in certain parts of the union, for the sake of union, and to save us from the greatest of all calamities, the total extinction of our credit in Europe." To his son-in-law, Thomas Mann Randolph, he revealed deeper anxiety: "If the states separate without funding, there is an end of the government: the only choice is among disagreeable things."

Madison, meanwhile, in a second prong of attack, informed the Massachusetts delegation that the Virginians might possibly be willing to abandon their long-standing rejection of assumption. "Madison at their head has made us private proposals," Representative Benjamin Goodhue confided to his brother, if the government adjourned to Philadelphia—thus placating the Pennsylvanians—and then more permanently "to the south." After idling for months in the political doldrums, assumption, too, suddenly seemed to have wind in its sails.

When the Pennsylvanians learned what Madison had told Massachusetts, they took a more serious look at Jefferson's offer. "It is now established beyond a doubt that the secretary of the Treasury guides the Movements of the Eastern Phalanx," Pennsylvania representative Peter Muhlenberg wrote to Benjamin Rush. "They are now ready to sacrifice every other object, provided they can thereby gain the assumption of the State Debts." If Pennsylvania had to choose between Hamilton and the Virginians, Muhlenberg reflected that he would pick the southerners, whom he deemed more likely to keep their word. Besides, "in the course of 15 or 20 years, Circumstances may alter cases." What Muhlenberg meant was, once the government was lodged in Philadelphia, its inhabitants ought to be clever enough to find a way to keep it there, no matter what they agreed to now.

A day or two later, one of the most fortuitous encounters in American history occurred when Jefferson ran into Hamilton in the street outside the president's house. As they paced back and forth in front of Washington's door, Hamilton, looking haggard and disheveled and "dejected beyond description," according to Jefferson, pleaded that the integrity of the Union hinged on assumption. If it failed to pass, he intended to resign. Could Jefferson speak to his southern friends and try to bring them around? The Virginian replied, why not sit down with Madison for a "friendly discussion"? Later that day, Jefferson sent notes to both men, inviting them to a dinner the next day at his home, adding genteelly that "men of sound heads and honest views needed nothing more than explanation and mutual understanding to enable them to unite in some measures which might enable us to get along."

Jefferson's living quarters were a far cry from the stateliness of Monticello. To make his "indifferent" home more tolerable, he built an extension on it to house his library, his proudest possession, and mounted a pair of engravings of President Washington, which would gaze with chilly dignity over what a cynic might unkindly have termed the first great backroom deal in American political history. He and his dining companions, most likely on June 20, comprised the most luminous stars of the government's younger generation. Compact and high-strung, Hamilton still radiated the martial style that he had acquired during the Revolution. Although their relationship had not yet splintered into the enmity that would characterize it later in the decade, the decidedly unmilitary Jefferson considered the treasury secretary something of a jumped-up provincial and suspected him even now of harboring "monarchist" tendencies that could threaten the republic. Madison formed a kind of balance wheel that occupied the political space between his two fellow diners: intimate of one and collaborator with the other, paramount exponent of the Federalist vision but already beginning his journey toward the hinterland of states' rights. Although his distance from Washington had grown, he was also still the most powerful member of Congress.

Another man was also present: James Hemings, Jefferson's slave and chef, the brother of the secretary of state's enslaved mistress, Sally Hemings, and the half brother of Jefferson's dead wife, Martha. Hemings's attentive, unacknowledged figure suggests, like a sort of moral parenthesis, the thwarted hopes of the nearly seven hundred thousand enslaved Americans whose destinies hinged on the decisions of the great men of the age. Jefferson and Madison ritually protested their distaste for the injustice of slavery but lived comfortably on the fruits of their slaves' labor. Hamilton, an enemy of slavery, believed that blacks' "natural faculties are probably as good as ours," as he wrote to John Jay, a fellow founding member of the New York Manumission Society. "The contempt we have been taught to entertain for the blacks makes us fancy many things that are founded in neither reason nor experience." He now had the power to throw the votes of his supporters behind a free-state capital. But he would not do it: his overriding object was passage of the assumption bill.

Years later, after Jefferson and Hamilton had become open antagonists and the treasury secretary was no longer alive to defend himself, Jefferson portrayed himself as the innocent victim of Hamilton's "duplicity." This was disingenuous. "The discussion took place," Jefferson wrote, in an 1818 memo, the only eyewitness account of what occurred that afternoon. "I could take no part in it, but an exhortatory one, because I was a stranger to the circumstances which should govern it." In the end, the two Virginians agreed that defeating Hamilton's financial plan had the potential to cause irreparable damage. So, in the name of national unity, they agreed to compromise. They would arrange for a certain number of Hamilton's opponents to switch their votes. However, wrote Jefferson, it was obvious that "this pill would be especially bitter to the Southern States, and that some concomitant measure should be adopted to sweeten it a little to them."

By the end of the dinner—given Jefferson's tastes, it was probably exquisite and French—it was agreed that Madison would permit assumption once again to be proposed in the House. He could not agree to vote for it himself, but he would oppose it less stridently, to protect himself from the vengeance of his Virginia constituents in the next election. More concretely, he promised to provide enough votes for assumption to ensure its passage. Hamilton's part of the bargain, the sweetener for the southerners, would be the permanent establishment of the federal city on the Potomac. As a sop, an essential one, to the Pennsylvanians, the Virginians would agree to allow the seat of government to remain in Philadelphia for ten to fifteen years while the new seat of government was being built. "In this way there will be something to displease & something to soothe every part of the Union," Jefferson wrote to Monroe later that night. "If this compromise failed, I fear one infinitely worse"— assumption with no limits at all, he meant, and the capital lost forever to the South.

This elaborate confection had other pieces. In a genteel version of a payoff, Hamilton agreed to a revaluation of Virginia's debt, guaranteeing that the state would enjoy a generous federal windfall from assumption, even though the state had long maintained that it had already paid off its debt. Hamilton had got what he most wanted, but he had also yielded a great deal.

Madison's strategic patience, Jefferson's fortuitous arrival on the scene, and Hamilton's exhaustion of his other options produced a bargain that could probably not have been accomplished earlier. That it took place at all seems obvious only with hindsight. Many members of Congress feared, with reason, that without a compromise to drain off bile-filled sectional jealousies, a collapse of the government would soon ensue. But the figurative, and perhaps actual, handshake across the dinner table was just the beginning.

According to historian Kenneth R. Bowling, Madison did not need more votes to pass his Potomac-and-Philadelphia bill; what he did need was Hamilton's influence over the New Englanders to prevent them from sabotaging the delicate negotiations between Pennsylvania and the south. This required considerable persuasion since most of the Yankees were "utterly disgusted" when they learned what was happening. "The Potowmack is to our eastern folks so disagreeable that we think We should never be able to justify our being accessory to so great and lasting an evil," Benjamin Goodhue of Massachusetts frostily commented.

By late June, Hamilton knew that he needed three more votes in the House to pass the assumption bill. In the Senate, despite the addition of Delaware's George Read, who was won over to the proassumption side by Robert Morris, Hamilton still lacked one vote to balance those of the two new antiassumption Rhode Island senators. Madison then made good on his dinner-table promise. He found Hamilton the votes he needed in the House, from Virginia and Maryland, from men based in areas most of which stood to benefit directly from the proposed Potomac capital. The pivotal senator was the aristocratic Charles Carroll, who owned a ten-thousand-acre, slave-worked estate on the Maryland side of the Potomac. In the House, Daniel Carroll was encouraged by Madison to believe, and possibly promised outright, that Georgetown would be included in the new federal district, doubtless spurring a surge in the worth of his local property. Madison also corralled George Gale, a longtime advocate for the Potomac from the Eastern Shore of Maryland; Richard Bland Lee of Virginia, who was probably told in private that Alexandria, which he represented, would also become part of the district; and Alexander White, who represented the upper Potomac. White was the hardest sell and went along only "with a revulsion of the stomach almost convulsive."

Meanwhile, Hamilton undertook to win over Pennsylvania's delegation through the leverage of the ever-pragmatic Robert Morris, who quickly reconciled himself to the deal: after all, the New Yorkers had been driven from the field, Pennsylvania had captured the temporary capital, and the Potomac would open a new field for his own speculative investments. Hamilton told Morris that he would no longer oppose Philadelphia, but the Pennsylvanian would have to accept a ten-year rather than a fifteen-year residence at Philadelphia—the maximum price that the southerners demanded for agreeing to go there at all. Morris further agreed that the Pennsylvanians would press their allies in Delaware and New Jersey to back the compromise.

Parking himself next to Maclay in the Senate chamber, Morris whispered with evident satisfaction, "The Business is settled at last."

At first Maclay didn't believe him, scribbling on a scrap of paper, "If Hamilton has his hand in the Residence now, he will have his Foot in it before the end of the Session."

Gradually, however, as the outlines of the deal became clear, Maclay realized that the most crucial "jockeying and bargaining" had taken place without him. Thinking he had been at the center of decision making, he discovered that he had merely been at its rim. Maclay then did what he later deemed the most embarrassing thing he had done in his life. He rose to his full height on the Senate floor and began ranting, declaring that Pennsylvania was owed the permanent capital, and that to deprive her of it was "a Species of Robbery!" But he stood apart and alone, a painful posture for a man so sensitive, so proud, and so desperate for respect.

Over several steamy, rain-soaked days the furious New Yorkers under the leadership of Senator Rufus King mounted a last-ditch attempt to broker a deal to keep the government in their city. "Cunning and intrigueing They Spare no pains to Coax & Cajole those with whom they think there is the least Chance of Success," Morris wrote to his wife. Baltimore, paired with a five-year residence in New York, was proposed and defeated. Then a two-year extension in New York; that failed, too. Splitting the next decade between New York and Philadelphia was then offered, and that, too, defeated. From his throne overlooking the floor, John Adams hectored the senators on the splendid character of New York City, annoying the Pennsylvanians, then declared that he would support a move to Philadelphia anyway, irritating the New Yorkers. King, according to Maclay, "sobbed, Wiped his Eyes and scolded & railed, and accused first everybody and then nobody of bargaining, contracting arrangements, and engagements that would dissolve the Union."

In the end, in what must have been an acutely painful conversation for all concerned, Hamilton urged his New York friends to abandon their effort and take the bird they had in hand: "The project of Phila & Potomack is bad, but it will insure the funding system and the Assumption. Agreeing to New York and Baltimore will defeat it."

The Potomac dream was now to become reality. But where on the river was it going to be? On June 28, Charles Carroll formally moved that the seat of government be established "at some place" between the Eastern Branch—today known as the Anacostia River, a few miles below

Georgetown—and tongue-twisting Conococheague Creek, which merges into the Potomac at Williamsport, Maryland, about sixty-five miles to the north as the crow flies. Beyond that, the exact location was left to the discretion of the executive. The president was directed to name a three-member commission to acquire and survey land, while government offices were required no later than the first Monday in December—just five months hence—to shift to Philadelphia, where they were to remain until permanent buildings were ready for them on the Potomac in December 1800. Most assumed that the commission would also pick the precise location for the new city.

Although many supposed that Georgetown was the most likely site, others—including James Monroe—assumed that "the fortunate spot" would be somewhere far upriver where the state was narrowest, so that the federal district might eventually incorporate parts of Virginia and Pennsylvania, an appealing prospect to those who saw the future seat of government as a symbol of nationhood that transcended the interest of individual states. Others scoffed: "Where in the name of common sense is Conogochegue?" demanded Elbridge Gerry, picking on just one of the prospective upriver sites. "You might as well induce a belief that you are in earnest by inserting Mississippi, Detroit, or Winnipipocket Pond," in faraway New Hampshire. "What are the members to do? Are they to carry their tents with them in summer, and repair to their barracks in winter?" Still others, tongue in cheek, claimed that the pronunciation of Conococheague made New England maidens blush at its sound.

Aedanus Burke scorned any arrangement that included Philadelphia—"a very bad neighborhood for the South Carolinians"—recalling how the Quakers had menacingly "hovered in the gallery" like malign spirits during the petition debate, back in February. "I would as soon pitch my tent beneath a tree in which was a hornets' nest, as I would, as a delegate from South Carolina, vote for placing the government in a settlement of Quakers," he barked. But even he had to admit that he was on the losing side.

In defense of the compromise, Richard Henry Lee confessed that assumption frankly repelled him, but regarded mutual concession as imperative for the sake of the country. In half-menacing, half-conciliatory language that southern politicians would perfect in decades to come, he warned northern opponents of the compromise not to offend the South. Give the *reasonable* men of the South what they wanted—that is, the seat of government—or else uncontrollable radicals and insurrectionists would tear the country apart. Don't dare to reject a bill so calculated to conciliate and unite and instead risk fueling the animosity that would only end in "the horrid and bloody calamities" of civil war. (Less flamingly, Lee complained that the New Yorkers had deliberately packed the House visitors' gallery with enticingly pretty girls, "as much as to say, as you Vote, so we will smile—A severe trial for susceptible minds.")

When Madison finally weighed in, he spoke as an avowed southerner. "We have it now in our power to procure a southern position," he strikingly declared. "The opportunity may not again speedily present itself." If the Potomac was struck out, then any other place might be inserted in its place: the Susquehanna, the Delaware, Baltimore, the Philadelphia suburbs. Moreover, amendment would also mean sending the bill back to the Senate. If that happened, would the House ever see it again? "By amending, we give up a certainty for an uncertainty. I beg leave to press it on gentlemen not to consent to any alteration lest it be wholly defeated, and the prospect of obtaining a southern position vanish forever." He may not have swayed many votes, but he had made crystal clear to any who wondered where his steady evolution away from drumbeating federalism was leading: southward.

Just hours after Washington signed the Potomac bill, the Senate voted 14 to 12 to add the assumption of $21.5 million in state war debts to the funding bill, as knots of excited representatives crowded against the iron rails that ran along the rear of the chamber. In the end, while assumption was shaped to satisfy Massachusetts and South Carolina, the two states that were most desperately in need of it, it also delivered a generous financial windfall to Virginia and North Carolina—in effect, a quid pro quo for their acquiescence to the temporary removal of the government to the repugnant Quakers' nest of Philadelphia. Massachusetts and South Carolina would each receive $4 million, followed by Virginia and North Carolina with $3.5 million and $2.4 million respectively. The allocations for other states ranged from $2.2 million for Pennsylvania to $200,000 for Rhode Island. Virginia's share was substantially more than the size of the debt that she had retired, as Madison privately confirmed to his father.

One knotty financial problem still remained: how much interest the government would pay holders of the various types of bonds and certificates. Investors naturally demanded the full 6 percent return that nearly all the government-issued paper originally promised, while the enemies of speculation argued for a rate of 4 or even 3 percent. A great deal of money was at stake, given the size of the debt. It was finally agreed that foreign creditors would be paid in full through new loans. Retirement of the domestic debt was more complex. After exchanging their old securities, creditors would be paid 4 percent interest on two-thirds of the new securities, beginning in 1792. The remaining one-third of the new securities would earn 6 percent, but those payments would not begin until 1800. Because it would take so long to pay the principal, the reduction of the interest rate from 6 to 4 percent amounted to an unacknowledged cut of about one-third in the amount of money the government would have to allot toward the debt over at least the next decade. Robert Morris, who shared the sentiments of speculators, who had hoped to be paid the higher rate for all the securities they held, threatened to vote *against* funding if the interest rate was set any lower than 6 percent. In the end, however, even he capitulated to the compromise, declaring, "Half a loaf is better than no bread."

With the passage of funding now all but assured, speculators raced to take advantage of last-minute bargains, dispatching fast boats southward to snap up discounted paper before rural holders of certificates heard news of the compromise. "Warn people from selling at 3/ or 4/ when they may soon get perhaps 10/," William Loughton Smith breathlessly advised his friend Edward Rutledge.

The volatile James Jackson of Georgia—whose state was allotted the comparatively paltry sum of $300,000—cried that the entire funding represented a vast and sinister plot by those who sought to absorb "the whole of the state powers within the vortex of the all devouring general government." Do not impose upon Americans "this enormous and iniquitous debt, [which] will beggar the people and bind them in chains!" he cried, "bellowing and rebellowing" so loudly with "his eyes uplifted to Heaven," one newspaper reported, that the Senate had to once again shut its windows to block him out, despite the summer heat. To this, Elbridge Gerry curtly retorted that Georgia was such "an infant state" and had contributed so little to the Revolutionary War that it deserved no more than it got.

On July 29, between three and four in the afternoon, the funding act was finally passed by both houses, bringing to an end the longest and most difficult debate of the First Congress. The Constitution had survived its first major crisis by means of the first publicly fought-out compromise in American history. The men such as Maclay who had condemned as dangerous to republican liberty the vote trading that made the compromise possible were proven wrong. An American tradition of bare-knuckle compromise had been born. Triumph though all this was for Madison the master strategist, he considered the sordid business "an unavoidable evil," he told Monroe. However, Madison sighed, "I cannot deny that the crisis demands a spirit of accommodation."

Members of Congress felt a general sense of relief. The dammed-up frustration of months broke, and the seeping fear of collective failure dissipated. When he learned that the seat-of-government bill had passed in the Senate, Representative Michael Jenifer Stone of Maryland trilled, "And forever thereafter the Seat of Government shall be—on the Banks of the river Potowmack! Joy! Joy to Myself! Joy to my Country! Joy to the United States! Joy to the lovers of Mankind!" Hamilton,

Madison, the New Englanders Ames and Sedgwick, and many others believed the Union had been saved, and they were not wrong. Washington, who considered the conjoined conundrums of the debt and the future capital "more in danger of having convulsed the government itself than any other points," was profoundly relieved, and Jefferson optimistically predicted that nothing "so generative of dissension can rise again."

Not everyone was that happy. Many republicans continued to regard assumption as a scandalous surrender to the malign designs of big-city financiers at home and abroad. "The Spanish cruelties in America & the English cruelties in the East Indies do not stain human Nature with a blacker hue than the conduct of the present Congress towards the Army that established our independence," fulminated the Philadelphia reformer Benjamin Rush. "The whole profits of the War will soon center in the hands of American Tories—Amsterdam Jews & London brokers—while the brave Men who deserved them will end their lives in [gaols] & hospitals, or beg their bread from door to door." Fear and loathing of Wall Street, soon to be the site of the nation's first stock exchange, would continue to deepen and grow, even as Hamilton's capitalist principles and debt-driven economics brought prosperity to Americans that was undreamed of in 1790.

New Yorkers were the most bitter of all. Their city would now never become the London or Paris that it might well have been had the capital remained there. Construction of the presidential palace would be halted. The grand plans for imperial boulevards and parks would remain stillborn. "The ingratitude of Congress stares them in the face," scowled DeWitt Clinton, the nephew of New York's governor. Wild, false rumors spread that mobs had swarmed Federal Hall and attacked the members, killing several and seriously wounding many more. All the gaudy processions, all the money that had been spent to renovate Federal Hall, the hospitality lavished on members of Congress, the balls, teas, levees—all of it was for nought.

The city's poets wept. Wrote one:

Have we not paid for chaplain's prayers,
That Heav'n might smile on state affairs?
Put some things up, pull'd others down,
And rais'd our streets through half the town?

Local newspapers denounced Congress as a collection "of rustic boors," hack lawyers, and planters "whose social collisions are with their hogs, negroes, and horses" and called for the impeachment of Morris and Madison, who, in the words of one correspondent, "together stood as guilty of betrayal as Judas himself." Morris was blamed unmercifully, far out of proportion to his actual responsibility for the compromise. Scurrilous cartoons showed him enticed by a transvestite prostitute serving as a procuress for Congress; pulling members toward Philadelphia with strings through their noses; and using Jefferson as a walking stick, with Hamilton and Madison dangling like ornaments from his watch chain.

Even the sacred Washington was no longer untouchable. "The Holy Name of the P—t is not much respected in the mouths of the profane," remarked DeWitt Clinton. Some citizens were so disgusted that they even condemned the mayor and the city council for commissioning a portrait of Washington to be hung in City Hall.

No one felt the pangs of defeat by realpolitik more than did Maclay. That Washington himself was implicated in such sordid dealings nearly broke his heart. "Alas! That the Affection nay Almost Adoration of the People should meet so unworthy a return," he ruefully opined. "The President has become in the hands of Hamilton The Dishclout of every dirty Speculation, as his name Goes to Wipe away blame and Silence all Murmuring."

Maclay felt not only disillusioned, but useless. He had been beaten on virtually every measure in which he took an interest. Philadelphians might now rejoice in having won for themselves the temporary seat of government, but they would be disappointed soon enough. New Englanders, too, he feared, would "become refractory and endeavor to Unhinge the Government" once the capital became embedded in the domain of the southern planter "surrounded with his slaves & dependants," and presidential patronage shifted to southern men. "I cannot however help concluding that all Things would have been better on the Susquehannah," he sighed.

CHAPTER 17

Indians

———•·———

What does Congress mean to do with those Creatures?

—Charles Thomson, June 1790

New Yorkers were agape at the sight: a sloop full of Creek Indians, feathered, beaded, and bejeweled, figures as much of romantic legend— and of menace—as they were living men, fresh from the wild interior of Georgia, now crossing the harbor from New Jersey in the shimmering July heat. A detachment of soldiers greeted them at Murray's Wharf, along with the entire membership of the Tammany Society, which, wearing fake Indian costumes, solemnly escorted them up Wall Street to Federal Hall, where the Indians exchanged salutes with members of Congress gathered on the second-floor balcony. The Indians moved on in a royal progress to the home of Secretary of War Knox, the Creeks' official host, where they smoked "the calumet of peace." They then continued to the president's home, a few doors away, where they were officially introduced to the chief executive. They finally wound up at the City Tavern, where they dined with "conviviality and good humor" as Knox's guests, along with members of Congress, assorted militia officers, and the "sachems" of the Tammany Society.

While Secretary of State Jefferson monitored the seismic political eruptions in faraway Europe, the nearest and most threatening powers to the United States were the native nations of the trans-Appalachian West from the Great Lakes to the Gulf of Mexico, where well-armed and defiant tribes—Wyandots, Shawnees, Cherokees, Creeks, and a half dozen others—formed a barrier against American settlers who were pressing ever more aggressively westward. Throughout the lawless and largely undefined borderland, whites and Indians murdered each other with near impunity, while reports of bloody raids, home burnings, kidnappings, and "outrages" against white women percolated eastward. (Americans usually characterized Indians as aggressors and savages, ignoring atrocities that settlers perpetrated against native peoples.) Reported one Ohio settler of his terrified wife, "She is almost every night dreaming of the Indians and, mistaking me for one of them, very frequently cries out in her sleep that I am scalping her." Another bitterly complained that Congress was allowing "the distant members of the Empire to be robbed, murdered, scalped, and carried away into captivity by an insignificant herd of tawny banditti." People in Kentucky talked seriously of seceding from the United States and affiliating with the Spanish west of the Mississippi for protection. "The emigration from this country to that is already alarming and unless greater security can be given there is no saying where it will stop," a correspondent wrote to James Madison. "No people will remain long under a Government which does not afford protection."

Allowing for exaggeration and self-serving disinformation by men with a financial stake in acquiring Indian lands—and there were many—the instability along the frontier was quite genuine. Marauding bands of Shawnees had compelled Knox to order the formation of a mixed force of regulars and militia under Brigadier Josiah Harmar to march on their strongholds in the Wabash Country, which straddled the border of the future states of Ohio and Indiana, while General Anthony Wayne reported that the security situation in Georgia was so bad as "to threaten this lately flourishing State with ruin & depopulation." Georgia officials estimated that between January and October 1789, the Creeks had killed 72 whites and 10 blacks, taken 30 whites and 110 slaves prisoner, wounded another 29 whites, burned 89 houses, and made off with almost 600 horses and 1,000 head of cattle. Representative James Jackson, a hardened Indian fighter, had declared in August 1789 that Georgia had been invaded and demanded that federal troops be dispatched to punish the Indians. Now the equally militant Pierce Butler of South Carolina warned in the Senate that unless the government took forceful action, the Georgians might seek succor "elsewhere"—presumably from Spain.

Meanwhile, settlers kept pouring through the gaps in the mountains, floating down the Ohio River and the Mississippi, and trekking into up-country Georgia and the Carolinas. "In spite of scalping the lands here will be settled," one determined Kentuckian wrote to George Washington. In November 1789, no fewer than three thousand westbound emigrants were camped at Wheeling alone, preparing to trade their wagons for flatboats for the journey to new lands in Kentucky and Ohio. Few Americans or Indians believed that emigration could be stopped completely. "Empire has been continually pointing its course westward," reflected Representative Thomas Scott of Pennsylvania. "Immigrations have been uniformly extending in that direction from the Garden of Eden to the present day."

The Creeks were hard-pressed not only by individual settlers, but also by well-financed land companies chartered by Georgia that were busily selling title to vast and sometimes overlapping tracts of Creek territory in western Georgia and the so-called Yazoo Country, encompassing parts of the present-day states of Mississippi and Alabama. Among the investors were many politically well-connected figures, including former Virginia governor Patrick Henry, war hero George Rogers Clark, Supreme Court justice James Wilson, and eventually Robert Morris, and an army of smaller speculators. George Washington, an aggressive land speculator elsewhere, disparaged the Yazoo companies as "Land Jobbers, who maugre every principle of Justice to the Indians, and policy to their country," and who "would, for their own immediate emolument, strip the Indns of all their territory." To the Creeks, the settlers were no more than a predatory "pack of Desperadoes" and "vagrants," declared the Creeks' leading chief, the remarkable Alexander McGillivray, the son of a Scottish trader and a mixed French-Indian mother, who was the tribe's last best hope of staving off the American invasion.

The Creeks were collectively strong enough to field as many as five thousand warriors, far more than the minuscule US Army, but, not an organized "tribe," they were more a scattering of bands and towns related by linguistic affinity. Their chiefs cooperated ad hoc rather than under McGillivray's command. Their well-developed economy combined hunting, farming, and cattle raising with extensive trade with both Anglo-Americans and the Spanish posts along the Gulf Coast from Florida to New Orleans. During the Revolutionary War, they were loosely aligned with England. When the British withdrew after the war, they shifted their diplomatic allegiance to Spain, for whom, in turn, the Creeks and other southeastern tribes served as a useful buffer against the encroaching Americans.

Although sometimes described by whites as a "king," McGillivray was just a first among equals, whose "open, generous mind," good judgment, and powers of persuasion won him the support of the majority of principal Creek chiefs. Racked by physical ailments—gout, rheumatism, migraine headaches, and probably some form of venereal disease—he was nonetheless an impressive figure, tall and slender, with strikingly long, tapering fingers and piercing eyes. He knew that the Creeks couldn't hold off the Georgians forever. McGillivray boasted that he could capture Savannah if he wanted and ravage Georgia at will. This may in fact have been the case. But he also understood that if he did so, the United States would declare war, crush him, and eventually drive what was left of his people from their homes. The Creeks' frontier towns had suffered greatly from American attacks, and they had no stomach for all-out war, while the speculators had succeeded in buying off some of the Chickasaws to the west, leaving the Creeks increasingly hemmed in. Despite his bravado, McGillivray had spent virtually his entire adult life either at war or in preparation for it; he personally wanted peace. He also realized that the weakness of the United States might be exploited to the Creeks' advantage. "It is better to treat with an enemy under Such circumstances than a more powerful one," he acutely remarked to a Spanish agent with whom he kept in regular contact. Even as he reassured his Spanish allies that he would remain loyal to them, he observed, "Everything urges us to a speedy issue with Wash[ington]."

During the Confederation years, the weak national government was no better able to impose its will in the shaping of Indian policy than it was in any other sphere, and the states had been left to deal with tribes as they wished. The Constitution had specified, however, that "trade and intercourse" with the tribes and the power of treaty making were both federal prerogatives. Knox and Washington seized the initiative almost immediately, in an effort to pry Indian affairs from the state legislatures, whose political interests and corruption by land speculators abetted the chronic instability on the frontier. They believed that if emigration could not be stopped, it could at least be controlled by the federal government in a way the protected Indian tribes from destruction. Knox, the most enlightened crafter of Indian policy the United States produced before the twentieth century, believed that Indians must be fairly compensated for lands already seized by whites, and that all future cessions of native land be negotiated peacefully and legally, and properly paid for. "To dispossess them on any other principle would be a gross violation of the fundamental Laws of nature," Knox asserted in 1788. "That the Indians possess the natural rights of man, and that they ought not wantonly to be divested thereof, cannot be well denied."

Ignoring Georgian protests that any federal action other than the deployment of troops constituted interference in the state's sovereign affairs, Knox, with Washington's support, dispatched Marinus Willett, a former army officer and sheriff of New York City, to the Creek country as the official ambassador of one nation to another. Willett assured McGillivray and his fellow chiefs that the new US government wanted none of their land for itself, and that President Washington desired to receive a tribal delegation in New York to negotiate a comprehensive treaty of peace. Thus the stage was set for the most picturesque episode in the history of the First Congress.

The Creeks' journey to New York in 1790 was the climax of nearly a year's negotiations. McGillivray and his party—the vividly named Bird Tail King, Big Fear, Blue Giver, Chickwockly, Stimalejie, Opay Mico, Stimafutchkee, nearly thirty chiefs in all—traveled north, some on horseback and others in wagons, through Guilford Court House in North Carolina, Richmond, Fredericksburg, and Philadelphia, reaching New York at the end of July. The treaty talks took place mostly in informal meetings over three weeks, while the Americans did their best to awe their guests with the might of the United States and the modernity of their government's home. The Indians were doubtless given a tour of Federal Hall and were perhaps taken to witness the impressive but still underemployed Supreme Court, which had begun its second brief session at the Royal Exchange Building, on August 2. Soldiers entertained the Creeks with displays of close-order drill and the firing of cannon. The president escorted them aboard an oceangoing merchant ship that had just arrived from Canton. At a "complimentary conference" put on at "the great Wigwam"—Federal Hall—members of the Tammany Society sang a medley of popular American songs, and the Creeks regaled their hosts with tribal dances. One afternoon after dinner, in an effort to impress the Indians with the sophistication of American culture, Washington led the chiefs to a room in his mansion for a surprise viewing of John Trumbull's full-length portrait of him. (Trumbull was the son of former governor Jonathan Trumbull of Connecticut, as well as a battlefield veteran of the Revolutionary War.) Few if any of the Creeks had seen a professional painting before, and "they were for a time mute with astonishment," Trumbull recalled. "At length one of the chiefs advanced toward the picture, and slowly stretched out his hand to touch it, and was still more astonished to feel, instead of a round object, a flat surface, cold to the touch. Another then approached, and placing one hand on the surface and the other behind, was still more astounded to perceive that his hands almost met."

The negotiations climaxed on August 7, when the Creeks approved a treaty of friendship—the first treaty of any kind to be completed under the Constitution. "In its consequences," Washington confidently informed the Senate, the treaty will "be the means of firmly attaching the Creeks and the neighboring Tribes to the interests of the United States." Five days later, the Senate gave its approval, against the opposition of the two disgruntled Georgia members and South Carolina's Pierce Butler. The next day, August 13, the treaty was formally ratified in the House chamber at Federal Hall under the eyes of the vice president, members of Congress, assorted dignitaries both foreign and domestic, and a horde of "respectable, curious, and highly gratified populace," including "a brilliant circle of ladies," Martha Washington among them, who packed helter-skelter into the visitors' gallery.

At twelve o'clock sharp, the Creek chiefs, "fancifully painted" and dressed in blue frock coats, strode into the chamber chanting a song that infused the staid ambience with a frisson of the wild frontier. "Suddenly rude and tumultuous sounds are heard—frightfully terrific they vibrate tremendously upon the ear," reported one enthralled eyewitness. Moments later, President Washington swept majestically into the chamber, wearing a suit of rich purple satin, and trailed by his cabinet secretaries and aides.

Washington's young secretary, Tobias Lear, read the provisions of the treaty aloud. After each sentence, an interpreter explained the sense of it to the Indians in their own language, and they responded with a loud cry of approval. Under the terms of the treaty, the Creeks would recognize American sovereignty over those parts of their territory that lay within the boundaries of the United States. They would also give up their claims to tribal lands that had already been seized by white settlers, in return for $10,000 in merchandise, and an annual federal subsidy of $1,500. Disputed territory that was claimed by Georgia—roughly between the present-day cities of Milledgeville and Atlanta—would be guaranteed to the Creeks. The federal government also promised to furnish "useful domestic animals and implements of husbandry," so that the Creeks might be led "to a greater degree of civilization and to become herdsmen and cultivators instead of remaining in a state of hunters." As a deterrent to unauthorized white settlement, the treaty explicitly gave the Creeks the right to punish as they saw fit any American who invaded their land. The Creeks, for their part, were required to deliver up any member of their tribe who committed robbery or a capital crime against an American citizen.

The American negotiators had pressed the Creeks to redirect their trade away from the Spanish ports to American ones. "The trade of the Indians is a main means of their political management," one American had bluntly noted. But the Creeks had refused, preferring to continue to play off the two powers against each other. However, a secret article of the treaty authorized Creek trade goods to pass through American ports free of duty if their regular channels of trade became obstructed. (Since conflict between Spain and Britain seemed imminent, this was a significant provision.) If the Creeks later chose to channel their trade through the United States, McGillivray was to be guaranteed personal control of it—a lucrative privilege that he already enjoyed with the Spanish. Another secret article appointed McGillivray an agent of the United States with the rank of brigadier and an annual salary of $1,200. Military commissions, large medals, and annuities of $100 a year were also assigned to six other chiefs.

When Lear finished reading, the president rose to his full height and delivered an "energetic and animated" speech, recommending "a spirit of Amity," and urging the Creeks to "endeavor to annihilate animosities, and to conciliate the Nations." He further begged "the great Spirit, the master of Breath," to forbid the infringement of a mutually beneficial contract formed under such happy auspices. He then presented to McGillivray a string of beads symbolic of amity, tobacco to be smoked in the pipe of friendship, and a pair of gold epaulets Washington had worn during the Revolutionary War. McGillivray in return promised that he would do all in his power to promote harmony, and to see that the treaty was upheld.

After this, each of the chiefs solemnly approached the president and intertwined his arm with Washington's in what a local newspaper termed the "shake of peace." Later that day, the St. Andrews Society of New York, a Scottish social organization, unanimously elected McGillivray an honorary member in a bibulous ceremony at the City Tavern, where the Creeks "Partook of a collation provided for the occasion, and mingled with great affability in the festivity of the evening."

The president was pleased at the outcome. "This event will leave us in peace from one end of our borders to the other, except where it may be interrupted by a small refugee banditti of Cherokees and Shawanese, who can easily be chastised or even extirpated if it shall become necessary," Washington triumphantly wrote to the Marquis de Lafayette, in Paris. "But this will only be done in an inevitable extremity, since the basis of our proceedings with the Indian Nations has been and shall be justice, during the period in which I may have anything to do in the administration of this government." Washington, unlike many of his contemporaries, took Indian land titles seriously.

Only the Georgians, who had largely been ignored during the negotiations, and their ally Butler, remained adamant. In essence, the US government had taken the Creeks' side against their states. The incensed representative James Jackson disgustedly declared that the government had "invited a savage of the Creek nation to the seat of government, caressed him in a most extraordinary manner, and sent him home loaded with favors." The Georgians were particularly galled by the provision that guaranteed the Creeks sovereignty over lands that Georgia had already sold to speculators. Jackson, no friend to the Yazoo speculators, blustered that Georgia's "rights" had been disgracefully sacrificed, and that decent citizens seeking to pursue their stolen property—for instance, slaves—into Indian country were liable to be tomahawked by savages who feared no punishment by the authorities. Of the secret provisions, he shrilled, "Will Congress permit the laws of the United States, like those of Caligula, to be placed where they cannot be read, and then punish the people for not obeying them?"

By all accounts, the Creeks went home happy. The Indians had, it seemed, ensured the protection of their core territory and even gained some valuable hunting lands in the bargain. McGillivray had carried off the negotiations with consummate skill. He had also done quite well for himself and his tribal allies in the secret articles. Although he swore allegiance to the United States, he also continued to profess loyalty to Spain and would continue to accept salaries from both countries until his premature death in 1793. "If I had not come to this city, Congress would undoubtedly have declared war against us; in which circumstances we would have had much to fear situated as we were," McGillivray wrote to the Spanish agent Carlos Howard. "We had no solid basis for supposing or hoping that Spain would go into a war in order to sustain our claims." McGillivray believed that he had gotten the solemn word of the United States to break up the Yazoo Company and other speculative schemes that threatened his people. He told Howard, "I am thankful that it did not turn out worse."

The Treaty of New York was hailed as a great success at the time of its signing, although it in fact brought only a brief interruption in the steady destruction of the Creek nation. The treaty would nevertheless serve as a model for agreements with other tribes along the frontier and help to reassure settlers elsewhere that the government was capable of dealing with the restive natives and aggressive whites and was determined to bring an end, peacefully if possible, to frontier violence. Washington and Knox had decisively removed treaty making from the vagaries of state politics. By employing a legal strategy akin to that used with foreign countries, the treaty also acknowledged (if ambiguously) the nationhood of tribes, shaping treaty making for decades to come, and laid the basis for tribal sovereignty today.

CHAPTER 18

Interlude II

———◆———

Musquitos, gnats, flees & bugs contended with each other for pref-
erence.

—Thomas Lee Shippen, September 1790

George Washington was relieved to see Congress finally wind to a close after months of its having been "perplexed and delayed" by so many "intricate" questions. Even before the session ended, he sailed for Rhode Island, eager to escape the city and to get some fresh air and exercise after the long sedentary months in New York. He had pointedly cold-shouldered Rhode Island during his earlier New England tour because it had not then ratified the Constitution. His present trip was intended both to soothe hurt feelings in the newest state and bolster the prestige of the beleaguered local Federalists. Accompanied by Thomas Jefferson, New York governor George Clinton, Supreme Court justice John Blair, William Loughton Smith of South Carolina, and several aides, Washington arrived at Newport after an "agreeable" two-day passage. The town's bells rang. Ships flew their colors. Salutes were fired. Crowds of citizens and all manner of official delegations inundated the president with gushing accolades, to which he usually replied with the florid boilerplate that was required: "I am inexpressibly happy that by the smiles of divine Providence my weak but honest endeavors to serve my country have hitherto been crowned with so much success." To the city's Jews, however, he declared with both force and striking sensitivity that the government of the United States "gives to bigotry no sanction, to persecution no assistance," adding, "May the Children of the Stock of Abraham, who dwell in this land, continue to merit and enjoy the good will of the other Inhabitants; while everyone shall sit in safety under his own vine and fig tree, and there shall be none to make him afraid." After a short stopover in Providence, where he was hailed with more bell ringing, cannon firing, dinners, toasts, and parades, one of which included "three negro scrapers"—fiddlers, presumably—"making a horrible noise," Washington reembarked for New York, which he reached on the afternoon of August 21, less than six days after his departure. By the standards of the time, it was a whirlwind tour.

On the morning of August 28, he left New York for good, accompanied by Martha, her grandchildren, four free white and four enslaved black servants, and several aides. A barge manned by thirteen men uniformed in white jackets and black caps picked them up at McComb's Wharf on the Hudson. Thirteen cannon were fired in salute. Then they, along with the country's government, were gone from New York, never to return.

While New Yorkers sulked—"Ungrateful men, and will ye go / and can ye—dare ye? Leave us so?" wailed a local poet—the government was on the move. The offices of the executive departments were being cleared, and their files and furniture boxed for shipping by water to New Brunswick, New Jersey, overland to Trenton, and then again by boat down the Delaware to Philadelphia. James Madison was busily packing his library: the collected letters of Cicero and Pliny, tracts on the corn trade, the orations of Demosthenes, the latest volume of Gibbon's *Decline and Fall*, an account of Captain Cook's voyages in the Pacific, a history of the Dutch Republic, numerous books in French, and works of theology. The Adamses, or at least Abigail, hated to leave New York. She was sorry to lose the "delicious spot" that she had so much enjoyed, with its venerable oaks and rolling grounds, and superb views of the Hudson River and the city's steeples. "I feel low Spirited," she told her sister Mary Cranch. Surrounded by crates and cases, Abigail unhappily imagined the effort it would take to make new friends in Philadelphia and "make and receive a hundred ceremonious visits, not one of ten from which I shall derive any pleasure or satisfaction." New York had been a hard trial for John Adams, who felt depleted and depressed. His popularity had continued to sink, and his sourish self-pity grew worse. "I have seen affection and gratitude and enthusiasm for others but never for me," he lamented. His enemies took constant pleasure "in throwing little slights, and Sly mortifications, and sometimes cruel insults in my way," while lesser men had run away with the people's passions and gained more influence over them than Adams felt (with some justice) that he, toiling day after day in the political vineyards, had earned and deserved. "I wish very heartily that a Change of Vice President could be made tomorrow," he wrote to Benjamin Rush. "I have been too ill-used in the office to be fond of it."

As the members of Congress fanned out toward their homes, some traveling by road, others by sea, apart from the New Yorkers, scarcely anyone remained behind. One of the few out of towners who did was the lordly and usually unsympathetic South Carolina aristocrat Senator Pierce Butler, who was waiting in helpless anguish for his beloved wife to die. "She is as helpless as an infant and reduced to a shadow," he wrote despairingly to a family minister. "She is in the hand of the Lord. It is my duty to submit to His sovereign Will—I will try to do so properly. Yet the Conflict is great." Butler, when he finally was able to depart New York, would leave with only his two grieving daughters.

The young law graduate Thomas Lee Shippen, who had spent the past months hobnobbing with political celebrities, had a "delightful" journey southward. (Travelers rarely used the word *delightful* to describe overland journeys along the country's corrugated roads.) A few miles south of Chester, Pennsylvania—just below Philadelphia—Shippen ran into James Madison and Thomas Jefferson, and they happily continued on together. To pass the time as they waited for a boat to carry them across the mouth of the Delaware River, they rowed themselves along the shore in a hired skiff and feasted on delicious crabs. At Annapolis, they checked into Mann's Inn—"among the most excellent in the world," Shippen enthused—and passed three pleasurable hours in the cupola of the statehouse, "from which you descry the finest prospect in the world, if extent, variety, Wood & Water in all their happiest forms can make one so." After that they enjoyed a dinner of turtle appetizingly seasoned with aged Madeira. Then the trip went abruptly downhill: the travelers next stopped at Queen Anne, "a dirty village" with accommodations to match, where "musquitos, gnats, flees & bugs contended with each other for preference." After a sleepless night, the trio recovered their spirits with breakfast at Bladensburg, at the establishment of an elderly black woman, Margaret Adams, whose inn was regarded as the best in that town. While they ate, she diverted them with an account of the resentment that had been directed at her by her fellow townsmen—evidently whites—because President Washington and his family had preferred to lodge with her when they last passed through. After trying, and failing, to "distress" her in every other way they could imagine, they pulled down her "temple of Cloacina"—that is, her privy. (Cloacina was the Roman goddess of sewers.) Adams amused the travelers by showing them its ruins, "a monument at the same time of the envy of her fellow citizens & her own triumph," Shippen recorded.

At Georgetown, the three toured the countryside round about like a party of ordinary tourists, taking in its "fine prospects," and breakfasting at the estate of one of the largest landowners of all, Notley Young, whose mansion overlooked the Potomac near the Eastern Branch. Afterward Jefferson and Madison conferred with several prominent men who owned land on the river to the south of Georgetown: Uriah Forrest, Francis Deakins, Benjamin Stoddert, and Daniel Carroll of Duddington. (The several similarly named Carrolls, like European grandees, were commonly known by the names of their estates.) Jefferson and Madison had more than sightseeing in mind. Another deal was in the making, a secret one, far from the prying eyes and attentive ears of Yankee congressmen.

The Residence Act that Congress had passed in the summer, pro-

viding for the establishment of a federal capital on the Potomac, had
set in motion a race against time. The opponents of the Potomac site
had succeeded in imposing a deadline: the government's most important
buildings—a meeting place for Congress, the president's mansion, and
accommodations for the executive departments—had to be completed
no later than December of 1800. If they weren't ready on schedule, Congress could, and very likely would, reverse its commitment to the Potomac. Congress had given George Washington executive authority to
name three commissioners to carry out the project, stipulating only that
the federal district was to be no more than one hundred square miles
in area, and somewhere between the Anacostia River and the Conococheague Creek. At least some northern members who had agreed to
the Residence Act had done so in the idealistic hope that the federal
city might be placed to the north and west near the narrow waist of
Maryland.

The Virginians had other ideas. First, they wanted to ensure that they
were not later outwitted by the wily Philadelphians, who would do all in
their power to hold on to the capital. "The essential point seems to be that
the Commission [should] be filled by men who prefer any place on the
Potowmac to any place elsewhere," Madison advised Washington. The
president also wanted something more: to situate the federal city beyond
the *southernmost* point that Congress had allowed, to encompass Washington's hometown of Alexandria, Virginia. In mid-September, Jefferson
penned a private memorandum that presumably reflected Washington's
desires. It included a hand-drawn map showing a simple grid of streets
laid out at the juncture of the Potomac and the Eastern Branch and emphasized the importance of moving forward with both speed and secrecy.
"If the present occasion of securing the Federal seat on the Potowmack
should be lost, it could never more be regained," Jefferson wrote, adding
that the project ought to be advanced "without recourse" to the legislatures of Maryland and Virginia: political competition between different
regional lobbies might well doom the Potomac's chances, as the hapless
Pennsylvanians had done to themselves in the prolonged debate over the

seat of government. Jefferson estimated that fifteen hundred acres of land would have to be acquired for the public buildings, streets, lodging houses for members of Congress, and "half a dozen taverns." Since it was widely assumed that land values would skyrocket once Washington's choice was revealed, Jefferson proposed that each landowner cede to the government half his property, which would then be sold to pay for the city's construction.

After a month spent tending to his affairs at Mount Vernon—hiring a new overseer, seeing to it that the mares were assigned to the right pastures and that the designated fields were prepared for sowing buckwheat and grass—the president returned to Georgetown on October 15, where he received a formal proposal from local landowners. Declaring that "in point of healthiness of situation, goodness of water & air," few spots anywhere else in the United States could compare for the establishment "of a City intended for the Seat of Empire," the proprietors offered four hundred acres of land, only a quarter of what Jefferson had asked for. But it was a start.

Two days later, Washington started upriver. He stopped first at the mouth of the Monocacy River, then at Shepherdstown, Virginia, and Sharpsburg, Maryland, where local landowners advanced the virtues of their area, and finally at the mouth of the Conococheague, where he was entertained by Williamsport's promoters. The president revealed no hint of his actual intentions. The entire trip seems to have been a piece of elaborate political theater rather than a bona fide fact-finding expedition, intended to foster the idea that the capital might well be placed upriver, a ploy that would enable Jefferson to extract the most favorable terms from the Georgetown landowners. Indeed, by mid-November, Washington was rumored to have ordered all three sites on the Potomac to be officially surveyed. Northerners were sufficiently bamboozled that they reiterated scoffing allegations that it would be lunacy to plant Congress in a place "dug out of the rocky wilderness," where, one Philadelphia satirist wrote, "it is already whispered that deers have been caught there with horns seven feet in length; the men too are said to be of extraordinary size, have no tails, and are extremely fond of peach brandy, though ever so hot from the still."

The last fleeting weeks of the recess ticked away all too quickly. Once again, businesses, legal practices, families, and plantations would have to take care of themselves, more or less, as Congress reconvened to consider Alexander Hamilton's proposed national bank, a revenue bill to pay for the interest on the assumed state debts, controversial defense proposals, and other "intricate" unfinished business. Many members would be lame ducks. The Second Congress would not begin its deliberations until October 1791, almost a year hence, but in many states elections for it were already under way. William Maclay was one who suspected that he would not be coming back. "I must stand with open breast to receive the wound inflicted by my adversaries," he reflected sadly. "Slander & defamation are the hooks applied to pull me down." Everywhere around him he heard whispers and innuendos. "It was painful," he confessed. "Every Body says *the People don't like You.*"

Before James Madison left his home for Philadelphia to reenter the fray, he gave detailed instructions to his overseer, Mordecai Collins, to avoid riding the horses without permission from James Madison Sr., to plant as many Irish potatoes as possible, and to "treat the Negroes with all the humanity & kindness consistent with their necessary subordination and work." Thomas Jefferson, too, was in similar haste to settle his affairs at Monticello. He reminded his overseer, Nicholas Lewis, that his daughters and son-in-law Thomas Mann Randolph would be remaining at the estate and were to be furnished with whatever they needed—corn, fodder, wheat, beeves, and firewood to be cut by "the plantation negroes." They were also to have free use of "the house-servants," including Betty Hemings.

From Mount Vernon, with his customary micromanaging zeal, George Washington was firing off barrages of querulous letters to his able secretary, Tobias Lear, who was responsible for wrapping up the president's affairs in New York and transferring his personal household to Philadelphia. Bring the washerwomen but not "the dirty figures" of Mrs. Lewis and her daughter; make sure the harness for the new coach was properly plated; and don't forget the repairs to the coach's pole end. When Washington learned that Pennsylvania had voted to erect a domed Palladian mansion for him, fueling his well-warranted suspicion that the state intended to hold on to the seat of government come what may, he made clear that he would not live in it. Instead, in volleys of letters to Lear, he grumblingly agreed to *rent* Robert Morris's residence on High Street, thus maintaining his role as a temporary tenant pending completion of the Potomac capital. (The state of Pennsylvania would pay the rent, but Washington had made his point.) As grand as Morris's house was, Washington complained that it was "less commodious" than his former residence in New York, that he didn't want any fancy renovations that would make his furniture look shabby, and that the layout would require visitors to climb two sets of stairs and pass his private rooms to reach his study, which was located in a converted bathroom.

More than minutiae preoccupied the president, however. Disturbing news came from Indian country, this time from the North. In July, the governor of the Northwest Territory, Arthur St. Clair, had dispatched a punitive expedition under Josiah Harmar, to chastise hostile Indians based around the headwaters of the Maumee and Wabash Rivers, in present-day Indiana. Harmar's mixed force of 1,453 militiamen and regulars had marched out of Fort Washington—today's Cincinnati—on October 1. Warned by their British allies of the American attack, the Indians evacuated and burned their main town of Kekionga on October 14. The undisciplined militia that made up four-fifths of Harmar's army broke ranks to pillage what was left of the town. The expedition then disappeared into the forest. For weeks there was no news of its fate. Washington's concern steadily deepened to distress. "Forebodings with respect to the expedition are of disappointment and a disgraceful termination," Washington uneasily wrote to Henry Knox in mid-November. "I gave up *all hope* of Success. My mind, from the silence which reigns, and other circumstances, is prepared for the worst." The outcome, when it became known, would be worse than Washington imagined.

CHAPTER 19

Freedom's Fav'rite Seat

———•◆•———

If New York wanted any revenge for the removal, the citizens might
be glutted if they would come here.

—Abigail Adams, November 1790

The temporary capital was a city of superlatives. "Philadelphia may
be considered the metropolis of the United States," the French traveler
Jacques Pierre Brissot de Warville had written in 1788. "It is certainly
the most beautiful and best-built city in the nation, and also the wealthiest. Here you find more well-educated men, more knowledge of politics
and literature, more political and learned societies than anywhere else in
the United States. Everywhere there is activity, industry, and competition." With forty-three thousand inhabitants, it boasted more commercial houses, more printing presses and newspapers, and more books in its
library than in any other city in America—not to mention the country's
first museum, where visitors could marvel at the painter Charles Willson
Peale's collection of stuffed birds and animals, Indian regalia, fossils, silk
slippers made for a Chinese woman's bound feet, a shark's jawbone, a
piece of the tree in which the deposed King Charles I had hidden during
the English Civil War, a live bear, a chicken with four legs, and portraits

of the distinguished figures of the American Revolution. In contrast to New York's rambling, filthy lanes, Philadelphia's geometrically planned, paved, and well-lit streets were a marvel. The inhabitants were another matter. Though appealingly plain in their speech and dress compared with New Yorkers, they were considered conceited. "They believe themselves to be the first people in America as well in manners as in arts, and like Englishmen they are at no pains to disguise their opinion," Theodore Sedgwick reported.

Quakers were no longer the majority of the population, but they still exerted influence on local mores out of proportion to their numbers. Their many charities distributed free medicine to the poor, offered care to needy mothers, provided for the mentally ill, lent assistance to prisoners in the city's model penitentiary, educated girls, and provided guidance and schooling for newly emancipated African-Americans. Philadelphia was headquarters to the Pennsylvania Abolition Society, the model for other northern emancipationist groups, which had proliferated after the Revolutionary War. The society's charter required all who considered themselves Christians "to use such means as are in their power to extend the blessings of freedom to every part of the human race," in particular to those of them "who are detained in bondage by fraud or violence." Not all opponents of slavery were so mild mannered. Perhaps the slave trade might best be restrained by the confiscation of slave ships, and the execution of their captains, suggested a correspondent to the *Pennsylvania Gazette*. "But death were too mild a punishment! Let the wretch be loaded with chains, and sunk to the middle of one of the swamps of Carolina or Georgia, there to plant rice for the remainder of his days, under the control of one of his own Negro passengers, who shall be authorised to use the cowskin at discretion." This kind of menacing thinking was just what southern slaveowners most feared.

Thanks to Quaker influence, no place in the United States was more hospitable to blacks than Philadelphia. In 1780, Quakers had led a successful campaign to enact a state emancipation law that would fully terminate slavery in Pennsylvania by 1799; by 1790, only 273 of the city's

2,100 black inhabitants were still enslaved. Free and fugitive alike, they flocked to Philadelphia from the surrounding hinterland. Under Pennsylvania law, any out-of-state slave who remained there for more than six months automatically became free, apart from those owned by members of Congress, who were specifically exempted from the law. The exemption did not apply to members of the executive branch, however, posing the same problem for George Washington as it did for other slaveowners. With several enslaved men and women on his household staff, Washington was careful to minimize risk. "The idea of freedom might be too great a temptation for them to resist," he advised Tobias Lear, directing him to see that each of Washington's slaves was temporarily rotated out of Pennsylvania before the expiration of the legal time limit. "I wish to have it accomplished under the pretext that may deceive both them and the Public," the president told Lear.

Even other Pennsylvanians found the Quakers' relentless right-mindedness more than a little oppressive. The "Gloomy Severity of the Quakers has proscribed all fashionable dress and Amusement," harrumphed William Maclay, whose own puritanical standards of behavior were rarely matched. "Denying themselves these enjoyments, they as much as in them lies, endeavor to deprive others of them also." Freewheeling New Yorkers, not surprisingly, were even more caustic. Philadelphians, the *New-York Daily Advertiser* sneered, were just plain boring: "In Philadelphia, the city tavern or coffee house is the receptacle of dullness and despondency." Philadelphians responded in kind, as a ditty that appeared in a local newspaper that autumn suggests: "*New York!* We envy not your cloyster / Inflam'd by beer and oysters."

By 1790, Quaker conservatism was yielding to more cosmopolitan attitudes as immigrants from Germany and Ireland, refugees from the revolution in France and the chaos in Saint Domingue (today Haiti), and newcomers from the states of the North and the South swelled the population. A Quaker-sponsored ban on theatrical performances had recently been repealed, making it possible to enjoy performances of Shakespeare's plays, as well as titillating fare such as Sheridan's *School for Scandal* and Garrick's *Clandestine Marriage* at the Southwark Theater. (Respectable patrons complained that tickets were so cheap that they allowed "bucks, bloods, and w—s and rogues to attend, who stole their seats at intermission.") Concerts abounded and dancing assemblies also flourished, although the snobbish wife of Maryland representative Joshua Seney sniffed that she had never seen "such a parsel of ugly women."

Even Philadelphia's staid religious life was sprouting exotic blooms, such as the popular evangelical preacher who, reported the sardonic George Thatcher, possessed "strong Lungs & a Stentorian voice, with the fist & hands of Vulcan," all of which "he kept in constant & violent exercise," seizing the pulpit and spewing "fear of hellfire, the devil and eternal damnation." The scene outside the church, where two rows of men formed up after the service, amused Thatcher even more. "These men seemed to look sharp upon the faces of the females & would now and then lay hold of one & another," he drily observed, having learned that such revival meetings were commonly frequented by men "to pick up girls & women—it being a place of general rendezvous for such Characters!"

From New Hampshire to Georgia, members of the government and their families set out for the temporary capital in the teeth of the worst winter yet on record. Their travails were even worse than usual. George Washington's driver proved so incompetent that he had to be removed from the coach and assigned to the wagon carrying the president's baggage, which he turned over twice. Abigail Adams lost all her best gowns when the ship carrying her family's possessions from New York sprang a leak. Four congressmen from Massachusetts were thrown from their stagecoach when it flipped over near New Brunswick, New Jersey, injuring Elbridge Gerry so severely that he was compelled to wear an enormous black patch over part of his scarred face. James Jackson's ship was so buffeted by storms that he demanded to be put ashore at Cape May, New Jersey, and traveled the rest of the way to Philadelphia bumping and pitching in a hired wagon. But no one could match the hair-raising ordeal of Aedanus Burke of South Carolina, who was shipwrecked at the mouth of the Delaware Bay, where during a terrifying night "boisterous weather" broke his ship's cables, shredded its sails, and drove it crashing over breakers and shoals onto the Delaware coast. "So much for attending Congress for a Southern Delegate," Burke drily commented.

Philadelphia's boosters greeted Congress with panegyrics:

Welcome, ye former warriors! Statesmen too!
Superior objects ye have now in view.
You come our former triumphs to complete,
And prove our city freedom's fav'rite seat.

Meanwhile, the city's streets thronged with newly arrived job seekers— secretaries and clerks, stenographers, printers, and itinerant journalists, along with every sort of tradesman from portrait painters, dancing masters, and chefs, to wigmakers and flower arrangers—who hoped to prosper from Congress's presence. Reported one newspaper, "Barbers and hair-dressers are flocking in from all parts of the continent, ready-armed with curling irons and craping tongs, the universal cry of all whom is 'Where shall we procure a house?'" As the demand for accommodations swelled, rents soared.

Secretary of War Knox's wife, Lucy, was so disgusted by the housing that was available that she threatened to put up in a tent, as she and her husband had during the Revolutionary War. George Washington, spared the indignity of begging for a roof, nevertheless found the presidential quarters uncomfortably cramped. As many as thirty people—the president, Martha and her two grandchildren, Washington's chief secretary, Lear, and his wife, Polly, three additional secretaries, and assorted valets, coachmen, footmen, porters, maids, housekeepers, and their families—were all wedged into Robert Morris's house and its outbuildings. Complained Abigail Adams, "If New York wanted any revenge for the removal, the citizens might be glutted if they would come here, where every article has become almost double in price." She disgustedly likened Philadelphians to plundering Spanish conquistadors: "One would suppose that the people thought Mexico was before them, and that Congress were the possessors" of it.

The Adamses had located a suitably grand dwelling overlooking the Schuylkill River more than two miles from the city, via a road that in the rain became a morass—"the horses sinking to their knees"—and in dry weather a washboard of ruts and potholes. On her arrival, Abigail found the house freezing cold, the rooms piled with boxes, barrels, and trunks, and painters with brushes still at work. She wasn't impressed with the setting either. "The Schuylkill is no more like the Hudson than I to Hercules," she sighed. Hiring servants in such an overheated market was yet another martyrdom. "Such a vile tribe you never was tormented with & I hope never will be," she lamented. Her cook lasted only three days: she "on Thursday got so drunk that she was carried to Bed, and so indecent that footman, Coachman & all were driven out of the House, and turned herself out of doors."

The Adamses' experience with their slatternly cook hinted at the darker side of Philadelphia life, where poverty, disease, and alcoholism festered in neighborhoods stinking of sewage and slaughterhouse offal just minutes' walk from the tidily laid-out streets that so impressed visitors. This world only occasionally touched the lives of members of Congress, as it did Senator Tristram Dalton of Massachusetts and his traveling companion Oliver Phelps, who had no sooner deposited their luggage in the stage office after their ordeal on the road—they had come in the same coach as the unfortunate Elbridge Gerry—and gone to a nearby tavern to take tea, than they were told that their trunks, containing all their clothes and thousands of dollars' worth of government securities, had been robbed. For even the most respectable poor, there was no safety net: the loss of a job might topple a man or a woman into penury overnight. Many wound up in the city's poorhouse, where they or their children could legally be sold into indentured servitude. Life was even more precarious for blacks. The same conditions that made Philadelphia a destination for fugitive slaves also made it a magnet for slave hunters, with its support industry of venal ship's captains, thugs for hire, and crooked innkeepers. A black child seized in Philadelphia could within hours be turned into a valuable commodity in the slave markets of Baltimore or Wilmington. Some children were literally snatched from the streets or lured aboard sloops in the Delaware River with promises of work, clothes, or food, then carried south for sale, a trade so repellent to antislavery Philadelphians that within a few years it would spur the creation of the Underground Railroad.

Congress was scheduled to open on December 3. The prodigiously wet weather of November turned increasingly frigid and miserable. Lonely and uncomfortable, Theodore Sedgwick wrote forlornly to his wife, Pamela, in Massachusetts, "Your Letters are almost the only things I have to Cheer me in this Gloomey season—Theay are Cordials To my Drooping Spirits—Indeed I feal Like a mourning dove without a Mate, a boddy without a head." Even George Thatcher, who as a Mainer was no stranger to brutal cold, found himself huddling next to his fire and rarely venturing out except to meet his colleagues. Thatcher was hardly alone; by December, the price of wood rose to an astronomical $8 per cord. Carriages gave way to sleighs on the snow-covered streets, while the appearance of bundled-up Dutchmen (as Pennsylvanians of German stock were called) in their distinctive fur caps seemed to bode even worse to come. Despite the horrible weather, the shipwrecks, and the overturned coaches, enough members of both the Senate and the House of Representatives arrived in time to form quorums on December 4, almost the first time since the Revolutionary War that any Congress had assembled so close to its appointed time—a sufficiently remarkable event that the French minister saw fit to report it to Paris as a sign of the increasing stability of the American government. Indeed, the punctuality of members was, in its prosaic way, a vital symbol of the commitment that they felt to this new form of government, which two years earlier many feared might never work at all. No one pretended to know what the future held, but none now imagined that there might not be a Second Congress, and many more to follow it. "I cannot foretell whether the Campaign will be a bloody one or not—it has opened with ominous circumstances, by taking the field as a season when other combatants go into winter quarters," William Loughton Smith of South Carolina wrote to a friend. No matter, he added, "We shall now go seriously to work."

On December 8, George Washington, dressed solemnly in black, entered the cramped redbrick building on Chestnut Street that the city of Philadelphia had designated as Congress Hall, to deliver to the assembled members of both houses what later ages would come to call the State of the Union address. The building had been erected a year earlier as a courthouse and had less than half the floor space of New York's Federal Hall. Although the ground-floor area allotted to the House of Representatives was marginally adequate, senators had to haul themselves to the second floor up a flight of stairs allegedly as steep as "an Indian ladder," to a chamber so crowded that when every member was present, it was said, "There is hardly space remaining sufficient to stow a large cat." ("All the puff about a national hall and a place for the President is vanished into smoke, and the mighty noise about elegant accommodation that used to stun our ears is sunk into a gentle whisper," an anonymous letter writer— probably a member of Congress—huffed.)

Washington was visibly becoming the pale, careworn figure familiar to Americans from the paintings of Rembrandt Peale and Gilbert Stuart. "His frame Would seem to Want filling Up," William Maclay noted. "His Motions rather slow than lively, his complexion pale Nay Almost Cadaverous." Yet he seemed to defy age. Facing members of the combined houses seated before him in tiered, semicircular rows of armchairs covered in red morocco, the president declared, "The abundant fruits of another year have blessed our Country with plenty." Looming behind him as he spoke were two giant portraits, of King Louis XVI of France and of Marie Antoinette, that had been donated to the Americans as symbols of friendship in 1784 and would preside incongruously over Congress's deliberations throughout the session. The speech was brief and matter-of-fact, rather like the sort of report Washington might expect from one of his wartime field officers or even one of his farm managers at Mount Vernon. Maclay, who had been so embarrassed for Washington nineteen months earlier, deemed his enunciation this time a "tolerable" improvement over his quivering delivery at his inauguration.

Security on the northwest frontier was deteriorating, Washington told Congress. The kind of treaty making that had brought the Creeks to heel had failed with the Miamis and Shawnees. "Certain *banditti* of Indians" had launched new attacks against American settlements "instead of listening to the humane invitations and overtures made on the part of the United States." The United States now had to demonstrate that it was "not less capable of punishing their crimes than it is disposed to respect their rights." Toward that end, he had ordered Josiah Harmar to march on the Indians' stronghold with eleven hundred men. "The event of the measure is yet unknown to me." (This was not quite true. Three days earlier, Washington had learned through unofficial channels that Harmar's command had been ambushed and cut to pieces, in the worst calamity yet to befall an American army. Within days, the news would be on everyone's lips.)

Further afield, Washington obliquely took note of the plight of the American sailors whom Barbary pirates continued to hold in "distressful" captivity at Algiers. He made no specific mention of Thomas Jefferson's humiliating efforts to negotiate a ransom, since—lacking a navy—the helpless United States could do nothing else to free its citizens. Of this, the president said rather weakly, "You will not think any deliberations misemployed which may lead to its relief and protection."

On the domestic front, he announced that Virginia's district of Kentucky would soon apply to become the fourteenth state. (Although he didn't mention it, Vermont was also on the brink of ratifying the Constitution.) He urged merchants to ship more of their cargo on American ships. He expressed hope that before the session concluded in March, Congress would address pending bills for the establishment of the militia, the founding of a national mint, rationalizing weights and measures, creating the post office, and drawing up routes for post roads.

The most significant part of Washington's speech was its most glaring omission. He failed even to hint at what everyone knew was likely to prove the most contentious issue of the session, the capstone of Alexander Hamilton's transformative financial plan: the establishment of a national bank. The president did extol the dramatic rise in national revenue, "beyond all expectation," as a happy sign of the nation's increased "respectability and credit." Loans had been completed in Holland with a speed that underscored a new European confidence in the nation's viability. There had been a correspondingly impressive rise in the value of public-debt certificates, which had a year earlier been virtually valueless and were now selling at par, or even above. He did not have to say that all this represented a vindication of Hamilton's promises. But of the bank, the great man said nothing. He doubtless knew that doing so would lead to a reopening of barely healed ideological wounds, and that to either endorse or oppose the bank would place him in a precarious no-man's-land between his most valued advisers.

CHAPTER 20

A Most Mischievous Engine

———•———

It is immaterial what serves the purpose of money.

—Alexander Hamilton, December 1790

Five days after Washington's speech, Hamilton submitted his official report on the prospective national bank. French minister Otto—no friend to the Anglophile secretary of the treasury—praised it lavishly as the best report that Hamilton had yet produced. Hamilton's efficiency was impressive. Even as he had been composing his watershed report, he was supervising the Treasury Department's relocation from New York with what biographer Ron Chernow aptly termed "almost martial precision." The department's main office ensconced itself at 100 Chestnut Street, around the corner from Hamilton's residence on South Third Street and a few blocks from Jefferson's house on Market Street, the War Department offices at Carpenter's Hall, and the Supreme Court's modest quarters at City Hall. Given that Treasury dwarfed all the other departments combined—with thirteen employees in the comptroller's office, nineteen in the register's, fourteen in the accounts office, twenty-one in the customs office, fifteen in the auditor's office, and more besides—getting them all moved, resettled, and back to work was a major success in itself, Chernow observes, as well as a vivid illustration of Hamilton's logistical talents.

In his report, Hamilton argued that by uniting "public authority and faith with private credit," a national bank would be an invaluable asset to the country: providing a repository for government funds, creating a trustworthy paper currency, servicing the national debt, managing foreign exchange, and creating a permanent pool of investment capital that would foster economic growth. Hamilton proposed an initial capitalization of $10 million, several times greater than the combined capital of the three existing banks in the United States. Of that amount, $8 million would be deposited by private investors, three-quarters of it in government securities. Converting state and federal debts into reserves that would underpin a new paper currency, Hamilton asserted, would cause the overall money supply to expand and in turn stimulate new investment activity. To succeed as a dynamic, profit-driven institution, he emphasized, the bank ought to be organized "under the guidance of *individual interest*," that is, according to the principles of free enterprise. The bank would operate as a limited-liability, profit-making institution governed by an independent board of directors subject to close federal oversight, to ensure "that so delicate a trust is executed with fidelity and care." Hamilton conceded that speculation would not be eradicated. He added, however, that "if the abuses of a beneficial thing are to determine its condemnation, there is scarcely a source of public prosperity which will not speedily be closed." Since, he told the president, "it is manifest that a *large commercial city* with a great deal of *capital* and *business* must be the fittest seat of the bank," it ought logically to be based in Philadelphia.

Hamilton correctly assumed that much of his audience knew next to nothing about banks or corporations and how they operated. So he offered a tutorial: "A National Bank is an institution of primary importance to the prosperous administration of the finances." In all "enlightened" commercial countries, trade and industry depended on banks, and governments counted on them to lend the large amounts of money that were needed on short notice in wartime. Because it was unlikely that all a bank's depositors would withdraw their money at the same time, banks could issue currency in much greater amounts than their reserves. Hamilton explained the elementary principles of lending and borrowing, trust and credit, and how banks multiplied the value of their deposits.

In 1790 most financial transactions took place in gold and silver specie. Employed merely as instruments of exchange, they were what Hamilton termed "dead stock." But deposited in banks, where they served to anchor paper currency that the banks issued, they "acquired life" and became "productive." Money deposited in a bank became the security upon which a depositor could borrow a much larger amount. "In this manner the credit keeps circulating, performing, in every stage, the office of money. Large sums are lent and paid, frequently through a variety of hands, without the intervention of a single piece of coin." Thus, "the money of one individual, while he is waiting for an opportunity to employ it, keeps the money itself in a state of incessant activity," earning profits, and driving investment and commerce that might otherwise never take place. "By contributing to enlarge the mass of industrious and commercial enterprise, banks become nurseries of national wealth."

In times of emergency, a national bank that was committed to serving the government would prove invaluable, since it would collect in a single place a deep well of capital that could quickly be drawn upon. The bank would also make it easier for citizens to pay taxes by eliminating the delay and risk of transporting quantities of specie over long distances. By drawing deposits from foreigners, the bank would still further increase the supply of money in the United States. In short, Hamilton challenged not just the members of Congress but Americans at large to think of money and its possibility in new ways. "It is immaterial what serves the purpose of money." Whether paper, gold, or silver, the effect upon industry was the same: "The intrinsic wealth of a nation is to be measured not by the abundance of the precious metals contained in it, but by the quantity of the productions of its labour and industry."

Congress would not be ready to grapple with Hamilton's report for several weeks yet. Few doubted that majorities existed to pass his proposals:

the enactment of assumption in the last session had demonstrated that Hamilton enjoyed sufficient legislative support. How willing the country was to undergo another divisive battle over radical—and, to some, threatening—financial principles that were still not well understood was another question.

While members were trying to digest this new Hamiltonian lump, they faced a small mountain of pending legislation that they hoped, somewhat delusionally as it turned out, to finish before they adjourned in March. Included were bills on navigation and shipowners' liability, on federal land offices and a postal system, on taxing whiskey, and—more fraught than most—on setting national standards for the organization of the state militias that were to be the country's first line of defense against insurrection or foreign invasion. The record of militiamen in the Revolutionary War was decidedly mixed. ("To place any dependence upon militia is assuredly resting on a broken staff," Washington declared disgustedly after the collapse of his forces at New York during the war.) Americans were now ashamed to learn that most of Harmar's militiamen had broken ranks to pillage Indian settlements, then fled when confronted by native warriors, leading to his catastrophic defeat. But popular faith in an idealized army of citizen soldiers remained widespread and opposition to a permanent military establishment intense. Far from the near sanctification of military service common in today's United States, the Americans of 1790 regarded a standing army virtually by definition as the coercive arm of oppressive government, owing loyalty not to the public but to kings and dictators.

The debate on the militia that followed was brief, but it foreshadowed a collision of fundamental values—coercion versus pacifism, the public interest versus individual conscience, universal service versus a volunteer army—that would continue to echo through American history. That there must be a well-organized militia no one doubted; that was, after all, the very point of the Second Amendment. The question was, who would be required to serve in it? The bill at hand specified simply "men between the ages of eighteen and twenty-five." But weren't there men who ought to be exempted? What about members of Congress? Appointed officials? Students and teachers? Those who objected to war on religious grounds?

The radically democratic—except when it came to slavery—Aedanus Burke of South Carolina argued that the ranks should be filled "with rich and poor alike, old and young, the powerful and the powerless, without distinction." James Madison saw no reason to exempt members of Congress, who "ought ever to bear a share of the burthens they lay on others," adding, "The greatest security for the preservation of liberty is for the government to have a sympathy with those on whom the laws act." However, Thomas Fitzsimons of Philadelphia protested that enrolling young apprentices would impose unjust hardship on towns and cities because it would discourage artisans from taking on trainees who were liable to be called away on militia duty. Other congressmen worried that boys would "contract vicious habits" by consorting with hard-drinking, whore-chasing veterans.

James Jackson, who had commanded militia on the bloody Georgia frontier, retorted that the youngest men made the best soldiers of all. They had no family responsibilities, they were "hot-blooded," and they were fired with ardor for personal honor. By the age of twenty-one, he sneered, they were almost worthless, having unfortunately learned "to dread dangers, which young men disregard." Jackson seemed to relish the spotlight more than ever, jumping up at every opportunity, needling, haranguing, and attacking with his customary fervor everything that annoyed him. (He turned everything into a fight; earlier, reacting to those who had suggested that the proposed whiskey tax would discourage drunkenness, he violently declared "that his constituents claim a right to get drunk, that they have long been in the habit of getting drunk, and that they will get drunk in defiance of all the excise duties which Congress might be weak or wicked enough to impose.")

Little of what was said up to this point seemed likely to provoke much of a reaction, except from the ever-bellicose Jackson. Then the Quakers arrived, with what one irritated Connecticut congressman impatiently dismissed as "their old teazing tricks." The Quakers were as absolute in their pacifism as they were in their opposition to slavery, and just as politically inept in their advocacy of it. Pacifism was a "Divine command," as the

Quaker Samuel Allinson wrote during their insistent lobbying campaign. "Whatever is morally & religiously right can never be politically wrong. War is unlawful, & equally so paying anything in support or lieu of it." The Quakers employed the same strategy they had in New York, crisscrossing the slippery, ice-crusted streets in subfreezing weather to lobby every member of Congress they could catch, laboring "to impress their minds with a due sense of the weight of the Subject," as James Pemberton put it, making it clear that the Quakers could neither serve in any militia nor pay any fee in lieu of service that could be construed as helping to finance war.

Jackson regarded the Quakers as hopeless idealists who "fancy that wars are now to cease, and all its horrors to be dispelled like a mist before the all-reviving ray of the sun of peace." Where would it end? How would Americans have fared if "this meek spirit of non-resistance" had held sway while the states were under attack by the British? If everyone who claimed to refuse to bear arms as a matter of conscience was to be exempted, Quakerism would speedily become the national religion. "People will sit at home in the hour of invasion, enjoying domestic ease, while their neighbor is torn from his family and exposed to perils and hardships." What would become of America's people, the government, and the nation? "They will be oppressed, overturned, and scattered in the air."

Against Jackson's warlike diatribe, Elias Boudinot posed a concept of moral conscience that was both rooted deep in Protestant tradition and looked forward to a modern understanding of individual rights, to which Jackson seemed oblivious. Boudinot, arguing that nothing was to be gained by forcing men to fight when they wouldn't do it, noted, "We are said to be a people who understand the civil rights of men, who venerate and support them. Do not let us then, at the outset, violate the great and important ones, the rights of conscience, and force men to that which their religious tenets teach them to abhor." Madison, who shared Boudinot's enlightened views, proposed an amendment to the bill to specifically exempt from military service those who were "conscientiously scrupulous of bearing arms," declaring, "It is the particular glory of this country to have secured the rights of conscience which in other nations are least understood or most strangely violated."

This contentious issue would not be concluded before the end of the session. For the time being, however, Jackson had the last, cynical word. Men were more awed by fear of the law than they were guided by religion, he replied harshly. If Madison thought that men were guided more by moral laws than municipal ones, then he hadn't looked carefully into the human heart. Men, Jackson said, "stand more in fear of the penalties inflicted in this world than of those of the world to come."

Despite fierce opposition from agrarian southerners and the inimitable William Maclay of Pennsylvania, passage of the national bank bill was never in doubt in the Senate. Pierce Butler of South Carolina claimed that the bank would "drain the Southern States of the little Cash they have," while Maclay warned that it would prove "a Most Mischievous engine" for "promoting the profits of unproductive Men." But the bank's supporters held an unbreachable majority, and the bill sailed through by a vote of 10–6 on January 20.

The bank's path was not quite so smooth in the House of Representatives, where it faced the determined opposition of James Madison. As much as any other issue facing the First Congress, the short but divisive battle over the bank widened the fissures between centralists and advocates of states' rights, and between the advocates of liberal versus strict construction of the Constitution, a rift that in turn nourished the growth of the political parties that would soon become the organizing engines of American politics. Opposition was also provoked by the bank's twenty-year charter, which further provided that it would remain in Philadelphia even after the federal government departed for the Potomac in 1800, leaving it in the clutches, so opponents feared, of self-serving financiers. On a personal plane, the bank controversy also boosted the rise of Alexander Hamilton within the president's circle and further weakened the intimacy that had existed between Washington and Madison, when he had served as the president's virtual prime minister during the early months of the First Congress. The configuration of executive power would afterward never be the same.

When the bill reached the floor of the House, James Jackson hurled himself at it as if it were an Indian war party, declaring that it would plunge the country into permanent debt and "an endless labyrinth of perplexities." However, the main attack came from Madison, on February 2. In contrast to Jackson's flailing polemics, Madison, in his measured way, first acknowledged the advantages that the bank might arguably bring: merchants could push their businesses further with less capital; they would be able to pay customs duties more efficiently; government could pay its debts more punctually when revenues were delayed; and usury would decrease because more money would be available at cheaper rates. But the bank's disadvantages were far greater: it would banish precious metals in favor of unreliable paper money; expose a trusting public to bank runs driven by false rumors, bad management, or an unfavorable balance of trade; and give unfair advantages to depositors and investors who resided near Philadelphia over those in distant, rural areas. But all these arguments, Madison said, were merely utilitarian. Something more profound was at issue: the bank was unconstitutional.

The only provisions of the Constitution under which a bank might even *arguably* be chartered, he said, were those that empowered government to collect taxes to pay the national debt, provide for the "common defense and general welfare," borrow money against the credit of the United States, or pass laws that were "necessary and proper" to execute powers defined elsewhere in the Constitution. But this bill met none of those criteria. The "necessary and proper" clause of the Constitution, upon which the edifice of Hamilton's reasoning rested, meant nothing more than the "technical means" of exercising governmental powers, Madison asserted. The proposed bank was in no way "necessary" to government; at best, it was merely "convenient." The Constitution granted the federal government only *limited* and *enumerated* powers and no others. By insidiously exploiting the dubious notion of *implied* powers, he charged, "implications thus remote and multiplied can be linked together" into a chain "that will reach every object of legislation, every object within the whole compass of political economy." Such a precedent would have terrible consequences: Congress could then incorporate *anything*—manufacturing companies, canal-building companies, fraudulent speculative schemes, or even religious societies that might dispatch religious teachers to every parish "and pay them out of the Treasury of the United States."

The power claimed by the bill, Madison powerfully concluded, was condemned by the silence of the Constitution; was condemned by the rule of interpretation arising out of the Constitution; was condemned by its tendency to destroy the main characteristic of the Constitution; was condemned by the expositions of the friends of the Constitution; was condemned by the apparent intention of the parties which ratified the Constitution; was condemned by the Amendments proposed by Congress themselves to the Constitution, and he hoped it would receive its final condemnation by the vote of this House.

The speech was a startling demonstration of how far Madison had traveled from principles that he had espoused as recently as the first session, when he was the driving engine of the administration's centralizing agenda. Now his assault against federal power sounded indistinguishable from that of the Antifederalists he had once scorned. His motives were certainly mixed. To at least some extent, his lofty assertion of principle was a smoke screen to conceal his parochial anxiety that establishment of the bank would permanently suck the seat of government away from the Potomac. When nothing else worked, Madison always resorted to a constitutional argument. It was his standard strategy. Nevertheless, the arguments he made were compelling. He feared, with some reason, that the bank would instigate a surge of unbridled speculation, and he genuinely worried that if loose construction of the Constitution prevailed, executive power might never again be reined in.

But he persuaded few if any members of the House. When the bill came to a vote six days later, only twenty congressmen supported him, a humiliating defeat for the man who was once treated as the paramount interpreter of the Constitution. This role was now passing to the ascendant Alexander Hamilton. The balloting also had a disturbing subtext: all but one of the twenty votes against the bank hailed from the South. (The exception was Jonathan Grout, an Antifederalist from western Massachusetts.) Of the thirty-nine votes in favor of the bank, all but five were from the North—yet another omen of the embryonic sectional divide that would dominate the nation's politics in years to come. Madison had not given up, however. The bank faced one more hurdle before it became law: the president. Carried from Congress Hall by a clerk of the House to the president's home on Market Street, a brisk five-minute walk away, the bill was placed in Washington's hands on February 14. There it sat, one day bleeding into the next, as Congress waited with mounting anxiety for him to act.

The pressure on Washington was immense. He was well aware of the deep suspicion of consolidated federal power that had been voiced both inside and outside Congress. But his personal views were more in tune with those of Hamilton and the northern Federalists than they were with his fellow Virginians. Madison recalled years later, "His belief in the utility of the establishment & his disposition to favor a liberal construction of the national powers formed a bias on one side." However, he shared Madison's worry that the bank would hobble, if not prevent, the removal of the national capital to the Potomac. Vetoing the bill might save the Potomac. But if his veto was overriden by Congress, would it permanently weaken the executive authority of the presidency? Did he even have the right to nullify a bill that had been passed by both houses of Congress with large majorities? But if it was indeed unconstitutional, wasn't it his duty to do so? He had little time to ponder such questions. If he did not exercise his veto within ten days, the bank bill would automatically become law. Washington's mind, as Madison understatedly put it, "was greatly perplexed."

In later years, the president's perplexities might have been addressed by the Supreme Court. But the court had never yet decided a case. Its members, rather than pondering great constitutional questions, were riding exhausting circuits among the newly established district courts and would not deliver their first decision until the summer of 1792. (Not until after 1801, when John Marshall became chief justice, would the court even begin to take on the role of supreme arbiter of constitutional law that it has enjoyed ever since.) Instead, the president turned to Attorney General Edmund Randolph, Secretary of State Jefferson, and Madison, upon whom Washington had always leaned, to explain the intricacies of the Constitution. Madison was no longer the only voice in his ear, however.

Madison reportedly said that if establishing a bank *was* constitutional, then federal power would inexorably grow beyond all bounds, and there would not be "a blade of grass in America which any man could with propriety call his own." Randolph asserted that if the Constitution's "necessary and proper" phrase had any meaning, it "does not enlarge the powers of Congress, but rather restricts them." (Randolph, the weakest member of the cabinet, was miserable in his ill-defined and ill-paid job—"a sort of mongrel between the states and the US," he complained to Madison.) Jefferson's reply was characteristically thorough. He quoted the declaration of the not-yet-ratified Tenth Amendment that all powers not delegated to the United States by the Constitution, nor prohibited by it to the states, were reserved to the states or to the people. "To take a single step beyond the boundaries thus specially drawn around the powers of Congress is to take possession of a boundless field of power," he advised the president. Yes, the Constitution allowed Congress to make laws "necessary and proper" for putting into effect its *enumerated* powers. But those powers could obviously be exercised without a bank, so nothing at all about it was "necessary." "Can it be thought that the Constitution intended that for a shade or two of *convenience* more or less, Congress should be authorised to break down the most antient & fundamental laws of the several States," namely those of mortmain, laws of alienage, rules of descent, acts of distribution, laws of escheat and forfeiture, laws of monopoly? "Nothing but a necessity invincible by any other means can justify such a prostration of Laws, which constitute the pillars of our whole System of jurisprudence." The veto, he reminded Washington, was the Constitution's shield against legislative "invasions," and that was what they now faced. Nevertheless, Jefferson recommended that Washington sign the bill anyway, since the legislature had approved it. (Many modern Americans may find Jefferson's stance startlingly inconsistent for a man who was largely in tune with the advocates of states' rights, but he shared his era's almost universal belief that Congress was the superior branch of government.)

Madison felt cautiously optimistic that he and his fellow Virginians had swayed the president against the bill. The Federalists had a hostage, however. For months, Congress, the country, and an army of land speculators had impatiently waited for Washington to announce his choice for the location of the permanent seat of government. When he finally broke his silence, the sound was politically deafening. "After duly examining and weighing the advantages and disadvantages of the several situations," he had disingenuously stated in a letter to Congress on January 24, 1791, he had decided to center the federal city on the expanse of rolling hills and water meadows that lay between the Anacostia River and Georgetown, Maryland—where he had secretly intended to establish it all along.

Many congressmen who believed when they had voted for the Potomac the previous summer that they would get a more northerly location in return were now furious. Not only did the site lie at the southernmost tip of the mandated zone, Washington wanted to extend it even farther southward to include his hometown of Alexandria, near his estate at Mount Vernon. Coincidentally or not, this would incorporate into the federal district 200 acres of Washington's own land, and several building lots that the president owned in downtown Alexandria. Almost one thousand acres belonging to the president's ward George Washington Parke Custis—the future site of Arlington National Cemetery—had already been included in the original grant. At the president's behest, without waiting for Congress's approval, Jefferson had already dispatched the surveyor Andrew Ellicott to Alexandria to lay out the boundaries of the new federal district.

Washington also announced that he had picked three men to serve as commissioners to oversee the development of the capital. All were old cronies: David Stuart was the administrator of Washington's private business affairs, his personal doctor, and the husband of Martha Washington's widowed daughter-in-law. Thomas Johnson, a former governor of Maryland, had nominated Washington as commander in chief of the Continental Army during the Revolution. And Daniel Carroll of Rock Creek, one of the congressmen who had switched his vote on Hamilton's assumption plan at Madison's request, owned a four-thousand-acre plantation that lay partly within what would become the federal district. None of the three had any experience in city planning, construction, or architecture. No one would dream of publicly accusing the sainted Washington of acting from outright self-interest. Nonetheless, many were shocked, although they expressed their dismay in private. "I have lived long enough to discover that almost all men form their opinions by their interest, without always knowing the governing principle of their motives or actions," Representative William Smith of Maryland observed, with evident sadness.

To accommodate Washington and his Potomac Valley friends, the original Residence Act, which provided for the temporary capital at Philadelphia and a permanent one on the Potomac, would have to be amended. If the president thought that Congress would blithely rubber-stamp his request, he was wrong. Barely six months earlier, the Residence Act had climaxed one of the most hard-fought battles of the First Congress; altering it now threatened to unravel the compromise that had been wrought over Jefferson's dinner table. Although no one explicitly declared that the president was faced with a quid pro quo—the capital for the bank—the reality was clear. Once again, the capital's future was entangled with Hamilton's financial plans.

None of this difficulty was on public display when Philadelphia celebrated the president's fifty-ninth birthday on February 22 with the kind of pomp and circumstance that Washington claimed to loathe, but did little to discourage. Artillery and light infantry paraded through the frosty streets. A thirteen-gun salute was fired. (At last, with North Carolina and Rhode Island safely in the Union, awkward eleven-gun salutes were a thing of the past.) Members of Congress, the heads of the executive departments, diplomats, clergymen, distinguished citizens, and uncounted strangers personally presented their greetings to the president at his home on Market Street. That evening, a grand ball was held at the Pennsylvania statehouse, next door to Congress Hall. For the occasion, a painting showing Washington trampling beneath his feet a Union Jack had been hung on one wall of the ballroom—a spectacle that noticeably irritated several British officers who were present. Three lusty huzzahs greeted Washington when he entered the room. Patriotic toasts were drunk to the nation, to Congress, the state of Pennsylvania, to both the king and the National Assembly of France (to carefully accommodate both French radicals and royalists), America's favorite Frenchman, the Marquis de Lafayette, the nation's allies, "the fine arts," Vice President Adams, and finally the president himself. As the president promenaded around the dance floor—despite his size and age, he was considered a splendid dancer—he could hardly fail to remember that he had only two days left to exercise his veto of the bank bill.

No one yet knew Washington's mind. Madison remained optimistic that he had swayed the president in favor of the bill's enemies. Tensions grew over the prospect of a legislative attempt to override the anticipated presidential veto. Rumors spread that if the bank was vetoed, Hamilton would resign, and the price of national securities would collapse. The only presidential adviser yet to weigh in was Hamilton himself, who, at Washington's request, had been working feverishly for most of the past week on a reply to the Virginians.

The treasury secretary must have made no more than a perfunctory appearance at the president's birthday gala. He worked through the rest of that night and into the next morning, with his wife, Elizabeth, copying out his words. By noon on the twenty-third, just twenty-four hours before the president's deadline, Hamilton handed his rebuttal to Washington. At forty pages and fifteen thousand words, it dwarfed his opponents' submissions.

Hamilton yielded no ground to the bank's enemies. He argued with all the vigor at his command on behalf of a liberal construction of the Constitution that would allow for flexibility, innovation, and what modern Americans would call an activist government. He dismissed Randolph's comments with near contempt, remarking tersely that the attorney general's critique was "so imperfect as to authorise no conclusion whatever." Hamilton skewered Madison by quoting his own words in *The Federalist*

Papers, where the Virginian had declared that if the Constitution had to include a full enumeration of all the powers "necessary and proper" to government, it would not only be ludicrously long, but also have to take account of "all the possible changes which futurity may produce." Madison had then succinctly stated, "No axiom is more clearly established in law or in reason than wherever the end is required, the means are authorized; wherever a general power to do a thing is given, every particular power for doing it is included." This was precisely the position that Madison was now denouncing as unconstitutional! Hamilton's response to the secretary of state, to which he devoted most of his effort, as historian Thomas McCraw has put it, "made Jefferson look like a naïf, a petulant child who knew little about constitutional law and nothing about finance."

Jefferson and Randolph, Hamilton said, denied the US government the authority to create corporations; if they were right, then "the United States would furnish the singular spectacle of a political society without sovereignty, or of a people governed without government." The incorporation of the bank was *precisely* the type of measure that had been envisioned by the Constitution in its "necessary and proper" clause. "Every power vested in a government is in its nature sovereign; and includes, by force of the term a right to employ all the means requisite, and fairly applicable to the attainment of the ends of such power; and which are not precluded by restrictions and exceptions specified in the Constitution, or not immoral, or not contrary to the essential ends of political Society." Hamilton also rejected the Virginians' contention that the bank invaded states' rights. If the national government could do nothing that might alter a state law, he argued, all its powers were simply meaningless. The federal regulation of export policy, for instance, obviously affected the existing laws of several states. The federal construction of lighthouses, beacons, and buoys along the coast—none of which were strictly "necessary," much less stipulated by the Constitution—were useful for society all the same; no one suggested that the federal government had no right to provide *them*.

Hamilton concluded with a ringing plea for the most liberal possible reading of the Constitution: "The powers contained in a constitution of government, especially those which concern the general administration of the affairs of a country, its finances, trade, defence &c ought to be construed liberally in advancement of the public good. The means by which national exigencies are to be provided for, national inconveniencies obviated, national prosperity promoted, are of such infinite variety, extent and complexity, that there must of necessity be great latitude of discretion in the selection and application of those means." Madison had now met his match, if not his superior, in the interpretation of the Constitution.

The rest of February 23 passed without any further news of the bill. On the morning of the twenty-fourth, John Rutledge wrote, "There was general uneasiness & the President stood on the brink of a precipice from which had he fallen he would have brought down with him much of that glorious reputation he has so deservedly established." The bank's partisans began venting their anger at the president, who they increasingly assumed was about to veto the bill. Remarked Madison, "The meanest motives were charged on him, and the most insolent menaces held over him." Years later, Madison recalled what happened next: "The time was running out, or indeed *was run* out; when just at this moment, Lear [Washington's private secretary] came in with the president's sanction. *I am satisfied that had it been his veto, there would have been an effort to nullify it.*" With the bank's future assured, Congress speedily passed by a large majority the president's bill to extend the federal district southward to include Alexandria, Virginia. After Washington's death, John Adams acerbically declared that the decision had raised the value of the Washington and Custis properties 1,000 percent.

Passage of the bank bill was a watershed. Madison had suffered yet another decisive defeat by Hamilton, who would continue to move closer to the president at the Virginian's expense. Hamilton's letters from this period are frustratingly unrevealing of his private feelings. (As Ron Chernow nicely puts it, "His grandiose plans left scant place for commonplace thoughts.") But it is impossible to imagine that he was not thrilled by his triumph: his enemies lay prostrate, his star was ascendant, and his plan for the nation's economic future was on the cusp of achievement. More broadly, visionary capitalism had once again triumphed over the agrarian values of a less complex and less dynamic America whose roots remained most deeply embedded in the South. Political power would remain lopsidedly tilted in the South's favor for decades to come, but the stage had now been set for the North's financial and economic ascendancy. Although the worst sectional animosity would remain largely veiled for another generation, southern distrust of the expanding federal government would never recede.

When writing to George Washington, Thomas Jefferson had couched his opposition to the national bank in the restrained language of the law. A year later, the secretary of state revealed deeper and more troubling feelings in an astonishing letter that he wrote to Madison, commenting on newly elected Virginia governor Henry Lee's desire to establish a state bank to compete with the national bank. "For any person to recognize a foreign legislature in a case belonging to the state itself is an act of treason against the state," Jefferson wrote. "And whosoever shall do any act under color of the authority of a foreign legislature—whether by signing notes, issuing or passing them, acting as director, cashier or any other office relating to it, shall be adjudged guilty of high treason and suffer death accordingly by the judgment of the state courts." The "foreign legislature" he was talking about was the Congress of the United States. It would be difficult to find a more fiery articulation of states' rights sentiment up to the eve of the Civil War.

American Dawn

———·•·———

It will be far more difficult to undo *than to* do.

—Alexander Hamilton, September 1790

T he last days of the First Congress's third and final session saw a tumbling and raucous rush of legislation that concluded by candlelight on the evening of March 3. "To speak in the uproar of business was like letting off a popgun in a Thunder Storm," in Maclay's words. The salary bill for executive officers and their clerks had to be dispatched. And the bill to recruit a new regiment to chastise the Indians of the Northwest. And the bill for the reduction of the public debt. And the bill for the collection of duties on teas. And the bill to reimburse witnesses and jurymen for their expenses attending federal court. And the bill to mitigate forfeitures. In the Senate, the new treaty of friendship with Morocco had to be approved. There was no time, in the end, to implement the post office or to establish a national mint or to enact the militia bill over which Congress had haggled back in January. These items would be shunted along to the Second Congress, which was scheduled to meet in December. "We used to canvass every Subject and dispute every inch," wrote Maclay, but now "all has been put off Untill this late Moment and the plea of want of time prevails. And every One that attempts to speak is Silenced with the Cry of the Question." (Before the development of the filibuster in the nineteenth century, "calling the previous question" was a parliamentary device to end debate and bring a measure to the floor for a speedy vote.)

When it was over, "the Members scampered down Stairs" from the Senate chamber, and along with their colleagues from the House, trickled out into the chill Philadelphia night. Most would depart for their distant homes as soon as they could. More than a third of them would not be coming back. Some had chosen not to run for reelection. Others had been defeated. There was no national schedule for congressional elections, so balloting had been taking place for months. Almost the entire Maryland delegation had been defeated. So had James Jackson of Georgia, who was beaten by his nemesis, former general Anthony Wayne, a "just reward," growled Theodore Sedgwick, for no man ever "sacrificed more largely than [Jackson had] done to popular whim and caprice." James Madison was easily returned, as were Sedgwick, William Loughton Smith, Fisher Ames, Elbridge Gerry, and Roger Sherman. The freethinking George Thatcher of Massachusetts's Maine district underwent four rematches before he finally attained the 50 percent of the vote required to send him back to Congress. Virginia had elected to the Senate the future president James Monroe, and in New York, the future vice president Aaron Burr replaced Hamilton's father-in-law, Philip Schuyler. (Burr, as is well known, would fatally dispatch Hamilton in a duel in 1804.)

Maclay had also been defeated, as he had anticipated. He remained for a while in the Senate chamber at the close of the session to collect his papers after most of his colleagues had gone. Only one of them, Tristram Dalton of Massachusetts, stopped to say good-bye to him, supposing that they would probably not see each other again soon. "As I left the Hall," wrote Maclay later that night, "I gave it a look with that kind of Satisfaction which A Man feels on leaving a place. Where he has been ill at ease, being fully satisfyed that many A Culprit has served Two Years at the Wheel-Barrow"—a punishment for felons—"without feeling half the pain & mortification that I experienced in my honorable Station."

Maclay's colleagues, however, felt an almost universal sense of satisfaction, no doubt leavened with sheer relief. Representative Alexander White of Virginia voiced the sentiments of many: "On a basis of what we have done, and the manner it has been done in the course of two years—I think we may return to our Countries without a Blush."

With the departure of Maclay and his colleagues, one of the great political epics in American history came to an end. The Revolution that began sixteen years earlier at Lexington and Concord was over. From a piece of paper, the members of the First Congress had made a government: the republican dream had been breathed into life, given political flesh and bone, pushed to its feet, and made to walk.

This was only the end of the beginning. The survivors of the recent elections would meet again in December and shoulder their political muskets once again. New lines would be drawn, new battles fought, friends and enemies bloodied in debate. Politicians and ordinary citizens looked forward with anticipation to what was to come. They believed in politics as a tool of national survival, and indeed as the only process that would ensure the triumph of the institutions they had created, and of which they were justly proud. The right to be political was what they had fought the Revolution for, and what they had overthrown the Confederation to improve. Politics, they knew, was the engine that made the machine of republican government work and would continue to drive it, they hoped, for untold generations to come.

Some of the achievements of the First Congress were inevitably incomplete. Problems left only half-solved or deferred would return to haunt, while some disputes were so fundamental that permanent solutions would remain elusive. Arguments over how flexibly or literally to interpret the Constitution would never end and would only grow more heated as the Supreme Court matured, states multiplied, and American society grew more complex. The deep-seated distrust of bankers and speculators that had boiled through the debates over Hamilton's financial plans would also remain a potent strain in American political life.

The National Bank (after its renewal in 1816) would survive only until 1836, when it would be terminated by Andrew Jackson, who had made its destruction a cornerstone of his populist appeal. The enlightened Indian policy that was manifested in the Creek treaty became a dead letter all too soon. With the relationship of Indians to the United States still undefined, the treaty might have set a precedent for accommodating native tribes somewhere within the constitutional order. But the treaty was never fully implemented. Alexander McGillivray, who died in 1793, would not live to see his people swept away by the land-hungry Georgians. In the Northwest, an army under Anthony Wayne would, in 1794, deliver a crushing defeat to the bellicose tribes there. Foreshadowing the systematic destruction of native peoples that was to come, the usually open-minded George Thatcher coldly reflected, "I think it must now be determined whether the Indians shall be exterminated, or the settlement of that Country be abandoned. There is no other alternative—Indians & white people cannot live in the neighborhood of each other."

The most consequential failure of the First Congress was its evasion of the corrosive problem of slavery when confronted with the Quaker petitions. Even members who loathed slavery feared that the new government could not risk an open debate on the subject without its splintering. They may have been right. But for the next seven decades this evasion encouraged southerners to bully any northern politicians who challenged slavery by threatening secession and war, as the number of enslaved Americans swelled from 323,000 in 1790 to almost 4 million in 1861, and the moral problem of slavery became ever more deeply enmeshed with the politics of states' rights. Representative Richard Bland Lee of Virginia, among others, foresaw eventual disunion as inevitable. He hoped only that it could be postponed until the South was in a stronger position. "The Southern States are too weak at present to stand by themselves," he privately remarked in 1790. But their time would come: "I flatter myself that we shall have the power to do ourselves justice, with dissolving the bond which binds us together."

The founders' dream of a government without political parties was also destined to be short-lived. The Federalist consensus that triumphed in New York and Philadelphia soon eroded and was in ruins before the decade was out. Antifederalists such as Elbridge Gerry, disaffected Federalists such as William Maclay, and southern partisans of states' rights such as Aedanus Burke would coalesce in what came to be known as the Democratic-Republican Party, which, under the leadership of Thomas Jefferson, would triumph in the presidential election of 1800, thereby giving force to the embryonic American political-party system. By the second decade of the nineteenth century, the Federalists would be a spent force, a regional party with little influence and few officeholders outside the Northeast. As the Federalists withered, their opponents steadily gathered strength, and in their descendant form as the antebellum Democratic Party, they would govern the United States almost continuously until the Civil War.

But all this remained in the womb of time. As the members of the First Congress took their leave from Philadelphia in March 1791, they believed with justice that they stood in the bright, clear light of an American dawn, with the republic securely founded on enlightened principles that would endure. When Congress convened in 1789, those who imagined that it would behave like a solemn conclave of classical philosophers rather than politicians were at first disappointed. Yet, month after month, men who were at times dismissed even by their peers as "rough and rude," "clumsy," and "quiddling" made the Constitution work even more successfully and flexibly than many of its ardent advocates had expected, proving to skeptical Europeans, and ultimately to the world, that a republic of the people could with ingenuity and determination not only save itself from disintegration but thrive.

Every member understood that the decisions he made would shape the republic for generations to come, and that mistakes would have consequences. "Whoever considers the nature of our government with discernment will see that though obstacles and delays will frequently stand in the way of the adoption of good measures, yet when once they are adopted, they are likely to be permanent," Alexander Hamilton presciently observed. "It will be far more difficult to *undo* than to *do*." The process was sometimes brutal, and it certainly did not conform to the idealized version of the founding held by many modern Americans. But it worked. Time would prove Hamilton right.

Like every Congress since, the First Congress was characterized by the collision of opposing interests, ideological dogmatism, preening egos, personal and sectional distrust, self-dealing, and the dragging inertia of time-serving mediocrity. But all its members shared a common fear of failure and a determination to make government work even if it meant compromising on matters of deep principle. "I have launched my barque on the federal ocean, and will endeavor to steer her appointed course," declared the Federalist John Vining of Delaware. "And should she arrive at her destined port with her invaluable cargo safe and unhurt, I shall not regret that in her voyage through these unexplored depths, she may have lost some small share of her rigging. Which may be considered as a cheap purchase for the safety of the whole." Even radical Antifederalists resigned themselves to outcomes they had fiercely resisted. Former governor Patrick Henry of Virginia, perhaps the loudest critic of the entire constitutional system, acquiesced with relative grace. "Altho' the Form of Governmt into which my Countrymen determined to place themselves had my Enmity, yet as we are one & all embarked, it is natural to care for the crazy Machine, at least so long as we are out of Sight of a Port to refit," he wrote to his protégé James Monroe.

Americans were rightfully proud of what their legislators had done. The prominent Connecticut lawyer John Trumbull wrote glowingly to his mentor John Adams at the close of the last session, "In no nation, by no Legislature, was ever so much done in so short a period for the establishment of Government, Order, public Credit & general tranquillity." Even the dyspeptic Adams himself mustered a rare burst of unadulterated joy: "The National Government has succeeded beyond the expectations even of the sanguine, and is more popular, and has given more general satisfaction than I expected ever to live to see." To a friend, Adams added, "I am happy that it has fallen to my share to do some thing towards setting the machine in motion."

The First Congress gave new and dramatic force to the republican idea. It did not create a democracy; that would evolve only slowly over time. Nearly all the political men of the 1790s, including George Washington, still believed that government was the proper province of the wealthy and wellborn. Yet, the triumph of the First Congress was not only a victory by, or for, the governing class. Madison and his colleagues had transformed the Constitution's parchment plan into muscular and enduring institutions that would be flexible enough to accommodate in years to come the rising power and democratic demands of Americans whose voices had been heard only distantly before in the corridors of power. As the historian Pauline Maier aptly put it, "The Constitution's success came less from a perfection in its design than from the sacrifices of men like Washington" and the dogged commitment of ordinary Americans "who refused to be told that the issues of their day were beyond their competence, tried to reconcile the ideals of the Revolution with the needs of the nation, and considered the impact of contemporary decisions not just on their own lives but for the future."

Ordinary Americans had changed. Under the Confederation, Americans had rarely heard news of any sort from Congress. Public opinion now mattered. Newly emboldened newspapers brought the doings of government to the door of every citizen, including the illiterate, who gathered in urban taverns and frontier hamlets to avidly hear the latest reports read to them by their literate neighbors. Well-informed men and women alike crowded into the visitors' gallery of the House of Representatives to listen to the debates and demanded to know why they couldn't pack into the Senate as well. In 1794, popular clamor would pry open the Senate's doors to the public, too. Men who had seen themselves primarily as citizens of their individual states had now mostly come to see themselves as the common citizens of a nation and embraced their new government as their own in a way that they had never done before. As Representative George Thatcher cockily reported to a friend in Maine, "Politics are the meat & drink of us the people, in a free government, & if it does not suit us, faith! we will correct the cook."

Afterword

———•◆•———

The achievements of the First Congress eventually grew dim as new struggles, new dreams, and new heroes occupied the hearts and minds of Americans, and the living memory of its members faded away.

Roger Sherman of Connecticut, the oldest member of the First Congress, was one of the first to go. Praised by Richard Henry Lee of Virginia as "our old republican friend," he was a living embodiment of stoic virtue and political probity. Reelected to the Second Congress in 1790, he was almost immediately chosen by the Connecticut legislature to represent his state in the US Senate. His career there ended suddenly with his death in 1793, at the age of seventy-two.

William Maclay never served in federal office again. He joined the emerging Democratic-Republican Party, a better fit for his hostility to strong central government than the Federalists, with whom he was so often at odds during the First Congress. He was elected several times to the Pennsylvania state legislature, where he voted for a constitutional amendment to restrict US Senate terms to three years, and against a formal expression of regret at George Washington's retirement from the presidency, and introduced a resolution declaring the state's opposition to war. He died in Harrisburg in 1804, at the age of sixty-six. His monument is his diary, which remained unpublished until 1880.

James Jackson's later career remained as volatile as his temperament. He went to court to challenge his defeat by Anthony Wayne; in a revote later in 1791, both men were defeated. Jackson rebounded with election to the US Senate in 1793, but was forced to resign two years later after being implicated in the massive land swindle known as the Yazoo Scandal. Despite this, he was elected governor of Georgia in 1798, and then again to the US Senate in 1801, where he served until his death in 1806, at age forty-eight.

Robert Morris became disenchanted with political life and retired from the Senate at the end of his term in 1795. He subsequently devoted himself to land speculation on a spectacular and disastrous scale, investing in vast tracts from western New York to Georgia, and within the new federal city on the Potomac. When his paper empire collapsed in 1798, he barricaded himself in his Pennsylvania home in a hopeless effort to fend off his creditors. After three years in debtors' prison, he lived out his last years in near poverty, in the care of his daughter. He died in 1806, at seventy-two.

Oliver Ellsworth of Connecticut, the godfather of the federal judicial system, was reelected to a second term in the Senate in 1790. He resigned to become the second chief justice of the Supreme Court, replacing John Jay in 1796. While he was still on the court, President John Adams sent him to Paris in 1799 as a special envoy in an ultimately successful though controversial effort to resolve the "Quasi-War" with France. Although he did not resign from the Supreme Court, Ellsworth never returned to the bench and died in Connecticut in 1807, aged sixty-two.

Termed the "American Demosthenes" for the coruscating quality of his oratory, Fisher Ames remained one of the most respected Federalist voices in the House of Representatives, where he continued to support the prerogatives and power of both the presidency and Congress. In 1796, he declined reelection and, although only in his forties, largely dropped out of public life, devoting his energies to overseeing a model farm that he owned in the Boston suburbs. Offered the presidency of Harvard College in 1805, he declined it on the grounds of ill health. He died from tuberculosis in 1808, aged fifty, deeply depressed at the direction of the country.

William Loughton Smith's letters, along with those of Fisher Ames, provide some of the best accounts of debate in the House of Representatives, as well as vivid descriptions of its personalities. Smith represented Charleston, South Carolina, as a Federalist until 1797, when John Adams appointed him the American minister to Portugal. Removed by Jefferson in 1801, he retired to Charleston, where he practiced law and married into the wealthy Izard family. He grew increasingly disenchanted with the Federalists and in 1808 formed an alliance with the Jeffersonians. He died ostracized by his former political friends in 1808, aged fifty-four.

Theodore Sedgwick remained one of Alexander Hamilton's staunchest advocates in Congress. In 1795, the Massachusetts legislature elected him to the Senate. He later ran for and won another single term in the House of Representatives. He retired from competitive politics after the Federalist defeat in 1800, but continued to serve on the Massachusetts Supreme Court and to tend to his beloved wife, Pamela, who suffered increasingly from chronic anxiety and depression. He died in 1813, aged sixty-six.

Elbridge Gerry, who was unpopular and often isolated in the First Congress, went on to enjoy a vigorous commercial and political life in Massachusetts. Despite his Antifederalist orientation, he supported his longtime friend John Adams for president in 1796 and was rewarded with an appointment to the diplomatic commission that Adams dispatched to France to mend strained relations. Failure of the mission, whose other members were John Marshall and Charles Cotesworth Pinckney, led to the Quasi-War of 1798. Gerry was later elected governor of Massachusetts as a Jeffersonian Republican; during his second term, in 1812, he bequeathed the term *gerrymandering* to the American lexicon after creating tortuous electoral districts designed to favor his party. Later that year, he was elected vice president on a ticket with James Madison. Two years later he became the first vice president to die in office. He was seventy years old.

John Adams, though strictly speaking not a member of the First Congress, was nevertheless one of its most active personalities in his capacity as president of the Senate. Near the end of the third session, he penned what might be considered a lasting epitaph for the vice presidency: "I find the office I hold, tho laborious, so wholly insignificant, So Stupidly pinched and betrayed that I wish myself again at the old Bar, old as I am. My own Situation is almost the only one in the World in which Firmness and Patience are Useless." Upon George Washington's retirement in 1797, Adams ascended to the highest office, to preside over what is widely regarded by historians as one of the least successful presidencies in American history. He retired with Abigail to their home in Quincy, Massachusetts, where he wrote copiously, complained incessantly about the nation's loss of its patriot virtues, and died on July 4, 1826, aged ninety, having lived long enough to see his son John Quincy Adams in the White House.

No man contributed more to the achievements of the First Congress than James Madison. He guided debate almost single-handedly during the first two sessions, played a critical role in strengthening the presidency, shaped the amendments that would become the Bill of Rights, helped forge the compromise that established the seat of government on the Potomac, and left his fingerprints on many other pieces of important legislation. Although his power diminished once Congress turned to financial policy, it is impossible to overrate his contribution to the Congress's success. He remained in the House of Representatives until 1797, continuing to evolve away from his early Federalist roots toward an embrace of states' rights that reflected the views of his Virginia constituents and the South generally. In 1800, he became Thomas Jefferson's secretary of state, then succeeded Jefferson in the presidency in 1809, presiding over the War of 1812 and the burning of Washington, DC, whose boosters in the First Congress had proclaimed it impregnable against foreign attack. He died in 1836, at the age of eighty-five.

The two cities where the First Congress met have changed beyond recognition. Apart from the pattern of cramped lanes at the tip of Manhattan Island, St. Paul's Chapel, and the rebuilt Trinity Church and Fraunces Tavern, where members met in their off-hours, nothing remains of the New York City that existed in 1789. Federal Hall was razed in 1812, the site of George Washington's first temporary home lies beneath the pilings of the Brooklyn Bridge, and the open fields where members of Congress rambled disappeared long ago under the city's advancing grid. The ghost of the First Congress has fared better in Philadelphia. There Congress Hall has been handsomely restored to its appearance in the 1790s and stands amid an ensemble of period buildings from which the accretions of the modern city have mostly been pared away. Recently the long-buried footprint of the president's mansion on Market Street was exposed by archaeologists and dedicated, in part, to memorializing George Washington's enslaved servants, a long overdue, though modest acknowledgment of slavery's central presence in the early republic.

Upon the close of the First Congress an acute foreign observer, Baron Hyde de Neuville, remarked with optimism edged with anxiety, "These rebel colonists are on their way to become one of the most powerful of nations. We shall one day see them the astonishment of Europe; and if they do not actually dictate laws to the two worlds, at least, they will be their example." He added, "Only let the Americans be wise."

Acknowledgments

———•◆•———

Several years ago, while writing a book on slavery and the founding of Washington, DC, I came to know Kenneth R. Bowling, whose many works on the early capital are wide-ranging, erudite, and infused with a wit that is rarely found in comparable scholarly work. *The First Congress* is derived in part from conversations that I had with Ken over several years, as I came to appreciate the immense resources that had been amassed by the First Federal Congress Project, of which he has been a longtime editor. Ken encouraged me to consider a history of the First Congress that would encompass its full, not to say stunning, range of accomplishments. Without his inspiration and guidance, this book would not exist.

No less essential to my work has been the ongoing support of the other members of the First Federal Congress Project: (project director) Charlene Bangs Bickford, Helen E. Veit, and William C. "Chuck" di Giacomantonio. The project, under the aegis of George Washington University, began more than half a century ago and is now nearing completion. It has brought together virtually every known piece of writing composed by or about the members of the First Congress—the obscure and eccentric as well as the august and famous—as well as the best official records of their debates. As an edifice of legislative history, it is unrivaled. Ken, Charlene, Helen, and Chuck made me welcome at the project's research office in Washington, DC, where they provided me access to their collections, as well as work space. All were extraordinarily generous with their time and thoughts, patiently answering countless questions that must sometimes have seemed naive or obtuse. Several members of the project read and commented on early drafts of this book. Whatever errors may remain are of course my own, and not theirs.

In addition, informal talks with US Senate historian Donald A. Richie and his predecessor Richard A. Baker were at various points in my research helpful in framing many of the issues that were central to the politics of the First Federal Congress.

I am deeply indebted to my editor, Bob Bender, whose insights, wise counsel, and gentle nudges in the direction of more precise and illuminating language improved this book in ways too numerous to mention. Johanna Li, also of Simon & Schuster, deftly piloted my manuscript through the shoals of the editing process with unflagging courtesy.

I owe much to my friend John Schmitz. Gifted with a brilliant design sensibility, John created the website which supports all my work, including this book, www.fergusbordewich.com, and was instrumental in assembling the portfolio of images that accompanies *The First Congress*. Marilyn Ibach of the Library of Congress Prints and Photographs Division provided invaluable assistance in tracking down several valuable images that had eluded me; she too has my gratitude.

My agent Elyse Cheney, as always, offered stalwart support and encouragement through the writing of *The First Congress*. Most of all, however, I must thank my wife, Jean, for her inexhaustible patience with a husband whose attention is so often diverted by the ghosts of the American past.

Notes

———•———

Abbreviations

DHFFC: Documentary History of the First Federal Congress
AHP: The Papers of Alexander Hamilton
TJP: The Papers of Thomas Jefferson
JMP: The Papers of James Madison
GWP: The Papers of George Washington

Introduction: Nebuchadnezzar's Monster

Page

2 *"the humiliating state"*: Ralph Izard to Thomas Jefferson, April 3, 1789, *DHFFC*, 15:190–91.

2 *"The people here"*: Catherine Green to Jeremiah Wadsworth, April 18, 1789, *DHFFC*, 15:280.

2 *"The people," condescendingly*: Beeman, *Plain, Honest Men*, 114.

3 *"a monument that"*: Élénor-François-Élie, Comte de Moustier, to Armand Marc, Comte de Montmorin de Saint-Hérem, June 9, 1789, *DHFFC*, 16:730.

3 *"trap to catch"*: Alexander White to Mary Wood, March 8, 1789, *DHFFC*, 15:45.

3 *"the great Increase"*: John Wendell to Elbridge Gerry, July 23, 1789, *DHFFC*, 16:1118–19.

3 *"Our present Confederacy"*: William Tudor to John Adams, July 9, 1789, *DHFFC*, 16:992–93.

5 *"as opposite"*: Martin, *Narrative of a Revolutionary Soldier*, 117.

5 *"for the transactions"*: George Clymer to Henry Hill, March 7, 1790, *DHFFC*, 18:765.

5 *"I fear much"*: Theodorick Bland to St. George Tucker, April 15, 1789, *DHFFC*, 15:265.

5 *"think the union"*: Bernhard, *Fisher Ames*, 106.

5 *"no more than general principles"*: "Americanus" in *Gazette of the United States*, June 10, 1789.

5 *"We are in a wilderness"*: James Madison to Thomas Jefferson, June 30, 1789, *DHFFC*, 16:890.

7 *Shays's Rebellion*: A particularly vivid account of the disorders in western Massachusetts will be found in Sedgwick, *In My Blood*, 80–91; see also Maier, *Ratification*, 15–17.

7 *"that mankind left"*: Maier, *Ratification*, 17.

7 *"lax and feeble cords"*: Tench Coxe to James Madison, April 21, 1789, *DHFFC*, 15:304–5.

7 *"Can we retain"*: Richard Peters to Fisher Ames, January 9, 1790, *DHFFC*, 17:164ff.

8 *"They will either throw"*: *Gazette of the United States*, May 30, 1789.

8 *"the insidious protection"*: Anthony Wayne to James Wilson, July 4, 1789, *DHFFC*, 16:940.

8 *In the Northwest*: Moustier to Montmorin, June 9, 1789, *DHFFC*, 16:735–37.

8 *Even more threatening*: McCraw, *Founders and Finance*, 1–5, 65–66, 93–94; and Chernow, *Alexander Hamilton*, 287ff.

8 *"I do believe"*: Theodore Sedgwick, *Congressional Register*, February 2, 1790.

8 *"In America we"*: Elbridge Gerry, May 12, 1789, *DHFFC*, 10:625.

9 *disparate kinds of money*: Monaghan and Lowenthal, *This Was New York*, 49; and Smith, *City of New York*, 110–11.

9 *This "abominable traffic"*: Brissot de Warville, *New Travels in the United States*, 155–56.

9 *"confusions, animosity and discord"*: Jeremiah Hill to George Thatcher, March 3, 1789, DHFFC, 15:6.

9 *"Is there not danger"*: John Adams to Nathaniel P. Sargeant, May 21, 1789, *DHFFC*, 15:610–11; also Adams to William Tudor, May 28, 1789, *DHFFC*, 15:640–41.

9 *"What has it"*: Adams to Sargeant, May 21, 1789.

10 *"a very scanty proportion"*: James Madison to Edmund Randolph, March 1, 1789, *DHFFC*, 15:2–3.

10 *"the yawning listlessness"*: Fisher Ames to George Richards Minot, May 27, 1789, in Allen, *Works of Fisher Ames*, 1:632–34.

11 *"keep* [the Constitution's] *friends"*: Royal Flint to Enos Hitchcock, March 11, 1789, *DHFFC*, 15:53.

11 *a cabal of "aristocratical men"*: Federal Farmer no. 1, in Allen and Lloyds, *Essential Antifederalist*, 75–83.

11 *"was a dangerous experiment"*: Federal Farmer no. 17, in Allen and Lloyds, *Essential Antifederalist*, 83–92.

12 *"monarchical, aristocratical, oligarchical"*: *New-York Daily Advertiser*, March 4, 1789.

12 *"a King as the King"*: Bartoloni de Tuazon, "Mr. President," 66.

12 *"We cannot yet"*: Benjamin Lincoln to John Adams, April 22, 1789, *DHFFC*, 15:317–18.

12 *"sow the seeds"*: Noah Webster to James Madison, August 14, 1789, *JMP*, 12:334–35.

12 *"The worship of"*: *Freeman's Journal*, March 4, 1789.

12 *"If we must"*: *New-York Daily Gazette*, June 3, 1789, in Bowling, "'A Tub to the Whale.'"

12 *"All eyes are"*: James Warren to Elbridge Gerry, April 19, 1789, *DHFFC*, 15:287.

13 *"In no nation"*: John Trumbull to John Adams, March 20, 1789, Adams Family Manuscript Trust, Massachusetts Historical Society.

14 *"These pilots, accustomed"*: Comte de Moustier to Comte de Montmorin, April 7, 1789, *DHFFC*, 15:217–19.

14 *"All ranks & degrees"*: James Kent to Elizabeth Hamilton, December 2, 1832, Hamilton-McLane Papers, LOC.

Chapter 1: An Ocean Always Turbulent

Page

16 *"rivulets of blood"*: Kaminski and Moore, *Assembly of Demigods*, 175.

16 *Washington wanted help*: George Washington to James Madison, January 2, 1789; Madison to Washington, January 14, 1789; and Washing-

ton to Madison, February 16, 1789, *GWP*, Presidential Series, 1:229–30, 1:243, 1:316–17; and Kenneth R. Bowling, interview with author, August 2, 2014.

17 *"sink it to hell"*: Schecter, *Battle for New York*, 165; see also 260, 265.

17 *Popular writers commonly:* Bartoloni de Tuazon, "Mr. President," 26ff, 49.

17 *"O WASHINGTON!":* Stiles, "United States Elevated to Glory."

17 *"the most unfeigned":* George Washington to Marquis de Lafayette, January 29, 1789, *GWP*, Presidential Series, 1:262–64.

17 *"the only man":* William Knox to Winthrop Sargent, March 13, 1789, *DHFFC*, 15:70.

17 *"a gloomy, stiff creature":* Martha Dangerfield Bland to Frances Bland Tucker, March 30, 1781; also, similar, Eliza House Trist to Thomas Jefferson, April 13, 1784, in Kaminski and Moore, *Assembly of Demigods*, 172.

18 *Although Madison spoke:* Fisher Ames to John Lowell, May 2, 1790, and William Pierce, September 1787, both in Kaminski and Moore, *Assembly of Demigods*, 173.

18 *"losing a vote":* Brookhiser, *James Madison*, 26.

18 *"Perhaps the strongest":* Chernow, *Alexander Hamilton*, 290.

19 *"Latent causes of faction":* Hamilton, Madison, and Jay, *Federalist Papers*, 60ff.

19 *suck "all power":* Ibid.

19 *"parchment barriers":* Ibid., 344ff.

20 *"Ambition must be made":* Ibid., 371–73.

20 *"Some unforeseen mischance":* George Washington to Marquis de Lafayette, January 29, 1789, *GWP*, Presidential Series, 1:262–64.

20 *"to yield your services":* John Armstrong Jr., January 27, 1789, *GWP*, Presidential Series, 1:253–54.

20 *"The event which":* George Washington to Samuel Vaughn, March 21, 1789, *GWP*, Presidential Series, 1:424–25.

21 *"All the Candidates":* James Madison to George Washington, March 5, 1789, *JMP*, 12:3.

21 *The traveler:* James Madison to George Washington, March 8, 1789, *DHFFC*, 15:44–55.

21 *"The people":* William Pickman to Benjamin Goodhue, March 3, 1789, *DHFFC*, 15:9.

21 *"Leaving my domestick":* John Langdon to Joshua Brackett, March 6, 1789, *DHFFC*, 15:39.

22 *"I am about"*: Bernhard, *Fisher Ames*, 74.

22 *"You are now"*: James Warren to Elbridge Gerry, March 3, 1789, *DHFFC*, 15:6.

22 *New York City*: Schecter, *Battle for New York*, 194–95, 204, 272–77, 285, 322; and Janvier, *In Old New York*, 46–47.

22 *"in a state"*: Smith, *City of New York*, 5.

22 *Now, however, the city*: Monaghan and Lowenthal, *This Was New York*, 20, 28–29, 66, 75–78, 143; Smith, *City of New York*, 5–10, 16, 35–36, 51, 101, 125, 198; and Brissot de Warville, *New Travels in the United States*, 143–45.

23 *"sweetening and salubrifying"*: Smith, *City of New York*, 88.

23 *"The Streets here"*: John Page to Robert Page, March 16, 1789, *DHFFC*, 15:71.

24 *"And what has added"*: Oliver Ellsworth to Abigail Ellsworth, March 29, 1789, *DHFFC*, 15:145.

24 *New Yorkers prided themselves*: Monaghan and Lowenthal, *This Was New York*, 55–58, 105; Smith, *City of New York*, 96–97; and James Madison to Thomas Jefferson, December 8, 1788, in Burnett, *Letters of Members*, 8:812–13.

25 *"The Tyrant Custom"*: Bowling and Veit, *Diary of William Maclay*, 248, 284; also Maclay to Tench Coxe, April 15, 1789, *DHFFC*, 15:267.

25 *"Great Baby House"*: William Maclay to Richard Willing, April 2, 1789, *DHFFC*, 15:185.

25 *"With so many windows"*: Federal Gazette, April 3, 1789, *DHFFC*, 15:195.

25 *the hall's harmonious redesign*: Stokes, *Iconography of Manhattan Island*, 1236–37; and Griswold, *Republican Court*, 120–22.

26 *"The Copartnership of"*: Smith, *City of New York*, 80.

26 *"The old government"*: "Letter from New York," *DHFFC*, 15:17.

26 *"will no doubt"*: Robert Morris to Mary Morris, March 4, 1789, *DHFFC*, 15:11–12.

26 *"The Public's expectation"*: Ibid.

Chapter 2: The Fostering Hand of Government

Page

27 *"When a Quorum"*: James Madison to George Washington, March 19, 1789, and March 26, 1789, *JMP*, 12:23, 12:28.

27 *"This is a very mortifying"*: Fisher Ames to George Richards Minot, March 25, 1789, *DHFFC*, 15:126.

28 *"Our Spirit of"*: John Sullivan to John Langdon, March 22, 1789, *DHFFC*, 15:94.

28 *"One of the Delaware"*: Fisher Ames to John Lowell, March 15, 1789, *DHFFC*, 15:66–67.

28 *"shipwrecked & landwrecked"*: George Washington to James Madison, March 22, 1789, *JMP*, 12:26; and Henry Lee to Madison, March 14, 1789, *JMP*, 12:12.

28 *"seized with a Chollick"*: Samuel Livermore to John Langdon, March 17, 1789, *DHFFC*, 15:70.

28 *"tumbling from one rock"*: Ann Gerry to Samuel Gerry, March 8, 1789, *DHFFC*, 15:43.

29 *"the wind blew"*: Robert Morris to Mary Morris, March 4, 1789, *DHFFC*, 15:11–12.

29 *"What must the world"*: Charles Thomson to George Read, March 21, 1789, *DHFFC*, 15:90–91.

29 *"suffer from the general indifference"*: Comte de Moustier to Comte de Montmorin, March 20, 1789, *DHFFC*, 15:83–85.

30 *"a more Centrical Situation"*: Thomas Hartley to Tench Coxe, March 16, 1789, *DHFFC*, 15:69.

30 *"Pennsylvania will obtain"*: Peter Muhlenberg to Benjamin Rush, March 18, 1789, *DHFFC*, 15:75–76.

30 *"You can scarce conceive"*: William Maclay to Tench Coxe, March 30, 1789, *DHFFC*, 15:159; also, Comte de Moustier to Comte de Montmorin, April 7, 1789, *DHFFC*, 15:217–19.

31 *"The eyes of"*: Ezra Ripley to George Thatcher, March 30, 1789, *DHFFC*, 15:160.

31 *"Woe betide you"*: John Murray to Benjamin Goodhue, April 4, 1789, *DHFFC*, 15:199.

31 *"his voice and manner"*: William A. Duer, "Reminiscences of an Old Yorker," *New York American Mail*, August 7, 1847.

31 "Fred Augustus": *New York Morning Post*, August 21, 1790; and author interview with Kenneth R. Bowling, March 4, 2015.

32 *"sufficient to give"*: James Madison to Edmund Pendleton, April 8, 1789, *JMP*, 12:51.

33 *"Is not my Election"*: John Adams to Benjamin Rush, May 17, 1789, *DHFFC*, 15:574; Adams to Nathaniel P. Sargeant, May 21, 1789, *DHFFC*, 15:610; *DHFFC*, 3:xxii; and Chernow, *Alexander Hamilton*, 271–73.

33 *"He was riven"*: Ellis, *Passionate Sage*, 52.

33 *"the first man"*: Thompson, *John Adams*, 38.

34 *"that these United Colonies"*: Ibid.

34 *"in effect, a one-man"*: Ellis, *Passionate Sage*, 42.

34 the *"monarchical" branch*: Elkins and McKitrick, *Age of Federalism*, 532–35.

34 *"Thus it is"*: Comte de Moustier to Comte de Montmorin, April 7, 1789, *DHFFC*, 15:217–19.

35 *"Action had been"*: McCullough, *John Adams*, 399.

35 *"tempestuous weather"*: Bowling, "Good-by 'Charlie.'"

35 *"conveniently waiting"*: Ibid.

35 *"Whatever may have"*: "Address to Charles Thomson," April 14, 1789, *GWP*, Presidential Series, 2:56.

35 *"I can assure you"*: George Washington to Henry Knox, April 1, 1789, *GWP*, Presidential Series, 2:2.

36 *"I walk on untrodden"*: George Washington to Catherine Sawbridge Macaulay Graham, January 9, 1790, in Jackson and Twohig, *Diaries of George Washington*, 5:551–54.

36 *He would quickly gain*: Tristram Lowther to James Iredell, May 9, 1789, *DHFFC*, 15:493.

36 *"demi-gods and Roman senators"*: Fisher Ames to George Richards Minot, May 27, 1789, in Allen, *Works of Fisher Ames*, 1:632–34.

37 *"There are many"*: Fisher Ames to George Richards Minot, April 4, 1789, *DHFFC*, 15:196–97.

37 *"Before I came"*: Fisher Ames to George Richards Minot, May 29, 1789, in Allen, *Works of Fisher Ames*, 1:635–38.

37 *"too meek to govern"*: William Constable to Gouverneur Morris, July 29, 1789, *DHFFC*, 15:1168; also Theodore Sedgwick to Pamela Sedgwick, March 4, 1790, *DHFFC*, 18:731–32.

37 *"that strength of nerves"*: Theodore Sedgwick to Benjamin Lincoln, July 19, 1789, in Kaminski and Moore, *Assembly of Demigods*, 177.

38 *Henry Knox estimated*: Henry Knox to George Washington, March 30, 1789, *GWP*, Presidential Series, 1:463.

38 *Ralph Izard of South Carolina:* Ralph Izard to Thomas Jefferson, April 3, 1789, *DHFFC*, 15:190–91.

38 *On April 9, Madison rose: New-York Daily Gazette,* April 10, 1789; Fisher Ames to George Richards Minot, May 18, 1789, in Allen, *Works of Fisher Ames,* 1:627–28; *DHFFC,* 4:339ff; *DHFFC,* 5:972ff; and *DHFFC,* 6:1954–55.

39 *"it is only against":* Comte de Moustier to Comte de Montmorin, June 9, 1789, *DHFFC,* 16:729.

39 *Commerce, he declared: DHFFC,* 10:1ff; *JMP,* 12:69ff; and generally, James Madison to Edmund Randolph, April 12, 1789, *JMP,* 12:75–76.

40 *"That nation is": DHFFC,* 10:262.

40 *New Englanders called:* Generally, William Taylor to George Thatcher, April 12, 1789, and Richard Bland Lee to Leven Powell, April 13, 1789, *DHFFC,* 15:255, 15:259.

40 *One South Carolinian: Congressional Register,* April 16 and 21, 1789, *DHFFC,* 10:163, 10:258.

40 *"like the industrious bee": Congressional Register,* April 21, 1789, *DHFFC,* 10:262.

40 *"It is to be feared":* Fisher Ames to John Lowell, April 8, 1789, *DHFFC,* 15:221–22.

41 *"not an article": DHFFC,* 10:93.

41 *James Jackson of Georgia: DHFFC,* 10:329; and *Gazette of the United States,* April 15, 1789.

41 *"has so intirely occupied us":* Bernhard, *Fisher Ames,* 84.

41 *"a necessary of life": DHFFC,* 10:100.

41 *All this was about:* Ibid., 328, 352, 368–69, 376–77; and Kurlansky, *Cod,* 80–89, 100.

41 *"These circumstances form": DHFFC,* 10:100–103; and Bernhard, *Fisher Ames,* 83.

42 *Madison appealed: JMP,* 12:69ff; *DHFFC,* 10:381–82, 10:189–90; and Bernhard, *Fisher Ames,* 85–86.

Chapter 3: A New Era

Page

43 *"As this delay":* George Washington to James Madison, March 30, 1789, *JMP*, 12:41–42.

43 *"You will see":* Griswold, *Republican Court*, 124.

44 *He had hoped:* George Washington to William Hartshorne, April 1, 1789, *GWP*, Presidential Series, 2:1.

44 *The entire route was aswarm: GWP*, Presidential Series, 2:59ff; Griswold, *Republican Court*, 125–30; Bartoloni de Tuazon, "Mr. President," 55–56; and Decatur, *Private Affairs of George Washington*, 4–5.

44 *"upon a scale":* Bartoloni de Tuazon, "Mr. President," 59–60.

44 *Finally on the morning:* Smith, *City of New York*, 219–25; and Griswold, *Republican Court*, 130.

45 *"as thick as the ears":* Stokes, *Iconography of Manhattan Island*, 5:1240.

45 *The panorama, Washington:* Schecter, *Battle for New York*, 76–77, 123, 255–56; George Thatcher to Sarah Thatcher, April 26, 1789, *DHFFC*, 15:365–67; Stokes, *Iconography of Manhattan Island*, 5:1238–42; *New-York Daily Gazette*, April 25, 1789; *Gazette of the United States*, April 29, 1789; and Jackson and Twohig, *Diaries of George Washington*, 5:44ff.

46 *A satirical and sacrilegious:* Bartoloni de Tuazon, "Mr. President," 50–51.

46 *he was "perfectly indifferent":* Ibid., 60.

46 *"which ought to disconcert":* Hugh Williamson to Reading Beatty, March 18, 1789, *DHFFC*, 15:77.

46 *"Benevolence and nobility":* Comte de Moustier to Comte de Montmorin, June 9, 1789, *DHFFC*, 16:732–33.

47 *Unless the president:* Hugh Williamson to Reading Beatty, April 23, 1789, *DHFFC*, 15:331.

47 *"There cannot be":* Bowling and Veit, *Diary of William Maclay*, 39.

48 *He wondered aloud:* Ibid., 6.

48 *"as if oppressed":* Ibid.

48 *"I have looked":* Ibid.

48 *In Massachusetts, Pennsylvania: DHFFC*, vol. 21, note for January 4, 1791.

49 *John Page and his friend:* February 25, 1790, *DHFFC*, 19:632.

50 *"I have seen him!":* Griswold, *Republican Court*, 138.

50 *"Her Mind was":* Lambert Cadwallader to James Armstrong Jr., May 8, 1789, *DHFFC*, 15:480.

50 *On the morning:* Griswold, *Republican Court,* 139.

50 *Maclay, togged out:* Bowling and Veit, *Diary of William Maclay,* 11–12.

50 *"How shall I behave":* Ibid.

50 *A little after noon:* Decatur, *Private Affairs of George Washington,* 9–10; Griswold, *Republican Court,* 120–22; Stokes, *Iconography of Manhattan Island,* 5:1238–42, 5:1236–37; and Ebenezer Hazard to Jeremy Belknap, April 25, 1789, *DHFFC,* 15:356–57.

51 *"People of every age":* Essex (MA) Journal, May 15, 1789.

51 *"He seemed to":* Bowling and Veit, *Diary of William Maclay,* 12–13; also *GWP,* Presidential Series, 2:154–57.

51 *The crowd hushed:* Griswold, *Republican Court,* 140–41; and Comte de Moustier to Comte de Montmorin, *DHFFC,* 15:403–6.

52 *"The scene was solemn":* Griswold, *Republican Court,* 140–41.

52 *"a coronation":* Bartoloni de Tuazon, "Mr. President," 63.

52 *"It is done":* Griswold, *Republican Court,* 140–41.

52 *"I was looking upon":* James Kent to Elizabeth Hamilton, February 20, 1832, *DHFFC,* vol. 22.

52 *"The magnitude and difficulty":* GWP, Presidential Series, 2:172–76.

54 *"This great Man":* Bowling and Veit, *Diary of William Maclay,* 12–13.

54 *"a very touching scene":* Fisher Ames to George Richards Minot, May 3, 1789, *DHFFC,* 15:436; and Ames to Nathaniel Bishop, May 1789, *DHFFC,* 15:631.

54 *"Time has made havoc":* Bernhard, *Fisher Ames,* 80.

54 *That evening:* Griswold, *Republican Court,* 143; Bowling and Veit, *Diary of William Maclay,* 12–13; Smith, *City of New York,* 226–35; and *DHFFC,* 10:412–15.

Chapter 4: Pomp and Quiddling

Page

56 *Elias Boudinot:* Elias Boudinot to Hannah Boudinot, April 14 and 21 and May 15, 1789, *DHFFC,* 15:260, 15:303, 15:557.

57 *"It will be attended":* The following account of the removal and Treasury debate is based on the *Congressional Register,* May 19 and 20, 1789; *New-York Daily Advertiser,* May 21, 1789; *Gazette of the United States,* May 21 and 23, 1789; and Fisher Ames to George Richards Minot, May 19, 1789, in Allen, *Works of Fisher Ames,* 1:627.

57   *"The creation of a financier"*: *DHFFC*, 10:736, 10:747ff.

57   *"I abhor now"*: Elbridge Gerry to John Wendell, March 22, 1789, *DHFFC*, 10:91–92.

58   *"Should there be"*: Elbridge Gerry to John Wendell, July 10, 1789, *DHFFC*, 16:998.

58   *the forty-four-year-old Gerry:* Elbridge Gerry to John Adams, June 16, 1784; Francis Dana to Elbridge Gerry, June 17, 1784; and unknown correspondent to Thomas Jefferson, October 11, 1787, in Kaminski and Moore, *Assembly of Demigods*, 39–40; also *DHFFC*, 16:619.

58   *"was his own conscience"*: Billias, *Elbridge Gerry*, 222.

58   *protect "the* governed*"*: Elbridge Gerry, "Open letter to voters of Middlesex," January 22, 1789, *DHFFC*, 15:112–13.

59   *Madison personally felt:* James Madison to Thomas Jefferson, May 27, 1789, *JMP*, 12:185.

59   *self-serving "Judas"*: "HZ" to George Washington, March 24, 1789, *GWP*, Presidential Series, 1:441.

59   *the first collision:* James Madison to Edmund Pendleton, June 21, 1789, *DHFFC*, 15:829; James Madison to Tench Coxe, June 24, 1789, *DHFFC*, 15:852–53; William Loughton Smith to Otho H. Williams, June 21, 1789, *DHFFC*, 15:830; James Madison to Thomas Jefferson, June 30, 1789, *DHFFC*, 15:893; and William Loughton Smith, August 21, 1789, *DHFFC*, 15:832.

60   *Oliver Ellsworth:* Bowling and Veit, *Diary of William Maclay*, 112.

61   *"whereas the president"*: William Loughton Smith to Edward Rutledge, August 9, 1789, *DHFFC*, 16:1264ff; also Smith to Rutledge, July 5, 1789, *DHFFC*, 16:959–61.

61   *"A new president"*: *DHFFC*, 10:737; also *JMP*, 2:170ff.

61   *"Things which alarm"*: William Loughton Smith to Edward Rutledge, June 21, 1789, *DHFFC*, 16:831–33.

61   *"Should Adams obtain"*: William Loughton Smith to Edward Rutledge, August 9, 1789, *DHFFC*, 16:1267.

62   *"These officers from"*: Ibid.

62   *Madison, whose direction:* James Madison to Edmund Randolph, May 31, 1789, *JMP*, 12:190; generally, *JMP*, 12:171ff.; and *DHFFC*, 10:727.

63   *a fourth executive department:* Bowling, "Good-by 'Charlie.'"

64   *Thomson fell victim:* Ibid.

64 *"a smooth, plausible Irishman":* Fisher Ames to George Richards Minot, May 18, 1789, in Allen, *Works of Fisher Ames*, 1:627.

64 *"I should contradict":* Bowling, "Good-by 'Charlie.'"

64 *the increasingly embattled vice president:* John Adams to Abigail Adams, June 6, 1789, *DHFFC*, 16:708; John Adams to Richard Peters, June 5, 1789, *DHFFC*, 16:704; John Adams to Cotton Tufts, June 12, 1789, *DHFFC*, 16:755; John Adams to John Lovell, June 4, 1789, *DHFFC*, 16:695; John Adams to William Tudor, May 3, 1789, *DHFFC*, 15:435–36; and John Adams to Nathaniel P. Sargeant, May 21, 1789, *DHFFC*, 15:610–11.

65 *"just playing the outrageous":* Comte de Moustier to Comte de Montmorin, May 17, 1789, *DHFFC*, 15:577–80.

65 *With his beloved wife:* Griswold, *Republican Court*, 168–69; and Abigail Adams to Mary Cranch, March 11, 1790, *DHFFC*, 18:22.

65 *"Don't babble":* John Adams to William Tudor, May 28, 1789, *DHFFC*, 15:640–41.

66 *"the want of titles":* John Adams to Jabez Bowen, June 26, 1789, *DHFFC*, 16:859.

66 *"Is it not":* William Grayson to Patrick Henry, June 12, 1789, *DHFFC*, 16:761.

66 *"is a declared partisan":* Comte de Moustier to Comte de Montmorin, June 9, 1789, *DHFFC*, 16:734.

66 *"Institutions of admirable Wisdom":* John Adams to Benjamin Rush, June 9, 1789, *DHFFC*, 16:727.

66 *"a monarchical Republic":* John Adams to William Tudor, June 28, 1789, *DHFFC*, 16:870–71.

66 *He feared executive despotism:* Ibid.; also John Adams to Benjamin Lincoln, May 8, 1789, *DHFFC*, 15:478–79; and John Adams to Benjamin Rush, June 9, 1789, *DHFFC*, 16:727.

67 *Although some wanted:* Thomas T. Tucker to St. George Tucker, May 13, 1789, *DHFFC*, 15:538.

67 *One republican slyly: Federal Gazette*, April 16, 1789.

67 *Adams tirelessly repeated:* Bartoloni de Tuazon, "Mr. President," 128–30; John Adams to William Tudor, May 3, 1789, *DHFFC*, 15:435–36; John Adams to William Tudor, May 9, 1789, *DHFFC*, 15:489; and Henry Lee to James Madison, March 14, 1789, *JMP*, 12:12.

67 *"Washington has studied":* Comte de Moustier to Comte de Montmorin, June 9, 1789, *DHFFC*, 16:733–34.

68 *Washington would itself:* Ibid., 734.

68 *Maclay, who set out:* Bowling and Veit, *Diary of William Maclay*, xi–xii, 5, 8, 18–19.

68 *"I believe I":* Ibid., 10.

69 *"I know not":* Ibid., 8.

69 *His arguments were:* Ibid., 28–29.

69 *"Does the dignity":* Gazette of the United States, May 13, 1789.

69 *Many Federalists thought:* Fisher Ames to George Richards Minot, May 27, 1789, in Allen, *Works of Fisher Ames*, 2:632–34; *DHFFC*, 10:582, 10:585, 10:598; and Bartoloni de Tuazon, "Mr. President," 176, 280.

69 *When the House voted:* Generally, *Congressional Register*, May 11, 1789.

70 *Maclay grimly predicted:* Bowling and Veit, *Diary of William Maclay*, 27–28.

70 *"What will the Common People":* Ibid., 29–32.

70 *Maclay's diary fairly crackles:* Ibid., 19, 28, 33, 37–38; and Bartoloni de Tuazon, "Mr. President," 169.

70 *On May 14:* Bowling and Veit, *Diary of William Maclay*, 37–39; and Bartoloni de Tuazon, "Mr. President," 161–62, 181.

71 *"Had the project":* James Madison to Thomas Jefferson, May 23, 1789, *DHFFC*, 15:619.

71 *this "Idolatrous Business":* Bowling and Veit, *Diary of William Maclay*, 39.

71 *"Your affectionate address":* JMP, 12:141, 12:167.

Chapter 5: A Very Perplexing Business

Page

72 *"very perplexing business":* Paine Wingate to Jeremy Belknap, May 12, 1789, *DHFFC*, 15:535.

72 *"In every step":* James Madison to Edmund Randolph, May 31, 1789, *JMP*, 12:190.

72 *"A great clumsy machine":* Fisher Ames to George Richards Minot, July 8, 1789, *DHFFC*, 16:978.

72 *"There are a great":* Robert Morris to Anthony Wayne, July 9, 1789, *DHFFC*, 16:988.

73 *"disappoint the wishes":* James Madison to Thomas Jefferson, May 27, 1789, *JMP*, 12:185.

73 *"the American areopagus":* Comte de Moustier to Comte de Montmorin, June 9, 1789, *DHFFC*, 16:729.

73 *"Once a system":* DHFFC, 10:383–84.

73 *Madison admitted:* Ibid., 297.

74 *"dropped upon you":* Bernhard, *Fisher Ames*, 71.

74 *Without the molasses: Congressional Register*, May 11, 1789.

74 *"The proposed duty":* Thomas B. Wait to George Thatcher, May 7, 1789, *DHFFC*, 15:471–72.

74 *"We are not": DHFFC*, 10:364–66, 10:375–80; Bernhard, *Fisher Ames*, 85–86; and Fisher Ames to Nathaniel Bishop, May 1789, in Allen, *Works of Fisher Ames*, 1:631.

74 *"Money is power":* Fisher Ames to George Richards Minot, May 16, 1789, in Allen, *Works of Fisher Ames*, 1:624–26.

75 *"unprincipled, light, frothy":* Thomas B. Wait to George Thatcher, March 14, 1789, *DHFFC*, 15:64.

75 *Thatcher hailed from:* di Giacomantonio, William C., "A Congressional Wife at Home: The Case of Sarah Thatcher," in Bowling and Kennon, *Neither Separate nor Equal: Congress in the 1790s*, 156, 174.

75 *A tax of $50: DHFFC*, 10:369.

75 *The mere mention:* Ibid., 372–74.

75 *Declaring that it was time: Congressional Register*, May 13, 1789; *New-York Daily Advertiser*, May 14, 1789; and *Gazette of the United States*, May 16, 1789.

76 *"Negroes sell at":* Edmund Randolph to James Madison, May 19, 1789, *JMP*, 12:168.

76 *The reaction to Parker: Congressional Register*, May 13, 1789; and *DHFFC*, 10:385.

77 *"It is to be hoped": JMP*, 12:160–63.

78 *the clatter and roar:* Monaghan and Lowenthal, *This Was New York*, 15–16, 23–24, 32, 97; and Elias Boudinot to Hannah Boudinot, April 14, 1789, *DHFFC*, 15:260.

78 *"You must shut":* Oliver Ellsworth to Abigail Ellsworth, April 18, 1789, *DHFFC*, 15:279.

78 *"These dull & gloomy":* George Thatcher to Sarah Thatcher, March 29, 1789, *DHFFC*, 15:152.

78 *"It would inform":* John Leland to James Madison, February 15, 1789, *JMP*, 442–43.

79 *On days off:* Griswold, *Republican Court*, 167–68; and Monaghan and Lowenthal, *This Was New York*, 39–41.

79 *the gay whirl of soirees:* Smith, *City of New York*, 97, 117–18; and Monaghan and Lowenthal, *This Was New York*, 55–58, 61, 105–7.

79 *"The Americans make":* Comte de Moustier to Comte de Montmorin, June 9, 1789, *DHFFC*, 16:735–37.

79 *"It is my wish":* George Washington to James Madison, March 30, 1789, *JMP*, 41–42.

80 *Besieged by:* Judith Sargent Murray to George Washington, February 25, 1789, et al., *GWP*, Presidential Series, 1:343–51.

80 *"fatal consequences":* George Washington to Samuel Vaughn, March 21, 1789, *GWP*, Presidential Series, 1:424–25.

80 *"But to mark":* George Washington to James Madison, May 12, 1789, *JMP*, 12:157.

80 *"I was unable":* George Washington to David Stuart, June 15, 1790, *DHFFC*, 19:1832–35.

81 *"a pretty high tone":* Alexander Hamilton to George Washington, May 5, 1789, *GWP*, Presidential Series, 2:211–14.

82 *"the Pompous People":* Bowling and Veit, *Diary of William Maclay*, 74.

82 *The four-story Georgian:* Griswold, *Republican Court*, 149–50, 167–68; Monaghan and Lowenthal, *This Was New York*, 96, 110; and Sarah Robinson to Kitty F. Wistar, April 30, 1789, *DHFFC*, 15:286n.

82 *"There is certain":* Monaghan and Lowenthal, *This Was New York*, 105; and Smith, *City of New York*, 240.

83 *"Nobody has ever":* Louis-Guillaume Otto to Comte de Montmorin, June 13, 1790, *DHFFC*, 19:1805–6.

Chapter 6: A Great and Delicate Subject

Page

84 *"that Great and Delicate":* Benjamin Harrison to James Madison, June 1, 1789, *DHFFC*, 16:680.

84 *"Whether he means":* George Clymer to Richard Peters, June 8, 1789, *DHFFC*, 16:722–23.

85 *Members strained:* "Notes for a speech," June 8, 1789, *DHFFC*, 16:723–

24; *New-York Daily Advertiser*, June 9, 1789; *Gazette of the United States*, June 10, 1789; and *Congressional Register*, June 8, 1789.

85 *"If this is"*: Comte de Moustier to Comte de Montmorin, June 8, 1789, *DHFFC*, 16:729–32.

87 *"with Fetters"*: Oliver Wolcott Sr. to Oliver Ellsworth, June 27, 1789, *DHFFC*, 16:868.

87 *"that I always"*: James Madison to "Resident," January 27, 1789, *JMP*, 428–29.

87 *"Poor Madison"*: Robert Morris to Francis Hopkinson, August 15, 1789, in Veit, Bowling, and Bickford, *Creating the Bill of Rights*, 278.

87 *"a little rebellion"*: Thomas Jefferson to James Madison, January 30, 1787, in Jefferson, *Writings*, 881ff.

87 *"the people are entitled"*: Thomas Jefferson to James Madison, December 20, 1787, in Jefferson, *Writings*, 914ff.

87 *"the inconveniencies of"*: Thomas Jefferson to James Madison, March 15, 1789, in Jefferson, *Writings*, 942ff.

87 *"Is it not"*: Rakove, *James Madison*, 86.

88 *"conciliatory sacrifices"*: James Madison to Thomas Jefferson, March 29, 1789, *JMP*, 12:37ff.

88 *"It will kill"*: James Madison to Robert Page, August 19, 1789, in Veit, Bowling, and Bickford, *Creating the Bill of Rights*, 282–83.

88 *"Their object is"*: William Grayson to Patrick Henry, June 12, 1789, *DHFFC*, 16:757ff.

88 *Having promised amendments:* Unless otherwise indicated, sources for following section are *New-York Daily Advertiser*, June 9, 1789; *Gazette of the United States*, June 10, 1989; and *Congressional Register*, June 8, 1789.

89 *Jefferson's prescient prediction:* Thomas Jefferson to James Madison, March 15, 1789, in Jefferson, *Writings*, 942ff.

89 *"the people have an indubitable"*: Veit, Bowling, and Bickford, *Creating the Bill of Rights*, 11–14.

90 *"hunted up all"*: Fisher Ames to Thomas Dwight, June 11, 1789, *DHFFC*, 16:748–49.

90 *"taking up the subject"*: Collier, *Roger Sherman's Connecticut*, 298.

91 *Livermore cuttingly added:* Elbridge Gerry to James Warren, July 10, 1789, *DHFFC*, 16:996.

91 *A skilled political infighter:* Billias, *Elbridge Gerry*, 221ff.

92 *if "ingenious men":* William Loughton Smith to Edward Rutledge, August 10, 1789, *DHFFC*, 16:1281–83.

92 *"Georgia is now":* *DHFFC*, 15:823.

92 *Thomas Scott of Pennsylvania:* *DHFFC*, 11:1095–96ff.

93 *"The people are waiting":* Gazette of the United States, June 9, 1789.

93 *"so many local":* Thomas Hartley to Jasper Yeates, June 19, 1789, *DHFFC*, 15:814.

93 *"whose face, manner":* Fisher Ames to George Richards Minot, May 18, 1789, in Allen, *Works of Fisher Ames*, 1:627.

93 *"a very perplexing business":* Paine Wingate to Jeremy Belknap, May 12, 1789, *DHFFC*, 15:535.

93 *senators continued to rehash:* Generally, Bowling and Veit, *Diary of William Maclay*, 51–84.

94 *"Members, both from":* Ibid., 74.

94 *senator Pierce Butler:* Ibid., 73.

94 *"I must go on":* Ibid., 58.

94 *"declare commercial War":* Ibid., 54.

94 *"if Commercial Treaties":* Ibid.

95 *"The Senate, God bless":* Fisher Ames to George Richards Minot, May 27, 1789, in Allen, *Works of Fisher Ames*, 1:632–34.

95 *"so Prund":* Peter Muhlenberg to Benjamin Rush, June 3, 1789, *DHFFC*, 15:691.

96 *"Hamilton is most":* James Madison to Thomas Jefferson, June 30, 1789, *DHFFC*, 15:893.

96 *"being unacquainted":* James Madison to Thomas Jefferson, May 27, 1789, *DHFFC*, 15:638.

96 *"No question has":* William Smith to Otho H. Williams, June 19, 1789, *DHFFC*, 15:815.

96 *James Jackson of Georgia:* Lamplugh, " 'Oh the Colossus!' "; more generally, Lamplugh, *Politics on the Periphery*, 83ff; and *DHFFC*, 14:555–61.

97 *Speaking, probably: Congressional Register*, June 19, 1789; and *DHFFC*, 11:999–1002.

97 *He reiterated that: Congressional Register*, June 22, 1789; and *DHFFC*, 11:1032.

98 *"My whole heart":* Fisher Ames to George Richards Minot, June 23, 1789, *DHFFC*, 15:840–41.

Chapter 7: Vile Politicks

Page

99 *"He has been"*: Bowling and Veit, *Diary of William Maclay*, 82–83, 87–90.

100 *"a Bile on"*: William Loughton Smith to Edward Rutledge, June 21, 1789, *DHFFC*, 16:833.

100 *"Cut away"*: Chernow, *Alexander Hamilton*, 283.

100 *"Do not flatter"*: Griswold, *Republican Court*, 179.

101 *"Our own citizens"*: *Gazette of the United States*, June 13, 1789; and *Congressional Register*, June 2, 1789.

101 *"I leave you"*: Ibid., July 1, 1789.

101 *"Where the money"*: Elbridge Gerry to John Wendell, July 10, 1789, *DHFFC*, 16:998.

101 *"We must therefore"*: Elbridge Gerry to James Warren, July 10, 1789, *DHFFC*, 16:996.

102 *"Upon the whole"*: William Loughton Smith to Edward Rutledge, July 5, 1789, *DHFFC*, 16:959–61; also Smith to Rutledge, June 6, 1789, *DHFFC*, 16:710–11.

102 *"steeped in Anglicism"*: James Madison to Thomas Jefferson, May 9, 1789, *JMP*, 12:142–43.

102 *"Our successors"*: James Madison to Thomas Jefferson, June 30, 1789, *DHFFC*, 15:890.

102 *"intrigue, cabal, management"*: Fisher Ames to George Richards Minot, July 8, 1789, *DHFFC*, 16:978; and *DHFFC*, 6:lvii–lxiii.

103 *"It is a novel thing"*: Richard Bland Lee to David Stuart, June 4, 1789, *DHFFC*, 15:698.

104 *"the mimicry of soldiership"*: Chernow, *Alexander Hamilton*, 284–85.

104 *In other words*: Nash, *Forgotten Fifth*, 26–36; and Kolchin, *American Slavery*, 72–73.

104 *"It is Sacrilege"*: Bowling and Veit, *Diary of William Maclay*, 112.

104 *Senators and representatives*: Ibid., 12–15.

105 *"consolidation is"*: Ibid., 114.

106 *"the eccentric impulses"*: Thomas Jefferson to Edmund Pendleton, August 26, 1776, *TJP*, 1:505.

106 *to "crush"*: Wood, *Empire of Liberty*, 403.

106 *"vicious" misbehavior:* James Madison to Samuel Johnston, July 31, 1789, *DHFFC*, 16:1184–85.

106 *"We see numbers":* Abigail Ellsworth to David Daggett, May 7, 1789, *DHFFC*, 15:473–74.

107 *"I think that":* Oliver Wolcott Sr. to Oliver Ellsworth, June 27, 1789, *DHFFC*, 16:867.

107 *"A perfect uniformity":* Casto, *Oliver Ellsworth*, 62.

107 *"a man of remarkable":* William Loughton Smith to Edward Rutledge, August 9, 1789, *DHFFC*, 16:1264ff.

107 *Maclay derided him:* Bowling and Veit, *Diary of William Maclay*, 24, 69, 273.

107 *"Intrigate & Laborious Work":* Richard Bassett to Benjamin Chew, June 1789, in Marcus, *Documentary History*, 4:401.

108 *"carry Law to":* Casto, *Oliver Ellsworth*, 67–68.

108 *Maritime issues loomed:* Ibid., 71–72.

108 *"to make headway":* Edmund Randolph to James Madison, June 30, 1789, in Marcus, *Documentary History*, 4:432.

108 *"foreign and hostile":* Fisher Ames to John Lowell, July 28, 1789, in Marcus, *Documentary History*, 4:480.

109 *estimated to cost:* Paine Wingate to Nathaniel Sargeant, July 18, 1789, in Marcus, *Documentary History*, 4:474.

109 *"Create Jealousies":* James Sullivan to John Langdon, August 18, 1789, *DHFFC*, 16:1351.

109 *"inferior to any":* Timothy Pickering to Paine Wingate, July 1, 1789, *DHFFC*, 16:910.

109 *"This Vile Bill":* Bowling and Veit, *Diary of William Maclay*, 105–6.

109 *"I stay here":* Ibid., 86–91, 104.

109 *"My mind revolts":* Ibid., 76.

109 *"inquisitorial power":* William Maclay to Tench Coxe, July 4, 1789, *DHFFC*, 16:938.

109 *"the Carcass":* Bowling and Veit, *Diary of William Maclay*, 97–98.

109 *"I have been pushed":* Ibid.

109 *Meanwhile, Ellsworth:* Both quotes in Lettieri, *Connecticut's Young Man*, 81.

110 *"hung like a Cat":* Bowling and Veit, *Diary of William Maclay*, 359.

110 *American financial unreliability:* McCraw, *Founders and Finance*, 46ff; and Casto, *Oliver Ellsworth*, 72–73.

111 *"a wanton Exercise":* Marcus, *Documentary History,* 4:471–72.

111 *"It certainly is":* Bowling and Veit, *Diary of William Maclay,* 473.

111 *"The most that can":* James Madison to Samuel Johnston, July 31, 1789, *DHFFC,* 16:1184–85.

112 *For those of:* Monaghan and Lowenthal, *This Was New York,* 151–55, 139, 143; Smith, *City of New York,* 202ff.

112 *"I am never":* George Thatcher to Sarah Thatcher, March 29, 1789, *DHFFC,* 16:152.

113 *"Classical history":* Monaghan and Lowenthal, *This Was New York,* 155.

113 *Members enjoyed:* Smith, *City of New York,* 183–87.

114 *Since the opening:* Ibid., 170–76.

114 *There shall the noblest: DHFFC,* 15:29.

Chapter 8: Propositions of a Doubtful Nature

Page

115 *"that Great and Delicate":* Benjamin Hawkins to James Madison, June 1, 1789, *DHFFC,* 16:680.

115 *"a mere musketo bite": Gazette of the United States,* August 22, 1789.

115 *"a few milk-and-water":* Pierce Butler to James Iredell, August 11, 1789; and Noah Webster to James Madison, August 14, 1789, in Veit, Bowling, and Bickford, *Creating the Bill of Rights,* 274, 276.

116 *As the constitutional:* Paul Finkelman, "James Madison and the Bill of Rights."

116 *Madison allotted:* Unless otherwise noted, the account of this debate is drawn from the *New-York Daily Advertiser,* August 14, 17, 19, and 20, 1787; *Gazette of the United States,* August 15, 19, 22, and 26, 1787; and *Congressional Register,* August 13, 14, 15, 17, 18, 19, 21, and 22, collected in Veit, Bowling, and Bickford, *Creating the Bill of Rights,* 104ff.

116 *He made clear:* James Madison to Edmund Randolph, August 21, 1789, in Veit, Bowling, and Bickford, *Creating the Bill of Rights,* 284.

116 *"While I approve": New-York Daily Advertiser,* August 17, 1789; and *Gazette of the United States,* August 19, 1789.

117 *"as a friend to": Congressional Register,* August 15, 1789.

117 *"exclude every proposition":* James Madison to Edmund Randolph, August 21, 1789, in Veit, Bowling, and Bickford, *Creating the Bill of Rights,* 284.

117 *"obstruct the wheels"*: Collier, *Roger Sherman's Connecticut*, 298.

118 *"Experience will shew"*: New Haven [CT] *Gazette*, December 18, 1788.

118 *"an old Puritan"*: *DHFFC*, 14:511.

118 *"as cunning as"*: Jeremiah Wadsworth to Rufus King, June 3, 1787, in Kaminski and Moore, *Assembly of Demigods*, 6.

118 *one of the most experienced*: Collier, *Roger Sherman's Connecticut*, 4–5, 161ff, 321–22; and *DHFFC*, 14:506ff.

119 *"I see nothing"*: George Washington to James Madison, May 31, 1789, *JMP*, 12:191.

120 *Daniel Carroll*: *New-York Daily Advertiser*, August 17, 1789; and *Gazette of the United States*, August 19, 1789.

121 *To Madison's disappointment*: Veit, Bowling, and Bickford, *Creating the Bill of Rights*, 11–14, 29–33.

122 *"We might as well"*: Collier, *Roger Sherman's Connecticut*, 299.

123 *Vining's committee also revised*: Veit, Bowling, and Bickford, *Creating the Bill of Rights*, 30.

123 *"the right to keep"*: Samuel Nasson to George Thatcher, July 9, 1787, *DHFFC*, 16:989–90.

124 *Gerry, for one*: Generally, Billias, *Elbridge Gerry*, 230ff.

125 *"little better than"*: Veit, Bowling, and Bickford, *Creating the Bill of Rights*, 175.

125 *"The antifederals in"*: William Loughton Smith to Edward Rutledge, August 15, 1789, *DHFFC*, 16:1327.

125 *"If it is in"*: William Loughton Smith to Edward Rutledge, August 9, 1789, *DHFFC*, 16:1264ff.

125 *Tucker bombarded the House*: *DHFFC*, 14:857ff.

127 *The shadow of Shays' Rebellion*: Sedgwick, *In My Blood*, 80ff; anonymous, in *New-York Daily Advertiser*, August 18, 1789.

Chapter 9: Paper Guarantees

Page

129 *On August 18*: *DHFFC*, 14:857ff.

130 *"ill-humour and rudeness"*: William Loughton Smith to Edward Rutledge, August 15, 1789, *DHFFC*, 16:1327.

130 *"the work has been"*: James Madison to Edmund Pendleton, August 21, 1789, in Veit, Bowling, and Bickford, *Creating the Bill of Rights*, 284.

130 *It was said:* Henry Sewall to Benjamin Shaw, August 18, 1789, *DHFFC*, 16:1350.

130 *"I feard lest":* Pamela Sedgwick to Theodore Sedgwick, August 22, 1789, *DHFFC*, 16:1374–75.

130 *"The weather was":* William Smith to Otho H. Williams, August 22, 1789, in Veit, Bowling, and Bickford, *Creating the Bill of Rights*, 285.

130 *"Such is the present":* Frederick A. Muhlenberg to Benjamin Rush, August 18, 1789, in Veit, Bowling, and Bickford, *Creating the Bill of Rights*, 280–81.

131 *"infinitely cold":* Comte de Moustier to Comte de Montmorin, October 3, 1789, *DHFFC*, 17:1659.

131 *One evening:* Bowling and Veit, *Diary of William Maclay*, 136–37.

132 *Benjamin Fishbourne: DHFFC*, 14:546ff; *DHFFC*, 17:1795; and William Smith to Otho H. Williams, *DHFFC*, 16:1281.

133 *Gunn "urged nothing":* "Letter from New York" to Benjamin Fishbourne, *DHFFC*, 16:1286–87.

133 *Wayne later interpreted: DHFFC*, 16:1240n.

133 *"shewed great want":* Benjamin Lincoln Lear, "Account of Washington's Attendance on the Senate," December 3, 1818, *DHFFC*, 16:1239–40.

133 *Washington again tempted fate:* Bowling and Veit, *Diary of William Maclay*, 128–31; Prucha, *American Indian Treaties*, 75ff.

136 *According to Maclay:* Bowling and Veit, *Diary of William Maclay*, 133.

136 *"the Waste of":* Robert Morris to Robert Page, August 24, 1789, in Veit, Bowling, and Bickford, *Creating the Bill of Rights*, 288; also Morris to James Warren, August 23, 1789, *DHFFC*, 16:1381; and Morris to Francis Hopkinson, August 15, 1789, *DHFFC*, 16:1324.

136 *"For a While":* Bowling and Veit, *Diary of William Maclay*, 135.

136 *"We might as well":* Richard Henry Lee to Patrick Henry, September 14, 1789, *DHFFC*, 17:1541–43.

137 *The Senate also made:* Veit, Bowling, and Bickford, *Creating the Bill of Rights*, 46–48.

138 *"After exhausting themselves":* Benjamin Goodhue to Salem Insurance Office, August 23, 1789, in Veit, Bowling, and Bickford, *Creating the Bill of Rights*, 285–86.

138 *"the late opponents":* James Madison to George Washington, November 20, 1789, *JMP*, 12:392.

138 *"He certainly does not"*: Abigail Adams to Mary Cranch, July 12, 1789, in Kaminski and Moore, *Assembly of Demigods*, 43.

138 *"The difficulty of"*: James Madison to Edmund Pendleton, September 14, 1789, in Veit, Bowling, and Bickford, *Creating the Bill of Rights*, 296.

138 *"rather have none"*: James Madison to Paine Wingate, September 17, 1789, in Veit, Bowling, and Bickford, *Creating the Bill of Rights*, 297.

139 *"argues a frivolity"*: Theodore Sedgwick to Pamela Sedgwick, August 20, 1789, in Veit, Bowling, and Bickford, *Creating the Bill of Rights*, 283.

139 *"the expectations of"*: William Ellery to Benjamin Harrison, August 24, 1789, in Veit, Bowling, and Bickford, *Creating the Bill of Rights*, 287.

139 *"had rendered Machiavelli"*: Bowling, "'A Tub to the Whale.'"

139 *"mutilated and enfeebled"*: Richard Henry Lee to Patrick Henry, September 27, 1789, in Veit, Bowling, and Bickford, *Creating the Bill of Rights*, 298.

139 *"little better than"*: Richard Henry Lee to Patrick Henry, September 14, 1789, in Veit, Bowling, and Bickford, *Creating the Bill of Rights*, 295.

139 *"I like it"*: Thomas Jefferson to James Madison, August 28, 1789, *DHFFC*, 16:1411–12.

141 *"unlike most modern"*: Amar, *Bill of Rights*, 284ff.

141 *the long-delayed judiciary bill*: The account of the ensuing debate draws mainly on these sources, unless otherwise noted: *Congressional Register*, August 8, 29, and 31, 1789; *Gazette of the United States*, September 2, 5, and 9, 1789; and *DHFFC*, 11:1329–32, 11:1348–93.

141 *He had earlier*: *DHFFC*, 14:666–68.

141 *"The air"*: Ibid., 599.

142 *"broken and interrupted"*: Charles Thomson to Hannah Thomson, October 20, 1783, in Kaminski and Moore, *Assembly of Demigods*, 38.

142 *"political experiment"*: Elbridge Gerry to John Wendell, September 14, 1789, in Veit, Bowling, and Bickford, *Creating the Bill of Rights*, 294.

Chapter 10: A Centre Without Parallel

Page

144 *"will lay a foundation"*: *Pennsylvania Gazette*, March 18, 1789.

145 *"While we had"*: *New-York Daily Advertiser*, September 4, 1789.

145 *More than thirty*: Thomas Jefferson, "Notes on the Permanent Seat of Con-

gress," April 13, 1784, in Padover, *Thomas Jefferson and the National Capital*, 6–9; *New-York Daily Gazette*, June 14, 1790; Bowling, *Creating the Federal City*, 23–37, 61–67; *DHFFC*, 11:1414, 11:1429–30; *Pennsylvania Gazette*, September 9, 1789; and Robert Morris to Mary Morris, March 4, 1789, *DHFFC*, 15:11–12.

146 *"For two or three":* George Thatcher to David Sewall, July 20, 1790, *DHFFC*, 20:2197–98.

146 *"that the heart":* *Congressional Register*, August 27, 1789.

146 *"where southern constitutions":* Timothy Pickering to Paine Wingate, April 15, 1789, *DHFFC*, 15:267; generally, *New-York Daily Advertiser*, September 9, 1789.

147 *"Like Electrified Clouds":* Benjamin Rush to John Adams, March 19, 1789, *DHFFC*, 15:79–81.

147 *Not until early:* "To the Citizens of New-York," *New-York Journal*, July 20, 1790; and Padover, *Thomas Jefferson and the National Capital*, 4–9.

147 *"the Cannons of":* "Political Opinions Particularly Respecting the Seat of the Federal Empire," in Bowling, *Creating the Federal City*, 55–56.

147 *"worth millions":* Michael Jenifer Stone to Walter Stone, July 1, 1790, *DHFFC*, 20:1997–98.

148 *"British hearted":* Benjamin Rush to John Adams, March 19, 1789, *DHFFC*, 15:79–81; also Rush to Adams, June 4, 1789, *DHFFC*, 16:699–700.

148 *"a permanent seat":* *Congressional Register*, August 27, 1789; *DHFFC*, 11:1340; also *DHFFC*, 14:802.

148 *"A permanent residential":* "Letter from New York," *Massachusetts Centinel*, September 6, 1789, in *DHFFC*, 17:1481; also Robert Morris to Mary Morris, September 6, 1789, *DHFFC*, 17:1479.

148 *"this vile":* Fisher Ames to George Richards Minot, September 6, 1789, *DHFFC*, 17:1470–71.

148 *New Englanders and:* Rufus King, "Summary of the Political Background to the Seat of Government Bill," September 26, 1789, *DHFFC*, 17:1619; *New-York Daily Advertiser*, September 9, 1789; and Thomas Fitzsimons to Tench Coxe, September 6, 1789, *DHFFC*, 17:1473–74.

149 *"lie by to mar":* George Clymer to Robert Page, September 6, 1789, *DHFFC*, 17:1472.

149 *"The real designs":* Fisher Ames to George Richards Minot, September 3, 1789, *DHFFC*, 17:1458.

149 *"sore & offended":* Thomas Fitzsimons to Tench Coxe, September 6, 1789, *DHFFC*, 17:1473–74; and *New-York Daily Advertiser*, September 5, 1789.

150 *"palladium of liberty": New-York Daily Advertiser*, September 4, 1789.

150 *On September 4: JMP*, 12:373–81.

151 *Alexandria congressman:* Unless otherwise noted, the following debate is based on these sources: *Congressional Register*, September 3, 17, 21, and 28, 1789; *New-York Daily Advertiser*, September 4, 5, 7, 8, and 22, 1789; *Pennsylvania Gazette*, September 9, 1789; *DHFFC*, 11:1400–1402, 11:1412–16, 11:1481–1512; Bowling, *Creation of Washington, D.C.*, 138–44, 153–57; Rappleye, *Robert Morris*, 462ff; Nuxoll, "The Financier as Senator," in Bowling and Kennon, *Neither Separate nor Equal*, 104–5; Fisher Ames to John Lowell, September 3, 1789, *DHFFC*, 17:1456–57; Fisher Ames to George Richards Minot, September 3, 1789, *DHFFC*, 17:1458; William Smith to Otho H. Williams, September 4, 1789, *DHFFC*, 17:1464; and Henry Wynkoop to Reading Beatty, September 4, 1789, *DHFFC*, 17:1464.

152 *Mumbet was well known:* Sedgwick, *In My Blood*, 69–77.

152 *"where Negro Slaves":* Benjamin Rush to John Adams, March 19, 1789, *DHFFC*, 15:79–81.

152 *that "odious distinction":* Thomas Dwight to Theodore Sedgwick, September 3, 1789, *DHFFC*, 17:1460–61.

152 *To the delight: Pennsylvania Gazette*, September 9 and 16, 1789; *Congressional Register*, September 7, 1789; *DHFFC*, 11:1438ff; and Fisher Ames to George Richards Minot, *DHFFC*, 17:1470–71.

153 *"I will not be":* William Maclay to Benjamin Rush, April 7, 1789, *DHFFC*, 15:217.

153 *the gregarious Robert Morris:* Bowling and Veit, *Diary of William Maclay*, 146ff; Nuxoll, "Financier as Senator," in Bowling and Kennon, *Neither Separate nor Equal*, 94–95; and Rappleye, *Robert Morris*, 10, 443–44, 464–65.

154 *African slaves: Pennsylvania Gazette*, May 11, 1758; May 6 and June 3, 1762; June 27, 1765; and Rappleye, *Robert Morris*, 140–41.

154 *"There has been a Violent":* Bowling and Veit, *Diary of William Maclay*, 144.

154 *"Thus barefacedly":* Ibid., 159.

154 *Morris's trump:* Robert Morris to Gouverneur Morris, September 27, 1789, *DHFFC*, 17:1627; also Arnebeck, *Through a Fiery Trial*, 15–17.

155 *Morris "flamed away"*: Bowling and Veit, *Diary of William Maclay*, 157ff.

156 *"a Monkey just put"*: Ibid., 33.

156 *"Thus fell our hopes"*: Ibid., 162–64.

156 *But Madison:* James Madison to Edmund Pendleton, September 23, 1789, *DHFFC*, 17:1603–4; and *Congressional Register*, September 28, 1789.

157 *"as sure as fate"*: *Independent Gazeteer*, in *DHFFC*, 17:1665–66.

157 *"And thus the house"*: Fisher Ames to Theodore Sedgwick, October 6, 1789, *DHFFC*, 17:1671–72; also Robert Morris to Gouverneur Morris, September 27, 1789, *DHFFC*, 17:1627.

157 *"You might search"*: John Adams to James Bridge, September 21, 1789, *DHFFC*, 17:1594.

157 *"expecting every man"*: Bowling and Veit, *Diary of William Maclay*, 141.

157 *"the yawning listlessness"*: Fisher Ames to George Richards Minot, May 27, 1789, in Allen, *Works of Fisher Ames*, 1:632–34.

157 *In May, optimists:* James Madison to Thomas Jefferson, May 9, 1789, *JMP*, 12:142–43.

157 *"left very strong impressions"*: William Grayson to Patrick Henry, September 29, 1789, *DHFFC*, 17:1638.

158 *"Never was a man"*: Pierce Butler to James Iredell, August 11, 1789, *DHFFC*, 16:1288–89.

158 *"It is impossible"*: Richard Henry Lee and William Grayson to the Speaker of the Virginia House of Delegates, September 28, 1789, in Veit, Bowling, and Bickford, *Creating the Bill of Rights*, 299.

159 *infested with "Intrigue"*: James Lovell to Elbridge Gerry, January 22, 1791, *DHFFC*, 21.

159 *George Washington appointed:* Friedman and Israel, *Justices of the United States Supreme Court*, 1:4–10; and Stahr, *John Jay*, 265–73.

160 *"so monstrous an appearance"*: William Grayson to Patrick Henry, September 29, 1789, *DHFFC*, 17:1638.

160 *"a resolute, frank, soldierly"*: Brissot de Warville, *New Travels in the United States*, 147.

160 *His "application is"*: Samuel Johnston to James Iredell, February 24, 1790, *DHFFC*, 18:624.

160 *"He knows everything, sir"*: Chernow, *Alexander Hamilton*, 286.

160 *"In undertaking the task"*: Alexander Hamilton to Marquis de Lafayette, October 6, 1789, in Hamilton, *Writings*, 521; also Chernow, *Alexander Hamilton*, 16–17; and Syrett, *Papers of Alexander Hamilton*, 5:365, 5:409.

161 *"It was indeed"*: George Washington to Catherine Sawbridge Macaulay Graham, January 9, 1790, in Jackson and Twohig, *Diaries of George Washington*, 5:551–54.

161 *"nowhere near as important"*: Comte de Moustier to Comte de Montmorin, October 3, 1789, *DHFFC*, 17:1659.

161 *"Every unpopular point"*: John Adams to William Cushing, September 8, 1789, *DHFFC*, 17:1485.

Chapter 11: Interlude I

Page

163 *"breath or spirits"*: Fisher Ames to Theodore Sedgwick, *DHFFC*, 17:1671.

163 *"It is fur"*: William Loughton Smith to Edward Rutledge, October 6, 1789, *DHFFC*, 17:1673–74.

164 *"long and tedeous"*: George Washington to Betty Washington Lewis, October 12, 1789, *GWP*, Presidential Series, 4:161.

164 *"to acquire knowledge"*: Washington's detailed account of his northern journey will be found in *GWP*, Presidential Series, 5:452–53, 5:460–82; and *GWP*, 4:162n.

164 *Before he departed:* "Thanks giving Proclamation," October 3, 1789, *GWP*, Presidential Series, 4:131–32; and Thompson, *"In the Hands of a Good Providence,"* 163–83.

166 *Washington pointedly spurned:* Jabez Bowen to John Adams, February 15, 1789, *DHFFC*, 18:533; and Nathaniel Bishop to Richard H. Lee, May 1, 1789, *DHFFC*, 15:423.

166 *"What security against"*: Fisher Ames to George Benson, June 13, 1789, *DHFFC*, 16:771.

167 *"the Botany Bay"*: "Letter from Newport," *New-York Daily Advertiser*, February 11, 1790, in *DHFFC*, 18:499.

167 *Instead of dignifying:* Jackson and Twohig, *Diaries of George Washington*, 5:483–97.

168 *"The ill-boding Politicians"*: George Washington to Catherine Sawbridge Macaulay Graham, January 9, 1990, *GWP*, Presidential Series, 4:551–54; also Theodorick Lee to John Langdon, November 14, 1789, *DHFFC*, 17:1710–11.

168 *"torrid" energy:* Chernow, *Alexander Hamilton*, 291.

169 *"No other moment"*: Ibid., 288–89.

169 *"better able to"*: McCraw, *Founders and Finance*, 6.

169 *"The people of this country"*: Jeremiah Wadsworth, October 26, 1789, *DHFFC*, 18:12–13.

169 *borrowing—"is to nations"*: Benjamin Rush to James Madison, March 10, 1790, *DHFFC*, 18:810–11.

170 *"When the country"*: Schecter, *Battle for New York*, 371–72.

170 *Several states that*: McCraw, *Founders and Finance*, 95–96.

171 *"We must pay it"*: DHFFC, 12:209.

171 *"Nay, I do not"*: Ibid., 256.

171 *"In considering plans"*: Alexander Hamilton to James Madison, October 12, 1789, *DHFFC*, 18:1.

171 *"wicked and impolitic"*: "The Observer," III, October 26, 1789, *DHFFC*, 18:12–13.

171 *"the boggy landscape"*: Ferling, *First of Men*, 381.

172 *"I contemn the grov'ling"*: McCraw, *Founders and Finance*, 16.

172 *"with incandescent brilliance"*: Ibid., 27.

172 *"turbulent and changing"*: Ibid., 81.

172 *"by the first ships"*: Angelica Schuyler Church to Alexander Hamilton, February 4, 1790, *AHP*, 6:245.

172 *"its most interested"*: Benjamin Lincoln to John Adams, April 22, 1789, *DHFFC*, 15:319.

172 *"have proved to be"*: McCraw, *Founders and Finance*, 64.

173 *During the presidential*: Chernow, *Alexander Hamilton*, 272–74, 285–86.

173 *"the artful machinations"*: "HZ" to George Washington, March 24, 1789, *GWP*, Presidential Series, 1:441; and McCraw, *Founders and Finance*, 38.

174 *George Beckwith*: Hamilton's relationship with Beckwith is described in Boyd, *Number 7*, 21–25.

174 *The putative secretary*: Thomas Jefferson to Nathaniel Cutting, November 21, 1789, *TJP*, 15:551; Jefferson to William Short, November 21, 1789, *TJP*, 15:552; Jefferson to John Jay, November 23, 1789, *TJP*, 15:553; and Jefferson to John Trumbull, November 25, 1789, *TJP*, 15:559.

175 *"plunge into the forests"*: Thomas Jefferson to William Short, December 14, 1789, *TJP*, 16:24–28.

175 *"favorable accounts"*: John Dawson to James Madison, December 17, 1789, *DHFFC*, 18:88; generally McCullough, *John Adams*, 244–45; and Smith, *Republic of Letters*, 638.

175 *"They were cheering"*: Gordon-Reed, *Hemingses of Monticello*, 392, 398–401.

175 *There was much:* James Brown to Thomas Jefferson, December 21, 1789, *TJP*, 16:38; and Alexander Donald to Jefferson, December 15, 1789, *TJP*, 16:28.

176 *"When I contemplate"*: Thomas Jefferson to George Washington, December 15, 1789, *TJP*, 16:34–35.

177 *"I was sorry"*: James Madison to George Washington, January 4, 1790, *DHFFC*, 18:140–41.

177 *"A Citizen of the World"*: Kenneth R. Bowling, "A Capital before a Capitol," in Bowling and Kennon, *Republic for the Ages*, 52–54.

177 *Walker's glorious vision:* Bowling, *Creating the Federal City*, 55–60; Bowling, *Creation of Washington, D.C.*, 163–67; Arnebeck, *Fiery Trial*, 18, 48, 158–60; and *Federal Gazette*, February 23, 1790.

178 *"in a gr[e]at Pain"*: Hugh Williamson to James Madison, May 21, 1789, *JMP*, 12:177.

178 *"to take rather too freely"*: Abigail Adams to Mary Cranch, January 5, 1790, *DHFFC*, 18:147–48.

179 *"The ladies all"*: Alexander White to Horatio Gates, March 1, 1790, *DHFFC*, 18:849–50.

179 *"[I] regained my flesh"*: James Madison to James Madison Sr., *DHFFC*, 18:286.

179 *"it will decide"*: Louis-Guillaume Otto to Comte de Montmorin, January 12, 1790, *DHFFC*, 17:197–99.

179 *"happy mixture of"*: Ibid.

180 *"Providing for the"*: http://ahp.gatech.edu/first_state_union_1790.html.

Chapter 12: The Labyrinth of Finance

Page

182 *the "extraordinary spirit"*: Paine Wingate to Jeremy Belknap, January 18, 1790, *DHFFC*, 18:248; generally, *New-York Journal*, January 14, 1790; *New-York Daily Advertiser*, January 14, 1790; and Stokes, *Iconography of Manhattan Island*, 1258–59.

183 *"Finances are now"*: Walter Rutherfurd to John Rutherfurd, January 8, 1790, *DHFFC*, 18:159.

183 *Alexander Hamilton was:* Alexander Hamilton to Andrew Craigie, January 7, 1790, *AHP*, 6:51.

183 *"What his plans"*: Benjamin Goodhue to Samuel Phillips Jr., January 11, 1790, *DHFFC*, 18:182.

184 *"I make no"*: Benjamin Goodhue to Samuel Phillips Jr., January 13, 1790, *DHFFC*, 18:205.

184 *Hamilton's report began:* Hamilton, *Writings*, 531–74; *AHP*, 6:51–63; and Brissot de Warville, *New Travels in the United States*, 48ff, 371ff.

185 *"by far the highest"*: McCraw, *Founders and Finance*, 95.

186 *"How can it be"*: Samuel Nasson to George Thatcher, March 2, 1790, *DHFFC*, 18:709.

186 *they were based:* Rappleye, *Robert Morris*, 236, 250.

186 *No American had:* McCraw, *Founders and Finance*, 99–100.

187 *"in the labyrinth"*: "Letter from a Citizen of Massachusetts at New York," *DHFFC*, 18:528.

187 *"I confess that"*: Otho H. Williams to William Smith, February 28, 1790, *DHFFC*, 18:682–83.

187 *"Finance is of"*: Jeremiah Wadsworth, "Observer," XVII, February 1, 1790, *DHFFC*, 17:382–89.

187 *"cut up by the roots"*: William Bradford Jr. to Elbridge Gerry, January 17, 1790, *DHFFC*, 18:235.

187 *"a masterly performance"*: Fisher Ames to William Tudor, January 17, 1790, *DHFFC*, 18:234.

187 *"Credit, public Credit"*: Robert Morris to George Harrison, March 13, 1790, *DHFFC*, 18:845.

187 *Wild rumors abounded: New-York Daily Advertiser*, February 13, 1790; and James Jackson to unknown correspondent, February 6, 1790, *DHFFC*, 18:429.

188 *"I sicken every time"*: Benjamin Rush to James Madison, March 10, 1790, *DHFFC*, 18:810–11.

188 *"will rank hereafter"*: Benjamin Rush to Thomas Fitzsimons, February 19, 1790, *DHFFC*, 18:577.

188 *"political tricks"*: Richard Henry Lee to James Madison, March 4, 1790, *DHFFC*, 18:725–27.

188 *The fiercest attack:* The account of the following debate is based mainly on the *Congressional Register*, January 28, 1790, in *DHFFC*, 12:107–14.

188 *William Duer:* Berkeley and Berkeley, *John Beckley*, 48–49; also McCraw, *Founders and Finance*, 103.

188 *"to buy up all"*: Hugh Williamson to John Gray Blount, February 24, 1790, *DHFFC*, 18:628.

188 *The volatile Jackson:* James Jackson to unknown correspondent, February 6, 1790, *DHFFC*, 18:429; Jackson to Samuel B. Webb, December 12, 1789, *DHFFC*, 18:74–75; Lamplugh, "'Oh the Colossus!,'" 83ff; and *DHFFC*, 14:555–61.

189 *"a dangerous leap"*: *Congressional Register*, February 10, 1790.

189 *"Though our present"*: Ibid., February 8, 1790.

189 *"For my part"*: Ibid.

189 *"I wish to God"*: Ibid., January 28, 1790.

189 *"Look at the gallant"*: Ibid.; *DHFFC*, 12:107, 12:113.

190 *Soldiers themselves had: DHFFC*, 12:258.

190 *"have since wedded"*: *Congressional Register*, February 10, 1790.

190 *"Must every transaction"*: Ibid., February 9, 1790.

190 *"The public faith"*: Ibid., January 28, 1790.

190 *"A love of property"*: Jeremiah Wadsworth, "Observer," XVI, January 25, 1790, *DHFFC*, 18:310–11.

191 *Like Jackson, Madison:* James Madison to Thomas Jefferson, January 24, 1790, *DHFFC*, 18:299.

191 *Madison admitted: New-York Daily Advertiser*, February 15, 1790; and *Congressional Register*, February 11, 1790.

191 *"A Public Debt"*: James Madison to Richard Henry Lee, April 13, 1790, *DHFFC*, 19:1220.

191 *"the sufferings of"*: *DHFFC*, 12:278ff.

191 *"something radically immoral"*: James Madison to Benjamin Rush, March 7, 1790, *DHFFC*, 18:769.

191 *Yet, he conceded: New-York Daily Advertiser*, February 15, 1790; and *Congressional Register*, February 11, 1790.

192 *Madison, "who, fearless": Massachusetts Centinel*, February 24, 1790, in *DHFFC*, 18:625.

192 *"A Madison above": Massachusetts Centinel*, February 27, 1790, in *DHFFC*, 18:663.

193 *"Hocus Pocus Humbug": New-York Daily Advertiser*, February 11, 1790, in *DHFFC*, 18:498.

193 *"Tho Mr. Madison"*: Thomas Fitzsimons to Benjamin Rush, February 14, 1790, *DHFFC*, 18:531.

193 *"it had more"*: Thomas Hartley to Jasper Yeates, February 14, 1790, *DHFFC*, 18:516.

Chapter 13: A Gross National Iniquity

Page

194 *"Blasting our Sanguwine"*: James Brown to John Adams, February 16, 1790, *DHFFC*, 18:545.

195 *the Supreme Court convened*: Friedman and Israel, *Justices of the United States Supreme Court*, 11.

195 *Secretary of War Knox's:* "A Plan for the General Arrangement of the Militia of the United States," January 18, 1790, *DHFFC*, 5:1435ff.

196 *"acquire such a habit"*: John Fisk to Benjamin Goodhue, February 15, 1790, *DHFFC*, 18:534.

196 *"consider man as created"*: Benjamin Rush to James Madison, February 27, 1790, *DHFFC*, 18:657.

196 *rejoined Madison: Congressional Register*, February 2, 1790; generally, *DHFFC*, 5:664ff; and *DHFFC*, 12:136.

196 *The naturalization bill:* For the debate, *DHFFC*, 5:1516ff; also *Congressional Register*, February 3, 1790.

197 *were "but leeches"*: *DHFFC*, 12:155.

197 *"overrun with the outcasts"*: Ibid., 154.

197 *"We must [then] add"*: Ibid., pp. 148, 152.

198 *"way-laid" members*: William Loughton Smith, quoted in di Giacomantonio, "'For the Gratification of a Volunteering Society'"; also *DHFFC*, 8:328; and *DHFFC*, 18:688–91.

198 *"with a sense of religious duty"*: Pennsylvania and New York memorials, *DHFFC*, 8:322–23.

199 *"Few appeared to"*: John Pemberton to James Pemberton, February 11, 1790, *DHFFC*, 18:496–97; generally, Newman, *Transformation of American Abolitionism*, 20–22, 41ff.

199 *"From a persuasion"*: Pennsylvania Abolition Society petition, *DHFFC*, 8:324–26.

199 *"Why increase the sons"*: Franklin, *Observations Concerning the Increase* (pamphlet).

200 *"an atrocious debasement"*: Isaacson, *Benjamin Franklin*, 464ff.

200 *"The Colour of a man":* Lowance, *Against Slavery,* 22–23.

201 *"reverse the order":* James Pemberton to James Phillips, November 18, 1784, Gilder Lehrman collection #GLCO4237, https://www.gilderlehrman .org.

201 *Nominally antislavery Senator:* Oliver Ellsworth to Abigail Ellsworth, March 7, 1790, *DHFFC,* 18:778–79.

201 *"The southern members":* John Pemberton to James Pemberton, February 11, 1790, *DHFFC,* 18:496–97.

201 *They accused the Quakers: Congressional Register,* February 11, 1790; *New-York Daily Advertiser,* March 25, 1790; and John Pemberton to James Pemberton, March 8, 1790, *DHFFC,* 18:789.

201 *"prayed us to establish":* Abraham Baldwin, *DHFFC,* 14:554–55; unless otherwise noted, the following account of the main debate is generally based on the *Congressional Register,* February 11, 1790.

202 *Congress was well within: DHFFC,* 14:802ff.

203 *"I look upon":* Ibid.

203 *"We had a great":* William Loughton Smith to Edward Rutledge, February 13, 1790, *DHFFC,* 18:511.

203 *"the condition of":* DHFFC, 8:327.

204 *"endeavored to convert":* William Loughton Smith to Edward Rutledge, February 28, 1790, *DHFFC,* 18:673–74; and Warner Mifflin to William Loughton Smith, March 10, 1790, *DHFFC,* 18:818–22.

205 *"with rather a sneer":* Bowling and Veit, *Diary of William Maclay,* 202; also John Pemberton to James Pemberton, February 15, 1790, *DHFFC,* 18:497, 18:540.

206 *"the Virginia straddle":* Ellis, *Founding Brothers,* 114–15.

206 *"in proportion as":* McCoy, *Last of the Fathers,* 234, 266.

206 *"might prove a great":* "Memorandum," October 20, 1789, *JMP,* 12:437–38; generally, Burstein and Isenberg: *Madison and Jefferson,* 201.

206 *Whatever his abstract:* Cyrus Griffin to James Madison, May 12, 1788; and James Madison to James Madison Sr., August 18, 1788, *JMP,* 11:44, 11:235–36.

207 *"Gentlemen need not":* JMP, 13:32.

207 *"shamefully indecent":* James. Madison to Edmund Randolph, March 21, 1790, *JWP,* 13:110.

207 *"one of that band":* DHFFC, 12:437.

207 *"the gallant earners"?:* James Madison to Benjamin Rush, March 7, 1790, *DHFFC,* 18:769.

207 *"the idea is much better":* James Madison to James Madison Sr., February 27, 1790, *DHFFC,* 18:654.

207 *"I feel disposed":* Benjamin Rush to James Madison, February 27, 1790, *DHFFC,* 18:655–56.

208 *Representative Peter Muhlenberg:* Peter Muhlenberg to Benjamin Rush, February 22, 1790, *DHFFC,* 18:605.

208 *Madison had by now: Congressional Register,* March 1, 1790, in *DHFFC,* 12:606ff.

208 *"hangs heavy on us":* Fisher Ames to William Tudor, March 3, 1790, *DHFFC,* 18:714.

208 *"by the mean":* Theodore Sedgwick to Pamela Sedgwick, March 4, 1790, *DHFFC,* 18:731–32.

209 *Although he knew:* George Washington to David Stuart, June 15, 1790, *DHFFC,* 19:1832–35.

209 *"vast and dangerous": DHFFC,* 14:598ff; unless otherwise noted, the following debate draws on the *Congressional Register,* February 23, 24, and 26, and March 1, 1790.

210 *Virginians, Madison among them:* James Madison to Edmund Pendleton, March 4, 1790, *DHFFC,* 18:729.

210 *"poor little Delaware":* Richard Bassett to George Read, March 1, 1790, *DHFFC,* 18:695; also *DHFFC,* 14:528.

210 *"blunders, vulgarisms, and Hibernianisms": DHFFC,* 14:837.

211 *Wedded though Gerry:* Billias, *Elbridge Gerry,* 223; and *Congressional Register,* February 23, and March 1 and 2, 1790.

212 *"A constant and":* Theodore Sedgwick to Pamela Sedgwick, March 14, 1790, *DHFFC,* 18:867.

212 *"Parties form":* Louis-Guillaume Otto to Comte de Montmorin, March 1, 1790, *DHFFC,* 18:699.

Chapter 14: The Trumpet of Sedition

Page

213 *The souring atmosphere:* Bowling and Veit, *Diary of William Maclay,* 209; William Smith to Otho H. Williams, March 14, 1790, *DHFFC,*

18:868; Theodore Sedgwick to Pamela Sedgwick, March 14, 1790, *DHFFC*, 18:867; Theodorick Bland to St. George Tucker, March 6, 1790, *DHFFC*, 18:747; and Robert Morris to Mary Morris, March 4, 1790, *DHFFC*, 18:730.

213 *draft report:* Draft Report, February 27, 1790, *DHFFC*, 18:333–36.

214 *When the House again:* Unless otherwise noted, the following debate is based on the *New-York Daily Advertiser*, March 16, 19, 20, 22, and 26, 1790; and the *New-York Daily Gazette*, March 26, 1790.

215 *"among my first wishes":* George Washington to John Frances Mercer, September 9, 1786, *GWP*, Confederation Series, 4:243–44.

215 *"very mal-apropos":* George Washington to David Stuart, March 28, 1790, *GWP*, Presidential Series, 5:287–88.

216 *compounding widespread dissension:* David Stuart to George Washington, June 2, 1790, *GWP*, Presidential Series, 5:459–60.

216 *"as great an":* Nash, *Race and Revolution*, 40.

216 *"Human fears":* John Pemberton to James Pemberton, March 2, 1790, *DHFFC*, 18:711.

216 *"the pet of Delaware":* DHFFC, 14:535–49.

217 *"It was a matter":* Ellis, *Founding Brothers*, 116; and John Pemberton to James Pemberton, February 23, 1790, *DHFFC*, 18:615.

217 *"The funding system":* John Pemberton to James Pemberton, March 16, 1790, *DHFFC*, 19:884.

217 *"like evil spirits":* William Loughton Smith to Edward Rutledge, February 28, 1790, *DHFFC*, 18:673–74; and John Pemberton to James Pemberton, March 2, 1790, *DHFFC*, 18:711.

217 *"as composed and resigned":* John Pemberton to James Pemberton, March 16, 1790, *DHFFC*, 19:884.

218 *By the time:* Report of the Committee of the Whole, March 22, 1790, *DHFFC*, 8:338.

218 *"with a view":* di Giacomantonio, " 'For the Gratification of a Volunteering Society.' "

218 *"effectively buried them":* Ibid.

219 *"Our early and":* William Loughton Smith to Edward Rutledge, February 28, 1790, *DHFFC*, 18:673–74.

219 *"It was a singular":* John Pemberton to James Pemberton, February 23, 1790, *DHFFC*, 18:615.

219 *"The slave business":* George Washington to David Stuart, March 28, 1790, in Ellis, *Founding Brothers*, 118.

219 *Sidi Mehemet Ibrahim: Federal Gazette*, March 23, 1790.

220 *"after as laborious":* Burstein and Isenberg, *Madison and Jefferson*, 212.

221 *"a universal anxiety":* James Madison to Thomas Jefferson, January 24, 1790, *DHFFC*, 18:299.

221 *"To have gone":* Thomas Jefferson to William Short, March 12, 1790, *TJP*, 16:228–29.

221 *Much had to be:* Thomas Jefferson to William Short, April 6, 1790, enclosure, *TJP*, 16:321–22; Jefferson to Short, March 12, 1790, *TJP*, 16:228–29; Jefferson to Thomas Garth, March 7, 1790, *TJP*, 16:209; and Jefferson to Madame de Tessé, March 11, 1790, *TJP*, 16:226–27.

221 *writing her en route:* Thomas Jefferson to Elizabeth Wayles Eppes, March 7, 1790, *TJP*, 16:208.

221 *"not eternally":* *TJP*, 16:225.

221 *He had left Monticello:* Thomas Jefferson to William Fitzhugh, March 11, 1790, *TJP*, 16:223; Burstein and Isenberg, *Madison and Jefferson*, 212; and Gordon-Reed, *Hemingses of Monticello*, 437ff.

222 *"Mr. Jefferson is here":* Abigail Adams to Mary Cranch, April 3, 1790, *DHFFC*, 19:1120.

222 *"I view great cities":* Gordon-Reed, *Hemingses of Monticello*, 445.

222 *At dinner tables: TJP*, 16:237n.

223 *"I like a little rebellion":* Thomas Jefferson to James Madison, January 30, 1787, in Jefferson, *Writings*, 881ff.

223 *Although he professed:* Jefferson, *Notes on the State of Virginia*, in *Writings*, 288–89, 264ff.

223 *congressmen had approvingly cited: New-York Daily Advertiser*, March 16, 20, and 22, 1790.

223 *"loose shackling air":* Bowling and Veit, *Diary of William Maclay*, 275.

224 *He suffered from nightmares:* Ibid., 277, 279.

224 *"Like most other":* Ibid., 147.

224 *"Oh, Man":* Ibid., 252.

224 *"The Very Goddess":* William Maclay to Benjamin Rush, June 18, 1790, *DHFFC*, 19:1805.

224 *"from the fever":* David Stuart to George Washington, June 2, 1790, *DHFFC*, 19:1679ff.

224 *"intemperate and bigotted zeal"*: William Loughton Smith to Tench Coxe, April 14, 1790, *DHFFC*, 19:1227–29.

225 *Madison, the leading enemy:* James Madison to Edmund Randolph, March 21, 1790, *JMP*, 13:110.

225 *"Our Fishery is"*: William Smith (of Boston) to John Adams, April 24, 1790, *DHFFC*, 19:1306.

225 *"disgusted many"*: Andrew Craigie to Daniel Parker, May 5, 1790, *DHFFC*, 19:1433.

225 *"unfounded facts"*: Gazette of the United States, May 29, 1790.

225 *"He becomes more and more"*: John Trumbull to John Adams, June 5, 1790, *DHFFC*, 19:1717.

225 *the debate ground on:* New-York Daily Advertiser, May 27, 1790.

225 *Assumption's supporters countered:* New-York Daily Advertiser, April 13 and 14, 1790; and Lloyd's Notes, April 15, 1790.

226 *"the novelty of it"*: New-York Daily Advertiser, May 5, 1790.

226 *"interests of the Union"*: Ibid., April 13, 1790.

226 *Patrick Henry, hinted:* David Stuart to George Washington, June 2, 1790, *DHFFC*, 19:1679ff.

226 *"I feel as if"*: New-York Daily Advertiser, March 12, 1790.

226 *Maclay, who went:* Bowling and Veit, Diary of William Maclay, 241–42.

Chapter 15: Cabals, Meetings, Plots, and Counterplots

Page

227 *"This question about Residence"*: George Thatcher to Nathaniel Wells, June 13, 1790, *DHFFC*, 19:1810–11.

228 *"the pecuniary business"*: New-York Daily Advertiser, July 8, 1790.

228 *"The business of"*: James Madison to Edmund Pendleton, June 22, 1790, *DHFFC*, 19:1902.

228 *"The Irritation is"*: Thomas Fitzsimons to Tench Coxe, April 13, 1790, *DHFFC*, 19:1218.

228 *"Tories, antifederalists"*: Benjamin Rush to James Madison, February 27, 1790, *DHFFC*, 18:655–56.

229 *"ministerial functions"*: Henry Lee to James Madison, April 3, 1790, *DHFFC*, 19:1113.

229 *"It is the River"*: Metcalf, *Waters of Potomac*, 83–84; generally, Bowling, *Creation of Washington, D.C.*, 117–19.

230 *"the greatest returns"*: George Washington to Marquis de Lafayette, October 10, 1784, *GWP*, Confederation Series, 2:86.

230 *"It is in fact"*: Bowling and Veit, *Diary of William Maclay*, 308.

230 *Southerners recalled that:* William Loughton Smith to Edward Rutledge, April 2, 1790, *DHFFC*, 19:1107–8; and Smith to Rutledge, July 5, 1789, *DHFFC*, 16:959ff; William Smith to Otho H. Williams, April 4, 1790, *DHFFC*, 19:1131; Bowling and Veit, *Diary of William Maclay*, 231; also, generally, *DHFFC*, 19:1151.

231 *The only way:* James Madison to Henry Lee, April 13, 1790, *DHFFC*, 19:1220; also Madison to Lee, October 4, 1789, *DHFFC*, 17:1667–68.

231 *"whose face, manner"*: Fisher Ames to George Richard Minot, May 18, 1789, *DHFFC*, 15:585–86.

231 *"He will absolutely"*: Bowling and Veit, *Diary of William Maclay*, 319.

232 *Morris's once-sterling reputation:* Rappleye, *Robert Morris*, 350–52, 480–81; and McCraw, *Founders and Finance*, 68–69.

232 *"His fortune carried"*: George Thatcher to Sarah Thatcher, October 1, 1788; and Smith, *Letters of Delegates*, 25:399–400.

232 *"poor Miserable Foundling"*: Robert Morris to Mary Morris, also note 1, *DHFFC*, 19:1357.

232 *"incessant disputation"*: George Clymer to Henry Hill, April 8, 1790, *DHFFC*, 19:1173.

232 *"It is truly"*: William Smith to Otho H. Williams, April 4, 1790, *DHFFC*, 19:1131.

232 *"Everything seems conducted"*: John Trumbull to John Adams, June 5, 1790, *DHFFC*, 19:1717.

233 *At this, Maclay:* Bowling and Veit, *Diary of William Maclay*, 254, 272.

233 *"Leave all that"*: Ibid., 272.

233 *"a mere shuttlecock"*: *New-York Daily Advertiser*, June 1, 1790.

233 *"Some are brushing"*: Ibid., June 10, 1790.

233 *"For this whole week"*: William Maclay to Benjamin Rush, June 5, 1790, *DHFFC*, 19:1713.

234 *"I could almost"*: Bowling and Veit, *Diary of William Maclay*, 279.

234 *"The plaguy Influenza"*: Richard Henry Lee to Thomas Lee Shippen, May 14, 1790, *DHFFC*, 19:1503.

234 *Theodorick Bland:* Note, *DHFFC*, 19:1672–74.

234 *"It was nothing but":* Bowling and Veit, *Diary of William Maclay*, 284–85.

234 *"Izard flamed":* Ibid., 286–87.

235 *Maclay, appalled:* Ibid., 264, 271.

235 *"in the greatest consternation":* Louis-Guillaume Otto to Comte de Montmorin, June 1, 1790, *DHFFC*, 19:1665; also, Maier, *Ratification*, 458–59.

235 *"They did not chuse":* William Ellery to Benjamin Harrison, June 12, 1790, *DHFFC*, 19:1787.

235 *Rhode Island's new senators:* William Ellery to Benjamin Harrison, June 12, 1790, *DHFFC*, 19:1787; and Henry Marchant to John Adams, June 12, 1790, *DHFFC*, 19:1791.

235 *As the days dragged: Gazette of the United States,* April 14, and May 5 and 19, 1790.

236 *"It is indeed": Connecticut Journal,* June 9, 1790.

236 *first copyright act: DHFFC,* 4:523–28.

236 *"There seems to be":* Bowling and Veit, *Diary of William Maclay*, 265.

236 *Lurid stories: DHFFC,* 19:1986–88; Bowling and Veit, *Diary of William Maclay*, 298; and Thomas Bird to George Washington, June 5, 1790, *GWP*, Presidential Series, 5:478–81.

237 *"Jealousies & distrusts":* George Washington to David Stuart, June 15, 1790, *DHFFC*, 19:1832–35.

Chapter 16: A Southern Position

Page

238 *"The New Yorkers":* Thomas Hartley to Jasper Yeates, June 9, 1790, *DHFFC*, 19:1765.

238 *"There is such":* Benjamin Goodhue to Stephen Goodhue, June 10, 1790, *DHFFC*, 19:1771.

239 *"Their declaration is":* Fisher Ames to Thomas Dwight, June 11, 1790, *DHFFC*, 19:1781–82.

239 *"Those who are fond": New-York Daily Gazette,* June 26, 1790.

239 *"with all the hurry":* George Thatcher to Nathaniel Wells, June 13, 1790, *DHFFC*, 19:1810ff.

240 *"Machinations may be"*: Richard Bland Lee to Theodorick Lee, June 15, 1790, *DHFFC*, 19:1828.

240 *"The Potowmac stands"*: James Madison to James Monroe, June 17, 1790, *DHFFC*, 19:1850.

240 *"The intrigues"*: Louis-Guillaume Otto to Comte de Montmorin, July 12, 1790, *DHFFC*, 19:2101–3.

241 *"I contained my indignation"*: Bowling and Veit, *Diary of William Maclay*, 291; the following account of negotiations is based primarily on Maclay, 291–94, 297n; and Bowling, *Creation of Washington, D.C.*, 182–83.

242 *"there will be no"*: Thomas Jefferson to James Monroe, June 20, 1790, *DHFFC*, 19:1881–82.

243 *"If the states"*: Thomas Jefferson to Thomas Mann Randolph, June 20, 1790, *DHFFC*, 19:1882.

243 *"Madison at their head"*: Benjamin Goodhue to Stephen Goodhue, June 17, 1790, *DHFFC*, 19:1848.

243 *"It is now established"*: Peter Muhlenberg to Benjamin Rush, June 17, 1790, *DHFFC*, 19:1850–51.

243 *"in the course of"*: Ibid.

243 *A day or two later*: Thomas Jefferson, undated from 1792–94, *DHFFC*, 19:1989–90; and Jefferson, February 4, 1818, *DHFFC*, 19:1991–92.

244 *Although their relationship*: Generally, Ellis, *Founding Brothers*, 69–72; Chernow, *Alexander Hamilton*, 174–75; and Brissot de Warville, *New Travels in the United States*, 91.

244 *James Hemings*: Cullen, *Jefferson's Memorandum Books*, 1:758–65; Stanton, *Free Some Day*, 17–24, 103–6; and *Notes on the State of Virginia*, in Jefferson, *Writings*, 288–89.

245 *"The contempt we"*: Chernow, *Alexander Hamilton*, 210–11, 214–16, 223; also Brookhiser, *Alexander Hamilton*, 14–16; *Minutes of the Manumission Society of New-York*; Hodges, *Root & Branch*, 166–67; and White, *Somewhat More Independent*, 85.

245 *"The discussion"*: Thomas Jefferson, February 4, 1818, *DHFFC*, 19:1991–92.

245 *"this pill would be"*: "Anas," in Jefferson, *Writings*, 668–69; also, 665–68.

246 *"In this way"*: Thomas Jefferson to James Monroe, June 20, 1790, *DHFFC*, 19:1881–82.

246   *Madison did not need:* Author interview with Kenneth Bowling, March 4, 2015; and Bowling, *Creation of Washington, D.C.*, 185–86.

246   *"The Potowmack is":* Benjamin Goodhue to Stephen Goodhue, June 22, 1790, *DHFFC*, 19:1900; also George Thatcher to David Sewall, July 4, 1790, *DHFFC*, 20:2024.

247   *"with a revulsion":* *DHFFC*, 19:1991–92; and Bowling, *Creation of Washington, D.C.*, 185–87.

248   *"jockeying and bargaining":* Bowling and Veit, *Diary of William Maclay*, 301–2.

248   *"a Species of Robbery!":* Ibid., 302–3.

248   *"Cunning and intrigueing":* Robert Morris to Mary Morris, July 2, 1790, *DHFFC*, 20:2005; also, Bowling and Veit, *Diary of William Maclay*, 307–8; and *DHFFC*, 19:1965–67.

248   *"sobbed, Wiped":* Bowling and Veit, *Diary of William Maclay*, 309.

248   *"The project of Phila":* *DHFFC*, 19:1986–88; Rufus King, "Notes," June 30, 1790, *DHFFC*, 19:1971–72; and Bowling and Veit, *Diary of William Maclay*, 306.

249   *"the fortunate spot":* James Monroe to James Madison, July 26, 1790, *DHFFC*, 20:2256.

249   *"Where in the name":* *New-York Daily Advertiser*, July 10, 1790.

249   *Still others, tongue in cheek:* Bowling, *Creation of Washington, D.C.*, 202.

249   *"a very bad neighborhood":* *Gazette of the United States*, July 14, 1790; and *New-York Daily Gazette*, July 8, 1790.

250   *"the horrid and bloody":* *New-York Daily Advertiser*, July 8, 1790.

250   *"as much as to say":* Richard Henry Lee to Thomas Lee Shippen, July 6, 1790, *DHFFC*, 20:2040.

250   *"We have it now":* *New-York Daily Advertiser*, July 8, 1790; and *New-York Daily Gazette*, July 10, 1790.

250   *Just hours after:* Bowling and Veit, *Diary of William Maclay*, 323; Theodore Sedgwick to Pamela Sedgwick, July 13, 1790, *DHFFC*, 20:2129; and James Madison to James Madison Sr., July 31, 1790, *DHFFC*, 20:2304.

251   *One knotty financial problem:* "Funding Act," *DHFFC*, 5:719; *New-York Daily Gazette*, July 30 and 31, 1790; William Loughton Smith to Edward Rutledge, July 30, 1790, *DHFFC*, 20:2288ff; and McCraw, *Founders and Finance*, 109.

251   *"Half a loaf":* Bowling and Veit, *Diary of William Maclay*, 327.

252 *"Warn people from":* William Loughton Smith to Edward Rutledge, July 17, 1790, *DHFFC*, 20:2157; also *Gazette of the United States*, September 4, 1790.

252 *The volatile James Jackson: New-York Daily Advertiser*, July 26, 1790.

252 *"an infant state": New-York Daily Advertiser*, July 29, 1790.

252 *"The Constitution had survived":* Bowling, *Creation of Washington, D.C.,* 206.

252 *"an unavoidable evil":* James Madison to James Monroe, July 25, 1790, *DHFFC*, 20:2248; also Thomas Jefferson to Thomas Mann Randolph, July 25, 1790, *DHFFC*, 20:2247.

252 *"And forever thereafter":* Michael Jenifer Stone to Walter Stone, July 1, 1790, *DHFFC*, 20:1997–98.

253 *"more in danger":* Bowling, *Creation of Washington, D.C.,* 197–98.

253 *"so generative of dissension":* Ibid.

253 *"The Spanish cruelties":* Benjamin Rush to Thomas Fitzsimons, August 5, 1790, *DHFFC*, 20:2344.

253 *"The ingratitude of ":* DeWitt Clinton to Charles Carter, July 20, 1790, *DHFFC*, 20:2194–95.

254 "Have we not": "The Removal," *New-York Daily Gazette*, August 10, 1790.

254 *"of rustic boors":* "A Citizen to the Citizens of New York," *New-York Journal*, July 20 and 27, 1790.

254 *Morris was blamed:* Robert Morris to Mary Morris, July 2, 1790, *DHFFC*, 20:2005; and Theodore Sedgwick to Pamela Sedgwick, July 4, 1790, *DHFFC*, 20:2019–22.

254 *"The Holy Name":* DeWitt Clinton to Charles Clinton, July 20, 1790, *DHFFC*, 20:2194–95.

254 *"Alas! That the":* Bowling and Veit, *Diary of William Maclay*, 321.

255 *"I cannot however":* Ibid., 331–32.

Chapter 17: Indians

Page

256 *New Yorkers were agape:* Stokes, *Iconography of Manhattan Island*, 1270; and Caughey, *McGillivray*, 43.

257 *Throughout the lawless:* James Seagrove to Pierce Butler, August 8, 1790, *DHFFC*, 20:2367.

257   *"She is almost"*: "Letter from a new Settler," *New-York Daily Advertiser*, April 15, 1790.

257   *"the distant members"*: *New-York Daily Advertiser*, May 25, 1790, *DHFFC*, 19:1393.

257   *"The emigration from"*: George Nichols to James Madison, May 8, 1789, *JMP*, 12:138–41.

257   *so alarming as "to threaten"*: Anthony Wayne to James Wilson, July 4, 1789, *DHFFC*, 16:940; *DHFFC*, 11:1197–98; and Foster, *James Jackson*, 41–42.

258   *the Georgians might seek:* Bowling and Veit, *Diary of William Maclay*, 243–45.

258   *"In spite of scalping"*: John Lewis to George Washington, April 1789, *GWP*, Presidential Series, 2:178–79.

258   *"Empire has been"*: *DHFFC*, 11:1096.

258   *Among the investors:* Sakolski, *Great American Land Bubble*, 124–31.

258   *"Land Jobbers, who"*: Ibid., 131.

258   *To the Creeks:* Caughey, *McGillivray*, 3ff, 23, 28–29; DePauw, *Senate Executive Journal*, 2:238; Alexander McGillivray to Carlos Howard, August 11, 1790, in Caughey, *McGillivray*, 273; McGillivray to William Pickman, May 8, 1790, in Caughey, *McGillivray*, 259–62; McGillivray to Esteban Miro, June 2, 1790, in Caughey, *McGillivray*, 265–66; George Beckwith, report, April 1790, *DHFFC*, 19:1387; and William Loughton Smith to Edward Rutledge, August 8, 1790, *DHFFC*, 20:2368ff.

259   *"open, generous mind"*: Caughey, *McGillivray*, 41.

260   *"It is better"*: Alexander McGillivray to Esteban Miro, June 2, 1790, in Caughey, *McGillivray*, 267.

260   *"Everything urges us"*: Alexander McGillivray to William Pickman, May 8, 1790, in Caughey, *McGillivray*, 259–62.

260   *Knox and Washington seized:* Prucha, *American Indian Treaties*, 59; and Prucha, *Great Father*, 17–23.

260   *"To dispossess them"*: Prucha, *Great Father*, 22.

261   *The Creeks' journey:* Prucha, *American Indian Treaties*, 75ff.

261   *Soldiers entertained:* Stokes, *Iconography of Manhattan Island*, 1271.

261   *"they were for a time"*: Prucha, *American Indian Treaties*, 77–81.

262   *"In its consequences"*: George Washington to the US Senate, August 7, 1790, *GWP*, Presidential Series, 6:213–14.

262 *The next day:* William Loughton Smith to Edward Rutledge, August 13, 1790, *DHFFC*, 20:2408.

262 *"Suddenly rude and":* Judith Sargent Murray to Judith Sargent, August 14, 1790, *DHFFC*, 20:2412–14.

262 *Under the terms:* Louis-Guillaume Otto to Comte de Montmorin, August 14, 1790, *DHFFC*, 20:2416–18; Secret Articles, DePauw, *Senate Executive Journal*, 2:243–49; Prucha, *American Indian Treaties*, 82–83; and Caughey, *McGillivray*, 44–46.

263 *"The trade of":* Prucha, *American Indian Treaties*, 82.

263 *"energetic and animated"* and following: Judith Sargent Murray to Judith Sargent, August 14, 1790, *DHFFC*, 20:2412–14.

264 *"Partook of":* Caughey, *McGillivray*, 278.

264 *"This event will":* George Washington to Marquis de Lafayette, August 11, 1790, *GWP*, Presidential Series, 6:234.

264 *"invited a savage":* Caughey, *McGillivray*, 45.

264 *"Will Congress permit":* Foster, *James Jackson*, 47.

265 *"If I had not":* Alexander McGillivray to Carlos Howard, August 11, 1790, in Caughey, *McGillivray*, 273–75.

Chapter 18: Interlude II

Page

266 *"perplexed and delayed":* George Washington to Marquis de Lafayette, August 11, 1790, *GWP*, Presidential Series, 6:233.

266 *His present trip: GWP*, Presidential Series, 6:279–87, 6:300–302.

267 *"Ungrateful men":* "Picture of New-York," August 1790, *DHFFC*, 20:2502–3.

267 *The offices of:* Henry Remsen Jr. to Thomas Jefferson, October 14, 1790, *TJP*, 17:595.

268 *the "delicious spot":* Abigail Adams to Thomas Brand Hollis, September 6, 1790, *DHFFC*, 20:2484; also, Abigail Adams to John Quincy Adams, July 8, 1790, *DHFFC*, 20:2051.

268 *"I feel low":* Abigail Adams to Mary Cranch, October 3, 1790, *DHFFC*, 20:2532.

268 *John Adams, who:* Abigail Adams to Mary Cranch, July 4, 1790, *DHFFC*, 20:2015; Abigail Adams to Mary Cranch, July 27, 1790, *DHFFC*, 20:2260;

and Louis-Guillaume Otto to Comte de Montmorin, June 13, 1790, *DHFFC*, 20:1805–6.

268 *"I have seen"*: John Adams to John Trumbull, April 2, 1790, *DHFFC*, 20:1101–2.

268 *"I wish very"*: John Adams to Benjamin Rush, April 18, 1790, *DHFFC*, 19:1260.

268 *"She is as"*: Pierce Butler to the Reverend Weedon Butler, September 1, 1790, *DHFFC*, 20:2476.

268 *To pass the time:* Thomas Lee Shippen to William Shippen, September 15, 1790, *DHFFC*, 20:2497–99.

269 *At Georgetown:* Ibid.; also, Arnebeck, *Through a Fiery Trial*, 25–26.

270 *Congress had given:* Thomas Jefferson to Charles Carroll, September 17, 1790, in Padover, *Thomas Jefferson*, 29–30.

270 *"The essential point"*: James Madison, "Memorandum on the Residence Act," ca. August 29, 1790, *JMP*, 13:294–95.

270 *"If the present"*: *TJP*, 17:454–56; "Proposals by Georgetown Landowners," October 13, 1790, *TJP*, 17:469ff; and "Report," September 14, 1790, *TJP*, 17:461–63.

271 *After a month:* George Washington to George Augustine Washington, August 20, 1790, *GWP*, Presidential Series, 6:311.

271 *Declaring that:* "Agreement of Georgetown Property Owners," October 13, 1790, *GWP*, Presidential Series, 6:554–56; and *TJP*, 17:454–56.

271 *Washington started upriver:* *GWP*, Presidential Series, 6:557n, also, 6:571; also, Louis-Guillaume Otto to Comte de Montmorin, November 15, 1790, *DHFFC*, 21:70–71.

271 *Washington was rumored:* *TJP*, 17:454–56.

271 *"dug out of"*: Bowling, *Creation of Washington, D.C.*, 201.

271 *"it is already"*: "Letter from Philadelphia," November 12, 1790, *DHFFC*, 21:67.

272 *"I must stand"*: Bowling and Veit, *Diary of William Maclay*, 345.

272 *"It was painful"*: Ibid., 350.

272 *"treat the Negroes"*: "Instructions for the Montpelier Overseer and Laborers," ca. November 8, 1790, *JMP*, 13:302–3.

272 *"the plantation negroes"*: Thomas Jefferson to Nicholas Lewis, November 7, 1790, *TJP*, 18:29.

272 *Bring the washerwomen:* George Washington to Theodorick Lee, Septem-

ber 9, 1790, *GWP*, Presidential Series, 6:408–10; and Lee to Washington, September 12, 1790, 419–22.

273 *"less commodious"*: George Washington to Theodorick Lee, September 5 and November 14, 1790, *GWP*, Presidential Series, 6:397–99, 6:653.

273 *More than minutiae: GWP*, Presidential Series, 6:362–64n; and Henry Knox to George Washington, October 25, 1790, *GWP*, Presidential Series, 6:582–83, and 6:584.

273 *"Forebodings with respect"*: George Washington to Henry Knox, November 19, 1790, *GWP*, Presidential Series, 6:668.

Chapter 19: Freedom's Fav'rite Seat

Page

274 *"Philadelphia may be"*: Brissot de Warville, *New Travels in the United States*, ixff, 240ff, 253–58, 260–62; Griswold, *Republican Court*, 238, 256–63; Nash, *First City*, 135–38; Kenneth R. Bowling, "The Federal Government and the Republican Court Move to Philadelphia, November 1790–March 1791," in Bowling and Kennon, *Neither Separate nor Equal*, 5–6, 19–21, 25; Anna Coxe Toogood, "Philadelphia as the Nation's Capital," in Bowling and Kennon, *Neither Separate nor Equal*, 34ff; di Giacomantonio, "'For the Gratification of a Volunteering Society'"; Newman, *Transformation of American Abolitionism*, 34–35; and *Pennsylvania Gazette*, July 7, 1790.

275 *"They believe themselves"*: Theodore Sedgwick to Pamela Sedgwick, January 9, 1791, *DHFFC*, 21:385–387.

275 *"to use such means"*: *Pennsylvania Gazette*, May 23, 1787.

275 *"But death were"*: Ibid., July 13, 1791.

275 *Thanks to Quaker*: Nash, *Race and Revolution*, 33–35; Moulton, *Journal and Major Essays of John Woolman*, 3–13, 137, 143, 233–35; and Winch, *Gentleman of Color*, 128–30.

276 *"The idea of"*: George Washington to Tobias Lear, April 12, 1791, *GWP*, Presidential Series, 8:84–86; also Bowling, *Creation of Washington, D.C.*, 211–12.

276 *The "Gloomy Severity"*: Bowling and Veit, *Diary of William Maclay*, 331–32.

276 *"In Philadelphia, the"*: *New-York Daily Advertiser*, October 28, 1790.

276 "New York!": "Peter Pindar," November 20, 1790, *DHFFC*, 21:85–86.

277 *"bucks, bloods, and"*: Bowling, "Federal Government and the Republican

Court," in Bowling and Kennon, *Neither Separate nor Equal*, 20; also Abigail Adams to Abigail Adams Smith, January 8, 1791, *DHFFC*, 21:363–64.

277 *"such a parsel":* Frances Seney to Hannah Nicholson, January 12, 1791, *DHFFC*, 21:409.

277 *possessed "strong Lungs":* George Thatcher to Nathaniel Barrell, January 30, 1791, *DHFFC*, 21:613–615.

277 *Their travails:* George Washington to Theodorick Lee, November 23, 1790, *GWP*, Presidential Series, 6:689; William Loughton Smith to Gabriel Manigault, December 19, 1790, *DHFFC*, 21:194; and James Jackson to John Milledge, December 1, 1790, *DHFFC*, 21:121–22.

278 *"So much for":* Aedanus Burke to "A Gentleman," November 27, 1790, *DHFFC*, 21:108–10.

278 "Welcome, ye former": "Stanzas on the Arrival of Congress," December 6, 1790, *DHFFC*, 21:134–35.

278 *"Barbers and hair-dressers":* Unidentified newspaper, November 1, 1790, *DHFFC*, 21:43; and William Loughton Smith to Edward Rutledge, November 24, 1790, *DHFFC*, 21:97–99.

278 *Knox's wife, Lucy:* Bowling, "Federal Government and the Republican Court," in Bowling and Kennon, *Neither Separate nor Equal*, 16.

278 *"If New York":* Abigail Adams to Abigail Adams Smith, November 21, 1790, *DHFFC*, 21:88–89.

279 *"the horses sinking":* Abigail Adams to Mary Cranch, January 9, 1791, *DHFFC*, 21:378–79.

279 *"The Schuylkill is":* Abigail Adams to Abigail Adams Smith, November 21, 1790, *DHFFC*, 21:88–89; and Abigail Adams to Mary Cranch, December 12, 1790, *DHFFC*, 21:160–61.

279 *"Such a vile tribe":* Abigail Adams to Mary Cranch, January 9, 1791, *DHFFC*, 21:378–79.

279 *Tristram Dalton of:* Fisher Ames to Thomas Dwight, December 12, 1790, *DHFFC*, 21:161–62; *A black child seized:* Winch, "Philadelphia and the Other Underground Railroad"; Wilson, *Freedom at Risk*, 10–11, 86; and Brissot de Warville, *New Travels in the United States*, 228.

280 *"Your Letters are":* Theodore Sedgwick to Pamela Sedgwick, January 16, 1791, *DHFFC*, 21:447–48.

280 *"I cannot foretell":* William Loughton Smith to Gabriel Manigault, December 19, 1790, *DHFFC*, 21:194.

281 *"There is hardly space"*: "Letter from New York to Mr. Dunlap," *Dunlap's American Daily Advertiser*, March 3, 1791; and Richard A. Baker, "The United States Senate in Philadelphia," in Bowling and Kennon, *House and Senate in the 1790s*, 293–96.

281 *"All the puff"*: "Letter from New York to Mr. Dunlap," *Dunlap's American Daily Advertiser*, February 20, 1790.

281 *"His frame Would"*: Bowling and Veit, *Diary of William Maclay*, 365–66.

281 *"The abundant fruits"*: "Address of the President to Congress," December 8, 1790, *JMP*, 13:311–14.

281 *deemed his enunciation:* Bowling and Veit, *Diary of William Maclay*, December 8, 1790, 340.

281 *"Certain* banditti*"*: "Address of the President to Congress," December 8, 1790, *JMP*, 13:311–14.

Chapter 20: A Most Mischievous Engine

Page

284 *French minister Otto:* Louis-Guillaume Otto to Comte de Montmorin, December 24, 1790, *DHFFC*, 21:218–19.

284 *"almost martial precision"*: Chernow, *Alexander Hamilton*, 338–39.

285 *"public authority and"*: Hamilton, *Report of the Secretary of the Treasury* (pamphlet); generally, also McCraw, *Founders and Finance*, 113–15; and Chernow, *Alexander Hamilton*, 346ff.

285 *"it is manifest"*: Alexander Hamilton to George Washington, March 27, 1791, *AHP*, 8:218.

287 *"To place any dependence"*: Chernow, *Alexander Hamilton*, 81.

288 *"with rich and poor"*: *General Advertiser*, December 24, 1790.

288 *"ought ever to bear"*: *Pennsylvania Packet*, December 18, 1790.

288 *"contract vicious habits"*: Ibid., December 25, 1790.

288 *James Jackson, who:* Ibid., December 24, 1790.

288 *"that his constituents"*: Christman, *First Federal Congress*, 204–5.

288 *"their old teazing tricks"*: Jonathan Trumbull to William Williams, December 18, 1790, *DHFFC*, 21:191–92.

288 *"Divine command"*: Samuel Allinson to Elias Boudinot, December 20, 1790, *DHFFC*, 21:198–99.

289   *"to impress their minds":* James Pemberton to Moses Brown, January 19, 1791, *DHFFC*, 21:472–73.

289   *Jackson regarded the Quakers:* The following debate is based on the *General Advertiser*, December 23 and 24, 1790; and *Pennsylvania Packet*, December 20, 24, 28, and 30, 1790.

290   *"drain the Southern States":* Pierce Butler to George Hooper, January 23, 1791, *DHFFC*, 21:501–502.

290   *a "Most Mischievous engine":* Bowling and Veit, *Diary of William Maclay*, 364.

290   *"promoting the profits":* Ibid., 362–63.

291   *When the bill reached:* The following debate is based on the *Gazette of the United States*, February 19 and 23, 1791.

292   *He feared:* Rakove, *James Madison*, 112–14.

293   *The pressure on Washington:* James Madison, "Detached Memorandum," after 1817, included in February 1791 of *DHFFC*, 21:810–12; *DHFFC*, 21:766–69 note, "Bank Bill Veto Controversy."

294   *"a blade of grass":* John Rutledge Jr. to William Short, March 30, 1791, *DHFFC*, 21:1049–50.

294   *Randolph asserted:* "Edmund Randolph's Opinion," February 12, 1791, *DHFFC*, 21:769–77.

294   *"a sort of mongrel":* Edmund Randolph to James Madison, February 27, 1791, *DHFFC*, 21:960.

294   *Jefferson's reply:* "Thomas Jefferson's Opinion," February 15, 1791, *DHFFC*, 21:777–81.

295   *"After duly examining":* George Washington, "A Proclamation," January 24, 1791, *GWP*, Presidential Series, 7:278–80.

295   *Coincidentally or not:* Bowling, *Creation of Washington, D.C.*, 209; Arnebeck, *Through a Fiery Trial*, 33; *DHFFC*, 6:1795.

295   *At the president's behest:* George Washington to Thomas Jefferson, January 2 and 4, and February 1, 1791; Thomas Jefferson to Daniel Carroll, January 24, 1791; Jefferson to Andrew Ellicott, February 2, 1791; and Andrew Ellicott to Thomas Jefferson, February 14, 1791, in Padover, *Thomas Jefferson and the National Capital*, 36–42.

296   *"I have lived":* William Smith to Otho H. Williams, February 3, 1791, *DHFFC*, 21:675–76.

296   *None of this difficulty: Gazette of the United States*, February 23, 1791; *Fed-*

eral Gazette, February 24, 1791; and Theodore Sedgwick to Pamela Sedgwick, February 23, 1791, *DHFFC*, 21:922–23.

297 *At forty pages:* "Alexander Hamilton's Opinion," February 23, 1791, *DHFFC*, 21:tk; and Chernow, *Alexander Hamilton*, 353.

298 *"No axiom is":* "Federalist No. 44," in Hamilton, Madison, and Jay, *Federalist Papers*, 323–24.

298 *"made Jefferson look":* McCraw, *Founders and Finance*, 116–18.

299 *"There was general":* John Rutledge Jr. to William Short, March 30, 1791, *DHFFC*, 21:1049–50.

299 *"The meanest motives":* James Madison to Thomas Jefferson, May 1, 1791, *DHFFC*, 22.

299 *"The time was":* Leibiger, *Founding Friendship*, 137.

299 *John Adams acerbically:* Bowling, *Creation of Washington, D.C.*, 213.

299 *"His grandiose plans":* Chernow, *Alexander Hamilton*, 332.

300 *"For any person":* Thomas Jefferson to James Madison, October 1, 1792, *AHP*, 12:85.

Epilogue: American Dawn

Page

301 *"To speak in":* Bowling and Veit, *Diary of William Maclay*, 398.

301 *"We used to canvass":* Ibid.

302 *"the Members scampered":* Paine Wingate to Josiah Bartlett, February 21, 1791, *DHFFC*, 21:898–99.

302 *"sacrificed more largely":* Theodore Sedgwick to Pamela Sedgwick, January 27, 1791, *DHFFC*, 21:561–62.

302 *"As I left":* Bowling and Veit, *Diary of William Maclay*, 400–401.

303 *"On a basis":* Christman, *First Federal Congress*, 211.

304 *"I think it must":* George Thatcher to Nathaniel Barrell, January 30, 1791, *DHFFC*, 21:613–15.

304 *"The Southern States":* Richard Bland Lee to Charles Lee, April 5, 1790, *DHFFC*, 19:1148.

305 *"rough and rude":* Bowling and Veit, *Diary of William Maclay*, 141; and Fisher Ames to George Richards Minot, July 8, 1789, *DHFFC*, 16:978.

305 *"Whoever considers the nature":* "Address to the Public Creditors," *AHP*, 7:1–5.

306 *"I have launched":* *New-York Daily Advertiser*, March 12, 1790.

306 *"Altho' the Form"*: Patrick Henry to James Monroe, January
DHFFC, 21:518–19.

306 *"In no nation"*: John Trumbull to John Adams, March 20, 1791
Family Manuscript Trust, Massachusetts Historical Society.

306 *"The National Government has"*: John Adams to William Stephens
March 14, 1791, *DHFFC*, 21:1028.

306 *"I am happy"*: John Adams to William Tudor, March 15, 1791, *DH*
21:1034–35.

306 *"The Constitution's success"*: Maier, *Ratification*, 467–68.

307 *"Politics are the meat"*: George Thatcher to Thomas B. Wait, December
1790, *DHFFC*, 21:194–97.

Afterword

Page

309 *"our old republican friend"*: *DHFFC*, 14:506.

309 *James Jackson's later:* Foster, *James Jackson*, 105ff.

310 *"American Demosthenes"*: *DHFFC*, 14:614–18.

312 *"I find the office"*: John Adams to John Trumbull, January 23, 1791,
DHFFC, 21:500–501.

313 *"These rebel colonists"*: Hyde de Neuville, *Memoirs of Baron Hyde de Neuville*, 1:237.

Selected Bibliography

———•—•———

Books

Abbott, W. W., Dorothy Twohig, et al., eds. *The Papers of George Washington*. Charlottesville: University of Virginia Press, 1987–.

Adams, John Quincy, and Charles Francis Adams. *The Life of John Adams*. 2 vols. New York: Haskell House, 1968.

Allen, W. B., ed. *Works of Fisher Ames*. 2 vols. Indianapolis: Liberty Classics, 1983.

Allen, W. B., and Gordon Lloyd, eds. *The Essential Antifederalist*. Lanham, MD: University Press of America, 1985.

Amar, Akhil Reed. *The Bill of Rights*. New Haven, CT: Yale University Press, 1998.

Arnebeck, Bob. *Through a Fiery Trial: Building Washington, 1790–1800*. Lanham, MD: Madison Books, 1991.

Bear, James A., and Lucia L. Stanton, eds. *Jefferson's Memorandum Books*. 2 vols. Princeton, NJ: Princeton University Press, 1997.

Beeman, Richard. *Plain, Honest Men: The Making of the American Constitution*. New York: Random House, 2010.

Berkeley, Edmund, and Dorothy Smith Berkeley. *John Beckley: Zealous Partisan in a Divided Nation*. Philadelphia: American Philosophical Society, 1973.

Bernhard, Winfred E. A. *Fisher Ames: Federalist and Statesman, 1758–1808*. Chapel Hill: University of North Carolina Press, 1965.

Bickford, Charlene Bangs, and Kenneth R. Bowling. *Birth of the Nation: The First Federal Congress, 1789–1791*. Lanham, MD: Madison House, 1989.

Billias, George Athan. *Elbridge Gerry: Founding Father and Republican States-man.* New York: McGraw-Hill, 1976.

Bowling, Kenneth R. *The Creation of Washington, D.C.: The Idea and Location of the American Capital.* Fairfax, VA: George Mason University Press, 1991.

———. *Creating the Federal City, 1774–1800: Potomac Fever.* Washington, DC: American Institute of Architects Press, 1988.

Bowling, Kenneth R., and Donald R. Kennon, eds. *The House and Senate in the 1790s: Petitioning, Lobbying, and Institutional Development.* Athens: Ohio University Press, 2002.

———, eds. *Neither Separate nor Equal: Congress in the 1790s.* Athens: Ohio University Press, 2000.

Bowling, Kenneth R., and Helen E. Veit, eds. *The Diary of William Maclay.* Baltimore: Johns Hopkins University Press, 1988.

Boyd, Julian P. *Number 7: Alexander Hamilton's Secret Attempts to Control American Foreign Policy.* Princeton, NJ: Princeton University Press, 1964.

———, ed. *The Papers of Thomas Jefferson.* Princeton, NJ: Princeton University Press, 1958, 1961.

Brissot de Warville, J. P. *New Travels in the United States of America, 1788.* Cambridge, MA: Harvard University Press, 1964.

Brookhiser, Richard. *James Madison.* New York: Basic Books, 2011.

———. *Alexander Hamilton, American.* New York: Touchstone, 1999.

Burnett, Edmund Cody. *The Continental Congress.* New York: Norton, 1964.

———. *Letters of Members of the Continental Congress.* Vol. 8. Washington, DC: Carnegie Institution, 1936.

Burstein, Andrew, and Nancy Isenberg. *Madison and Jefferson.* New York: Random House, 2010.

Casto, William R. *Oliver Ellsworth and the Creation of the Federal Republic.* New York: Second Circuit Committee on History and Commemorative Events, 1997.

Caughey, John Walton. *McGillivray of the Creeks.* Norman: University of Oklahoma Press, 1938.

Cheney, Lynne. *James Madison: A Life Reconsidered.* New York: Viking, 2014.

Chernow, Barbara Ann. *Robert Morris: Land Speculator, 1790–1801.* New York: Arno Press, 1978.

Chernow, Ron. *Alexander Hamilton.* New York: Penguin, 2004.

Christman, Margaret C. S. *The First Federal Congress, 1789–1791.* Washington, DC: Smithsonian Institution Press, 1989.

Collier, Christopher. *Roger Sherman's Connecticut: Yankee Politics and the American Revolution.* Middletown, CT: Wesleyan University Press, 1971.

Daniels, Marcus. *Scandal & Civility: Journalism and the Birth of American Democracy.* New York: Oxford, 2009.

Decatur, Stephen, Jr. *Private Affairs of George Washington from the Records and Accounts of Tobias Lear, Esquire, His Secretary.* Boston: Houghton Mifflin, 1933.

DePauw, Linda Grant, ed. *Senate Executive Journal and Related Documents.* Vol. 2. Baltimore: Johns Hopkins University Press, 1974.

Dumbauld, Edward. *The Bill of Rights.* Norman: University of Oklahoma Press, 1957.

Elkins, Stanley, and Eric McKitrick. *The Age of Federalism: The Early American Republic, 1788–1800.* New York: Oxford University Press, 1993.

Ellis, Joseph J. *His Excellency George Washington.* New York: Knopf, 2004.

———. *Founding Brothers: The Revolutionary Generation.* New York: Vintage, 2002.

———. *Passionate Sage: The Character and Legacy of John Adams.* New York: Norton, 2001.

Farrand, Max, ed. *The Records of the Federal Convention of 1787.* New Haven, CT: Yale University Press, 1937.

Ferguson, E. J. *The Power of the Purse: A History of American Public Finance, 1776–1790.* Chapel Hill: University of North Carolina Press, 1961.

Ferling, John E. *The First of Men: A Life of George Washington.* Knoxville: University of Tennessee Press, 1988.

Finkelman, Paul. *Slavery and the Founders: Race and Liberty in the Age of Jefferson.* New York: M. E. Sharpe, 2001.

Flexner, James Thomas. *George Washington: Anguish and Farewell, 1793–1799.* Boston: Little, Brown, 1969.

———. *George Washington and the New Nation, 1783–1793.* Boston: Little, Brown, 1969.

Foster, William Omer, Sr. *James Jackson: Duelist and Militant Statesman, 1757–1806.* Athens: University of Georgia Press, 1960.

Friedman, Leon, and Fred L. Israel. *The Justices of the United States Supreme Court, 1789–1969: Their Lives and Major Opinions.* Vol. 1. New York: Chelsea House, 1969.

Goldstone, Lawrence. *Dark Bargain: Slavery, Profits, and the Struggle for the Constitution.* New York: Walker, 2005.

Gordon-Reed, Annette. *The Hemingses of Monticello: An American Family.* New York: Norton, 2008.

Greene, Jack P., and J. R. Pole. *The Blackwell Encyclopedia of the American Revolution.* Cambridge: Blackwell, 1991.

Griswold, Rufus Wilmot. *The Republican Court; or, American Society in the Days of Washington.* New York: Haskell House, 1971.

Gutheim, Frederick. *The Potomac.* New York: Holt, Rinehart and Winston, 1949.

Hamilton, Alexander, James Madison, and John Jay. *The Federalist Papers.* New York: Pocket Books, 2004.

———. *Writings.* New York: Library of America, 2001.

Hodges, Graham Russell. *Root & Branch: African Americans in New York & East Jersey, 1613–1863.* Chapel Hill: University of North Carolina Press, 1999.

Horton, James Oliver, and Lois Horton. *In Hope of Liberty: Culture, Community, and Protest among Northern Free Blacks, 1700–1860.* New York: Oxford University Press, 1997.

Hutchinson, William T., William M. E. Rachal, et al., eds., *The Papers of James Madison.* Chicago: University of Chicago Press, 1962–.

Hyde de Neuville, Jean-Guillaume. *Memoirs of Baron Hyde de Neuville: Outlaw, Exile, Ambassador.* 2 vols. London: Sands & Co., n.d.

Isaacson, Walter. *Benjamin Franklin: An American Life.* New York: Simon & Schuster, 2003.

Jackson, Donald, and Dorothy Twohig. *The Diaries of George Washington.* Charlottesville: University of Virginia Press, 1979.

Janvier, Thomas. *In Old New York.* New York: Harper & Brothers, 1894.

Jefferson, Thomas. *Writings.* New York: Library of America, 1984.

Kaminski, John P., and Timothy D. Moore. *An Assembly of Demigods: Word Portraits of the Delegates to the Constitutional Convention by Their Contemporaries.* Madison, WI: Parallel Press, 2012.

Kennon, Donald, ed., *A Republic for the Ages: The United States Capitol and the Political Culture of the Early Republic.* Charlottesville: University of Virginia Press, 1999.

Kolchin, Peter. *American Slavery, 1619–1877.* New York: Hill & Wang, 1993.

Kurlansky, Mark. *Cod: A Biography of the Fish That Changed the World.* New York: Vintage, 1999.

Labunski, Richard. *James Madison and the Struggle for the Bill of Rights.* New York: Oxford, 2006.

Lamplugh, George R. *Politics on the Periphery: Factions and Parties in Georgia, 1783–1806.* Newark: University of Delaware Press, 1986.

Larkin, Jack. *The Reshaping of Everyday Life, 1790–1840.* New York: Harper & Row, 1989.

Leibiger, Stuart. *Founding Friendship: George Washington, James Madison, and the Creation of the American Republic.* Charlottesville: University of Virginia Press, 1999.

Lettieri, Ronald John. *Connecticut's Young Man of the Revolution: Oliver Ellsworth.* Hartford: American Revolution Bicentennial Committee of Connecticut, 1978.

Lowance, Mason, ed. *Against Slavery: An Abolitionist Reader.* New York: Penguin, 2000.

Maier, Pauline. *Ratification: The People Debate the Constitution, 1787–1788.* New York: Simon & Schuster, 2010.

Main, Jackson Turner. *The Anti-federalists: Critics of the Constitution, 1781–1788.* New York: Norton, 1974.

Marcus, Maeva, ed. *The Documentary History of the Supreme Court of the United States.* Vol. 4. New York: Columbia University Press, 1992.

Martin, Joseph Plumb. *A Narrative of a Revolutionary Soldier.* New York: Signet Classic, 2001.

McCoy, Drew R. *The Last of the Fathers: James Madison and the Republican Legacy.* New York: Cambridge University Press, 1989.

McCraw, Thomas K. *The Founders and Finance: How Hamilton, Gallatin, and Other Immigrants Forged a New Economy.* Cambridge, MA: Belknap Press, 2012.

McCullough, David. *John Adams.* New York: Simon & Schuster, 2001.

Metcalf, Paul. *Waters of Potowmack.* Charlottesville: University of Virginia Press, 2002.

Monaghan, Frank, and Marvin Lowenthal. *This Was New York: The Nation's Capital in 1789.* Garden City, NY: Doubleday, Doran, 1943.

Moulton, Phillips P., ed. *The Journal and Major Essays of John Woolman.* Richmond, IN: Friends United Press, 1971.

Nash, Gary B. *The Forgotten Fifth: African Americans in the Age of Revolution*. Cambridge, MA: Harvard University Press, 2006.

———. *First City: Philadelphia and the Forging of Historical Memory*. Philadelphia: University of Pennsylvania Press, 2002.

———. *Race and Revolution*. Lanham, MD: Rowman & Littlefield: 1990.

Newman, Richard S. *The Transformation of American Abolitionism: Fighting Slavery in the Early Republic*. Chapel Hill: University of North Carolina Press, 2002.

Padover, Saul K., ed. *Thomas Jefferson and the National Capital*. Washington, DC: US Government Printing Office, 1946.

Prucha, Francis Paul. *American Indian Treaties: The History of a Political Anomaly*. Berkeley: University of California Press, 1994.

———. *The Great Father: The United States Government and the American Indians*. Lincoln: University of Nebraska Press, 1984.

Rakove, Jack N. *James Madison and the Creation of the American Republic*. New York: Longman, 2002.

Rappleye, Charles. *Robert Morris: Financier of the American Revolution*. New York: Simon & Schuster, 2010.

Sakolski, A. M. *The Great American Land Bubble: The Amazing Story of Land-Grabbing, Speculations, and Booms from Colonial Days to the Present Times*. New York: Harper & Brothers, 1932.

Schecter, Barnet. *The Battle for New York: The City at the Heart of the American Revolution*. New York: Penguin, 2002.

Schwartz, Bernard. *A History of the Supreme Court*. New York: Oxford University Press, 1993.

Sedgwick, John. *In My Blood: Six Generations of Madness and Desire in an American Family*. New York: HarperCollins, 2007.

Smith, James Morton. *The Republic of Letters: The Correspondence between Thomas Jefferson and James Madison, 1776–1826*. Vol. 1. New York: Norton, 1995.

Smith, Paul H., ed. *Letters of Delegates to Congress*. Vol. 25. Washington, DC: Library of Congress, 1998.

Smith, Thomas E. V. *The City of New York in the Year of Washington's Inauguration, 1789*. Riverside, CT: Chatham Press, 1972.

Stahr, Walter. *John Jay: Founding Fathers*. New York: Hambledon & London, 2005.

Stanton, Lucia. *Free Some Day: The African-American Families of Monticello.* Monticello, VA: Thomas Jefferson Foundation, 2000.

———. *Slavery at Monticello.* Monticello, VA: Thomas Jefferson Foundation, 1996.

Stewart, David O. *Madison's Gift: Five Partnerships That Built America.* New York: Simon & Schuster, 2015.

Stokes, I. N. Phelps. *The Iconography of Manhattan Island, 1498–1909.* Vol. 5. New York: Arno Press, 1967.

Syrett, Harold C., ed. *The Papers of Alexander Hamilton.* New York: Columbia University Press, 1961–87.

Thompson, C. Bradley. *John Adams and the Spirit of Liberty.* Lawrence: University Press of Kansas, 1998.

Thompson, Mary V. *"In the Hands of a Good Providence": Religion in the Life of George Washington.* Charlottesville: University of Virginia Press, 2008.

Veit, Helen E., Kenneth R. Bowling, and Charlene Bangs Bickford. *Creating the Bill of Rights: The Documentary Record from the First Federal Congress.* Baltimore: Johns Hopkins University Press, 1991.

White, Leonard D. *The Federalists: A Study in Administrative History.* New York: Free Press, 1965.

White, Shane. *Somewhat More Independent: The End of Slavery in New York City, 1770–1810.* Athens: University of Georgia Press, 1991.

Wiencek, Henry. *Master of the Mountain: Thomas Jefferson and His Slaves.* New York: Farrar, Straus & Giroux, 2012.

Wills, Gary. *James Madison.* New York: Times Books, 2002.

Wilson, Carol. *Freedom at Risk: The Kidnapping of Free Blacks in America, 1780–1865.* Lexington: University Press of Kentucky, 1994.

Winch, Julie. *A Gentleman of Color: The Life of James Forten.* New York: Oxford University Press, 2002.

Wood, Gordon S. *The Idea of America: Reflections on the Birth of the United States.* New York: Penguin, 2011.

———. *Empire of Liberty: A History of the Early Republic, 1789–1815.* New York: Oxford University Press, 2009.

———. *The Radicalism of the American Revolution.* New York: Knopf, 1992.

Wright, Robert E., and David J. Cowen. *Financial Founding Fathers: The Men Who Made America Rich.* Chicago: University of Chicago Press, 2006.

Zilversmit, Arthur. *The First Emancipation: The Abolition of Slavery in the North.* Chicago: University of Chicago Press, 1970.

Articles, Pamphlets, and Other Sources

Bartoloni de Tuazon, Mary Kathleen. "Mr. President: Washington, the Presidency, & the Indispensable Title Controversy of 1789." PhD thesis, George Washington University, 2010.

Bowling, Kenneth R. "'A Tub to the Whale': The Founding Fathers and the Adoption of the Federal Bill of Rights." *Journal of the Early Republic* 8, no. 3 (Fall 1988).

———. "Good-by 'Charle': The Lee-Adams Interest and the Political Demise of Charles Thompson, Secretary of Congress, 1774–1789." *Pennsylvania Magazine of History and Biography* 100, no. 3 (July 1976).

di Giacomantonio, William C. "'For the Gratification of a Volunteering Society': Antislavery and Pressure Group Politics in the First Federal Congress." *Journal of the Early Republic* 15 (Summer 1995).

Finkelman, Paul. "James Madison and the Bill of Rights: A Reluctant Paternity." *Supreme Court Review* 301 (1990).

Franklin, Benjamin. *Observations Concerning the Increase of Mankind, Peopling of Countries, &c.* Pamphlet. S. Kneeland, 1755.

Frost, J. William. "Quaker Antislavery: From Dissidence to Sense of the Meeting." Unpublished paper. Friends Historical Library, Swarthmore College. http://www.swarthmore.edu/Library/friends/Frost.

Hamilton, Alexander. *Report of the Secretary of the Treasury on the Subject of a National Bank.* Pamphlet. New York: S. Whiting & Co., 1811.

Lamplugh, George R. "'Oh the Colossus! The Colossus!': James Jackson and the Jeffersonian Republican Party in Georgia, 1796–1806." *Journal of the Early Republic* 9 (Autumn 1989).

Langdon, John. *Remarks on the Report of the Secretary of the Treasury to the House of Representatives.* Pamphlet. May 1790.

"Memorial of the Pennsylvania Society for Promoting the Abolition of Slavery to the Senate and Representatives of the United States." February 3, 1790. PAS Collection, Historical Society of Pennsylvania. http://www.digitallibrary .hsp.org.

Minutes of the Manumission Society of New-York. Vol. 6. New-York Historical Society.

Stiles, Ezra. "The United States Elevated to Glory and Honor." Sermon. 1783. University of Nebraska-Lincoln Digital Commons. http://digitalcommons .unl.edu/etas.

Winch, Julie. "Philadelphia and the Other Underground Railroad." *Pennsylvania Magazine of History and Biography* 111, no. 1 (January 1987).

Newspapers

Congressional Register
Connecticut Journal
Dunlap's American Daily Advertiser
Federal Gazette
Gazette of the United States
General Advertiser
Lloyd's Notes
New-York Daily Advertiser
New-York Daily Gazette
New-York Journal
Pennsylvania Gazette
Pennsylvania Packet

Index

———•———

abolitionists, 75, 152, 198, 215, 219, 275
Adams, Abigail, 65, 138, 178–79, 222, 267–68, 277, 278–79, 312
Adams, John, 3–4, 33–35, 64–67, 297
  background of, 33–34
  capital site selection and, 152, 156, 248, 299
  on congressional colleagues, 9, 64–65, 118, 157
  Continental Congress and, 33
  criticism and dislike of, 48, 49, 66, 68, 70, 156, 162
  debates over Washington's title as president and, 47, 67, 68, 69–70
  election as vice president, 32–33, 64
  first congressional session and, 161–62
  on First Congress's success, 306
  foreign policy and, 172
  Franklin and, 34, 205
  on his role as vice president, 47–48, 50, 67, 268, 311–12
  Hamilton and election of, 173
  Independence Day celebrations and, 103
  Indian policy and, 262
  later political career of, 312
  letters to, 12, 13, 306
  Maclay on, 48, 50, 51, 68, 70, 104, 105, 134, 156, 205
  on Morris, 153
  Moustier on, 65, 66
  move from New York by, 267–68
  move to Philadelphia by, 268, 277, 278–79
  on the new government, 65–66
  New York City life and, 178–79, 268
  oratorical skill of, 47–48
  personality of, 33, 80, 161–62
  popularity of, 34–35, 47, 268
  presidency of, 311, 312
  presidential power viewed by, 60, 105

Quakers and, 205
on Rhode Island's refusal to ratify Constitution, 194
slavery debate and, 205
tie-breaking votes cast by, 105, 156, 161–62, 233
vice presidency of, 13, 32–33, 34–35, 47, 48, 71, 161–62, 268
Washington's inauguration and, 50, 51
as Washington's possible successor, 61, 66, 100
Washington's relationship with, 71, 131
Adams, John Quincy, 312
Adams, Margaret, 269
Adams, Samuel, 36, 165
African Americans. *See also* slaves
  free blacks and, 23, 149, 196, 214–15, 273–74
  in Philadelphia, 273–74
Alabama, 4, 133, 258
Alexandria, Virginia, as capital site, 30, 145
Allinson, Samuel, 289
amendment proposals. *See also* Bill of Rights; bill of rights proposal
  ad hoc committee to study, 117, 119
  as bill of rights, 117, 119–20
  conference committee on, 137–38
  cruel and unusual punishments ban (Eighth Amendment) and, 120, 122–23
  House approval of, 136
  House debate on, 115–28
  later aura attached to, 140–41
  Madison's proposals and, 88–91, 92, 93, 107, 119, 120, 121, 123, 126, 138–39
  Madison's proposed preamble to the Constitution and, 89, 92, 121, 139
  minimalist language of, 139–40
  mood after final passage of, 138–40
  national bank bill debate and, 292
  passage of, 117, 138–39, 158–59

amendment proposals (*cont.*)
  placement of, either before or after text of the
    Constitution, 121–22
  proposed right of instruction by citizens on
    voting by congressmen and, 127–28
  religious freedom (First Amendment) and,
    119, 120–21, 136, 137–38
  Senate debate and changes to, 136–37
  state ratification conventions on wording of,
    121, 122, 125, 127, 128
  state ratification of, after congressional
    passage, 140–41
  states' rights and, 86–87, 90, 92, 121, 125–26
  Washington's request to Congress to act on,
    116
  Washington's support for, 87, 115–16, 119
  week-long congressional debate on details of,
    116
Ames, Fisher
  amendment debates and, 90, 124
  background of, 36
  capital site debate and, 146, 149, 157, 253
  on congressional colleagues, 10, 28, 36–37,
    64, 93, 148, 149, 157, 231, 310–11
  debate over presidential powers and, 98
  federal assumption of state debts and, 239
  foreign policy and, 173–74
  as House member, xiv, 22, 36, 72, 148, 157,
    163, 302
  later political career of, 310
  on Madison, 37, 208
  on national unity, 5
  oratorical skill of, 73–74, 310
  public credit proposals and, 187, 190
  on Rhode Island's refusal to ratify
    Constitution, 166–67
  slavery debate and, 216
  trade and taxation bills and, 40, 41–42,
    73–74, 95
  travel between congressional sessions by, 163
  Washington's inauguration and, 54
Anacostia River, and capital site proposals, 147,
  177, 248–49, 270, 295
Antifederalists, 159, 306
  amendment debates and, 84, 85, 87, 88, 90,
    91, 98, 116, 117, 120, 123–24, 125, 126,
    127, 128, 136, 138, 139, 158–59, 178, 180,
    183
  beliefs of, 11
  capital site debate and, 228
  federal assumption of the states' debts and,
    209
  Hamilton's public credit proposal and, 185
  judicial bill and, 142–43
  later political parties and, 305
  Rhode Island and, 235
  states' rights and, 90, 107
  Washington and, 17

apprentices, 288
archives, federal, 176, 194–95
Armstrong, John Jr., 20
army
  Indian skirmishes and, 259, 273, 282, 304
  Knox's proposal on, 195–96
  need to raise standing, 14, 86, 123–24, 171,
    180, 195
  president as commander in chief of, 97
  required service in, 287–88
  Washington's call for creation of, 180
Articles of Confederation, 6, 86, 90, 105–06,
  126, 129, 142, 227, 233
Ashe, John Baptista, xv
assembly, freedom of, 90, 119, 123, 127
assumption debate. *See* federal assumption of
  state debts
Attorney General of the United States
  creation of office of, 95, 107
  Randolph as first, 108, 160, 294, 297

Baldwin, Abraham, xiv, 201
Baltimore, as capital site, 30, 145, 146, 228, 235,
  240, 248, 250
Bank of New York, 168, 173, 187
Barbary pirates, 38, 193, 220, 222, 282
Bard, Samuel, 23, 100
Bassett, Richard, xiii
Battle of Long Island (1776), 17, 22, 45, 167
Beckley, John, 183, 190–91
Beckwith, George, 174
Benson, Egbert, xv
Billias, George A., 58
Bill of Rights
  later aura attached to, 140–41
  passage of, 13, 136–37
bill of rights proposal. *See also* amendments
  amendment debate on, 85, 86, 89, 117, 119–20
  Jefferson's support for, 87, 89
  Madison and, 86, 87, 117, 312
  use of term, 86, 117, 140
Bird, Thomas, 237
black Americans. *See also* slaves
  free blacks and, 23, 149, 196, 214–15, 273–74
  in Philadelphia, 273–74
Blair, John, 195, 266
Bland, Theodorick, xv, 5, 28, 61, 213, 234
Bloodworth, Timothy, xv
Boudinot, Elias, 187
  background of, 10–11
  capital site debate and, 153
  on congressional colleagues, 56
  copyright act introduced by, 236
  debt bill and, 226
  as House member, xv, 56, 226
  Indians and, 56
  moral conscience exemption for military
    service and, 289

personality of, 56
slavery debate and, 56, 216
Treasury Department proposal of, 56–57
Bourn, Benjamin, xv
Bowling, Kenneth R., 35, 246
Bradford, William Jr., 187
Brissot de Warville, Jacques Pierre, 273
Bronx, New York, as capital site, 30, 145
Brookhiser, Richard, 18
Brown, John, xv
Bryan, Samuel, 139
Burke, Aedanus
  amendment debate and, 125
  capital site debate and, 249
  Hamilton and, 230–31
  as House member, xv
  immigration policy and, 197
  militia plan and, 288
  revenue bills and, 93
  slavery debate and, 206, 210–11, 215
  states' rights and, 305
  travel to Philadelphia by, 277–78
Burr, Aaron, 23, 105, 302
Butler, Pierce, xiv
  amendment debate and, 115, 116
  capital site debate and, 258
  federal power and, 158
  import duties and, 94
  Indian policy and, 262, 264, 268
  judicial system bill and, 111
  national bank and, 290
  slavery debate and, 205, 234

Cadwalader, Lambert, xv
capitalism
  agrarian values versus, 300
  Hamilton's study of, 172
capital site
  central location and conditions desired for, 146
  Constitutional mandate for, 144, 227–28
  as symbol for new nation, 144–45, 228, 249
capital site debate, 193, 219, 227–34, 238–43, 246–51. See also Potomac River Valley as capital site
  activity between congressional sessions on, 177–78
  bargaining, alliances, and vote trading in, 148–49, 233, 234, 239–40, 248, 250
  critics of final decision in, 253–55
  federal assumption of state debts plan and, 243, 250
  final vote on bill on, 13, 140, 252–53, 270
  Hamilton's involvement in, 230–31, 234, 240, 241–44, 245–47, 248–49
  House and, 148–53, 156–57
  investors and speculators and, 231, 251–52, 271

Jefferson's meetings on, 14, 243–46, 296
Jefferson's memorandum and map on, 270–71
Maclay's work on bills for, 254–55
Madison's funding proposal and final vote on, 250–51
Madison's preferences in, 21, 149, 150–51, 156–57, 229, 231, 240, 250, 270
Marylanders and, 30, 178, 231, 239
meaning of "seat of government" and, 150
Morris's proposed compromise and, 232–33
national bank proposal and, 290, 292, 293, 299
New Englanders and, 148, 149, 152, 232–33, 238–39, 255
New Jersey members and, 30, 149, 232–33, 247
New York City as temporary seat of government, 149, 152, 153, 238, 242, 248
New Yorkers and, 30, 148, 149, 154, 228, 238, 247, 248, 250, 253–54
Pennsylvanians and, 30, 145, 146–47, 148–49, 152–57, 224–25, 228, 231, 233–34, 238, 239–40, 241, 243, 248, 270–71
Philadelphia as temporary seat of government, 149, 233, 234–35, 239–40, 242, 243, 245–46, 247, 248, 249, 251, 254–55, 267, 274, 296
Philadelphians and, 30, 270, 271–72
plan for implementing, 270–72
population center as factor in, 146, 148, 150
range of sites proposed in, 30, 44, 136, 145–48, 177–78, 228–29, 240, 249
reactions to passage of bill on, 253–55
Rhode Island members and, 235
secession threat and, 151, 219
sectional fissures in Congress over, 157–58, 228–29, 232–33
Senate and, 153–56
sense of relief at resolution of, 252–53
separate questions about permanent and temporary sites in, 227
slavery concerns related to, 149, 151–52, 178
southerners' suspicion of northerners and, 218–19
Susquehanna bill and, 152–57
Washington's preferences for, 18, 44, 153, 229, 230, 231, 237, 254, 270, 271–72, 273, 299
capital site development
  commissioners to oversee, 249, 270, 295–96
  national bank proposal and, 293, 296
  Residence Act (1790) on, 269–70, 296
  Washington's interests and, 147, 153, 229–30, 296, 299
Carroll, Charles, xiii, 50, 104, 230, 247, 248–49
Carroll, Daniel, xiv, 93, 120, 247, 269, 295–96
census, 4, 13, 176, 196, 198
Chernow, Ron, 168, 169, 284–85, 299

Cherokee Indians, 4, 257, 264
circuit courts, 107–09, 159
citizenship, naturalization bill on requirements
  for, 196–97, 198
Civil War, 219, 300
Clark, George Rogers, 258
Clarkson, Thomas, 198
Clinton, DeWitt, 253, 254
Clinton, George, 33, 45, 173, 253, 266
Clymer, George, xv, 5, 84, 226, 232
Coasting Act (1789), 102–03
Coles, Isaac, xv
Collection Act (1789), 103
collectors, for customs, 39, 103, 126, 135, 159,
  168
Columbia, Pennsylvania, as capital site, 145,
  148, 150, 151
committee of the whole, 32
Confederation Congress, 11
  Adams in, 33
  Indian policy under, 261
  last days of, 2, 21
  Madison and, 18
  members of, 22, 58
  national debt and, 170
  official end of, 26
  president of, 35
  protection of settlers by, 8
  public opinion of ordinary Americans and, 307
  seat of government under, 144
  state representation in, 6
Congress (in general)
  Constitution's "necessary and proper" clause
    on powers of, 121, 291–92, 294
  legislative power shared between Senate and
    House in, 71
  powers allotted to, 294
  sectional divide in, 293, 300
  as superior branch of government, 295
Congress, First
  achievements of, 303–04
  earliest surviving record of oral testimony
    before a committee of, 203–04
  first-session accomplishments of, 158–61, 180
  first State of the Union speech in, 180–81
  first use of tie-breaking vote cast by vice
    president in, 105
  Independence Day celebrations and, 103–04
  members of, xiii–xv
  New York City's summer heat affecting
    meetings of, 84, 130–31, 134, 252
  political fissures in, 157–58
  public opinion of ordinary Americans and,
    307
  second session, 160
  spectators viewing debates by, 239
  success of Constitution and, 307
  third session of, 280–81, 301–02

  tie-breaking votes cast by vice president in,
    105, 156, 161–62, 233
  visitors' gallery use and, 150, 217, 250, 307
  Washington's concerns about wrangling in,
    237
Congress, Second, 280, 303
  bills deferred to, 301
  member reelection to, 272, 302, 309, 309, 310
Congress Hall, Philadelphia, 281, 313
congressional districts, debate over size of, 6,
  124, 128, 136, 200
congressmen
  access to Washington by, 81
  daily life in New York City of, 77, 79, 112–14,
    194–95, 213, 312, 313
  end of third session and, 302–303
  first death of, while serving, 234
  as lame-duck members in third session, 272
  lasting impact of decisions made by, 305–06
  leisure activities of, 112–13
  Maclay on, 157, 224
  move from New York City by, 268
  newspapers read by, 113
  proposed right of instruction by citizens on
    how to vote by, 127–28
  reading habits of, 112–13
  rivalries and conflicts among, 160–61
  salary per diem of, 232
  sense of satisfaction and relief at end of First
    Congress, 303
  term limits proposed for, 86, 116, 117–18,
    125
  travel between congressional sessions by, 163
  travel to New York City by, 28–29, 179
  travel to Philadelphia by, 277–78
Congress of the Confederation. See
  Confederation Congress
Connecticut, 4
  amendments ratified by, 140
  federal assumption of state debts and, 210
  members of First Congress from, xiii, xiv
  tobacco grown in, 93
Conococheague Creek, as capital site, 249, 270,
  271
Constitution
  Adams on, 66
  "advice and consent" duty of Senate under,
    59–60, 132–35
  amendments proposed for. See amendment
    proposals; Bill of Rights; bill of rights
    proposal
  capital site mandated in, 144, 227–28
  executive department appointees under,
    104–05
  federal assumption of state debts under, 226
  First Congress and success of, 307
  funding bill as major crisis for, 252
  Gerry's opposition to, 57–58

Hamilton as interpreter of, 292, 298–99
Indian policy under, 260
Madison as interpreter of, 59, 97–98, 292, 294, 299, 307
Madison's grasp of, 10
Madison's proposed preamble to, 89, 92, 121, 139
national bank debate and, 290, 291, 298–99
"necessary and proper" clause of, 121, 291, 294, 298
North Carolina's ratification of, 86, 87, 178, 180
opposition to, 32, 85–86
passage of first amendments to, 13, 136, 140–41, 312
presidential power over executive departments under, 59–63
president's role defined in, 46–47, 53
revenue authority of Congress under, 27–28
Rhode Island's ratification of, 86, 166–67, 180, 183, 194, 235
slavery under, 200, 214
states' conditions for ratification of, 53, 86–87, 121, 127–28, 146
states' rights under, 125–26
Vermont's ratification of, 282
vice president's role defined in, 47, 48
Constitutional Convention, 1, 20, 107
antislavery debate in, 200
bill of rights debate at, 85–86
Franklin at, 200
Gerry at, 22, 57, 85
Great Compromise on representation in, 10, 118
Hamilton at, 172
Madison and, 18
population size and representation in, 6
public support for second, 138
Washington at, 18–19
Contee, Benjamin, xiv
Continental Army, 232, 295
Continental Congress, 8, 10, 11, 17, 20, 33, 58, 107, 118, 154, 186
copyright system, 13, 63, 176, 222, 236
court system
    federal. See justice system
    state, 109–10, 111–12
Coxe, Tench, 241
creditors. See payment to creditors with government securities
Creek Indians
    attacks on settlers by, 257–58
    land speculators and, 258–59, 264
    McGillivray's leadership of, 259–60
    settlers' seizure of land of, 259, 260, 262, 263
    treaty with, 133–35, 261–65, 304
    visit to New York City by, 256, 261–65
    Washington and, 260–61

cruel and unusual punishments, ban on (Eighth Amendment), 120, 122–23
Cushing, William, 195
Custis, George Washington Parke, 295, 299

Dalton, Tristram, xiii, 279, 302
Daubing, Mary, 50
debt
    federal. See national debt
    state. See federal assumption of state debts (assumption plan)
Decker, Joseph, 113
Declaration of Independence, 10, 34, 89, 118
Declaration of Rights and Grievances, 34
Delaware, 4
    capital site debate and, 247
    federal assumption of state debts and, 210
    members of First Congress from, xiii, xiv, 28
Delaware Indians, 64
Democratic Party, 304
Democratic-Republican Party, 305, 309
Department of Foreign Affairs, 29, 58–59, 64, 95, 96, 104–05. See also Department of State
Department of State, 13, 64, 105, 168, 176–77. See also Department of Foreign Affairs
Department of War, 13, 15, 58, 68, 95, 168, 284
Dickinson, Philemon, xiii
di Giacomantonio, William C., 218
discrimination plan. See payment to creditors with government securities
Duane, James, 100
Duer, William, 31, 188
duties
    Collection Act on, 103
    congressional bills on, 13, 38, 39, 41, 93, 95, 301
    government income from, 108
    Madison's desire to enact, 38, 39, 94, 102
    national bank proposal and, 291
    objections to, 40, 74, 94, 101, 288
    portion of as reserves, 186

education, Washington's remarks on, 181
elections, federal
    of Adams as vice president, 33, 64, 173
    congressional power to oversee, 31, 86
    for First Congress, 20, 21, 28
    presidential (1800), and political parties, 305
    proposed amendment on power over, 125, 126–27
    of Washington as president, 33, 35, 173
elections, state, and reelection of congressmen, 193, 272, 302
Ellicott, Andrew, 295
Ellis, Joseph J., 33, 34, 206
Ellsworth, Abigail, 24

Ellsworth, Oliver
    amendment debate and, 136
    background of, 107
    import duties and, 108
    judicial branch creation and, 10, 107, 109–10,
        111–12, 310
    later political career of, 310
    letters to daughter from, 78
    on New York City, 24
    presidential power over executive departments
        and, 60, 104–05
    as Senate member, xiii, 136
    slavery debate and, 201
    on vice president's duties, 48
Elmer, Jonathan, xiii
executive departments
    "advice and consent" duty of Senate on
        appointees to, 59–60
    creation of, 13, 58–59, 64, 95, 104, 160
    debate on presidential power over, 59–63, 64,
        96–98, 104–05, 132–33
    Home Department proposal and, 63, 64, 176
    move from New York City by, 267
    president's appointments approved for, 160

federal assumption of state debts (assumption
        plan), 209–12, 225–26, 238
    capital site debate and, 243, 250
    critics of resolution of, 253
    Hamilton's funding plan delayed by, 227
    Hamilton's proposal on, 185, 209, 211, 225
    House debate over, 209–12, 225–26,
        246–47
    House initial defeat of, 226
    Madison's suggested compromise on,
        211–12, 225, 245, 247, 296
    passage of, 246–47, 250–51
    public opinion on, 214
    revenue bill to pay for, 272
    secession threat and, 226
    Senate and, 239, 246–47
    states' rights and, 226
    windfalls for states in, 250–51
federal court system. See justice system
Federal Farmer (author), 11
Federal Hall, New York City
    First Congress's use of, 2, 25–26, 30, 77–78,
        253
    later razing of, 313
    Maclay on design of, 25
    New York City's summer heat affecting
        meetings in, 84, 130–31, 134, 252
    opposition to using as capital site, 145
    painted image of, in theatrical production,
        114
    second congressional session opening at,
        179–81
Federalist Papers, The, 19, 59, 173, 297–98

Federalists, 20, 21, 28
    amendment debates and, 88, 92, 117–18, 120,
        122, 124, 128, 136, 138, 139, 158–59
    beliefs of, 11, 12
    capital site debate and, 178, 295
    federal assumption of the states' debts and,
        209
    federal power and, 293
    foreign policy and, 172–73
    judicial bill and, 142
    later political parties and, 305
    Madison and, 208
    public credit proposals and, 187–88, 192–93
    Rhode Island and, 167, 266
    seats held by, 11
    Washington and, 17
Ferling, John E., 171
Few, William, xiii, 235
filibuster, 201, 302
Finkelman, Paul, 116
First Amendment (religious freedom), 119,
    120–21, 136, 137–38
Fishbourne, Benjamin, 132–33
Fitzsimons, Thomas
    on apprentices in militias, 288
    capital site debate and, 231
    federal assumption of state debts (assumption
        plan) and, 226, 228
    on Hamilton's report on public credit, 193
    as House member, xv
    import duties and, 41, 93, 101
    Quaker petitions to end slavery and, 198
Floyd, William, xv
Foreign Affairs Department, 29, 58–59, 64, 95,
    96, 104, 105. See also State Department
Foster, Abiel, xiv, 203, 218
Foster, Theodore, xiv, 225
Franklin, Benjamin
    Adams and, 34, 205
    antislavery petition from, 199–200
    Washington's visit to, 222
free assembly, right to, 90, 119, 123, 127
free blacks, 23, 149, 196, 214–15, 273–74
Freeman's Journal, 12
French Revolution, 58, 85, 171, 223
fugitive slaves, 276, 279–80
funding bill
    assumption debate as distraction from, 227,
        239
    compromise and vote trading in, 242–43,
        248, 250–51, 252
    Madison as strategist for, 191, 225, 230–31,
        252
    opposition to, 188, 225–26, 230, 233–34,
        251
    passage of, 251–52
    slavery debate as distraction from, 206, 216,
        217, 224

Gale, George, xiv, 247
Georgetown, Maryland, as capital site, 145, 146,
    147, 177, 230, 242, 247, 249, 269, 271, 295
Georgia, 4
    amendment debate and, 92
    amendments ratified by, 140
    Creek Indian treaty and, 262, 264, 304
    Creek land ownership in, 258, 262, 264, 304
    federal assumption of state debts and, 217, 252
    Indian attacks in, 8, 92, 126, 257–58, 261
    Indian treaties with, 134
    Indian tribes in, 4
    later political career of, 311
    members of First Congress from, xiii, xiv
    slave ownership in, 76, 77, 201, 203, 214
    slavery debate and, 77, 201, 214, 217–18
    Yazoo Company land speculators in, 258–59,
        265, 310
Germantown, Pennsylvania, as capital site, 149,
    154–57, 232, 242
Gerry, Elbridge, 12
    amendment debate and, 91, 121, 122, 124,
        126, 127, 128, 130, 138
    background of, 58
    beliefs of, 10, 305
    capital site debate and, 233, 249
    Constitutional Convention and, 22, 57
    Constitution opposed by, 57–58
    federal assumption of state debts and, 252
    as House member, xiv, 302
    judicial bill and, 142–43
    on national debt, 8, 211–12, 226
    on the new government, 57
    personality of, 58
    presidential power over executive departments
        and, 60–61
    revenue bills and, 101
    slavery debate and, 202
    travel between congressional sessions by, 163,
        277, 278
    Treasury Department proposal and, 57
gerrymandering, 311
Giles, William Branch, xv
Gilman, Nicholas, xiv
Goodhue, Benjamin, xiv, 31, 93, 183–84, 239,
    243, 246
Gordon-Reed, Annette, 175
government securities. See payment to creditors
    with government securities
Graham, Catherine Macaulay, 36, 161
Grayson, William, xiv, 88, 105, 136, 157–58,
    194
Great Compromise, Constitutional Convention,
    10, 118
Greene, Nathanael, 103–04, 132–33, 230
Griffin, Samuel, xv
Grout, Jonathan, xiv
Gunn, James, xiii, 132–33

Hamilton, Alexander
    Adams and, 33
    background of, 160, 169, 171–72
    banks and, 172–73
    Burke's insult and threatened duel with,
        230–31
    Burr's duel with, 302
    capital site debate and, 230, 252
    as Constitution's interpreter, 292, 298–99
    critics and enemies of, 103–04, 173, 186,
        187–90
    federal assumption of state debts and proposal
        of, 185, 209, 211, 225
    federal economic policy developed by, 13–14,
        168–69, 299–300
    financial knowledge of, 172–73, 253, 299–300
    financial plan of, 168–73, 245, 303
    foreign policy and, 172–73
    influence of, 33, 103, 299–300
    Jefferson and, 244, 245, 284
    on lasting impact of congressional decisions,
        305–06
    military experience of, 172
    national bank proposal of, 272, 283, 284–86,
        290, 297–98
    national security and, 170–71
    New York City and, 23
    payment to creditors with old government
        securities (discrimination plan) proposal of,
        185–86, 191, 207, 208
    personality of, 112
    political power of, 173–74
    public credit report to Congress by, 181,
        183–90
    revenue and tax proposals of, 171
    slavery views of, 104, 172, 215–16, 230,
        245
    speech on Greene and militias in
        Revolutionary War, 103–04, 230
    Treasury Department move to Philadelphia
        and, 284–85
    as treasury secretary, 13, 59, 96, 160, 168,
        173–74, 284
    Washington's desire for advice from, 81, 297
    work between congressional sessions by,
        168–69
Hamilton, Elizabeth Schuyler, 103, 297
Hancock, John, 33, 34, 166
Hancock, Maryland, as capital site, 145, 151
Harmar, Josiah, 257, 273, 282, 287
Hartley, Thomas, xv, 93, 193, 238
Hathorn, John, xv
Hawkins, Benjamin, xiii
Hemings, Betty, 272
Hemings, James, 174, 221, 244
Hemings, Robert, 221, 222
Hemings, Sally, 174, 244
Henry, John, xiii

Henry, Patrick, 17, 88, 139, 157–58, 226, 258, 306
Hiester, Daniel, xv
Home Department proposal, 63, 64, 176
House of Representatives. *See also* Congress
  committees of, 31–32, 77, 95
  legislative power shared with Senate, 71
  members of first, xiv–xv
  Speaker of, 10, 31
Howard, Carlos, 265
Huger, Daniel, xv
Humphreys, David, 16, 44, 46, 52, 55, 82, 179
Huntington, Benjamin, xiv, 120–21
Hyde de Neuville, Jean-Guillaume, Baron, 313

immigration
  ambivalence about, 196
  naturalization bill and citizenship requirements and, 180, 196–97, 198
  population changes and, 4, 276
  Washington's remarks on, 180
Independence Day celebrations, New York City, 103–04
Indian policy, 256–65
  Constitution on, 260
  Creek Indians and, 133–35, 261–65, 304
  Knox as secretary of war and, 14, 133, 256, 257, 260, 265, 273
  militia bill and, 301
  treaties and, 133–35, 235, 261–65, 282, 304
  Washington and, 258, 260–61, 264, 273, 282
Indians. *See also specific tribes*
  census proposal and, 196
  Harmar's militia against, 257, 273, 282, 287
  land speculators and, 258–59, 261
  settlers' need for protection from, 178, 257–58, 282
  settlers' seizure of land of, 259, 260
  Thomson's attitudes toward, 63–64
  Washington's remarks on, 180
  Wayne's defeat of, 304
Iredell, James, 158
Izard, Ralph, xiv
  on Adams, 70
  American commerce and, 38
  capital site debate and, 234
  on new government, 3
  slavery debate and, 205
  wealth of, 11

Jackson, Andrew, 304
Jackson, James, 133
  amendment proposals and, 91, 122, 124
  federal assumption of state debts and, 252
  Hamilton's public credit proposal and, 188–89, 191
  as House member, xiv, 277, 288, 302
  immigration proposals and, 197

  Indian policy and, 258, 264
  later political career of, 309–10
  military background of, 11, 96, 258, 288
  militia bill debate and, 288, 290
  national bank bill and, 291
  personality of, 188
  population of congressional district of, 6, 124
  presidential power over executive departments and, 60, 96, 97
  Quakers' pacifism and, 288–89, 290
  revenue bills and, 126
  as Senate member, 310
  slavery debate and, 76–77, 202, 203, 206, 207, 214, 216, 217, 220
  trade bills and, 41
  Washington's title as president and, 96–97
Jackson, William, 164, 179
Jay, John
  Confederation Congress and, 29, 58, 68
  Federalist policies of, 19, 113, 173
  foreign affairs and, 58, 59, 68, 96, 173, 174
  slavery and, 245
  Supreme Court and, 14, 96, 159, 160, 179, 195, 237, 310
  as vice presidential candidate, 32
  Washington and, 131, 179
Jefferson, Polly, 174, 221, 278
Jefferson, Thomas, 2, 17
  advice on Constitution from, 294, 298
  amendment debate and, 87, 139
  bill of rights support from, 87, 89
  capital site debate and, 14, 243–46, 253, 254, 295, 296
  capital site memorandum and map of, 270–71
  Congress and states' rights and, 294–95
  court system and, 106
  Democratic-Republican Party under, 305
  as diplomat in Paris, 58–59, 68, 96, 160, 174–75, 221
  family of, 174, 221, 278
  foreign policy duties of, 174, 223
  Hamilton and, 244, 245, 284
  health of, 234
  Jay and, 174–75
  later political career of, 311, 312
  Maclay on, 223
  Madison's friendship with, 17, 71, 73, 87, 96, 102, 163, 176–77, 220–21, 222, 223, 268–69, 300
  move from New York City by, 268–69
  move to New York City by, 221–22
  move to Philadelphia by, 272
  national bank bill and, 294, 296, 298, 300
  Potomac River Valley and, 147, 269
  as secretary of state, 14, 58, 96, 160, 174–75, 176–77, 220–21, 222–23, 257
  slavery debate and, 198, 206, 223, 244
  slaves owned by, 174, 175, 223, 230, 244–45

states' rights and, 300
  Washington and, 220, 221, 266, 294, 298
Jews, Washington on, 267
Johnson, William Samuel, xiii
Johnston, Samuel, xiii, 111, 235
joint conference committees, 95
judicial branch. *See* justice system
jury duty, 106, 301
jury trials, right to, 90, 111, 138
justice system, 105–12
  Articles of Confederation on, 105–06
  creation of, 106–12
  dislike for lawyers and, 106
  Ellsworth's role in, 107, 109–10, 111–12
  federal crimes in, 159–60
  first-session congressional accomplishments
    in, 159–60
  House judiciary bill on, 141–43
  judicial districts in, 107–08, 159
  jury duty and, 106
  state courts and, 109–10, 111–12
  state legislatures and, 106–07

Kent, James, 14
Kentucky, 4
  British agents in, 21
  Indian attacks in, 257, 258
  as new state, 140, 282
King, Rufus, xiii, 173, 248
Knox, Henry
  duties and, 38
  Indian policy and, 14, 133, 256, 257, 260, 265
  militia proposal of, 195–96
  as secretary of war, 14, 29, 38, 58, 68, 133,
    160, 195, 256
  Washington and, 35, 44, 55, 68, 179, 260,
    265, 273
Knox, Lucy, 79, 278

Lafayette, Gilbert du Motier, Marquis de, 160,
  264, 297
land speculation
  capital site selection and, 231, 251–52, 271
  Creek Indian lands and, 258–59
Langdon, John, xiii, 22
Laurance, John, xv, 198–99
Lear, Tobias, 44, 164, 262, 263, 272–73, 276,
  278, 299
Lee, Billy, 44, 46
Lee, Henry, 228–29, 300
Lee, Richard Bland, xv, 103, 151, 152–53, 240,
  247, 304
Lee, Richard Henry, 234
  amendment debate and, 136, 139
  background of, 10
  capital site debate and, 250
  debates over Washington's title as president
    in, 69

duties and revenue bills and, 94
Hamilton's public credit proposal and, 188,
  191
on new government, 158
as Senate member, xiv, 10, 12, 32, 36, 250
on Shays's Rebellion, 7
L'Enfant, Peter (Pierre), 2–3, 25, 27, 48
Leland, John, 78–79
Leonard, George, xiv
Lewis, Betty Washington, 164
Lewis, Nicholas, 272
Lincoln, Benjamin, 12, 172
Livermore, Samuel
  amendment debate and, 91, 115, 116, 122–23
  census proposal and, 196
  as House member, xiv, 28
  judicial bill and, 141, 142
Livingston, Robert R., 51–52, 55, 59, 95, 173
Long Island, Battle of (1776), 17, 22, 45, 167

Maclay, William, xiii
  on Adams, 48, 50, 51, 68, 70, 104, 105, 134,
    156, 205
  background of, 68
  capital site legislation and, 153, 155–56, 230,
    231–32, 233, 234–35, 241–42, 247–48,
    252, 254–55
  capital site proposals and, 30, 81–82, 136,
    154, 155
  on congressional colleagues, 54, 68–69, 94,
    107, 109, 136, 157, 224, 226, 241, 242, 247,
    248, 301
  on congressional debates, 71, 111, 114, 155,
    205, 233, 234–35, 230, 236, 252, 254, 272,
    290, 301
  debate over executive powers and, 104–05
  defeat for reelection and retirement of, 302,
    309
  Democratic-Republican Party and, 305, 309
  diary of, 30, 309
  Hamilton's funding bill and, 233–34
  health of, 223–24
  on his congressional service, 302
  on Jefferson, 223
  on judicial system proposals, 68, 107, 109,
    111
  on Madison, 99
  on Morris, 231–32, 233
  national bank bill and, 290
  on New Yorkers, 25, 79, 82, 112, 153, 213,
    233, 236, 242
  public debt proposals and, 189, 226
  on Quakers, 276
  on treaties, 94–95
  on Washington, 54, 81–82, 99, 131–32, 135,
    230, 254, 281–82
McCraw, Thomas K., 169, 172, 185, 298
McCullough, David, 35

McGillivray, Alexander, 259–60, 261, 263–64, 265, 304
Madison, James Jr., 76
  amendment debate and, 84–85, 87–88, 115–17, 120–22, 128, 130, 138–39, 159
  amendments proposed by, 88–91, 92, 93, 107, 119, 120, 121, 123, 126, 138–39
  Ames on, 37
  bill of rights proposal by, 86, 87, 117, 312
  campaign against Monroe by, for House seat, 16, 87
  capital site funding proposal of, 250–51, 253, 254, 293, 312
  capital site preferences of, 149, 150–51, 156–57, 229, 231, 240, 250, 270
  on congressional colleagues, 10
  congressional debates over national revenues and taxes and, 72, 73, 74–75
  constituent letters to, 78–79
  on Constitution, 87–88
  Constitutional Convention and, 18–19, 20, 21
  as Constitution's interpreter, 59, 97–98, 292, 294, 299, 307
  Continental Congress and, 17
  domination of First Congress by, 9–10, 71, 193
  executive department powers and, 58–60, 62–63, 96, 97–98
  federal assumption of state debts and, 211–12, 225, 245, 251, 296
  federal court system creation and, 108, 111
  foreign policy and, 174
  as funding bill strategist, 191, 225, 230–31, 252
  Hamilton's relationship with, 193
  health of, 163, 179
  Indian policy and, 257
  Jefferson's friendship with, 17, 71, 73, 87, 96, 102, 163, 176–77, 220–21, 222, 223, 268–69, 300
  judicial bill and, 142
  later political career of, 312
  leadership of, 31, 88, 312
  militia bill debate and, 288, 289–90
  Moustier on, 85
  move from New York by, 267, 268–69
  move to Philadelphia by, 272
  national bank opposition of, 290, 291–92, 293, 294, 295, 297–98, 299
  on the new government, 5, 71, 291–92
  Patrick Henry and, 17, 88
  payment to creditors with government securities and, 191–92, 207–09
  Potomac River Valley and, 147, 269
  presidency of, 311, 312
  presidential powers supported by, 96, 97–98
  public credit proposals and, 188, 190–93, 207–09
  ratification of Constitution and, 19, 86–87
  reelection concerns of, 193, 272, 302
  as representative from Virginia, xv, 9, 16
  revenue bills and, 39–42, 73, 93, 94, 102
  second congressional session opening and, 179
  slavery debate and, 77, 205–07, 217–18, 244
  slaves owned by, 244–45, 272
  travel between congressional sessions by, 163
  on Washington's character, 18–19, 293
  Washington's friendship with, 10, 15–17, 68, 79–80, 99, 290, 294
  Washington's inaugural address written by, 16, 52, 71, 87, 116
  Washington's title as president and, 69, 71
Maier, Pauline, 307
Marshall, John, 293, 311
Martin, Joseph, 170
Maryland, 4
  capital site debate and, 30, 178, 231, 239
  federal assumption of state debts and, 210, 211, 247
  members of First Congress from, xiii, xiv
  Potomac as capital site and, 178, 270
  reelection of members from, 302
Mason, George, 28, 85
Massachusetts, 4
  amendments ratified by, 140
  federal assumption of state debts and, 210, 225, 250, 251
  members of First Congress from, xiii, xiv
  postwar debt of, 170
  voting instructions to senators issued by legislature in, 48–49
Mathews, George, xiv
middle states, 4
Mifflin, Warner, 204–05
militia. See also army
  amendment (Second Amendment) on, 123–24, 137, 287
  collision of fundamental values in debate on, 287
  debate on bills on, 282, 287–90, 301
  defense against Indians using, 257, 273, 282, 287, 301
  Hamilton's speech on Greene and, 103–04, 230
  Knox's proposal on, 195–96
  Madison on, 289–90
  moral conscience exemption for service in, 289–90
  Washington on bill for, 282
mint, founding of, 176, 201, 282
Mississippi, 4
Mississippi River, 4, 174, 258
molasses, taxes on, 39, 41–42, 73, 74, 75, 101–02, 140

Monroe, James, 306
  capital site debates and, 240, 242, 246, 249, 252
  election to Senate of, xiv, 302
  Madison's campaign against, for House seat, 16, 87
Monticello, Virginia, 175–76, 221, 244, 272
Moore, Andrew, xv
Morocco, treaty with, 301
Morris, Gouverneur, 154, 174
Morris, Robert, 29
  amendment debate and, 136
  background of, 26, 153–54, 232, 241
  capital site debate and, 136, 149, 153–56, 157, 232–33
  capital site legislation and, 234, 239, 241–42, 248, 251, 254
  Confederation Congress and, 26
  federal assumption of state debts bill and, 246–47, 251
  financial dealings of, 26, 153–54, 187, 231–32, 251, 258, 310
  Hamilton's financial policies and, 160, 186, 187
  later career of, 310
  Maclay on, 231–32, 233
  on Madison, 87
  as Senate member, xiii, 11, 36, 64, 104, 136, 156, 213, 231–32, 241–42
  on new government, 26, 27, 72
  retirement of, 310
  Treasury Department and, 59, 160
  Washington and, 160, 273
Mount Vernon, Virginia, 15, 18, 44, 80, 82, 164, 271, 272, 281, 295
Moustier, Élénor-François-Élie, Comte de, 38, 83
  on Adams, 34, 65, 66
  on American political process, 14, 29, 39, 73
  on Americans' love of entertaining, 79
  Federal Hall remodeling and, 3
  on Madison, 85
  on Washington, 46–47, 67
Muhlenberg, Frederick Augustus, xv, 11, 30, 31–32, 130–31, 208
Muhlenberg, John Peter, xv, 30, 208, 243
Mumbet (former slave), 151–52

national bank, 13, 290–95
  capital site debate and, 290, 292, 293, 299
  congressional debate on, 286–93
  Constitutional powers and, 290, 291, 298–99
  Hamilton's proposal for, 272, 283, 284–86, 290, 297–98
  Jefferson's opposition to, 294, 296, 298, 300
  Jackson's termination of, 304
  Madison's opposition to, 290, 291–92, 293, 294, 295, 297–98, 299
  Washington's delay on, 293–95, 297, 299

national debt
  bill to reduce, 301
  Hamilton's view of, as creative tool, 185–86, 209
  national bank and, 291
  overdue loans to foreign bankers and, 169–70
  state debts and. See federal assumption of state debts (assumption plan)
national security
  Hamilton's concerns about, 170–71
  Washington on, 180
naturalization bill, 180, 196–97
Native Americans. See Indians
naval officers, for tariffs, 39, 132–34, 159
navy
  American sailors in captivity in Algiers and, 220, 222, 282
  initial lack of, 108, 282
  national defense and need for, 170–71
Newark, Delaware, as capital site, 145
Newburgh conspiracy, 20
New England
  capital site debate and, 148, 149, 152, 232–33, 238–39, 255
  federal assumption of state debts and, 211
  revenue debate and, 40–42, 93–94
  slavery debate and, 216
  Washington's tour through, 164–68
New Hampshire, 4
  federal assumption of state debts and, 210
  members of First Congress from, xiii, xiv
  slavery in, 203
New Jersey, 4
  capital site debate and, 30, 149, 232–33, 247
  federal assumption of state debts and, 210
  members of First Congress from, xiii, xv
newspapers
  congressional activity reported in, 307
  congressmen's preferences for, 113
  in New York City, 23, 113, 236–37
New York City
  as capital site possibility, 30, 145, 146, 149, 189, 228, 239, 248
  congressmen's social life in, 112–14, 130, 179, 224, 312, 313
  congressmen's workdays in, 77–79
  Creek Indians' visit to, 256, 261–65
  description of life in, 22–24, 182–83, 236–37
  difficulties of travel to, 28–29, 179, 188
  disappointment in, after capital site decision rejection of, 253–54
  dislike of, 153, 189
  fashion in, 24–25
  Hamilton's political power in, 173
  Independence Day celebrations in, 103–04
  Jefferson on social life of, 222
  later changes to, 312–13

New York City (*cont.*)
  Maclay on life in, 25, 79, 82, 112, 153, 213,
    233, 236, 242
  newspapers in, 23, 113, 236–37
  new year celebrations in, 178–79
  port traffic in, 38, 40
  revenue bills and business interests in, 102
  summer heat in, 84, 112, 130–31, 134, 252
  temporary seat of government in, 149, 152,
    153, 238, 242, 248
  Washington's departure from, 267
  Washington's inauguration celebrated in, 50,
    54–55
  Washington's residences of, 45, 82, 100, 194,
    312–13
  Washington's social life in, 79–80, 82, 83
New-York Daily Advertiser (newspaper), 12, 92,
    113, 183, 192–93, 233, 276
New York Manumission Society, 104, 198–99
New York Society Library, 112–13
New York State, 4
  capital site debate and, 30, 148, 149, 154, 228,
    238, 247, 248, 250, 253–54
  federal assumption of state debts and, 210, 211
  Hamilton's political power in, 173
  Indian tribes in, 4
  members of First Congress from, xiii, xv
  Quaker antislavery activities in, 198–99
  ratification of Constitution and, 86
North
  capital site debate and, 152, 270, 271
  conflicts over slavery and, 152
  Constitutional Convention on demographic
    advantage of, 6
  Knox's militia proposal and, 195
  national bank bill passage and, 293
  sectional divide in Congress and, 293, 300
  slavery debate and, 206, 218
  southerners' suspicion of, 218–19
  states included in, 4
  Washington's tour through, 164–68
North Carolina, 4
  federal assumption of state debts and, 210,
    212, 250
  freed blacks in, 203
  members of First Congress from, xiii, xv
  oath on support for Constitution in, 4
  ratification of Constitution by, 86, 87, 178,
    180
  slave ownership in, 214
  smugglers in, 73
  voting instructions to senators issued by
    legislature in, 48–49
northwest frontier, military action against
    Indians in, 273, 282, 301, 304
Northwest Territory, 8, 273
Notes on the State of Virginia (Jefferson), 198,
    223

O'Connor, John, 147
Ohio, 4, 145
  Indian attacks in, 257, 258
Osgood, Samuel, 96
Otis, Samuel, 52
Otto, Louis-Guillaume, 83, 179–80, 240, 284

pacifism, 180, 196, 202, 287, 288–89
Page, John, xv, 23–24, 49, 123, 197–98
Parker, Josiah, xv, 75–76, 77, 101
Partridge, George, xiv
patent office, 13, 63, 176
Paterson, William, xiii, 104–05, 108
payment to creditors with government securities
    (discrimination plan)
  critics of proposals on, 189–90, 193
  Hamilton's proposal on, 185–86, 191, 207,
    208
  interest to be paid in, 251
  Madison on, 191–92, 207–09
  Rush on defeat of plan for, 207–08
  speculators and, 251–52
Pemberton, James, 198, 201, 202, 216, 289
Pemberton, John, 198, 199, 201, 202, 204,
    216–17, 219
Pennsylvania, 4
  capital site debate and, 30, 145, 146–47,
    148–49, 152–57, 224–25, 228, 231,
    233–34, 238, 239–40, 241, 243, 248,
    270–71
  federal assumption of state debts and, 210, 251
  members of First Congress from, xiii, xv
  Philadelphia as capital site and donation from,
    154–55
  slavery in, 275–76
  voting instructions to senators issued by
    legislature in, 48–49
Pennsylvania Abolition Society, 198, 199, 220,
    275
Perkins, Elisha, 100
Phelps, Oliver, 279
Philadelphia
  Abigail Adams on, 278–79
  congressmen's move to, 277–78
  Congress's sessions in, 280–81, 301–02, 313
  description of life in, 274–77, 279–80
  free blacks in, 273–74
  fugitive slaves in, 279–80
  Germantown suburb of, as capital site, 149,
    154–57, 232, 242
  later changes to, 313
  Morris's background in, 153–54
  national bank location in, 285, 290, 291
  opposition to capital in, 249, 251, 254
  as permanent capital site, 30, 145, 146–47,
    152, 153, 154–55, 156, 228, 231, 239
  Quaker antislavery activities in, 198–99,
    275–76

slavery in, 154, 279–80, 313
  as temporary capital site, 149, 233, 234–35,
    239–40, 242, 243, 245–46, 247, 248, 249,
    251, 254–55, 267, 274, 296
  Washington's birthday celebration in, 296–97
  Washington's move to, 267, 272–73, 313
  Washington's residence in, 273, 278, 313
Pickering, Timothy, 95–96, 146
Pinckney, Charles Cotesworth, 311
political parties, 304–05
postal system, 180, 235–36, 282, 287, 301
Potomac River Valley as capital site
  compromise selection of, 245–48, 250
  deadline for completion of buildings on, 270
  debate on, 30, 44, 147, 149, 150–51, 152,
    153, 155, 156, 177–78, 189, 228, 231, 235,
    239–40
  investors and speculators and, 310
  location proposals for seat of government in,
    150–51, 177, 248–50, 269–72, 293
  Madison and, 231, 312
  national bank bill's impact on, 292, 293
  proposed commercial development of, 147,
    177, 229–30
  public enthusiasm for selection of, 177–78
  speculation and, 229–30
  Washington's preference for capital site on,
    231, 253, 271–72, 273, 295, 296
  Washington's promotion of development of,
    147, 153, 229–30, 299
president of Confederation Congress, 35
president of United States, 35
  Constitution on duties of, 46–47, 53
  debates over title for, 47, 64, 66–68, 69–71,
    97
  executive branch appointees and powers of,
    60, 96–98, 104–05, 132–33
  negotiation of treaties by, 132–35
  oath of office of, 51–52
  term limits proposed for, 86, 116, 117–18,
    125
  veto power of, 19–20, 293, 294
  Washington on responsibilities of, 36, 79–81
  Washington's election as, 32, 35
  Washington's invention of public image of,
    83, 179–80
  Washington's shaping of powers of, 13, 68,
    161
privateers and privateering, 108
public credit proposals, 182–93, 207–12. See
    also federal assumption of state debts
    (assumption plan); payment to creditors
    with government securities (discrimination
    plan)
  American future cited in debates on, 190
  critics of Hamilton's proposals on, 186,
    187–90
  Federalists on, 187–88, 192–93

Hamilton's report to Congress on, 183–87,
    199, 209
  Madison on, 188, 190–93, 207–09
  need for borrowing and, 184, 185
  payments to veterans and, 189, 190, 191, 207
  public reaction to congressional debate on,
    187
  revenue projections to offset, 186–87
  speculators and, 188, 189, 190
  war debt amount and, 184–85
  Washington's remarks on, 181
public debt. See national debt
Punishment of Crimes Act (1790), 159–60
Putnam, Israel, 167
Putnam, Rufus, 7–8

Quakers
  Adams and, 205
  capital site debate and, 249
  congressional committee on antislavery
    petitions from, 203–04, 213–14
  congressional debate on petitions from, 183,
    198–205, 213–16, 223, 224, 249, 304
  criticism of, 216, 217, 219, 224, 276
  influence of, 196, 275
  lobbying against slavery by, 198
  Madison's view of petitions of, 206–07,
    217–18
  opposition to slavery by, 149, 172, 183,
    200–01, 275, 288
  pacifism of, 196, 288–89
  in Philadelphia, 24, 149, 251, 275
  reaction of slaveholders to petitions of, 201–03
  right of free assembly and, 123
  significance of antislavery campaign of,
    218–19
  southerners' opinion of, 217–19, 249
Quasi-War, 310, 311

Randolph, Edmund, 72, 108, 160, 176, 207,
    294, 297, 298
Randolph, John, 51
Randolph, Thomas Mann Jr., 221, 243, 272
Read, George, xiii, 29, 105, 246
religious freedom (First Amendment), 119,
    120–21, 136, 137–38
"Report on the Militia" (Knox), 195–96
"Report on Public Credit" (Hamilton), 183–87,
    209
representatives. See House of Representatives
Residence Act (1790), 269–70, 296. See also
    capital site development
revenue bills. See also duties; taxation
  congressional debates on, 93–95, 100–03
  Constitution on congressional authority for,
    27–28, 86
  disagreement over sources in, 72–77
  federal assumption of state debts and, 272

revenue bills (*cont.*)
  Madison's proposals for, 39–42, 102
  need for revenue stream and, 3, 13, 37, 38, 93
  opposition to, 57, 116
Revolutionary War
  Creek Indians in, 259
  French support in, 174
  Hamilton's speech on Greene and militias in,
    103–04, 230
  payments to veterans of, 189, 190, 191, 207
  privateers in, 108
  slaves' participation in, 104
  state debts from. *See* federal assumption of
    state debts (assumption plan)
Rhode Island, 4
  capital site debate and, 235
  federal assumption of state debts bill and,
    247, 251
  members of First Congress from, xiv, xv
  ratification of Constitution by, 86, 166–67,
    180, 183, 194, 235
  smugglers in, 73
  Washington and, 166–67, 266–67
rum, taxes on, 41, 73, 74, 75, 114
Rush, Benjamin, 33, 146–47, 148, 152, 169, 188,
  196, 207–08, 222, 243, 253, 268
Rutledge, Edward, 125, 203, 252
Rutledge, John, 33, 299

St. Clair, Arthur, 273
Schureman, James, xv
Schuyler, Philip, xiii, 103, 173, 174, 302
Scott, Thomas, xv, 8, 92, 148, 190, 202–03, 258
Second Amendment, 90, 123–24, 137, 287
securities. *See* payment to creditors with
  government securities
Sedgwick, Pamela, 130, 139, 208, 280, 311
Sedgwick, Theodore, 130, 213
  amendment debate and, 123, 127–28, 139
  federal assumption of state debts, 212, 225,
    226, 253
  as House member, xiv, 302
  immigration policy and, 197
  on Jackson's electoral defeat, 302
  judicial bill and, 142, 151–52
  later political career of, 311
  letters to wife from, 139, 208, 280
  on Madison, 208
  national defense and, 171
  on Philadelphia, 275, 280
Senate. *See also* Congress
  "advice and consent" duty of, 59–60, 132–35
  committees of, 32, 70, 77, 95
  legislative power shared with House, 71
  members of first, xiii–xiv
  state legislatures' instructions to senators in,
    on how to vote, 48–49
  as "upper house," 101

Seney, Joshua, xiv
Sevier, John, xv
Shawnee Indians, 257, 264, 282
Shays, Daniel, 7
Shays's Rebellion, 7, 127, 152, 211
Sherman, Roger
  on Adams, 47
  amendments and, 90–91, 117–18, 120,
    121–22, 130, 139, 226
  background and family of, 118–19
  constituents and, 2, 128
  Constitutional Convention's Great
    Compromise and, 10, 118
  as House member, xiv, 36, 117, 302
  personality of, 118
  as Senate member, 309
  tax legislation and, 93
Shippen, Thomas Lee, 268–69
Short, William, 221, 223
Silvester, Peter, xv
Sixth Amendment, 138
slavery
  amendment debates and, 125
  capital site debates and, 149, 151–52, 178
  Congress's evasion of settling problem of,
    304
  federal court system and, 112
  Hamilton's views on, 104, 172, 215–16, 230,
    245
  North-South conflict over, 152
  opposition to, 75, 76
  in Philadelphia, 154, 279–80, 313
  Quaker petitions to end, 183, 198–205,
    213–16, 223, 224, 249, 304
  "the Virginia straddle" on, 206
slavery debate, 198–220
  Franklin on, 199–200, 219–20
  funding bill and, 206, 216, 217, 224
  Hamilton and, 215–16
  House committee and oral testimony in,
    203–05, 213–14
  House debate on, 198–203, 214–16, 218
  Jefferson on, 198, 206, 223, 244
  Madison and, 77, 205–07, 217–18, 244
  Quaker petitions and, 183, 198–205, 213–16,
    223, 224, 249, 304
  secession threat in, 3, 77, 218, 304
  sectional fissures and, 216
  states' rights and, 304
  Washington on, 215, 219
slaves
  census proposal and, 196
  congressional districts including, 124, 200
  Constitutional Convention on, 6
  fugitive slaves, 276, 279–80
  Jefferson's ownership of, 174, 175, 223, 230,
    244–45
  Knox's militia proposal and, 195–96

Madison's ownership of, 244–45, 272
manumission of, 201, 206
Revolutionary War participation of, 104
Sedgwick's defense of, 151–52
Washington's ownership of, 215, 276, 313
slave trade
  debate over. See slavery debate
  decline in volume of, 76
  Madison's opposition to, 77, 206
  proposed taxes on slaves in, 75–77, 214, 218
  "the Virginia straddle" on, 206
Sinnickson, Thomas, xv
Smith, Adam, 169, 172, 193
Smith, William (Maryland representative), xiv,
  130, 213, 232, 296
Smith, William Loughton (South Carolina
  representative)
  amendment debate and, 92, 125
  background of, 62
  on congressional colleagues, 310–11
  as House member, xv, 28, 62, 280–81, 302
  later political career of, 311
  national debt and, 171, 224
  opposition to, 62, 92
  payment to creditors with old government
    securities and, 252
  presidential powers viewed by, 61–62
  revenue bills and, 101–02
  slavery debate and, 92, 202, 203, 204–05,
    215, 217
  travel between congressional sessions by, 163
  on Washington's health, 100
smugglers and smuggling, 40, 73, 101, 108, 168
Society of Friends. See Quakers
Sons of St. Tammany, 236
South
  capital site proposals and, 146, 147, 149, 151,
    157–58, 178, 228–29, 231, 235, 243, 247,
    250
  congressional district sizes in, 124
  Constitutional Convention on representation
    from, 6
  Hamilton disliked by, 230
  Knox's militia proposal and, 195–96
  later political parties and, 305
  national bank bill and, 290
  political power rooted in, 300
  sectional divide in Congress and, 293, 300
  slavery debate and, 152, 200, 201–03, 206,
    216, 217, 218, 224, 304
  states included in, 4
  suspicion of North held by, 218–19
South Carolina, 4
  amendment debate and, 92
  capital site choice and, 249
  federal assumption of state debts and, 210,
    211, 250, 251
  members of First Congress from, xiv, xv

postwar debt of, 170
revenue taxes and, 101
slave ownership in, 76, 77, 92, 104, 125, 201,
  214
slavery debate and, 77, 125, 201, 214, 216,
  217–18
Spain, 94, 258
  Creek Indian trade with, 259, 260, 263, 265
  Western settlement and, 7
Speaker, House of Representatives, 10, 31
speculators
  capital site selection and, 231, 251–52, 271
  Creek Indian lands and, 258–59
Stanton, Joseph Jr., xiv, 235
State Department, 13, 64, 105, 168, 176–77.
  See also Foreign Affairs Department
state legislatures
  amendments proposals and, 53, 117
  capital site debate and, 270
  early laws and statutes written in, 106
  Indian affairs and, 260
  justice system and, 106–07
  oath on support for Constitution in, 4
  private debt and, 110
  state judges and, 142
  voting instructions to senators issued by,
    48–49
State of the Union speeches, 180–81, 281–83
state ratification conventions, 235
  amendment debate and, 53, 121, 122, 125,
    127, 128
  bill of rights and, 86
states
  bill of rights enacted in, 89
  postwar debt of. See federal assumption of
    state debts (assumption plan)
  powers reserved to, 294
  reelection concerns of congressmen from, 193,
    272, 302
states' rights
  amendment debate and, 86–87, 90, 92, 121,
    125–26
  Antifederalists' support for, 90, 107, 116, 120
  Democratic-Republican Party and, 305
  federal assumption of state debts and, 170,
    185, 211, 226
  federal court system and, 107
  federal power in conflict with, 1, 129, 140,
    226
  House members' support for, 69, 125, 141,
    202, 312
  later political parties and, 305
  Madison on, 90
  Jefferson and, 295, 300
  national bank proposal and, 290, 298
  proposed amendment protecting, 86
  slavery debate and, 304
Steele, John, xv

Stiles, Ezra, 17
Stone, Michael Jenifer, xiv, 141–42, 209–10, 211, 252
Strong, Caleb, xiii, 94, 104
Stuart, David, 224, 237, 295
Sturges, Jonathan
Sullivan, John, 28
Sumter, Thomas, xv
Supreme Court, 5
    bill of rights and, 141
    creation of, 13, 107–08, 111
    first justices on, 195
    first meeting of, 195
    Jay as chief justice at, 14, 96, 159, 160, 179, 195, 310
    Madison's proposal for, 20
surveyors, 39, 159
Susquehanna River, as capital site, 30, 145, 148–49, 150, 152–57, 189, 228, 231, 232, 241, 250, 255

Tammany Hall, New York City, 236
Tammany Society, 256, 261
tariffs
    bureaucracy for collection of, 39, 159
    congressional debate over, 114
    Madison's proposed bill for, 39
    opposition to, 38
    passage of, 13, 159
taxation
    census proposal and, 196
    imported slaves in slave trade and, 75–77, 214, 218
    Jackson on need for, 189
    proposed amendment on, 126
    of whiskey, 287
Tennessee, 4
Tenth Amendment, 129, 294
thanksgiving proclamation, 164
Thatcher, George
    capital site debate and, 146, 227, 240, 280
    Hamilton's public credit proposal and, 186
    as House member, xiv, 6, 26, 75, 112, 302
    on Indian policy, 304
    on Morris's fortune, 232
    new government and, 26, 31
    personality of, 75, 78
    on Philadelphia's religious life, 277
    on politics, 307
    tax policies and, 75, 76
    on Washington's visit to New York City, 45–46
Thomson, Charles, 2, 29, 35, 44, 63–64, 195
tobacco, taxes on, 93
Tories, 10, 17, 62, 102, 106, 211, 228, 253
Treasury Department
    creation of, 13, 95
    debate over nature of, 57, 97

Hamilton as secretary of, 13, 59, 96, 160, 168, 173–74, 284
    national bank debate and, 292
    size of, 168, 284
    state war debts and securities issued by, 185
treaties
    "advice and consent" duty of Senate on, under the Constitution, 132–35
    Hamilton and, 174
    with Indians, 133–35, 235, 261–65, 282, 304
    with Morocco, 301
Treaty of New York, with Creek Indians, 133–35, 261–65
Treaty of Paris (1783), 110
Trenton, New Jersey, as capital site, 30, 145, 146, 149, 232, 233, 242
Trumbull, John (lawyer), 13, 232, 306
Trumbull, John (painter), 208, 261–62
Trumbull, Jonathan (Sr.), 261
Trumbull, Jonathan Jr., xiv
Tucker, St. George, 49
Tucker, Thomas Tudor, xv, 69, 125–26, 127, 129
Tudor, William, 3–4

Underground Railroad, 280

Van Rensselaer, Jeremiah, xv
Vaughn, Samuel, 20
Vermont, 4, 167
    as new state, 13
    ratification of Constitution by, 282
veterans, payments to, 189, 190, 191, 207
veto power of president, 19–20, 293, 294
vice president
    Adams on role of, 47–48, 50, 161–62
    Constitution on duties of, 47, 48
    first use of tie-breaking vote cast by, 105
Vining, John
    amendment debate and, 93, 117, 119, 123
    capital site debate and, 145, 153
    as House member, xiv, 306
    Quaker abolitionism and, 216
    states' rights and, 226
Virginia, 4
    capital site debate and, 30, 147, 149, 155, 178, 228–29, 231, 238, 239, 240, 243, 245–46, 270–71
    federal assumption of state debts and, 210, 246, 247, 250, 251
    members of First Congress from, xiv, xv
    Potomac as capital site and, 178, 270
    slavery debate and, 206, 216

Wadsworth, Jeremiah, xiv, 169, 171, 187, 190
Walker, George, 177
Walker, John, xiv

War Department, 13, 15, 58, 68, 95, 168, 284
Washington, George
  Adams as successor to, 61, 66, 100
  Adams as vice president and, 71
  amendment debate and, 87, 115–16, 119,
    138
  appearance in Senate by, 132–35
  background of, 35–36, 79
  cabinet of, 63
  capital site bill signed by, 250
  capital site commission appointed by, 249, 270
  capital site preferences of, 18, 44, 153, 229,
    230, 231, 237, 254, 270, 271–72, 273, 299
  concerns about congressional wrangling by,
    237, 253
  congressmen's access to, 81
  Constitutional Convention and, 18–19
  Creek Indians' visit with, 256, 260, 261–64
  critics of, 46, 51, 81–82, 254
  daily routine of, 83
  death of mother of, 43
  debates over title for, 47, 64, 66–68, 69–71,
    97
  election of, 32, 35–36
  ethical standards of, 80, 99, 161
  executive branch powers and, 80
  farming background of, 79, 164–65
  federal assumption of the states' debts and,
    209
  federal power and, 293
  first congressional session and changes in, 161
  Hamilton's friendship with, 172, 209, 254,
    290, 299
  Hamilton's suggestions to, 81, 297
  health of, 99–100, 103, 104, 131, 145, 164,
    166, 234
  inaugural address of, 16, 51, 52–54, 71, 87,
    116
  inauguration of, 50–55, 64
  Indian policy and, 258, 260–61, 264, 282
  Jefferson and, 96, 176, 177, 220, 221
  journey to New York City by, 43–46
  Maclay on, 54, 81–82, 99, 131–32, 135, 230,
    254, 281–82
  Madison's friendship with, 10, 15–17, 68,
    79–80, 99, 290, 294
  Mount Vernon life of, 15, 80, 271, 272, 281,
    295
  Moustier on, 46–47, 67, 131
  move to Philadelphia by, 272–73, 277
  national bank bill and, 293–95, 297, 299
  on new government, 43, 161, 237, 307
  New York City residences of, 45, 82, 100, 194,
    312–13
  New York City social life of, 79–80, 82, 114
  oath of office taken by, 51–52, 80, 161
  Otto on demeanor of, 83, 179–80
  personality of, 35, 36, 80, 131, 133, 135, 166

  Philadelphia residence of, 273, 278, 313
  Philadelphia's celebration of birthday of,
    296–97
  plea for clemency from, 237
  popularity of, 44, 45–46, 50, 51, 113, 161
  Potomac capital site favored by, 231, 253,
    271–72, 273, 295, 296
  Potomac River Valley development promotion
    by, 147, 153, 229–30, 299
  presidential powers given to, 60, 61
  presidential powers shaped by, 13, 68, 161
  presidential public image invented by, 83,
    179–80
  public appearances by, 103, 165–68, 266–67,
    269, 281–82, 296–97
  public receptions and levees held by, 81, 82,
    83, 100, 131–32, 168, 179, 253, 273
  relationship with Congress, 46–47
  religious belief of, 164
  on responsibilities of being president, 36,
    79–81
  retirement from presidency by, 309, 312
  Rhode Island and, 166–67, 266–67
  salary as president, 53
  seclusion and aura of mystery of, 81, 83
  second congressional session opening speech
    of, 179–81
  as slaveowner, 215, 276, 313
  slavery debate and, 215, 219
  State of the Union speeches by, 180–81,
    281–83
  thanksgiving proclamation by, 164
  travel through northern states between
    congressional sessions by, 164–68
  Treasury Department and, 59
  Trumbull's portrait of, 261–62
  as unifying symbol for new nation, 145
  wife Martha's unhappiness with public life
    with, 82–83
Washington, Martha, 82–83, 131, 168, 179, 237,
  262, 267, 278, 295
Wayne, Anthony, 8, 132–33, 257, 302, 304,
  309–10
Webster, Noah, 12
Well Meaning Club, 105
West
  area included in, 4
  capital site debate and population shift
    toward, 146, 148, 150, 178, 229
  concerns about settlement of, 7–8
  Constitutional Convention on representation
    from, 6
  military defense of, 171, 180, 282, 301, 304
  proposed new slave states in, 6
  settlers' need for protection from Indians in,
    178, 257–58, 282
  Washington's ownership of lands in, 20,
    229

Whigs, 17
White, Alexander, xv, 179, 226, 247, 303
Willett, Marinus, 260
Williamson, Hugh, xv, 188
Wilmington, Delaware, as capital site, 145, 153, 235
Wilson, James, 195, 258

Wingate, Paine, xiii, 93, 138
Wolcott, Oliver Sr., 107
Woolman, John, 200
Wynkoop, Henry, xv

Yazoo Company land speculators, 258–59, 265, 310